Single-Case Research Designs

METHODS FOR CLINICAL AND APPLIED SETTINGS

ALAN E. KAZDIN

Western Psychiatric Institute and Clinic
University of Pittsburgh School of Medicine

New York   Oxford
OXFORD UNIVERSITY PRESS
1982

Library of Congress Cataloging in Publication Data
Kazdin, Alan E.
Single-case research designs.
Bibliography: p.
Includes index.
1. Case method. 2. Experimental design.
3. Psychological research. 4. Psychology, Applied—Research.
5. Psychiatric research. I. Title.
BF76.5.K33 616.89′00724 81-18786
ISBN 0-19-503020-6 ISBN 0-19-503021-4 (pbk.) AACR2

Printing (last digit): 9 8 7 6

Printed in the United States of America

To my sister, Jackie

Preface

Most empirical investigations that evaluate treatment and intervention techniques in clinical psychology, psychiatry, education, counseling, and related professions use traditional between-group research designs. When the design requirements can be met, between-group designs can address a wide range of basic and applied questions. The difficulty is that traditional design strategies are not well suited to the many applied situations in which treatment focuses on the individual subject. Many of the demands of between-group designs (e.g., identification of homogeneous groups of subjects, random assignment of subjects to groups, standardization of treatments among subjects) are not feasible in applied settings where only one or a few patients, children, residents, or families may be the focus of a particular intervention.

Single-case designs have received increased attention in recent years because they provide a methodological approach that permits experimental investigation with one subject. In the case of clinical work, the designs provide an alternative to uncontrolled case studies, the traditional means of evaluating interventions applied to single cases. Beyond investigation of individual subjects, the designs greatly expand the range of options for conducting research in general. The designs provide a methodological approach well suited to the investigation of individuals, single groups, or multiple groups of subjects. Hence, even in cases where investigation of the individual subject is not of interest, the designs can complement more commonly used between-group design strategies.

The utility of the designs has been illustrated repeatedly in applied settings, including clinics, schools, the home, institutions, and the community for a variety of populations. In most instances, single-case demonstrations have been used to investigate behavior modification techniques. Indeed, within behavior modification, the area known as *applied behavior analysis* has firmly established the utility of single-case designs and has elaborated the range of design options suitable for investigation. Despite the tendency to associate single-case designs with a particular content area, the methodology is applicable to a variety of areas of research. The designs specify a range of conditions that need to be met; these conditions do not necessarily entail a commitment to a particular conceptual approach.

Although single-case designs have enjoyed increasingly widespread use, the methodology is rarely taught formally in undergraduate or graduate courses. Moreover, relatively few texts are available to elaborate the methodology. Consequently, several myths still abound regarding what single-case research can and cannot accomplish. Also, the designs are not used as widely as they might be in situations that could greatly profit from their use. This book elaborates the methodology of single-case research and illustrates its use in clinical and other areas of applied research.

The purpose of this book is to provide a relatively concise description of single-case experimental methodology. The methodology encompasses a variety of topics related to assessment, experimental design, and data evaluation. An almost indefinite number of experimental design options are available within single-case research. No attempt is made here to catalogue all possible assessment or design strategies within single-case research. Rather, the goal is to detail the underlying rationale and logic of single-case designs and to present major design options. Single-case methodology is elaborated by describing the designs and by evaluating their advantages, limitations, and alternatives in the context of clinical and applied research.

The book has been written to incorporate several recent developments within single-case experimental research. In the area of assessment, material is presented on methods of selecting target areas for treatment, alternative assessment strategies, and advances in methods for evaluating interobserver agreement for direct observations of performance. In the area of experimental design, new design options and combinations of designs are presented that expand the range of questions that can be asked about alternative treatments. In the area of data evaluation, the underlying rationale and methods of evaluating intervention effects through visual inspection are detailed. In addition, the use of statistical tests for single-case data, controversial issues raised by these tests, and alternative statistics are presented. (For the interested reader, two appendixes are provided to elaborate the application of visual inspection methods and alternative statistical tests.)

In addition to recent developments, several topics are included in this book that are not widely discussed in currently available texts. The topics include the use of social validation techniques to evaluate the clinical or applied significance of intervention effects, pre-experimental single-case designs as techniques to draw scientific inferences, and experimental designs to study maintenance of behavior. In addition, the limitations and special problems of single-case designs are elaborated. The book not only seeks to elaborate single-case designs but also to place the overall methodology into a larger context. Thus, the relationship of single-case and between-group designs is also discussed.

Several persons contributed to completion of the final book. I am especially grateful to Professor J. Durac, who provided incisive comments on an earlier draft, for his cogent recommendations to organize the references alphabetically. Gratitude is also due to Nicole and Michelle Kazdin, my children, who trimmed several sections of the first draft, only a few of which were eventually found. Preparation of the manuscript and supporting materials was greatly facilitated by Claudia L. Wolfson, to whom I am indebted. I am grateful as well for research support as part of a Research Scientist Development Award (MH00353) and other projects (MH31047) from the National Institute of Mental Health, which were provided during the period in which this book was written.

Pittsburgh   A.E.K.
May 1981

Contents

1. Introduction and Historical Perspective, 3

   Historical Overview, 4
   Contemporary Development of Single-Case Methodology, 10
   Overview of the Book, 15

2. Behavioral Assessment, 17

   Identifying the Focus of Assessment and Treatment, 17
   Strategies of Assessment, 26
   Conditions of Assessment, 39
   Summary and Conclusions, 46

3. Interobserver Agreement, 48

   Basic Information on Agreement, 48
   Methods of Estimating Agreement, 52
   Base Rates and Chance Agreement, 59
   Alternative Methods of Handling
      Expected ("Chance") Levels of Agreement, 62
   Sources of Artifact and Bias, 67
   Acceptable Levels of Agreement, 72
   Summary and Conclusions, 74

4. Experimentation, Valid Inferences,
   and Pre-Experimental Designs, 76

   Experimentation and Valid Inferences, 76
   Pre-Experimental Single-Case Designs, 87
   Pre-Experimental and Single-Case Experimental Designs, 100
   Summary and Conclusions, 101

5. Introduction to Single-Case Research and ABAB Designs, 103

   General Requirements for Single-Case Designs, 104
   ABAB Designs, 109
   Basic Characteristics of the Designs, 110
   Design Variations, 115
   Problems and Limitations, 121
   Evaluation of the Design, 124
   Summary and Conclusions, 125

6. Multiple-Baseline Designs, 126

   Basic Characteristics of the Designs, 126
   Design Variations, 132
   Problems and Limitations, 141
   Evaluation of the Design, 148
   Summary and Conclusions, 150

7. Changing-Criterion Designs, 152

   Basic Characteristics of the Designs, 153
   Design Variations, 157
   Problems and Limitations, 160
   Evaluation of the Design, 169
   Summary and Conclusions, 170

8. Multiple-Treatment Designs, 172

   Basic Characteristics of the Designs, 173
   Major Design Variations, 173
   Additional Design Variations, 185
   Problems and Considerations, 188
   Evaluation of the Designs, 196
   Summary and Conclusions, 198

9. Additional Design Options, 200

   Combined Designs, 200
   Problems and Considerations, 207

Designs to Examine Transfer of Training
  and Response Maintenance, 208
Between-Group Designs, 219
Summary and Conclusions, 228

10. Data Evaluation, 230

Visual Inspection, 231
Statistical Evaluation, 241
Clinical or Applied Significance of Behavior Change, 251
Summary and Conclusions, 259

11. Evaluation of Single-Case Designs: Issues and Limitations, 262

Common Methodological Problems and Obstacles, 263
General Issues and Limitations, 275
Summary and Conclusions, 287

12. Summing Up: Single-Case Research in Perspective, 290

Characteristics of Single-Case Research, 291
Single-Case and Between-Group Research, 294

Appendix A. Graphic Display of Data for Visual Inspection, 296

Basic Types of Graphs, 296
Descriptive Aids for Visual Inspection, 307
Conclusion, 317

Appendix B. Statistical Analyses for Single-Case Designs:
Illustrations of Selected Tests, 318

Conventional t and F Tests, 318
Time-Series Analysis, 321
Randomization Tests, 324
R_n Test of Ranks, 329
Split-Middle Technique, 333
Conclusion, 337

References, 339

Author Index, 359

Subject Index, 365

Single-Case Research Designs

1

Introduction and Historical Perspective

Single-case designs have been used in many areas of research, including psychology, psychiatry, education, rehabilitation, social work, counseling, and other disciplines. The designs have been referred to by different terms, such as *intrasubject-replication designs, N = 1 research, intensive designs,* and so on.[1] The unique feature of these designs is the capacity to conduct experimental investigations with the single case, i.e., one subject. Of course, the designs can evaluate the effects of interventions with large groups and address many of the questions posed in between-group research. However, the special feature that distinguishes the methodology is the provision of some means of rigorously evaluating the effects of interventions with the individual case.

Single-case research certainly is not the primary methodology taught to students or utilized by investigators in the social and biological sciences. The dom-

1. Although several alternative terms have been proposed to describe the designs, each is partially misleading. For example, "single-case" and "N = 1" designs imply that only one subject is included in an investigation. This is not accurate and, as mentioned later, hides the fact that thousands or over a million subjects have been included in some "single-case" designs. The term "intrasubject" is a useful term because it implies that the methodology focuses on performance of the same person over time. The term is partially misleading because some of the designs depend on looking at the effects of interventions across subjects. "Intensive designs" has not grown out of the tradition of single-case research and is used infrequently. Also, the term "intensive" has the unfortunate connotation that the investigator is working intensively to study the subject, which probably is true but is beside the point. For purposes of conformity with many existing works, "single-case designs" has been adopted as the primary term in the present text because it draws attention to the unique feature of the designs, i.e., the capacity to experiment with individual subjects, and because it enjoys the widest use.

inant views about how research should be done still include many misconceptions about or oversimplifications of single-case research. For example, a widely held belief is that single-case investigations cannot be "true experiments" and cannot reveal "causal relations" between variables, as that term is used in scientific research. Among those who grant that causal relations can be demonstrated in such designs, a common view is that single-case designs cannot yield conclusions that extend beyond the one or few persons included in the investigation. Single-case designs, however, are important methodological tools that can be used to evaluate a number of research questions with individuals or groups. It is a mistake to discount them without a full appreciation of their unique characteristics and their similarities to more commonly used experimental methods. The designs should not be proposed as flawless alternatives for more commonly used research design strategies. Like any type of methodology, single-case designs have their own limitations, and it is important to identify these.

The purpose of this book is to elaborate the methodology of single-case experimentation, to detail major design options and methods of data evaluation, and to identify problems and limitations. Single-case designs can be examined in the larger context of clinical and applied research in which alternative methodologies, including single-case designs and between-group designs, make unique as well as overlapping contributions. In the present text, single-case research is presented as a methodology in its own right and not necessarily as a replacement for other approaches. Strengths and limitations of single-case designs and the interrelationship of single-case to between-group designs are addressed.

Historical Overview

Single-case research certainly is not new. Although many of the specific experimental designs and methodological innovations have developed only recently, investigation of the single case has a long and respectable history. This history has been detailed in various sources and, hence, need not be reviewed here at length (see Bolgar, 1965; Dukes, 1965; Robinson and Foster, 1979). However, it is useful to trace briefly the investigation of the single case in the context of psychology, both experimental and clinical.

Experimental Psychology

Single-case research often is viewed as a radical departure from tradition in psychological research. The tradition rests on the between-group research approach that is deeply engrained in the behavioral and social sciences. Interestingly, one need not trace the history of psychological research very far into the past to learn that much of traditional research was based on the careful investigation of individuals rather than on comparisons between groups.

In the late 1880s and early 1900s, most investigations in experimental psychology utilized only one or a few subjects as a basis of drawing inferences. This approach is illustrated by the work of several prominent psychologists working in a number of different areas.

Wundt (1832–1920), the father of modern psychology, investigated sensory and perceptual processes in the late 1800s. Like others, Wundt believed that investigation of one or a few subjects in depth was the way to understand sensation and perception. One or two subjects (including Wundt himself) reported on their reactions and perceptions (through introspection) based on changes in stimulus conditions presented to them. Similarly, Ebbinghaus' (1850–1909) work on human memory using himself as a subject is widely known. He studied learning and recall of nonsense syllables while altering many conditions of training (e.g., type of syllables, length of list to be learned, interval between learning and recall). His carefully documented results provided fundamental knowledge about the nature of memory.

Pavlov (1849–1936), a physiologist who contributed greatly to psychology, made major breakthroughs in learning (respondent conditioning) in animal research. Pavlov's experiments were based primarily on studying one or a few subjects at a time. An exceptional feature of Pavlov's work was the careful specification of the independent variables (e.g., conditions of training, such as the number of pairings of various stimuli) and the dependent variables (e.g., drops of saliva). Using a different paradigm to investigate learning (instrumental conditioning), Thorndike (1874–1949) produced work that is also noteworthy for its focus on a few subjects at one time. Thorndike experimented with a variety of animals. His best-known work is the investigation of cats' escape from puzzle boxes. On repeated trials, cats learned to escape more rapidly with fewer errors over time, a process dubbed "trial and error" learning.

The above illustrations list only a few of the many prominent investigators who contributed greatly to early research in experimental psychology through experimentation with one or a few subjects. Other key figures in psychology could be cited as well (e.g., Bechterev, Fechner, Köhler, Yerkes). The small number of persons mentioned here should not imply that research with one or a few subjects was delimited to a few investigators. Investigation with one or a few subjects was once common practice. Analyses of publications in psychological journals have shown that from the beginning of the 1900s through the 1920s and 30s research with very small samples (e.g., one to five subjects) was the rule rather than the exception (Robinson and Foster, 1979). Research typically excluded the characteristics currently viewed as essential to experimentation, such as large sample sizes, control groups, and the evaluation of data by statistical analysis.

The accepted method of research soon changed from the focus of one or a few subjects to larger sample sizes. Although this history is extensive in its own right, certainly among the events that stimulated this shift was the development of statistical methods. Advances in statistical analysis accompanied greater appreciation of the group approach to research. Studies examined intact groups and obtained correlations between variables as they naturally occurred. Thus, interrelationships between variables could be obtained without experimental manipulation.

Statistical analyses came to be increasingly advocated as a method to permit group comparisons and the study of individual differences as an alternative to experimentation. All of the steps toward the shift from smaller to larger sample sizes are difficult to trace, but they include dissatisfaction with the yield of small sample size research and the absence of controls within the research (e.g., Chaddock, 1925; Dittmer, 1926) as well as developments in statistical tests (e.g., Gosset's development of the Studentized t test in 1908). Certainly, a major impetus to increase sample sizes was R. A. Fisher, whose book on statistical methods (Fisher, 1925) demonstrated the importance of comparing groups of subjects and presented the now familiar notions underlying the analyses of variance. By the 1930s, journal publications began to reflect the shift from small sample studies with no statistical evaluation to larger sample studies utilizing statistical analyses (Boring, 1954; Robinson and Foster, 1979). Although investigations of the single case were reported, it became clear that they were a small minority (Dukes, 1965).

With the advent of larger-sample-size research evaluated by statistical tests, the basic rules for research became clear. The basic control-group design became the paradigm for psychological research: one group, which received the experimental condition, was compared with another group (the control group), which did not. Most research consisted of variations of this basic design. Whether the experimental condition produced an effect was decided by statistical significance, based on levels of confidence (probability levels) selected in advance of the study. Thus larger samples became a methodological virtue. With larger samples, experiments are more powerful, i.e., better able to detect an experimental effect. Also, larger samples were implicitly considered to provide greater evidence for the generality of a relationship. If the relationship between the independent and dependent variables was shown across a large number of subjects, this suggested that the results were not idiosyncratic. The basic rules for between-group research have not really changed, although the methodology has become increasingly sophisticated in terms of the number of design options and statistical techniques that can be used for data analysis.

Clinical Research

Substantive and methodological advances in experimental psychology usually influence the development of clinical psychology. However, it is useful to look at clinical work separately because the investigation of the individual subject has played a particularly important role. The study of individual cases has been more important in clinical psychology than in other areas of psychology. Indeed, the definition of clinical psychology frequently has explicitly included the study of the individual (e.g., Korchin, 1976; Watson, 1951). Information from group research is important but excludes vital information about the uniqueness of the individual. Thus, information from groups and that from individuals contribute separate but uniquely important sources of information. This point was emphasized by Allport (1961), a personality theorist, who recommended the intensive study of the individual (which he called the *idiographic approach*) as a supplement to the study of groups (which he called the *nomothetic approach*). The study of the individual could provide important information about the uniqueness of the person.

The investigation of the individual in clinical work has a history of its own that extends beyond one or a few theorists and well beyond clinical psychology. Theories about the etiology of psychopathology and the development of personality and behavior in general have emerged from work with the individual case. For example, psychoanalysis both as a theory of personality and as a treatment technique developed from a relatively small number of cases seen by Freud (1856–1939) in outpatient psychotherapy. In-depth study of individual cases helped Freud conceptualize basic psychological processes, developmental stages, symptom formation, and other processes he considered to account for personality and behavior.

Perhaps the area influenced most by the study of individual cases has been the development of psychotherapy techniques. Well-known cases throughout the history of clinical work have stimulated major developments in theory and practice. For example, the well-known case of Little Hans has been accorded a major role in the development of psychoanalysis. Hans, a five-year-old boy, feared being bitten by horses and seeing horses fall down. Freud believed that Hans's fear and fantasies were symbolic of important psychological processes and conflicts, including Hans's attraction toward his mother, a wish for his father's demise, and fear of his father's retaliation (i.e., the Oedipal complex). The case of Little Hans was considered by Freud to provide support for his views about child sexuality and the connection between intrapsychic processes and symptom formation (Freud, 1933).

In the 1880s, the now familiar case of Anna O. was reported, which had a great impact on developments in psychotherapy (Breuer and Freud, 1957). Anna O. was a twenty-one-year-old woman who had many hysterical symptoms, including paralysis and loss of sensitivity in the limbs, lapses in awareness, distortion of sight and speech, headaches, a persistent nervous cough, and other problems as well. Breuer (1842–1925), a Viennese physician, talked with Anna O. and occasionally used hypnosis to help her discuss her symptoms. As Anna O. talked about her symptoms and vividly recalled their first appearance, they were eliminated. This "treatment" temporarily eliminated all but a few of the symptoms, each one in turn as it was talked about and recalled. This case has been highly significant in marking the inception of the "talking cure" and cathartic method in psychotherapy. (The case is also significant in part because of the impetus it provided to an aspiring young colleague of Breuer, namely, Freud, who used this example as a point of departure for his work.)

From a different theoretical orientation, a case study on the development of childhood fear also had important clinical implications. In 1920, Watson and Rayner reported the development of fear in an eleven-month-old infant named Albert. Albert initially did not fear several stimuli that were presented to him, including a white rat. To develop Albert's fear, presentation of the rat was paired with a loud noise. After relatively few pairings, Albert reacted adversely when the rat was presented by itself. The adverse reaction appeared in the presence of other stimuli as well (e.g., a fur coat, cotton-wool, Santa Claus mask). This case was interpreted as implying that fear could be learned and that such reactions generalized beyond the original stimuli to which the fear had been conditioned. The above cases do not begin to exhaust the dramatic instances in which intensive study of individual cases had considerable impact in clinical work. Individual case reports have been influential in elaborating relatively infrequent clinical disorders, such as multiple personality (Prince, 1905; Thigpen and Cleckley, 1954), and in suggesting viable clinical treatments (e.g., Jones, 1924).

Case studies occasionally have had remarkable impact when several cases were accumulated. Although each case is studied individually, the information is acculumated to identify more general relationships. For example, modern psychiatric diagnosis, or the classification of individuals into different diagnostic categories, began with the analysis of individual cases. Kraepelin (1855–1926), a German psychiatrist, identified specific "disease" entities or psychological disorders by systematically collecting thousands of case studies of hospitalized psychiatric patients. He described the history of each patient, the onset of the disorder, and its outcome. From this extensive clinical material, he elaborated various types of "mental illness" and provided a general model for contemporary approaches to psychiatric diagnosis (Zilboorg and Henry, 1941).

Although the intensive study of individual cases has served as a major tool for studying clinical disorders and their treatment, the investigative methods did not develop quite to the point of analogous work in experimental psychology. In experimental research, the focus on one or a few cases often included the careful specification of the independent variables (e.g., events or conditions presented to the subject such as the particular pairing of stimuli [Pavlov] or the types of lists committed to memory [Ebbinghaus]). And the dependent measures often provided convincing evidence because they were objective and replicable (e.g., latency to respond, correct responses, or verbalizations of the subject). In clinical research, the experimental conditions (e.g., therapy) typically were not really well specified and the dependent measures used to evaluate performance usually were not objective (e.g., opinions of the therapist). Nevertheless, the individual case was often the basis for drawing inferences about human behavior.

General Comments

Investigation of the single case has a history of its own not only in experimental and clinical psychology, but certainly in other areas as well. In most instances, historical illustrations of single-case research do not resemble contemporary design procedures. Observation and assessment procedures were rarely systematic or based on objective measures, although, as already noted, there are stark exceptions. Also, systematic attempts were not made within the demonstrations to rule out the influence of extraneous factors that are routinely considered in contemporary experimental design (see Cook and Campbell, 1979).

We can see qualitative differences in clinical work, as, for example, in the case study of Anna O., briefly noted above, and single-case investigations of the sort to be elaborated in later chapters. The distinction between uncontrolled case studies and single-case experiments reflects the differential experimental power and sophistication of these two alternative methods, even though both may rely on studying the individual case. Thus, the single-case historical precedents discussed to this point are not sufficient to explain the basis of current experimental methods. A more contemporary history must fill the hiatus between early experimental and clinical investigations and contemporary single-case methodology.

Contemporary Development of Single-Case Methodology

Current single-case designs have emerged from specific areas of research within psychology. The designs and approach can be seen in bits and pieces in historical antecedents of the sort mentioned above. However, the full emergence of a distinct methodology and approach needs to be discussed explicitly.

The Experimental Analysis of Behavior

The development of single-case research, as currently practiced, can be traced to the work of B. F. Skinner (b. 1904), who developed programmatic animal laboratory research to elaborate operant conditioning. Skinner was interested in studying the behavior of individual organisms and determining the antecedent and consequent events that influenced behavior. In Skinner's work, it is important to distinguish between the content or substance of his theoretical account of behavior (referred to as *operant conditioning*) and the methodological approach toward experimentation and data evaluation (referred to as the *experimental analysis of behavior*). The substantive theory and methodological approach were and continue to be intertwined. Hence, it is useful to spend a little time on the distinction.

Skinner's research goal was to discover lawful behavioral processes of the individual organism (Skinner, 1956). He focused on animal behavior and primarily on the arrangement of consequences that followed behavior and influenced subsequent performance. His research led to a set of relationships or principles that described the processes of behavior (e.g., reinforcement, punishment, discrimination, response differentiation) that formed operant conditioning as a distinct theoretical position (e.g., Skinner, 1938, 1953a).

Skinner's approach toward research, noted already as the experimental analysis of behavior, consisted of several distinct characteristics, many of which underlie single-case experimentation (Skinner, 1953b). First, Skinner was interested in studying the frequency of performance. Frequency was selected for a variety of reasons, including the fact that it presented a continuous measure of ongoing behavior, provided orderly data and reflected immediate changes as a function of changing environmental conditions, and could be automatically recorded. Second, one or a few subjects were studied in a given experiment. The effects of the experimental manipulations could be seen clearly in the behavior of individual organisms. By studying individuals, the experimenter could see lawful behavioral processes that might be hidden in averaging performance across several subjects, as is commonly done in group research. Third, because of the lawfulness of behavior and the clarity of the data from continuous frequency measures over time, the effects of various procedures on performance could be seen directly. Statistical analyses were not needed. Rather, the changes in performance could be detected by changing the conditions presented to the subject and observing systematic changes in performance over time.

Investigations in the experimental analysis of behavior are based on using the subject, usually a rat, pigeon, or other infrahuman, as its own control. The designs, referred to as intrasubject-replication designs (Sidman, 1960), evaluate the effect of a given variable that is replicated over time for one or a few subjects. Performances before, during, and after an independent variable is presented are compared. The sequence of different experimental conditions over time is usually repeated within the same subject.

In the 1950s and 1960s, the experimental analysis of behavior and intrasubject or single-case designs became identified with operant conditioning research. The association between operant conditioning as a theory of behavior and single-case research as a methodology became somewhat fixed, in part because of their clear connection in the various publication outlets and professional organizations. Persons who conducted research on operant conditioning topics usually used single-case designs, and persons who usually used single-case designs were trained and interested in operant conditioning. The connection between a particular theoretical approach and a research methodology is not a necessary one, as will be discussed later, but an awareness of the connection is important for an understanding of the development and current standing of single-case methodology.

Applied Behavior Analysis

As substantive and methodological developments were made in laboratory applications of operant conditioning, the approach was extended to human behavior. The initial systematic extensions of basic operant conditioning to human behavior were primarily of methodological interest. Their purpose was to demonstrate the utility of the operant approach in investigating human performance and to determine if the findings of animal laboratory research could be extended to humans.

The extensions began primarily with experimental laboratory research that focused on such persons as psychiatric patients and normal, mentally retarded, and autistic children (e.g., Bijou, 1955, 1957; Ferster, 1961; Lindsley, 1956, 1960) but included several other populations as well (see Kazdin, 1978c). Systematic behavioral processes evident in infrahuman research were replicated with humans. Moreover, clinically interesting findings emerged as well, such as reduction of symptoms among psychotic patients during laboratory sessions (e.g., Lindsley, 1960) and the appearance of response deficits among mentally retarded persons (e.g., Barrett and Lindsley, 1962). Aside from the methodological extensions, even the initial research suggested the utility of operant conditioning for possible therapeutic applications.

Although experimental work in operant conditioning and single-case research continued, by the late 1950s and early 1960s an applied area of research began to emerge. Behaviors of clinical and applied importance were focused on directly, including stuttering (Goldiamond, 1962), reading, writing, and arithmetic skills (Staats et al., 1962, 1964), and the behavior of psychiatric patients on the ward (e.g., Ayllon, 1963; Ayllon and Michael, 1959; King, Armitage, and Tilton, 1960).

By the middle of the 1960s, several programs of research emerged for applied purposes. Applications were evident in education and special education settings, psychiatric hospitals, outpatient treatment, and other environments (Ullmann and Krasner, 1965). By the late 1960s, the extension of the experimental analysis of behavior to applied areas was recognized formally as *applied behavior analysis* (Baer, Wolf, and Risley, 1968). Applied behavior analysis was defined as an area of research that focused on socially and clinically important behaviors related to matters such as psychiatric disorders, education, retardation, child rearing, and crime. Substantive and methodological approaches of the experimental analyses were extended to applied questions.

Applied behavior analysis emerged from and continues to be associated with the extensions of operant conditioning and the experimental analysis of behavior to applied topics. However, a distinction can be made between the substantive approach of operant conditioning and the methodology of single-case designs. Single-case designs represent important methodological tools that extend beyond any particular view about behavior and the factors by which it is influenced. The designs are well suited to investigating procedures developed from operant conditioning. Yet the designs have been extended to a variety of interventions out of the conceptual framework of operant conditioning. Single-case designs can be evaluated in their own right as a methodology to contribute to applied and experimental work. The purpose of the present book is to elaborate single-case designs, their advantages and limitations.

Additional Influences

Developments in the experimental and applied analysis of behavior explain the current evolution and use of single-case designs. However, it is important to bear in mind other factors that increase interest in a research methodology to study the individual case. In many areas of the so-called "mental health" or "helping" professions (e.g., psychiatry, clinical psychology, counseling, social work), there is often a split between research and practice. The problem is not confined to one discipline but can be illustrated by looking at clinical psychology, where the hiatus between research and practice is heavily discussed (Azrin, 1977; Barlow, 1981; Bornstein and Wollersheim, 1978; Hersen and Barlow, 1976; Leitenberg, 1974; Raush, 1974). Traditionally, after completing training, clinical psychologists are expected to be skilled both in conducting research and in administering direct service, as in clinical treatment. Yet, serious questions have been raised about whether professionals are trained to perform the functions of both scientist and practitioner.

In clinical psychology, relatively little time among professionals is devoted to research. The primary professional activity consists of direct clinical service (Garfield and Kurtz, 1976). Those who do conduct research are rarely engaged in clinical practice. Researchers usually work in academic settings and lack access to the kinds of problems seen in routine clinical and hospital care. Treatment research conducted in academic settings often departs greatly from the conditions that characterize clinical settings such as hospitals or outpatient clinics (Kazdin, 1978b; Raush, 1974). Typically, such research is conducted under carefully controlled laboratory conditions in which subjects do not evince the types or the severity of problems and living situations characteristic of persons ordinarily seen in treatment. In research, treatment is usually standardized across persons to ensure that the investigation is properly controlled. Persons who administer treatment are usually advanced students who closely follow the procedures as prescribed. Two or more treatments are usually compared over a relatively short treatment period by examining client performance on standardized measures such as self-report inventories, behavioral tests, and global ratings. Conclusions about the effectiveness of alternative procedures are reached on the basis of statistical evaluation of the data.

The results of treatment investigations often have little bearing on the questions and concerns of the practitioner who sees individual patients. Clinicians often see patients who vary widely in their personal characteristics, education, and background from the college students ordinarily seen in research. Also, patients often require multiple treatments to address their manifold problems.

The clinician is not concerned with presenting a standardized technique but with providing a treatment that is individualized to meet the patient's needs in an optimal fashion. The results of research that focuses on *statistically significant* changes may not be important; the clinician is interested in producing a *clinically significant* effect, i.e., a change that is clearly evident in the patient's everyday life. The results of the average amount of change that serves as the basis for drawing conclusions in between-group research does not address the clinician's need to make decisions about treatments that will alter the individual client.

Researchers and clinicians alike have repeatedly acknowledged the lack of relevance of clinical research in guiding clinical practice. Indeed, prominent clinical psychologists (e.g., Rogers, Matarazzo) have noted that their own research has not had much impact on their practice of therapy (Bergin and Strupp, 1972). Part of the problem is that clinical investigations of therapy are invariably conducted with *groups* of persons in order to meet the demands of traditional experimental design and statistical evaluation. But investigation of groups and conclusions about average patient performance may distort the primary phenomenon of interest, viz., the effects of treatments on individuals. Hence, researchers have suggested that experimentation at the level of individual case studies may provide the greatest insights in understanding therapeutic change (Barlow, 1980, 1981; Bergin and Strupp, 1970, 1972).

The practicing clinician is confronted with the individual case, and it is at the level of the clinical case that empirical evaluations of treatment need to be made. The problem, of course, is that the primary investigative tool for the clinician has been the uncontrolled case study in which anecdotal information is reported and scientifically acceptable inferences cannot be drawn (Bolgar, 1965; Lazarus and Davison, 1971). Suggestions have been made to improve the uncontrolled case study to increase its scientific yield, such as carefully specifying the treatment, observing performance over time, and bringing to bear additional information to rule out possible factors that may explain changes over the course of treatment (Barlow, 1980; Kazdin, 1981). Also, suggestions have been made for studying the individual case experimentally in clinical work (e.g., Chassan, 1967; Shapiro, 1961a, 1961b; Shapiro and Ravenette, 1959). These latter suggestions propose observing patient behavior directly and evaluating changes in performance as treatment is systematically varied over time. Single-case experimental designs discussed in this book codify the alternative design options available for investigating treatments for the individual case.

Single-case designs represent a methodology that may be of special relevance to clinical work. The clinician confronted with the individual case can explore the effects of treatment by systematically applying selected design options. The net effect is that the clinician can contribute directly to scientific knowledge about intervention effects and, by accumulating cases over time, can establish general relationships otherwise not available from uncontrolled cases. Clinical research will profit from treatment trials where interventions are evaluated under the usual circumstances in which they are implemented rather than in academic or research settings.

In general, single-case research has not developed from the concerns over the gap between research and practice. However, the need to develop research in clinical situations to address the problem of direct interest to clinicians makes the extension of single-case methodology beyond its current confines of special interest. The designs extend the logic of experimentation normally applied to between-group investigations to investigations of the single case.

Overview of the Book

This text describes and evaluates single-case designs. A variety of topics are elaborated to convey the methodology of assessment, design, and data evaluation in applied and clinical research. Single-case designs depend heavily on assessment procedures. Continuous measures need to be obtained over time. Alternative methods for assessing behavior commonly employed in single-case designs and problems associated with their use are described in Chapter 2. Apart from the methods of assessing behavior, several assurances must be provided within the investigation that the observations are obtained in a consistent fashion. The techniques for assessing consistency between observers are discussed in Chapter 3.

The crucial feature of experimentation is drawing inferences about the effects of various interventions or independent variables. Experimentation consists of arranging the situation in such a way as to rule out or make implausible the impact of extraneous factors that could explain the results. Chapter 4 discusses the factors that experimentation needs to rule out to permit inferences to be drawn about intervention effects and examines the manner in which such factors can be controlled or addressed in uncontrolled case studies, pre-experimental designs, and single-case experimental designs.

The precise logic and unique characteristics of single-case experimental designs are introduced in Chapter 5. The manner in which single-case designs test predictions about performance within the same subject underlies all of the designs. In Chapters 5 through 9, several different designs and their variations, uses, and potential problems are detailed.

Once data within an experiment are collected, the investigator selects techniques to evaluate the data. Single-case designs have relied heavily on visual inspection of the data rather than statistical analyses. The underlying rationale and methods of visual inspection are discussed in Chapter 10. Statistical analyses in single-case research and methods to evaluate the clinical significance of intervention effects are also discussed in this chapter. (For the reader interested in extended discussions of data evaluation in single-case research, visual inspection and statistical analyses are illustrated and elaborated in Appendixes A and B, respectively.) Although problems, considerations, and specific issues associated with particular designs are treated throughout the text, it is useful to evaluate single-case research critically. Chapter 11 provides a discussion of issues, problems, and limitations of single-case experimental designs. Finally, the contribution of single-case research to experimentation in general and the interface of alternative research methodologies are examined in Chapter 12.

2
Behavioral Assessment

Traditionally, assessment has relied heavily on psychometric techniques such as various personality inventories, self-report scales, and questionnaires. The measures are administered under standardized conditions. Once the measure is devised, it can be evaluated to examine various facets of reliability and validity. In single-case research, assessment procedures are usually devised to meet the special requirements of particular clients, problems, and settings. The measures often are improvised to assess behaviors suited to a particular person. To be sure, there are consistencies in the strategies of measurement across many studies. However, for a given area of research (e.g., child treatment) or intervention focus (e.g., aggressiveness, social interaction) the specific measures and the methods of administration often are not standardized across studies.

Assessment in single-case research is a process that begins with identifying the focus of the investigation and proceeds to selecting possible strategies of assessment and ensuring that the observations are obtained consistently. This chapter addresses initial features of the assessment process, including identifying the focus of assessment, selecting the assessment strategy, and determining the conditions under which assessment is obtained. The next chapter considers evaluation of the assessment procedures and the problems that can arise in collecting observational data.

Identifying the Focus of Assessment and Treatment

The primary focus of assessment in single-case designs is on the behavior that is to be changed, which is referred to as the *target behavior*. The behavior that needs to be altered is not always obvious; it often depends on one's conceptualization of deviant behavior and personal values regarding the desirability of some behaviors rather than others. Thus, behaviors focused on in applied and clinical research occasionally are debated. For example, recent controversies have centered on the desirability of altering one's sexual attraction toward the same sex, feminine sex-role behavior in young males, and mildly disruptive behaviors among children in school (e.g., Davison, 1976; Nordyke, Baer, Etzel, and LeBlanc, 1977; Rekers, 1977; Winett and Winkler, 1972; Winkler, 1977).

Even when there is agreement on the general target problem, it may be difficult to decide the specific behaviors that are to be assessed and altered. For example, considerable attention is given in behavioral research to the training of "social skills" among psychiatric patients, the mentally retarded, delinquents, children and adults who are unassertive, and other populations (e.g., Bellack and Hersen, 1979; Combs and Slaby, 1977). However, social skills is only a very general term and may encompass a variety of behaviors, ranging from highly circumscribed responses such as engaging in eye contact while speaking, facing the person with whom one is conversing, and using appropriate hand gestures, to more global behaviors such as sustaining a conversation, telephoning someone to arrange a date, and joining in group activities. These behaviors and several others can be used to define social skills. However, on what basis should one decide the appropriate focus for persons who might be considered to lack social skills?

Relatively little attention has been devoted to the process by which target behaviors are identified. In general, applied behavior analysis is defined by the focus on behaviors that are of applied or social importance (Baer et al., 1968). However, this general criterion does not convey how the specific target behaviors are identified in a given case.

Deviant, Disturbing, or Disruptive Behavior

The criteria for identifying target behaviors raise complex issues. Many behaviors are clearly of clinical or applied importance; the focus is obvious because of the frequency, intensity, severity, or type of behavior in relation to what most people do in ordinary situations. A pivotal criterion often only implicit in the selection of the behavior is that it is in some way deviant, disturbing, or disruptive. Interventions are considered because the behaviors:

1. may be important to the client or to persons in contact with the client (e.g., parents, teachers, hospital staff);
2. are or eventually may be dangerous to the client or to others (e.g., aggressive behavior, drug addiction);

3. may interfere with the client's functioning in everyday life (e.g., phobias, obsessive-compulsive rituals); and
4. indicate a clear departure from normal functioning (e.g., bizarre behaviors such as self-stimulatory rocking, age-inappropriate performance such as enuresis or thumbsucking among older children).

The above factors generally are some of the major criteria utilized for identifying abnormal and deviant behavior (e.g., Ullmann and Krasner, 1975) independently of single-case research. In fact, however, interventions usually are directed at behaviors that fall into the above categories. For example, interventions evaluated in single-case research often focus on self-care skills, self-injurious behavior, hyperactivity, irrational verbalizations, obsessive-compulsive acts, and disruptive behavior and lack of academic skills in the classroom.

Typically, the specific target focus is determined by a consensus that behaviors meet some or all of the above criteria. A systematic evaluation of what behaviors need to be changed is not made because the behaviors appear to be and often obviously are important and require immediate intervention. Deviant behaviors in need of intervention often seem quite different from behaviors seen in everyday life and usually can be readily agreed upon as in need of treatment.[1]

Social Validation

The above criteria suggest that identifying behavior that is deviant, disturbing, or disruptive is all that is required to decide the appropriate focus. However, the specific behaviors in need of assessment and intervention may not always be obvious. Even when the general focus may seem clear, several options are available for the precise behaviors that will be assessed and altered. The investigator wishes to select the particular behaviors that will have some impact on the client's overall functioning in everyday life.

Recently, research has begun to rely on empirically based methods of identifying what the focus of interventions should be. In applied behavior analysis, the major impetus has stemmed from the notion of *social validation,* which generally refers to whether the focus of the intervention and the behavior changes that have been achieved meet the demands of the social community of

---

1. The above criteria refer primarily to selection of the target behaviors for individual persons. However, many other behaviors are selected because they reflect larger social problems. For example, interventions frequently focus on socially related concerns such as excessive consumption of energy in the home, use of automobiles, littering, shoplifting, use of leisure time, and others. In such cases, behaviors are related to a broader social problem rather than to the deviant, disturbing, or disruptive performance of a particular client.

which the client is a part (Wolf, 1978). Two social validation methods can be used for identifying the appropriate focus of the intervention, namely, the social comparison and subjective evaluation methods.

Social Comparison. The major feature of the social comparison method is to identify a peer group of the client, i.e., those persons who are similar to the client in subject and demographic variables but who differ in performance of the target behavior. The peer group consists of persons who are considered to be functioning adequately with respect to the target behavior. Essentially, normative data are gathered with respect to a particular behavior and provide a basis for evaluating the behavior of the client. The behaviors that distinguish the normative sample from the clients suggest what behaviors may require intervention.

The use of normative data to help identify behaviors that need to be focused on in intervention studies has been reported in a few studies. For example, Minkin et al. (1976) developed conversational skills among predelinquent girls who resided in a home-style treatment facility. The investigators first sought to determine the specific conversational skills necessary for improving interpersonal interactions by asking normal junior high school and college students to talk normally. Essentially, data from nonproblem youths were obtained to assess what appropriate conversations are like among youths adequately functioning in their environment. From the interactions of normal youths, the investigators tentatively identified behaviors that appeared to be important in conversation, namely, providing positive feedback to another person, indicating comprehension of what was said, and asking questions or making a clarifying statement.

To assess how well these behaviors reflected overall conversational skills, persons from the community (e.g., homemakers, gas station attendants) rated videotapes of the students. Ratings of the quality of the general conversational skills correlated significantly with the occurrence of behaviors identified by the investigators. The delinquent girls were trained in these behaviors with some assurance that the skills were relevant to overall conversational ability. Thus, the initial normative data served as a basis for identifying specific target behaviors related to the overall goal, namely, developing conversational skills.

Another example of the use of normative data to help identify the appropriate target focus was reported by Nutter and Reid (1978), who were interested in training institutionalized mentally retarded women to dress themselves and to select their own clothing in such a way as to coincide with current fashion. Developing skills in dressing fashionably represents an important focus for persons preparing to enter community living situations. The purpose of the study was to train women to coordinate the color combinations of their clothing. To determine the specific color combinations that constituted currently popular fashion, the investigators observed over 600 women in community settings where the institutionalized residents would be likely to interact, including a local shopping mall, restaurant, and sidewalks. Popular color combinations were identified, and the residents were trained to dress according to current fashion. The skills in dressing fashionably were maintained for several weeks after training.

In the above examples, investigators were interested in focusing on specific response areas but sought information from normative samples to determine the precise behaviors of interest. The behavior of persons in everyday life served as a criterion for the particular behaviors that were trained. When the goal is to return persons to a particular setting or level of functioning, social comparison may be especially useful. The method first identifies the level of functioning of persons performing adequately (or well) in the situation and uses the information as a basis for selecting the target focus.

Subjective Evaluation. As another method of social validation, subjective evaluation consists of soliciting the opinions of others who by expertise, consensus, or familiarity with the client are in a position to judge or evaluate the behaviors in need of treatment. Many of the decisions about the behaviors that warrant intervention in fact are made by parents, teachers, peers, or people in society at large who identify deviance and make judgments about what behaviors do and do not require special attention. An intervention may be sought because there is a consensus that the behavior is a problem. Often it is useful to evaluate the opinions of others systematically to identify what specific behaviors present a problem.

The use of subjective evaluation as a method for identifying the behaviors requiring intervention was illustrated by Freedman, Rosenthal, Donahoe, Schlundt, and McFall (1978). These investigators were interested in identifying problem situations for delinquent youths and the responses they should possess to handle these situations. To identify problem situations, psychologists, social workers, counselors, teachers, delinquent boys, and others were consulted. After these persons identified problem situations, institutionalized delinquents rated whether the situations were in fact problems and how difficult the situations were to handle.

After the problem situations were identified (e.g., being insulted by a peer, being harassed by a school principal), the investigators sought to identify the appropriate responses to these situations. The situations were presented to delinquent and nondelinquent boys, who were asked to respond as they typically would. Judges, consisting of students, psychology interns, and psychologists, rated the competence of the responses. For each of the problem situations, responses were identified that varied in their degree of competence. An inventory of situations was constructed that included several problem situations and response alternatives that had been developed through subjective evaluations of several judges.

In another study with delinquents, subjective judgments were used to identify the behaviors delinquents should perform when interacting with the police (Werner, Minkin, Minkin, Fixsen, Phillips, and Wolf, 1975). Police were asked to identify important behaviors for delinquents in situations in which delinquents were suspects in their interactions with police. The behaviors consisted of facing the officer, responding politely, and showing cooperation, understanding, and interest in reforming. The behaviors identified by the police served as the target behaviors focused on in training.

In another example, Mithaug and his colleagues wished to place severely and profoundly handicapped persons in workshop and activity centers (Johnson and Mithaug, 1978; Mithaug and Hagmeier, 1978). These investigators were interested in identifying the requisite behaviors that should be trained among their clients. The requisite behaviors were determined by asking administrative and supervisory personnel at facilities in several states to identify the entry skills required of the clients. Personnel responded to a questionnaire that referred to a large number of areas of performance (e.g., interactions with peers, personal hygiene). The questions allowed personnel to specify the precise behaviors that needed to be developed within several areas of performance. The behaviors could then serve as the basis for a comprehensive training program.

In the above examples, persons were consulted to help identify behaviors that warranted intervention. The persons were asked to recommend the desired behaviors because of their familiarity with the requisite responses for the specific situations. The recommendations of such persons can then be translated into training programs so that specific performance goals are achieved.

General Comments. Social comparison and subjective evaluation methods as techniques for identifying the target focus have been used relatively infrequently.[2] The methods provide empirically based procedures for systematically selecting target behaviors for purposes of assessment and intervention. Of course, the methods are not without problems (see Kazdin, 1977b). For exam-

---

2. Social comparison and subjective evaluation methods have been used somewhat more extensively in the context of evaluating the outcomes of interventions (see Chapter 10).

ple, the social comparison method suggests that behaviors that distinguish normals from clients ought to serve as the basis for treatment. Yet, it is possible that normative samples and clients differ in many ways, some of which may have little relevance for the functioning of the clients in their everyday lives. Just because clients differ from normals in a particular behavior does not necessarily mean that the difference is important or that ameliorating the difference in performance will solve major problems for the clients.

Similarly, with subjective evaluation, the possibility exists that the behaviors subjectively judged as important may not be the most important focus of treatment. For example, teachers frequently identify disruptive and inattentive behavior in the classroom as a major area in need of intervention. Yet, improving attentive behavior in the classroom usually has little or no effect on children's academic performance (e.g., Ferritor, Buckholdt, Hamblin, and Smith, 1972; Harris and Sherman, 1974). However, focusing directly on improving academic performance usually has inadvertent consequences on improving attentiveness (e.g., Ayllon and Roberts, 1974; Marholin, Steinman, McInnis, and Heads, 1975). Thus, subjectively identified behaviors may not be the most appropriate or beneficial focus in the classroom.

Notwithstanding the objections that might be raised, social comparison and subjective evaluation offer considerable promise in identifying target behaviors. The objections against one of the methods of selecting target behaviors usually can be overcome by employing both methods simultaneously. That is, normative samples can be identified and compared with a sample of clients (e.g., delinquents, mentally retarded persons) identified for intervention for behaviors of potential interest. Then, the differences in specific behaviors that distinguish the groups can be evaluated by raters to examine the extent to which the behaviors are viewed as important.

Defining the Target Focus

Target Behaviors. Independently of how the initial focus is identified, ultimately the investigator must carefully define the behaviors that are to be observed. The target behaviors need to be defined explicitly so that they can be observed, measured, and agreed on by those who assess performance and implement treatment. Careful assessment of the target behavior is essential for at least two reasons. First, assessment determines the extent to which the target behavior is performed before the program begins. The rate of preprogram behavior is referred to as the *baseline* or *operant rate*. Second, assessment is required to reflect behavior change after the intervention is begun. Since the major purpose of the program is to alter behavior, behavior during the program must be compared with behavior during baseline. Careful assessment throughout the program is essential.

Careful assessment begins with the definition of the target response. As a general rule, a response definition should meet three criteria: objectivity, clarity, and completeness (Hawkins and Dobes, 1977). To be *objective,* the definition should refer to observable characteristics of behavior or environmental events. Definitions should not refer to inner states of the individual or inferred traits, such as aggressiveness or emotional disturbance. To be *clear,* the definition should be so unambiguous that it could be read, repeated, and paraphrased by observers. Reading the definition should provide a sufficient basis for actually beginning to observe behavior. To be *complete,* the boundary conditions of the definition must be delineated so that the responses to be included and excluded are enumerated.

Developing a definition that is complete often creates the greatest problem because decision rules are needed to specify how behavior should be scored. If the range of responses included in the definition is not described carefully, observers have to infer whether the response has occurred. For example, a simple greeting response such as waving one's hand to greet someone may serve as the target behavior (Stokes, Baer, and Jackson, 1974). In most instances, when a person's hand is fully extended and moving back and forth, there would be no difficulty in agreeing that the person was waving. However, ambiguous instances may require judgments on the part of observers. A child might move his or her hand once (rather than back and forth) while the arm is not extended, or the child may not move his or her arm at all but simply move all fingers on one hand up and down (in the way that infants often learn to say good-bye). These latter responses are instances of waving in everyday life because we can often see others reciprocate with similar greetings. For assessment purposes, the response definition must specify whether these and related variations of waving would be scored as waving.

Before developing a definition that is objective, clear, and complete, it may be useful to observe the client on an informal basis. Descriptive notes of what behaviors occur and which events are associated with their occurrence may be useful in generating specific response definitions. For example, if a psychiatric patient is labeled as "withdrawn," it is essential to observe the patient's behavior on the ward and to identify those specific behaviors that have led to the use of the label. The specific behaviors become the object of change rather than the global concept.

Behavior modification programs have reported clear behavioral definitions that were developed from global and imprecise terms. For example, the focus of treatment of one program was on aggressiveness of a twelve-year-old institutionalized retarded girl (Repp and Deitz, 1974). The specific behaviors included biting, hitting, scratching, and kicking others. In a program conducted in the home, the focus was on bickering among the children (Christophersen, Arnold, Hill, and Quilitch, 1972). Bickering was defined as verbal arguments between any two or all three children that were louder than the normal speaking voice. Finally, one program focused on the poor communication skills of a schizophrenic patient (Fichter, Wallace, Liberman, and Davis, 1976). The conversational behaviors included speaking loud enough so another person could hear him (if about ten feet away) and talking for a specified amount of time. These examples illustrate how clear behavioral definitions can be derived from general terms that may have diverse meanings to different individuals.

Stimulus Events. Assessing the occurrence of the target behavior is central to single-case designs. Frequently it is useful to examine antecedent and consequent events that are likely to be associated with performance of the target behavior. For example, in most applied settings, social stimuli or interactions with others constitute a major category of events that influence client behavior. Attendants, parents, teachers, and peers may provide verbal statements (e.g., instructions or praise), gestures (e.g., physical contact), and facial expressions (e.g., smiles or frowns) that may influence performance. These stimuli may precede (e.g., instructions) or follow (e.g., praise) the target behavior.

Interventions used in applied behavior analysis frequently involve antecedent and consequent events delivered by persons in contact with the client. From the standpoint of assessment, it is useful to observe both the responses of the client and the events delivered by others that constitute the intervention. For example, in one report, the investigators were interested in evaluating the effect of nonverbal teacher approval on the behavior of mentally retarded students in a special education class (Kazdin and Klock, 1973). The intervention consisted of increasing the frequency that the teacher provided nonverbal approval (e.g., physical patting, nods, smiles) after children behaved appropriately. To clarify the effects of the program, verbal and nonverbal teacher approval were assessed. The importance of this assessment was dictated by the possibility that verbal rather than nonverbal approval may have increased and accounted for changes in the students' behavior. Interpretation of the results was facilitated by findings that verbal approval did not increase and nonverbal approval did during the intervention phases of the study.

The antecedent and consequent events that are designed to influence or alter the target responses are not always assessed in single-case experiments. However, it is quite valuable to assess the performance of others whose behaviors are employed to influence the client. The strength of an experimental demonstration can usually be increased by providing evidence that the intervention was implemented as intended and varied directly with the changes in performance.

Strategies of Assessment

Assessment of performance in single-case research has encompassed an extraordinarily wide range of measures and procedures. The majority of observations are based on directly observing overt performance. When overt behaviors are observed directly, a major issue is selecting the measurement strategy. Although observation of overt behavior constitutes the vast bulk of assessment in single-case research, other assessment strategies are used, such as psychophysiological assessment, self-report, and other measures unique to specific target behaviors.

Overt Behavior

Assessment of overt behavior can be accomplished in different ways. In most programs, behaviors are assessed on the basis of discrete response occurrences or the amount of time that the response occurs. However, several variations and different types of measures are available.

Frequency Measures. Frequency counts require simply tallying the number of times the behavior occurs in a given period of time. A measure of the frequency of the response is particularly useful when the target response is discrete and when performing it takes a relatively constant amount of time each time. A discrete response has a clearly delineated beginning and end so that separate instances of the response can be counted. The performance of the behavior should take a relatively constant amount of time so that the units counted are approximately equal. Ongoing behaviors, such as smiling, sitting in one's seat, lying down, and talking, are difficult to record simply by counting because each response may occur for different amounts of time. For example, if a person talks to a peer for fifteen seconds and to another peer for thirty minutes, these might be counted as two instances of talking. A great deal of information is lost by simply counting instances of talking, because they differ in duration.

Frequency measures have been used for a variety of behaviors. For example, in a program for an autistic child, frequency measures were used to assess the number of times the child engaged in social responses such as saying "hello" or sharing a toy or object with someone and the number of self-stimulatory behaviors such as rocking or repetitive pulling of her clothing (Russo and Koegel, 1977). With hospitalized psychiatric patients, one program assessed the frequency that patients engaged in intolerable acts, such as assaulting someone or setting fires, and social behaviors, such as initiating conversation or responding to someone else (Frederiksen, Jenkins, Foy, and Eisler, 1976). In an investigation designed to eliminate seizures among brain-damaged, retarded, and autistic children and adolescents, treatment was evaluated by simply counting the number of seizures each day (Zlutnick, Mayville, and Moffat, 1975). There are additional examples of discrete behaviors that can be easily assessed with frequency counts, including the number of times a person attends an activity or that one person hits another person, number of objects thrown, number of vocabulary words used, number of errors in speech, and so on.

Frequency measures require merely noting instances in which behavior occurs. Usually there is an additional requirement that behavior be observed for a constant amount of time. Of course, if behavior is observed for twenty minutes on one day and thirty minutes on another day, the frequencies are not directly comparable. However, the *rate of response* each day can be obtained by dividing the frequency of responses by the number of minutes observed each day. This measure will yield frequency per minute or rate of response, which is comparable for different durations of observation.

A frequency measure has several desirable features for use in applied settings. First, the frequency of a response is relatively simple to score for individuals working in natural settings. Keeping a tally of behavior usually is all that is required. Moreover, counting devices, such as wrist counters, are available to facilitate recording. Second, frequency measures readily reflect changes over time. Years of basic and applied research have shown that response frequency is sensitive to a variety of interventions. Third, and related to the above, frequency expresses the amount of behavior performed, which is usually of concern to individuals in applied settings. In many cases, the goal of the program is to increase or decrease the number of times a certain behavior occurs. Frequency provides a direct measure of the amount of behavior.

Discrete Categorization. Often it is very useful to classify responses into discrete categories, such as correct–incorrect, performed–not performed, or appropriate–inappropriate. In many ways, discrete categorization resembles a frequency measure because it is used for behaviors that have a clear beginning and end and a constant duration. Yet there are at least two important differences. With a frequency measure, performances of a particular behavior are tallied. The focus is on a single response. Also, the number of times the behavior may occur is theoretically unlimited. For example, how often one child hits another may be measured by frequency counts. How many times the behavior (hitting) may occur has no theoretical limit. Discrete categorization is used to measure whether several different behaviors may have occurred or not. Also, there is only a limited number of opportunities to perform the response.

For example, discrete categorization might be used to measure the sloppiness of one's college roommate. To do this, a checklist can be devised that lists several different behaviors, such as putting away one's shoes in the closet, removing underwear from the kitchen table, putting dishes in the sink, putting food away in the refrigerator, and so on. Each morning, the behaviors on the checklist could be *categorized* as performed or not performed. Each behavior is measured separately and is categorized as performed or not. The total number of behaviors performed correctly constitutes the measure.

Discrete categories have been used to assess behavior in many applied programs. For example, Neef, Iwata, and Page (1978) trained mentally retarded and physically handicapped young adults to ride the bus in the community. Several different behaviors related to finding the bus, boarding it, and leaving the bus were included in a checklist and classified as performed correctly or incorrectly. The effect of training was evaluated by the number of steps performed correctly.

In a very different focus, Komaki and Barnett (1977) improved the execution of plays by a football team of nine- and ten-year-old boys. Each play was broken down into separate steps that the players should perform. Whether each act was performed correctly was scored. A reinforcement program increased the number of steps completed correctly. In a camp setting, the cabin-cleaning behaviors of emotionally disturbed boys were evaluated using discrete categorization (Peacock, Lyman, and Rickard, 1978). Tasks such as placing coats on hooks, making beds, having no objects on the bed, putting toothbrushing materials away, and other specific acts were categorized as completed or not to evaluate the effects of the program.

Discrete categorization is very easy to use because it merely requires listing a number of behaviors and checking off whether they were performed. The behaviors may consist of several different steps that all relate to completion of a task, such as developing dressing or grooming behaviors in retarded children. Behavior can be evaluated by noting whether or how many steps are performed (e.g., removing a shirt from the drawer, putting one arm through, then the other arm, pulling it on down over one's head, and so on). On the other hand, the behaviors need not be related to one another, and performance of one may not necessarily have anything to do with performance of another. For example, room-cleaning behaviors are not necessarily related; performing one correctly (making one's bed) may be unrelated to another (putting one's clothes away). Hence, discrete categorization is a very flexible method of observation that allows one to assess all sorts of behaviors independently of whether they are necessarily related to each other.

Number of Clients. Occasionally, the effectiveness of behavioral programs is evaluated on the basis of the number of clients who perform the target response. This measure is used in group situations such as a classroom or psychiatric hospital where the purpose is to increase the overall performance of a particular behavior, such as coming to an activity on time, completing homework, or speaking up in a group. Once the desired behavior is defined, observations consist of noting how many participants in the group have performed the response. As with frequency and categorization measures, the observations require classifying the response as having occurred or not. But here the *individuals* are counted rather than the number of times an individual performs the response.

Several programs have evaluated the impact of treatment on the number of people who are affected. For example, in one program, mildly retarded women in a halfway house tended to be very inactive (Johnson and Bailey, 1977). A reinforcement program increased participation in various leisure activities (e.g., painting, playing games, working on puzzles, rugmaking) and was evaluated on the number of participants who performed these activities. Another program increased the extent that senior citizens participated in a community meal program that provided low-cost nutritious meals (Bunck and Iwata, 1978). The program was evaluated on the number of new participants from the community who sought the meals. In another program, the investigators were interested in reducing speeding among highway drivers (Van Houten, Nau, and Marini, 1980). To record speeding, a radar unit was placed unobtrusively along the highway. A feedback program that publicly posted the number of speeders was implemented to reduce speeding. The effect of the intervention was evaluated on the percentage of drivers who exceeded the speed limit.

Knowing the number of individuals who perform a response is very useful when the explicit goal of a program is to increase performance in a large group of subjects. Developing behaviors in an institution and even in society at large is consistent with this overall goal. Increasing the number of people who exercise, give to charity, or seek treatment when early stages of serious diseases are apparent, and decreasing the number of people who smoke, overeat, and commit crimes all are important goals that behavioral interventions have addressed.

A problem with the measure in many treatment programs is that it does not provide information about the performance of a particular individual. The number of people who perform a response may be increased in an institution or in society at large. However, the performance of any particular individual may be sporadic or very low. One really does not know how a particular individual is affected. This information may or may not be important, depending upon the goals of the program. As noted earlier, applied behavioral research often focuses on behaviors in everyday social life in which the performance of members of large groups of subjects is important, such as the consumption of energy, performance of leisure activity, and so on. Hence, the number of people who perform a response is of increased interest.

Interval Recording. A frequent strategy of measuring behavior in an applied setting is based on units of time rather than discrete response units. Behavior is recorded during short periods of time for the total time that it is performed. The two methods of time-based measurement are interval recording and response duration.

With interval recording, behavior is observed for a single block of time such as thirty or sixty minutes once per day. A block of time is divided into a series of short intervals (e.g., each interval equaling ten or fifteen seconds). The behavior of the client is observed during each interval. The target behavior is scored as having occurred or not occurred during each interval. If a discrete behavior, such as hitting someone, occurs one or more times in a single interval, the response is scored as having occurred. Several response occurrences within an interval are not counted separately. If the behavior is ongoing with an unclear beginning or end, such as talking, playing, and sitting, or occurs for a long period of time, it is scored during each interval in which it is occurring.

Intervention programs in classroom settings frequently use interval recording to score whether students are paying attention, sitting in their seats, and working quietly. An individual student's behavior may be observed for ten-second intervals over a twenty-minute observational period. For each interval, an observer records whether the child is in his or her seat working quietly. If the child remains in his seat and works for a long period of time, many intervals will be scored for attentive behavior. If the child leaves his seat (without permission) or stops working, inattentive behavior will be scored. During some intervals, a child may be sitting in his or her seat for half of the time and running around the room for the remaining time. Since the interval has to be scored for either attentive or inattentive behavior, a rule must be devised as to how to score behavior in this instance. Often, getting out of the seat will be counted as inattentive behavior within the interval.

Interval recording for a single block of time has been used in many programs beyond the classroom setting. For example, one program focused on several inappropriate behaviors (e.g., roughhousing, touching objects, playing with merchandise) that children performed while they accompanied their parents on a shopping trip (Clark et al., 1977, Exp. 3). Observers followed the family in the store to record whether the inappropriate behaviors occurred during consecutive fifteen-second intervals. Interval assessment was also used in a program to develop conversational skills in delinquent girls (Minkin et al., 1976). Observations were made of whether appropriate conversational behaviors occurred (asking questions of another person and making comments that indicated understanding or agreement with what the other person said) during ten-second intervals while the youths conversed.

In using an interval scoring method, an observer looks at the client during the interval. When one interval is over, the observer records whether the behavior occurred. If an observer is recording several behaviors in an interval, a few seconds may be needed to record all the behaviors observed during that interval. If the observer recorded a behavior as soon as it occurred (before the interval was over), he or she might miss other behaviors that occurred while the first behavior was being scored. Hence, many investigators use interval-scoring procedures that allow time to record after each interval of observation. Intervals for observing behavior might be ten seconds, with five seconds after the interval for recording these observations. If a single behavior is scored in an interval, no time may be required for recording. Each interval might be ten seconds. As soon as a behavior occurred, it would be scored. If behavior did not occur, a quick mark could indicate this at the end of the interval. Of course, it is desirable to use short recording times, when possible, because when behavior is being recorded, it is not being observed. Recording consumes time that might be used for observing behavior.

A variation of interval recording is *time sampling*. This variation uses the interval method, but the observations are conducted for brief periods at different times rather than in a single block of time. For example, with an interval method, a child might be observed for a thirty-minute period. The period would be broken down into small intervals such as ten seconds. With the time-sampling method, the child might also be observed for ten-second intervals, but these intervals might be spread out over a full day instead of a single block of time.

As an illustration, psychiatric patients participating in a hospital reinforcement program were evaluated by a time-sampling procedure (Paul and Lentz, 1977). Patients were observed each hour, at which point an observer looked at the patient for a two-second interval. At the end of the interval, the observer recorded the presence or absence of several behaviors related to social interaction, activities, self-care, and other responses. The procedure was continued throughout the day, sampling one interval at a time. The advantage of time sampling is that the observations represent performance over the entire day. Performance during one single time block (such as the morning) might not represent performance over the entire day.

There are significant features of interval recording that make it one of the most widely adopted strategies in applied research. First, interval assessment is very flexible because virtually any behavior can be recorded. The presence or absence of a response during a time interval applies to any measurable response. Whether a response is discrete and does not vary in duration, is continuous, or sporadic, it can be classified as occurring or not occurring during a brief time period. Second, the observations resulting from interval recording can easily be converted into a percentage. The number of intervals during which the response is scored as occurring can be divided by the total number of intervals observed. This ratio multiplied by 100 yields a percentage of intervals that the response is performed. For example, if social responses are scored as occurring in twenty of forty intervals observed, the percentage of intervals of social behavior is 50 percent $(20/40 \times 100)$. A percentage is easily communicated to others by noting that a certain behavior occurs a specific percentage of time (intervals). Whenever there is doubt as to what assessment strategy should be adopted, an interval approach is always applicable.

Duration. Another time-based method of observation is duration or amount of time that the response is performed. This method is particularly useful for ongoing responses that are continuous rather than discrete acts or responses of extremely short duration. Programs that attempt to increase or decrease the length of time a response is performed might profit from a duration method.

Duration has been used in fewer studies than has interval observation. As an example, one investigation trained two severely withdrawn children to engage in social interaction with other children (Whitman, Mercurio, and Caponigri, 1970). Interaction was measured by simply recording the amount of time that the children were in contact with each other. Duration has been used for other responses, such as the length of time that claustrophobic patients spent sitting voluntarily in a small room (Leitenberg, Agras, Thomson and Wright, 1968), the time delinquent boys spent returning from school and errands (Phillips, 1968), and the time students spent working on assignments (Surratt, Ulrich, and Hawkins, 1969).

Another measure based on duration is not how long the response is performed but rather how long it takes for the client to begin the response. The amount of time that elapses between a cue and the response is referred to as *latency.* Many programs have timed response latency. For example, in one report, an eight-year-old boy took extremely long to comply with classroom instructions, which contributed to his academic difficulties (Fjellstedt and Sulzer-Azaroff, 1973). Reinforcing consequences were provided to decrease his response latencies when instructions were given. Compliance with instructions became much more rapid over the course of the program.

Assessment of response duration is a fairly simple matter, requiring that one start and stop a stopwatch or note the time when the response begins and ends. However, the onset and termination of the response must be carefully defined. If these conditions have not been met, duration is extremely difficult to employ. For example, in recording the duration of a tantrum, a child may cry continuously for several minutes, whimper for short periods, stop all noise for a few seconds, and begin intense crying again. In recording duration, a decision is required to handle changes in the intensity of the behavior (e.g., crying to whimpering) and pauses (e.g., periods of silence) so they are consistently recorded as part of the response or as a different (e.g., nontantrum) response.

Use of response duration is generally restricted to situations in which the length of time a behavior is performed is a major concern. In most programs, the goal is to increase or decrease the frequency of a response rather than its duration. There are notable exceptions, of course. For example, it may be desirable to increase the length of time that some students study. Because interval measures are so widely used and readily adaptable to virtually all responses, they are often selected as a measure over duration. The number or proportion of intervals in which studying occurs reflects changes in study time, since interval recording is based on time.

Other Strategies

Most assessment in single-case research has focused on overt behavior, using one of the strategies mentioned above. Other strategies are available that are used in a sizable portion of investigations. Three general strategies in particular can be delineated, including response-specific, psychophysiological, and self-report measures. Although the formats of these measures sometimes overlap with the overt behavioral assessment strategies discussed earlier (e.g., frequency, duration), the strategies discussed below are somewhat different from merely observing overt performance in the usual way.

Response-Specific Measures. Response-specific measures are assessment procedures that are unique to the particular behaviors under investigation. Many behaviors have specific measures peculiar to them that can be examined directly. For example, interventions designed to reduce overeating or cigarette smoking can be evaluated by assessing the number of calories consumed or cigarettes smoked. Calories and cigarettes could be considered as simple frequency measures in the sense that they are both tallies of a particular unit of performance. However, the measures are distinguished here because they are peculiar to the target behavior of interest and can be used to assess the impact of the intervention directly. Response-specific measures are used in a large number of investigations. For example, Foxx and Hake (1977) were interested in decreasing the use of automobiles among college students in an effort to conserve gasoline. Driving was assessed directly by measuring mileage from odometer readings of each student's car. Chapman and Risley (1974) were interested in reducing the amount of litter in an urban housing area. Assessment consisted of counting the pieces of litter (e.g., paper, wood, glass, food, broken toys, or other items). Schnelle et al. (1978) were interested in preventing burglaries by altering the types of police patrols in a city. The occurrence of burglaries was noted in routine police records and could be tallied.

The above examples illustrate only a few of the measures that might be called response-specific. In each case, some feature of the response or the situation in which behavior was observed allowed an assessment format peculiar to the behavior of interest. Response-specific measures are of use because they directly assess the response or a product of the response that is recognized to be of obvious clinical, social, or applied significance. Also, assessment is often available from existing data systems or records that are part of the ongoing institutional or social environment (e.g., crime rate, traffic accidents, hospital admissions). When decisions about assessment are being made, the investigator may wish to consider whether the response can be assessed in a direct and unique way that will be of clear social relevance. Response-specific measures often are of more obvious significance to persons unfamiliar with behavioral research to whom the results may need to be communicated than are specially devised overt behavioral measures.

Psychophysiological Assessment. Frequently, psychophysiological responses have been assessed in single-case designs. Psychophysiological responses directly reflect many problems of clinical significance or are highly correlated with the occurrence of such problems. For example, autonomic arousal is important to assess in disorders associated with anxiety or sexual arousal. One can observe overt behavioral signs of arousal. However, physiological arousal can be assessed directly and is a crucial component of arousal in its own right.

Much of the impetus for psychophysiological assessment in single-case research has come from the emergence of biofeedback, in which the client is presented with information about his or her ongoing physiological processes. Assessment of psychophysiological responses in biofeedback research has encompassed diverse disorders and processes of cardiovascular, respiratory, gastrointestinal, genitourinary, musculoskeletal, and other systems (see Blanchard and Epstein, 1977; Knapp and Peterson, 1976; Yates, 1980). Within the various systems, the number of psychophysiological responses and methods of assessment are vast and cannot begin to be explored here (see Epstein, 1976; Kallman and Feuerstein, 1977).

Some of the more commonly reported measures in single-case research include such psychophysiological measures as heart or pulse rate, blood pressure, skin temperature, blood volume, muscle tension, and brain wave activity. For example, Beiman, Graham, and Ciminero (1978) were interested in reducing the hypertension of two adult males. Clients were taught to relax deeply when they felt tense or anxious or felt pressures of time or anger. Blood pressure readings were used to reflect improvements in both systolic and diastolic blood pressure. As another example of psychophysiological assessment, Lubar and Bahler (1976) were interested in reducing seizures in several patients. Cortical activity (of the sensorimotor cortex) was measured by electroencephalogram (EEG) recordings. The measures were used to examine the type of activity and to provide feedback to increase the activity (sensorimotor rhythm) that would interfere with seizure activity.

Paredes, Jones, and Gregory (1977) were interested in training an alcoholic to discriminate his blood alcohol levels. Training persons to discriminate blood alcohol levels is sometimes an adjunct to treatment of alcoholics, the rationale being that if persons can determine their blood alcohol concentrations, they can learn to stop drinking at a point before intoxication. Blood alcohol concentrations were measured by a breathalyzer, a device into which a person breathes that reflects alcohol in the blood.

The above examples provide only a minute sample of the range of measures and disorders encompassed by psychophysiological assessment. Diverse clinical problems have been studied in single-case and between-group research, including insomnia, obsessive-compulsive disorders, pain, hyperactivity, sexual dysfunction, tics, tremors, and many others (Yates, 1980). Depending on the target focus, psychophysiological assessment permits measurement of precursors, central features, or correlates of the problem.

Self-Report. Single-case designs have focused almost exclusively on overt performance. Clients' own reports of their behaviors or their perceptions, thoughts, and feelings, may, however, be relevant for several clinical problems. Emphasis has been placed on overt actions rather than verbal behavior, unless verbal behavior itself is the target focus (e.g., irrational speech, stuttering, threats of aggression).

Part of the reason for the almost exclusive focus on overt performance rather than self-report (verbal behavior) can be traced to the conceptual heritage of applied behavior analysis (Kazdin, 1978c). This heritage reflects a systematic interest in how organisms behave. In the case of humans, what people say about their performance may be of considerable interest, but it is not always related to how they act, to the problems they bring to treatment, or to the extent to which their behavior is altered after treatment.

As a method of assessment, self-report often is held to be rather suspect because it is subject to a variety of response biases and sets (e.g., responding in a socially desirable fashion, agreeing, lying, and others) which distort one's own account of actual performance. Of course, self-report is not invariably inaccurate, nor is direct behavioral assessment necessarily free of response biases or distortion. When persons are aware that their behavior is being assessed, they can distort both what they say and what they do. Self-report does tend to be more readily under control of the client than more direct measures of overt behavior, however, and hence it is perhaps more readily subject to distortion.

In many cases in clinical research, whether single-case or between-group, self-report may represent the only modality currently available to evaluate treatment. For example, in the case of private events such as obsessive thoughts, uncontrollable urges, or hallucinations, self-report may be the only possible method of assessment. When the client is the only one with direct access to the event, self-report may have to be the primary assessment modality.

For example, Gullick and Blanchard (1973) treated a male patient who complained of obsessional thoughts about having blasphemed God. His recurring thoughts incapacitated him so that he could not work or participate in activities with his family. Because thoughts are private events, the investigators instructed the patient to record the duration of obsessional thoughts and evaluated alternative treatments on the basis of changes in self-reported data.

Even when self-report is not the only measure, it often is an important measure because the person's private experience may be relevant to the overall problem. It is possible that overt performance may be observed directly and provide important data. However, self-report may represent a crucial dimension in its own right. For example, considerable research has been devoted to the treatment of headaches. Various measures can be used, including psychophysiological measures (e.g., muscle tension, electrical activity of the cortex, skin temperature) (Blanchard and Epstein, 1977), or such measures as medical records or reports from informants (e.g., Epstein and Abel, 1977). These measures are only imperfect correlates of reported headaches and are not substitutes for self-reports of pain. Self-report obviously is of major importance because it typically serves as the basis for seeking treatment. Hence, in most intervention studies, verbal reports are solicited that include self-report ratings of intensity, frequency, and duration of headaches.

Similarly, many intervention studies focus on altering sexual arousal in persons who experience arousal in the presence of socially inappropriate and censured stimuli (e.g., exhibitionistic, sadistic, masochistic stimuli or stimuli involving children, infrahumans, or inanimate objects). Direct psychophysiological assessment of sexual arousal is possible by measuring vaginal or penile blood volume to evaluate changes in arousal as a function of treatment. Yet it is important as well to measure what persons actually say about what stimuli arouse them, because self-report is a significant response modality in its own right and does not always correlate with physiological arousal. Hence, it is relevant to assess self-report along with other measures of arousal.

For example, Barlow, Leitenberg, and Agras (1969) altered the pedophilic behavior (sexual attraction to children) of a twenty-five-year-old male. Assessment measured physiological arousal but also subjective measures of arousal. The patient was instructed to record in everyday situations the times he was sexually aroused by the sight of an immature girl. The number of self-reported instances of arousal decreased over the course of treatment.

Selection of an Assessment Strategy

In most single-case designs, the investigator selects one of the assessment strategies based on overt performance (e.g., frequency, interval measures). Some behaviors may lend themselves well to frequency counts or categorization because they are discrete, such as the number of profane words used, or the number of toileting or eating responses; others are well suited to interval recording, such as reading, working, or sitting; and still others are best assessed by duration, such as time spent studying, crying, or getting dressed. Target behaviors usually can be assessed in more than one way, so there is no single strategy that must be adopted. For example, an investigator working in an institution for delinquents may wish to record a client's aggressive behavior. Hitting others (e.g., making physical contact with another individual with a closed fist) may be the response of interest. What assessment strategy should be used?

Aggressive behavior might be measured by a *frequency* count by having an observer record how many times the client hits others during a certain period each day. Each hit would count as one response. The behavior also could be observed during *interval recording*. A block of time such as thirty minutes could be set aside for observation. The thirty minutes could be divided into ten-second intervals. During each interval, the observer records whether any hitting occurs. A *duration* measure might also be used. It might be difficult to time the duration of hitting, because instances of hitting are too fast to be timed with a stopwatch unless there is a series of hits (as in a fight). An easier duration measure might be to record the amount of time from the beginning of each day until the first aggressive response, i.e., a *latency* measure. Presumably, if a program decreased aggressive behavior, the amount of time from the beginning of the day until the first aggressive response would increase.

Although many different measures can be used in a given program, the measure finally selected may be dictated by the purpose of the program. Different measures sometimes have slightly different goals. For example, consider two behavioral programs that focused on increasing toothbrushing, a seemingly simple response that could be assessed in many different ways. In one of the programs, the *number of individuals* who brushed their teeth in a boys' summer camp was observed (Lattal, 1969). The boys knew how to brush their teeth and an incentive system increased their performance of the response. In another program that increased toothbrushing, the clients were mentally retarded residents at a state hospital (Horner and Keilitz, 1975). The residents were unable to brush their teeth at the beginning of the program, so the many behaviors involved in toothbrushing were developed. *Discrete categorization* was used to assess toothbrushing, where each component step of the behavior (wetting the brush, removing the cap, applying the toothpaste, and so on) was scored as performed or not performed. The percentage of steps correctly completed measured the effects of training. Although both of the above investigations assessed toothbrushing, the different methods reflect slightly different goals, namely getting children who can brush to do so or training the response in individual residents who did not know how to perform the response.

Many responses may immediately suggest their own specific measures. In such cases, the investigator need not devise a special format but can merely adopt an existing measure. Measures such as calories, cigarettes smoked, and miles of jogging are obvious examples than can reflect eating, smoking, and exercising, relatively common target responses in behavioral research.

When the target problem involves psychophysiological functioning, direct measures are often available and of primary interest. In many cases, measures of overt behavior can reflect important physiological processes. For example, seizures, ruminative vomiting, and anxiety can be assessed through direct observation of the client. However, direct psychophysiological measures can be used as well and either provide a finer assessment of the target problem or evaluate an important and highly related component.

Characteristics of the target problem may dictate entirely the type of assessment, as in the case of private events, noted earlier. Self-report may be the only available means of evaluating the intervention. More commonly, use of self-report as an assessment modality in single-case research results from evaluating multifaceted problems where self-report represents a significant component in its own right. For example, self-report is an important dimension in problems related to anxiety, sexual arousal, and mood disorders where clients' perceptions may serve as the major basis for seeking treatment.

To a large extent, selection of an assessment strategy depends on characteristics of the target response and the goals of the intervention. In any given situation, several assessment options are likely to be available. Decisions for the final assessment format are often made on the basis of other criteria than the target response, including practical considerations such as the availability of assessment periods, observers, and so on.

Conditions of Assessment

The strategies of assessment refer to the different methods of recording performance. Observations can vary markedly along other dimensions, such as the manner in which behavior is evoked, the setting in which behaviors are assessed, whether the persons are aware that their behaviors are assessed, and whether human observers or automated apparatus are used to detect performance. These conditions of assessment are often as important as the specific strategy selected to record the response. Assessment conditions can influence how the client responds and the confidence one can have that the data accurately reflect performance.

Naturalistic versus Contrived Observations

Naturalistic observation in the present context refers to observing performance without intervening or structuring the situation for the client. Ongoing performance is observed as it normally occurs, and the situation is not intentionally altered by the investigator merely to obtain the observations. For example, observations of interactions among children at school during a free-play period would be considered naturalistic in the sense that an ordinary activity was observed during the school day (Hauserman, Walen, and Behling, 1973). Similarly, observation of the eating of obese and nonobese persons in a restaurant would constitute assessment under naturalistic conditions (Gaul, Craighead, and Mahoney, 1975).

Although direct observation of performance as it normally occurs is very useful, naturalistic observation often is not possible or feasible. Many of the behaviors of interest are not easily observed because they are of low frequency, require special precipitating conditions, or are prohibitive to assess in view of available resources. Situations often are contrived to evoke responses so that the target behavior can be assessed.

For example, Jones, Kazdin, and Haney (1981) were interested in evaluating the extent to which children could escape from emergency fire situations at home. Loss of life among children at home and in bed at night make emergency escape skills of special importance. Direct assessment of children in their homes under conditions of actual fires was obviously not possible. Hence, contrived situations were devised at the children's school by using simulated bedrooms that included a bed, window, rug, and chair, and looked like an ordinary bedroom. How children would respond under a variety of emergency situations was assessed directly. Training was evaluated on the number of correct responses (e.g., crawling out of bed, checking to see whether the bedroom door was hot, avoiding smoke inhalation) performed in the contrived situation.

Naturalistic and contrived conditions of assessment provide different advantages and disadvantages. Assessment of performance under contrived conditions provides information that often would be too difficult to obtain under naturalistic conditions. The response might be seen rarely if the situation were not arranged to evoke the behavior. In addition, contrived situations provide consistent and standardized assessment conditions. Without such conditions, it may be difficult to interpret performance over time. Performance may change or fluctuate markedly as a function of the constantly changing conditions in the environment.

The advantage of providing standardization of the assessment conditions with contrived situations bears a cost as well. When the situation is contrived, the possibility exists that performance may have little or no relation to performance under naturalistic conditions. For example, family interaction may be observed in a clinic situation in which parents and their children are given structured tasks to perform. The contrived tasks allow assessment of a variety of behaviors that might otherwise be difficult to observe if families were allowed to interact normally on their own. However, the possibility exists that families may interact very differently under contrived conditions than they would under ordinary circumstances. Hence, a major consideration in assessing performance in contrived situations is whether that performance represents performance under noncontrived conditions. In most behavioral assessment, the relationship between performance under contrived versus naturalistic conditions is assumed rather than demonstrated.

Natural versus Laboratory (or Clinic) Settings

The previous discussion examined how the situation was structured or arranged to obtain behavioral observations, namely, in naturalistic or contrived conditions. A related dimension that distinguishes observations is where the assessment is conducted. Observations can be obtained in the natural environment or in the laboratory or clinical setting. The setting in which the observations are actually conducted can be distinguished from whether or not the observations are contrived.

Ideally, direct observations are made in the natural setting in which clients normally function. Such observations may be especially likely to reflect performance that the client has identified as problematic. Naturalistic settings might include the community, the job, the classroom, at home, in the institution, or some other settings in which clients ordinarily function. For example, in one investigation an adult male who was extremely anxious and deficient in verbal skills was trained to speak in an organized and fluent fashion (Hollandsworth, Glazeski, and Dressel, 1978). Observations were made in the natural environment to examine the client's verbal skills after treatment. Specifically, observers posing as shoppers were sent to the store where the client worked. Observations of interactions with customers were sampled directly. It is important to note also that the observations were contrived. The assessors engaged in behaviors that permitted assessment of the behaviors of interest. They could have simply observed other shoppers, but this would have reduced the control and standardization they had over the conditions of assessment.

Often behavioral observations are made in the home of persons who are seen in treatment. For example, to treat conduct problem children and their families, observers may assess family interaction directly in the home (Patterson, 1974; Reid, 1978). Restrictions may be placed on the family, such as having them remain in one or a few rooms and not spend time on the phone or watch television to help standardize the conditions of assessment. The assessment is in a naturalistic setting even though the actual circumstances of assessment are slightly contrived, i.e., structured in such a way that the situation probably departs from ordinary living conditions. Assessment of family interaction among conduct problem children has also taken place in clinic settings in addition to the natural environment (e.g., Eyberg & Johnson, 1974; Robinson and Eyberg, 1980). Parents and their children are presented with tasks and games in a playroom setting, where they interact. Interactions during the tasks are recorded to evaluate how the parents and child respond to one another. Interestingly, the examples here with conduct problem children convey differences in whether the assessment was conducted in naturalistic (home) or clinic settings. However, in both situations, the assessment conditions were contrived in varying degrees because arrangements were made by the investigator that were likely to influence interactions.

Assessment in naturalistic settings raises obvious problems. A variety of practical issues often present major obstacles, such as the cost required for conducting observations and reliability checks, ensuring and maintaining standardization of the assessment conditions, and so on. Clinic and laboratory settings have been relied on heavily because of the convenience and standardization of assessment conditions they afford. In the vast majority of clinic observations, contrived situations are used, such as those illustrated earlier. When clients come to the clinic, it is difficult to observe direct samples of performance that are not under somewhat structured, simulated, or contrived conditions.

Obtrusive versus Unobtrusive Assessment

Independently of whether the measures are obtained under contrived or naturalistic conditions and in clinic or natural settings, observations of overt behavior may differ in whether they are *obtrusive,* i.e., whether the subjects are aware that their behaviors are assessed. The obtrusiveness of an assessment procedure may be a matter of degree, so that subjects may be aware of assessment generally, aware that they are being observed but unsure of the target behaviors, and so on. The potential issue with obtrusive assessment is that it may be *reactive,* i.e., that the assessment procedure may influence the subject's performance.

Observations of overt performance may vary in the extent to which they are conducted under obtrusive or unobtrusive conditions. In many investigations that utilize direct observations, performance is assessed under obtrusive conditions. For example, observation of behavior problem children in the home or the clinic is conducted in situations in which families are aware that they are being observed. Similarly, clients who are seen for treatment of anxiety-based problems usually are fully aware that their behavior is assessed when avoidance behavior is evaluated under contrived conditions.

Occasionally, observations are conducted under *un*obtrusive assessment conditions (Kazdin, 1979a, 1979c). For example, Bellack, Hersen, and Lamparski (1979) evaluated the social skills of college students by placing them in a situation with a confederate. The situation was contrived to appear as if the subject and confederate had to sit together during a "scheduling mix-up." The confederate socially interacted with the subject, who presumably was unaware of the assessment procedures. The interaction was videotaped for later observation of such measures as eye contact, duration of responding, smiles, and other measures. As another example, McFall and Marston (1970) phoned subjects who completed an assertion training program. The caller posed as a magazine salesperson and completed a prearranged sequence of requests designed to elicit assertive behavior. Because the phone call was under the guise of selling magazines, it is highly unlikely that the persons were aware that their behaviors were being assessed.

In another example, Fredericksen et al. (1976) evaluated the effects of treatment designed to train psychiatric patients to avoid abusive verbal outbursts on the ward. Situations on the ward that previously had precipitated these outbursts were arranged to occur (i.e., contrived) after treatment. When the contrived situations were implemented, the patients' responses (e.g., hostile comments, inappropriate requests) were assessed unobtrusively by staff normally present on the ward. (This example is interesting for reasons other than the use of unobtrusive assessment. Although the observations were contrived, the situations were those that had normally occurred on the ward so that they may be viewed from the patients' standpoint as naturalistic situations.)

Unobtrusive behavioral observations are reported relatively infrequently (see Kazdin, 1979c). In many situations, clients may not know all the details of assessment but are partially aware that they are being evaluated (e.g., children in a classroom study). Completely withholding information about the assessment procedures raises special ethical problems that often preclude the use of unobtrusive measures based on direct observations of overt performance (Webb, Campbell, Schwartz, Sechrest, and Grove, 1981).

Human Observers versus Automated Recording

Another dimension that distinguishes how observations are obtained pertains to the data collection method. In most applied single-case research, human observers assess behavior. Observers watch the client(s) and record behavior according to one of the assessment strategies described earlier. All of the examples discussed above illustrating assessment under naturalistic versus contrived conditions, in natural and laboratory settings, and with obtrusive or unobtrusive measures relied upon human observers. Observers are commonly used to record behavior in the home, classroom, psychiatric hospital, laboratory, community, and clinical settings. Observers may include special persons introduced into the setting or others who are already present (e.g., teachers in class, spouses or parents in the home).

In contrast, observations can be gathered through the use of apparatus or automated devices. Behavior is recorded through an apparatus that in some way detects when the response has occurred, how long it has occurred, or other features of performance.[3] With automated recording, humans are involved in assessment only to the extent that the apparatus needs to be calibrated or that persons must read and transcribe the numerical values from the device, if these data are not automatically printed and summarized.

A major area of research in which automated measures are used routinely is biofeedback. In this case, psychophysiological recording equipment is required to assess ongoing physiological responses. Direct observation by human observers could not assess most of the responses of interest because they are undetectable from merely looking at the client (e.g., brain wave activity, muscle tension, cardiac arrhythmias, skin temperature). Some physiological signs might be monitored by observers (e.g., pulse rate by external pressure, heart rate by stethoscope), but psychophysiological assessment provides a more sensitive, accurate, and reliable recording system.

Automated assessment in single-case research has not been restricted to psychophysiological assessment. A variety of measures has been used to assess responses of applied interest. For example, Schmidt and Ulrich (1969) were interested in reducing excessive noise among children during a study period in a fourth-grade classroom. To measure noise, a sound level meter was used. At regular intervals, an observer simply recorded the decibel level registered on the meter. Similarly, Meyers, Artz, and Craighead (1976) were interested in controlling noise in university dormitories. Microphones in each dormitory recorded the noise. Each noise occurrence beyond a prespecified decibel level automatically registered on a counter so that the frequency of excessive noise occurrences was recorded without human observers.

Leitenberg et al. (1968) were interested in assessing how long a claustrophobic patient could remain in a small room while the door was closed. The patient was told that she should leave the room when she felt uncomfortable. An automated timer connected to the door measured the duration of her stay in the room. Finally, Van Houten et al. (1980) recorded speeding by drivers on

---

3. Automated recording here refers to apparatus that registers the responses of the client. In applied research, apparatus that aids human observers are often used, such as wrist counters, event recorders, stop watches, and audio and video tape recorders. These devices serve as useful aids in recording behavior, but they are still based on having human observers assess performance. Insofar as human judgment is involved, they are included here under human observations.

a highway. The cars' speed was assessed automatically by a radar unit commonly used by police. An observer simply recorded the speed registered on the unit.

As evident from some of the above examples, human observers can be completely removed from assessment by means of automated recordings. In other instances, human observers have a minimal role. The apparatus registers the response in a quantitative fashion, which can be simply copied by an observer. The observer merely transcribes the information from one source (the apparatus) to another (data sheets), a function that often is not difficult to program automatically but may be easier to achieve with human observers.

The use of automated records has the obvious advantage of reducing or eliminating errors of measurement that would otherwise be introduced by the presence of human observers.[4] Humans must subjectively decide whether a response has begun, is completed, or has occurred at all. Limitations of the "apparatus" of human observers (e.g., the scanning capability of the eyes), subjective judgment in reaching decisions about the response, and the assessment of complex behaviors with unclear boundary conditions may increase the inaccuracies and inconsistencies of human observers. Automated apparatus overcomes many of the observational problems introduced by human observers.

To be sure, automated recordings introduce their own problems. For example, equipment can and often does fail, or it may lose its accuracy if not periodically checked and calibrated. Also, equipment is often expensive and less flexible in terms of the range of behaviors that can be observed or the range of situations that can be assessed. For example, Christensen and Sprague (1973) were interested in evaluating treatments to reduce hyperactivity among children in a classroom setting. To record the children's hyperactivity, stabilimetric cushions were attached to each chair. The cushions automatically assessed in-seat movements. The cushions were connected to a counter that recorded movements per minute. The advantages of automated recording in this example are obvious. However, some flexibility in assessment was lost. Hyperactivity is manifest in the classroom in a variety of ways beyond movements that children make in their seats. Human observers are more likely to be able to sample a wider range of behaviors (e.g., running around the room, remaining in one's seat but looking around the class, throwing objects at others, shouting) and to record across a wider range of situations (e.g., classroom, playground).

Apparatus that automatically records responses overcomes significant problems that can emerge with human observers. In addition, automated recordings often allow assessment of behavior for relatively long periods of time. Once the

4. The errors introduced by humans in recording behavior will be discussed in the next chapter.

device is in place, it can record for extended periods (e.g., entire school day, all night during sleep). The expense of human observers often prohibits such extended assessment. Another advantage may relate to the impact of the assessment procedure on the responses. The presence of human observers may be obtrusive and influence the responses that are assessed. Automatic recording apparatus often quickly becomes part of the physical environment and, depending on the apparatus, may less readily convey that behavior is being monitored.

General Comments

The conditions under which behavioral observations are obtained may vary markedly. The dimensions that distinguish behavioral observations discussed above do not exhaust all of the possibilities. Moreover, for purposes of presentation, three of the conditions of assessment were discussed as either naturalistic *or* contrived, in natural *or* laboratory settings, and as obtrusive *or* unobtrusive. Actually, these characteristics vary along continua. For example, many clinic situations may approximate or very much attempt to approximate a natural setting. As an illustration, the alcohol consumption of hospitalized alcoholics is often measured by observing patients as they drink in a simulated bar in the hospital. The bar is in a clinic setting. Yet the conditions closely resemble the physical environment in which drinking often takes place.

The range of conditions under which behavioral observations can be obtained provides many options for the investigator. When the strategies for assessment (e.g., frequency, interval observations) are added, the diversity of observational practices is even more impressive. Thus, for behaviors related to aggressiveness, social skills, and anxiety, several options for direct behavioral observation are available. An interesting issue yet to be fully addressed in behavioral assessment is the interrelationship among alternative measures that can be used for particular behaviors.

Summary and Conclusions

Assessment in single-case research raises a variety of issues related to the identification of target behaviors and the selection of alternative strategies for their assessment. Identification of the focus of assessment is often obvious because of the nature of the client's problem (e.g., severe deficits or excesses in performance) or the goals of the program (e.g., reduction of traffic accidents or consumption of energy). In such cases the focus is relatively straightforward and does not rely on systematic or formal evaluation of what needs to be assessed. The selection of target behaviors occasionally relies on empirically based social validation methods. The target focus is determined by empirically evaluating the performance of persons who are functioning adequately and whose behaviors might serve as a useful performance criterion for a target client *(social comparison method)* or by relying on the judgments of persons regarding the requisite behaviors for adaptive functioning *(subjective evaluation method)*.

When the target behavior is finally decided on, it is important that its definition meet several criteria: *objectivity, clarity,* and *completeness.* To meet these criteria not only requires explicit definitions, but also decision rules about what does and does not constitute performance of the target behavior. The extent to which definitions of behavior meet these criteria determines whether the observations are obtained consistently and, indeed, whether they can be obtained at all.

Typically, single-case research focuses on direct observations of overt performance. Different strategies of assessment are available, including *frequency counts, discrete categorization, number of clients* who perform the behavior, *interval recording,* and *duration.* Other strategies include response measures peculiar to the particular responses, psychophysiological recording, and self-report. Depending on the precise focus, measures other than direct observation may be essential.

Apart from the strategies of assessment, observations can be obtained under a variety of conditions. The conditions may vary according to whether behavior is observed under *naturalistic or contrived situations,* in *natural or laboratory settings,* by *obtrusive* or *unobtrusive* means, and whether behavior is recorded by *human observers or* by *automated apparatus.* The different conditions of assessment vary in the advantages and limitations they provide, including the extent to which performance in the assessment situation reflects performance in other situations, whether the measures of performance are comparable over time and across persons, and the convenience and cost of assessing performance.

3

Interobserver Agreement

When direct observations of behavior are obtained by human observers, the possibility exists that observers will not record behavior consistently. However well specified the responses are, observers may need to make judgments about whether a response occurred or may inadvertently overlook or misrecord behaviors that occur in the situation. Central to the collection of direct observational data is evaluation of agreement among observers. *Interobserver agreement*, also referred to as *reliability*, refers to the extent to which observers agree in their scoring of behavior.[1] The purpose of the present chapter is to discuss interobserver agreement and the manner in which agreement is assessed.

Basic Information on Agreement
Need to Assess Agreement

Agreement between different observers needs to be assessed for three major reasons. First, assessment is useful only to the extent that it can be achieved with some consistency. For example, if frequency counts differ depending upon who is counting, it will be difficult to know the client's actual performance. The

---

1. In applied research, "interobserver agreement" and "reliability" have been used interchangeably. For purposes of the present chapter, the "interobserver agreement" will be used primarily. "Reliability" as a term has an extensive history in assessment and has several different meanings. Interobserver agreement specifies the focus more precisely as the consistency between or among observers.

client may be scored as performing a response frequently on some days and infrequently on other days as a function of who scores the behavior rather than actual changes in client performance. Inconsistent measurement introduces variation in the data, which adds to the variation stemming from ordinary fluctuations in client performance. If measurement variation is large, no systematic pattern of behavior may be evident. Any subsequent attempt to alter performance with a particular intervention might be difficult to evaluate. And any change in behavior might not be detected by the measure because of inconsistent assessment of performance. Stable patterns of behavior are usually needed if change in behavior is to be identified. Hence, reliable recording is essential. Agreement between observers ensures that one potential source of variation, namely, inconsistencies among observers, is minimal.

A second reason for assessing agreement between observers is to minimize or circumvent the biases that any individual observer may have. If a single observer were used to record the target behavior, any recorded change in behavior may be the result of a change in the observer's definition of the behavior over time rather than in the actual behavior of the client. Over time the observer might become lenient or stringent in applying the response definition. Alternatively, the observer might expect and perceive improvement based on the implementation of an intervention designed to alter behavior, even though no actual changes in behavior occur. Using more than one observer and checking interobserver agreement provide a partial check on the consistency with which response definitions are applied over time.

A final reason that agreement between observers is important is that it reflects whether the target behavior is well defined. Interobserver agreement on the occurrences of behavior is one way to evaluate the extent to which the definition of behavior is sufficiently objective, clear, and complete—requirements for response definitions discussed in the last chapter. Moreover, if observers readily agree on the occurrence of the response, it may be easier for persons who eventually carry out an intervention to agree on the occurrences and to apply the intervention (e.g., reinforcing consequences) consistently.

Agreement versus Accuracy

Agreement between observers is assessed by having two or more persons observe the same client(s) at the same time. The observers work independently for the entire observation period, and the observations are compared when the session is over. A comparison of the observers' records reflects the consistency with which observers recorded behavior.

It is important to distinguish agreement between observers from accuracy of the observations. *Agreement* refers to evaluation of how well the data from separate observers correspond. High agreement means that observers correspond in the behaviors they score. Methods of quantifying the agreement are available so that the extent to which observers do correspond in their observations can be carefully evaluated.

A major interest in assessing agreement is to evaluate whether observers are scoring behavior accurately. *Accuracy* refers to whether the observers' data reflect the client's actual performance. To measure the correspondence between how the client performs and observers' data, a standard or criterion is needed. This criterion is usually based on consensus or agreement of several observers that certain behaviors have or have not occurred.

Accuracy may be evaluated by constructing a videotape in which certain behaviors are acted out and, hence, are known to be on the tape with a particular frequency, during particular intervals, or for a particular duration. Data that observers obtain from looking at the tape can be used to assess accuracy, since "true" performance is known. Alternatively, client behavior under naturalistic conditions (e.g., children in the classroom) may be taped. Several observers could score the tape repeatedly and decide what behaviors were present at any particular point in time. A new observer can rate the tape, and the data, when compared with the standard, reflect accuracy. When there is an agreement on a standard for how the client actually performed, a comparison of an observer's data with the standard reflects accuracy, i.e., the correspondence of the observers' data to the "true" behavior.

Although investigators are interested in accuracy of observations, they usually must settle for interobserver agreement. In most settings, there are no clear criteria or permanent records of behavior to determine how the client really performed. Partially for practical reasons, the client's behavior cannot be videotaped or otherwise recorded each time a check on agreement is made. Without a permanent record of the client's performance, it is difficult to determine how the client actually performed. In a check on agreement, two observers usually enter the situation and score behavior. The scores are compared, but neither score necessarily reflects how the client actually behaved.

In general, both interobserver agreement and accuracy involve comparing an observer's data with some other source. They differ in the extent to which the source of comparison can be entrusted to reflect the actual behavior of the client. Although accuracy and agreement are related, they need not go together. For example, an observer may record accurately (relative to a preestablished standard) but show low interobserver agreement (with another observer whose observations are quite inaccurate). Conversely, an observer may show poor accuracy (in relation to the standard) but high interobserver agreement (with another observer who is inaccurate in a similar way). Hence, interobserver agreement is not a measure of accuracy. The general assumption is that if observers record the same behaviors, their data probably reflect what the client is doing. However, it is important to bear in mind that this is an assumption. Under special circumstances, discussed later in the chapter, the assumption may not be justified.

Conducting Checks on Agreement

In an investigation, an observer typically records the behavior of the client on a daily basis over the entire course of the investigation. Occasionally, another observer will also be used to check interobserver agreement. On such occasions, both observers will record the client's behavior. Obviously, it is important that the observers work independently, not look at each other's scoring sheets, and refrain from discussing their observations. The purpose of checking agreement is to determine how well observers agree when they record performance independently.

Checks on interobserver agreement are usually conducted on a regular basis throughout an investigation. If there are several different phases in the investigation, interobserver agreement needs to be checked in each phase. It is possible that agreement varies over time as a function of changes in the client's behavior. The investigator is interested in having information on the consistency of observations over the course of the study. Hence, interobserver agreement is checked often and under each different condition or intervention that is in effect.

There are no precise rules for how often agreement should be checked. Several factors influence decisions about how often to check interobserver agreement. For example, with several observers or a relatively complex observational system, checks may need to be completed relatively often. Also, the extent to which observers in fact agree when agreement is checked may dictate the frequency of the checks. Initial checks on agreement may reveal that observers agree all or virtually all of the time. In such cases, agreement may need to be checked occasionally but not often. On the other hand, with other behaviors and observers, agreement may fluctuate greatly and checks will be required more often. As a general rule, agreement needs to be assessed within each phase of the investigation, preferably at least a few times within each phase. Yet checking on agreement is more complex than merely scheduling occasions in which two observers score behavior. How the checks on agreement are actually conducted may be as important as the frequency with which they are conducted, as will be evident later in the chapter.

Methods of Estimating Agreement

The methods available for estimating agreement partially depend on the assessment strategy (e.g., whether frequency or interval assessment is conducted). For any particular observational strategy, several different methods of estimating agreement are available. The major methods of computing reliability, their application to different observational formats, and considerations in their use are discussed below.

Frequency Ratio

Description. The frequency ratio is a method used to compute agreement when comparisons are made between the totals of two observers who independently record behaviors. The method is often used for frequency counts, but it can be applied to other assessment strategies as well (e.g., intervals of behavior, duration). Typically, the method is used with free operant behavior, that is, behavior that can theoretically take on any value so that there are no discrete trials or restrictions on the number of responses that can occur. For example, parents may count the number of times a child swears at the dinner table. Theoretically, there is no limit to the frequency of the response (although laryngitis may set in if the response becomes too high). To assess agreement, both parents may independently keep a tally of the number of times a child says particular words. Agreement can be assessed by comparing the two totals the parents have obtained at the end of dinner. To compute the frequency ratio, the following formula is used:

$$\text{Frequency Ratio} = \frac{\text{Smaller total}}{\text{Larger total}} \times 100$$

That is, the smaller total is divided by the larger total. The ratio usually is multiplied by 100 to form a percentage. In the above example, one parent may have observed twenty instances of swearing and the other may have observed eighteen instances. The frequency ratio would be $\frac{18}{20}$ or .9, which, when multiplied by 100, would make agreement 90 percent. The number reflects the finding that the totals obtained by each parent differ from each other by only 10 percent (or 100 percent agreement minus obtained agreement).

Problems and Considerations. The frequency ratio is used relatively often. Although the method is quite simple and easy to describe, there is general agreement that the method leaves much to be desired. A major problem is that frequency ratios reflect agreement on the total number of behaviors scored by each observer. There is no way of determining within this method of agreement whether observers agreed on any particular instance of performance (Johnson and Bolstad, 1973). It is even possible, although unlikely, that the observers may never agree on the occurrence of any particular behavior; they may see and record different instances of the behavior, even though their totals could be quite similar. In the above example, one parent observed eighteen and the other twenty instances of swearing. It is possible that thirty-eight (or many more) instances occurred, and that the parents never scored the same instance of swearing. In practice, of course, large discrepancies between two observers scoring a discrete behavior such as swearing are unlikely. Nevertheless, the frequency ratio hides the fact that observers may not have actually agreed on the instances of behavior.

The absence of information on instances of behavior makes the agreement data from the frequency ratio somewhat ambiguous. The method, however, has still proved quite useful. If the totals of two observers are close (e.g., within a 10 to 20 percent margin of error), it serves a useful guideline that they generally agree. The major problem with the frequency ratio rests not so much with the method but with the interpretation that may be inadvertently made. When a frequency ratio yields a percentage agreement of 90 percent, this does *not* mean that observers agreed 90 percent of the time or on 90 percent of the behaviors that occurred. The ratio merely reflects how close the totals fell within each other.

The frequency ratio of calculating agreement is not restricted to frequency counts. The method can also be used to assess agreements for duration, interval assessment, and discrete categorization. In each case the ratio is computed for each session in which reliability is assessed by dividing the smaller total by the larger total. For example, a child's tantrums may be observed by a teacher and teacher's aide using interval (or duration) assessment. After the session is completed, the total number of intervals (or amount of time in minutes) of tantrum behavior are compared and placed into the ratio. Although the frequency ratio can be extended to different response formats, it is usually restricted to frequency counts. More exact methods of computing agreement are available for other response formats to overcome the problem of knowing whether observers agreed on particular instances or samples of the behavior.

Point-by-Point Agreement Ratio

Description. An important method for computing reliability is to assess whether there is agreement on each instance of the observed behavior. The point-by-point agreement ratio is available for this purpose whenever there are discrete opportunities (e.g., trials, intervals) for the behavior to occur (occur– not occur, present–absent, appropriate–inappropriate). Whether observers agree is assessed for each opportunity for behavior to occur. For example, the discrete categorization method consists of several opportunities to record whether specific behaviors (e.g., room-cleaning behaviors) occur. For each of several behaviors, the observer can record whether the behavior was or was not performed (e.g., picking up one's clothing, making one's bed, putting food away). For a reliability check, two observers would record whether each of the behaviors was performed. The totals could be placed into a frequency ratio, as described above.

Because there were discrete response categories, a more exact method of computing agreement can be obtained. The scoring of the observers for each response can be compared directly to see whether both observers recorded a particular response as occurring. Rather than looking at totals, agreement is evaluated on a response-by-response or point-by-point basis. The formula for computing point-by-point agreement consists of:

$$\text{Point-by-Point Agreement} = \frac{A}{A + D} \times 100$$

Where A = agreements for the trial or interval
       D = disagreements for the trial or interval

That is, agreements of the observers on the specific trials are divided by the number of agreements plus disagreements and multiplied by 100 to form a percentage. Agreements can be defined as instances in which both observers record the same thing. If both observers recorded the behavior as occurring or they both scored the behavior as not occurring, an agreement would be scored. Disagreements are defined as instances in which one observer recorded the behavior as occurring and the other did not. The agreements and disagreements are tallied by comparing each behavior on a point-by-point basis.

A more concrete illustration of the computation of agreement by this method is provided using interval assessment, to which point-by-point agreement ratio is applied most frequently. In interval assessment, two observers typically record and observe behavior for several intervals. In each interval (e.g., a ten-second period), observers record whether behavior (e.g., paying attention in class) occurred or not. Because each interval is recorded separately, point-by-point agreement can be evaluated. Agreement could be determined by comparing the intervals of both observers according to the above formula.

In practice, agreements are usually defined as agreement between observers on occurrences of the behavior in interval assessment. The above formula is unchanged. However, agreements constitute only those intervals in which both observers marked the behavior as occurring. For example, assume observers recorded behavior for fifty ten-second intervals and both observers agreed on the occurrence of the behavior in twenty intervals and disagreed in five intervals. Agreement (according to the point-by-point agreement formula) would be $20/(20 + 5) \times 100$, or 80 percent. Although observers recorded behavior for fifty intervals, all intervals were not used to calculate agreement. An interval is counted only if at least one observer recorded the occurrence of the target behavior.

Excluding intervals in which neither observer records the target behavior is based on the following reasoning. If these intervals were counted, they would be considered as agreements, since both observers "agree" that the response did not occur. Yet in observing behavior, many intervals may be marked without the occurrence of the target behavior. If these were included as agreements, the estimate would be inflated beyond the level obtained when occurrences alone were counted as agreements. In the above example, behavior was not scored as occurring by either observer in 25 intervals. By counting these as agreements, the point-by-point ratio would increase to 90 percent ($45/(45 + 5) \times 100 = 90$ percent) rather than the 80 percent obtained originally. To avoid this increase, most investigators have restricted agreements to response occurrence. Whether agreements should be restricted to intervals in which both observers record the response as occurring or as not occurring raises a complex issue discussed in a separate section below.

Problems and Considerations. The point-by-point agreement ratio is one of the more commonly used methods in applied research (Kelly, 1977). The advantage of the method is that it provides the opportunity to evaluate observer agreement for each response trial or observation interval and is more precise than the frequency ratio, which evaluates agreement on totals. Although the method is used most often for interval observation, it can be applied to other methods as well. For example, the formula can be used with frequency counts when there are discrete trials (e.g., correct arithmetic responses on a test), discrete categories, or the number of persons observed to perform a response. In any assessment format in which agreement can be evaluated on particular responses, the point-by-point ratio can be used.

Despite the greater precision of assessing exact agreement, many questions have been raised as to the method of computing agreement. For interval observations, investigators have questioned whether "agreements" in the formula should be restricted to intervals where both observers record an occurrence of the behavior or also should include intervals where both score a nonoccurrence. In one sense, both indicate that observers were in agreement for a particular interval. The issue is important because the estimate of reliability depends on the frequency of the client's behavior and whether occurrence and/or nonoccurrence agreements are counted. If the client performs the target behavior relatively frequently or infrequently, observers are likely to have a high proportion of agreements on occurrences or nonoccurrences, respectively. Hence, the estimate of reliability may differ greatly depending on what is counted as an agreement between observers and how often behavior is scored as occurring.

Actually, the issue raised here is a larger one that applies to most of the methods of computing agreement. The extent to which observers agree is partially a function of frequency of the client's performance of the behavior (House and House, 1979; Johnson & Bolstad, 1973). With relatively frequent occurrences or intervals in which occurrences are recorded, agreement tends to be high. A certain level of agreement occurs simply as a function of "chance." Thus, the frequency of the behavior has been used to help decide whether agreements on occurrences or nonoccurrences should be included in the formula for point-by-point ratio agreement.

Pearson Product-Moment Correlation

Description. The previous methods refer to procedures for estimating agreement on any particular occasion in which reliability is assessed. In each session or day in which agreement is assessed, the observers' data are entered into one of the formulas provided above. Of course, a goal is to evaluate agreement over the entire course of the investigation encompassing each of the phases in the design. Typically, frequency or point-by-point agreement ratios are computed during each reliability check and the mean level of agreement and range (low and high agreement levels) of the reliability checks are reported.

One method of evaluating agreement over the entire course of an investigation is to compute a Pearson product-moment correlation (r). On each occasion in which interobserver agreement is assessed, a total for each observer is provided. This total may reflect the number of occurrences of the behavior or total intervals or duration. Essentially, each reliability occasion yields a pair of scores, one total from each observer. A correlation coefficient compares the totals across all occasions in which reliability was assessed. The correlation provides an estimate of agreement across all occasions in which reliability was checked rather than an estimate of agreement on any particular occasion.

   The correlation can range from −1.00 through +1.00. A correlation of 0.00 means that the observers' scores are unrelated. That is, they tend not to go together at all. One observer may obtain a relatively high count of the behavior and the other observer's score may be high, low, or somewhere in between. The scores are simply unrelated. A positive correlation between 0.00 to +1.00, particularly one in the high range (e.g., .80 or .90), means that the scores tend to go together. When one observer scores a high frequency of the behavior, the other one tends to do so as well, and when one scores a lower frequency of the behavior, so does the other one. If the correlation assumes a minus value (0.00 to −1.00) it means that observers tend to report scores that were in opposite directions: when one observer scored a higher frequency, the other invariably scored a lower frequency, and vice versa. (As a measure of agreement for observational data, correlations typically take on values between 0.00 and +1.00 rather than any negative value.)

   Table 3-1 provides hypothetical data for ten observation periods in which the frequency of a behavior was observed. Assume that the data were collected for twenty days and that on ten of these days (every other day) two observers independently recorded behavior (even-numbered days). The correlation between the observers across all days is computed by a commonly used formula (see bottom of Table 3-1).

Table 3-1. Scores for two observers to compute Pearson product-moment correlation

Days of agreement check	Observer 1 Totals = X	Observer 2 Totals = Y
2	25	29
4	12	20
6	19	17
8	30	31
10	33	33
12	18	20
14	26	28
16	15	20
18	10	11
20	17	19

Σ = sum
X = scores of observer 1
Y = scores of observer 2
XY = cross products of scores
N = number of checks

$$r = \frac{N\Sigma XY - \Sigma X \Sigma Y}{[N\Sigma X^2 - (\Sigma X)^2]\,[N\Sigma Y^2 - (\Sigma Y)^2]}$$
$$r = +.93$$

Problems and Considerations. The Pearson product-moment correlation assesses the extent to which observers covary in their scores. *Covariation* refers to the tendency of the scores (e.g., total frequencies or intervals) to go together. If covariation is high, it means that both tend to obtain high scores on the same occasions and lower scores on other occasions. That is, their scores or totals tend to fluctuate in the same direction from occasion to occasion. The correlation says nothing about whether the observers agree on the total amount of a behavior in any session. In fact, it is possible that one observer always scored behavior as occurring twenty (or any constant number) times more than the other observer for each session in which agreement was checked. If this amount of error were constant across all sessions, the correlation could still be perfect ($r = +1.00$). The correlation merely assesses the extent to which scores go together and not whether they are close to each other in absolute terms.

Since the correlation does not necessarily reflect exact agreement on total scores for a particular reliability session, it follows that it does not necessarily say anything about point-by-point agreement. The correlation relies on totals from the individual sessions, and so the observations of particular behaviors are lost. Thus, as a method of computing interobserver agreement, the Pearson product-moment correlation on totals of each observer across sessions provides an inexact measure of agreement.

Another issue that arises in interpretation of the product-moment correlation pertains to the use of data across different phases. In single-case designs, observations are usually obtained across several different phases. In the simplest case, observations may be obtained before a particular intervention is in effect, followed by a period in which an intervention is applied to alter behavior. When the intervention is implemented, behavior is likely to increase or decrease, depending on the type of intervention and the purpose of the program.

From the standpoint of a product-moment correlation, the change in frequency of behavior in the different phases may affect the estimate of agreement obtained by comparing observer totals. If behavior is high in the initial phase (e.g., hyperactive behaviors) and low during the intervention, the correlation of observer scores may be somewhat misleading. Both observers may tend to have high frequencies of behavior in the initial phase and low frequencies in the intervention phase. The tendency of the scores of observers to be high or low together is partially a function of the very different rates in behavior associated with the different phases. Agreement may be inflated in part because of the effects of the different rates between the phases. Agreement within each of the phases (initial baseline [pretreatment] phase *or* intervention phase) may not have been as high as the calculation of agreement between both phases. For the product-moment correlation, the possible artifact introduced by different rates of performance across phases can be remedied by calculating a correlation separately for each phase. The separate correlations can be averaged (by Fisher's z transformation) to form an average correlation.

General Comments

The above methods of computing agreement address different characteristics of the data. Selection of the method is determined in part by the observational strategy employed in the investigation and the unit of data. The unit of data refers to what the investigator uses as a measure to evaluate the client's performance on a day-to-day basis. For example, the investigator may plot total frequency or total number of occurrences on a graphical display of the data. Even though an exact (e.g., point-by-point) method of agreement will be calculated, it is important to have an estimate of the agreement between observers on the totals. In such a case, a frequency ratio or product-moment correlation may be selected. Similarly, the investigator may observe several different disruptive behaviors in the home or in a classroom. If total disruptive behaviors are used as a summary statistic to evaluate the client's performance, it would be useful to estimate agreement on these totals. On the other hand, if one particular behavior is evaluated more analytically, separate agreement may be calculated for that behavior.

Even though agreement on totals for a given observation session is usually the primary interest, more analytic point-by-point agreement may be examined for several purposes. When point-by-point agreement is assessed, the investigator has greater information about how adequately several behaviors are defined and observed. Point-by-point agreement for different behaviors, rather than a frequency ratio for the composite total, provides information about exactly where any sources of disagreements emerge. Feedback to observers, further training, and refinement of particular definitions are likely to result from analysis of point-by-point agreement. Selection of the methods of computing agreement is also based on other considerations, including the frequency of behavior and the definition of agreements, two issues that now require greater elaboration.

Base Rates and Chance Agreement

The above methods of assessing agreement, especially the point-by-point agreement ratio, are the most commonly used methods in applied research. Usually, when the estimates of agreement are relatively high (e.g., 80 percent or $r = .80$), investigators assume that observers generally agree in their observations.

However, investigators have been alert to the fact that a given estimate such as 80 or 90 percent does not mean the same thing under all circumstances. The level of agreement is in part a function of how frequently the behavior is scored as occurring.

If behavior is occurring with a relatively high frequency, observers are more likely to have high levels of agreement with the usual point-by-point ratio formula than if behavior is occurring with a relatively low frequency. The *base rate* of behavior, i.e., the level of occurrence or number of intervals in which behavior is recorded as occurring, contributes to the estimated level of agreement.[2] The problem of high base rates has been discussed most often in relation to point-by-point agreement as applied to interval data (Hawkins and Dotson, 1975; Hopkins and Hermann, 1977; Johnson and Bolstad, 1973; Kent and Foster, 1977). The possible influence of high or low frequency of behavior on interobserver agreement applies to other methods as well but can be illustrated here with interval methods of observation.

A client may perform the response in most of the intervals in which he or she is observed. If two observers mark the behavior as occurring in many of the intervals, they are likely to agree merely because of the high rate of occurrence. When many occurrences are marked by both observers, correspondence between observers is inevitable. To be more concrete, assume that the client performs the behavior in 90 of 100 intervals and that both observers coincidentally score the behavior as occurring in 90 percent of the intervals. Agreement between the observers is likely to be high simply because of the fact that a large proportion of intervals was marked as occurrences. That is, agreement will be high as a function of chance.

Chance in this context refers to the level of agreement that would be expected by *randomly* marking occurrences for a given number of intervals. Agreement would be high whether or not observers saw the same behavior as occurring in each interval. Even if both observers were blindfolded but marked a large number of intervals as occurrences, agreement might be high. Exactly how high chance agreement would be depends on what is counted as an agreement. In the point-by-point ratio, recall that reliability was computed by dividing agreements by agreements plus disagreements and multiplying by 100. An agreement usually means that both observers recorded the behavior as occurring. But if behavior is occurring at a high rate, reliability may be especially high on the basis of chance.

---

2. The base rate should not be confused with the baseline rate. The base rate refers to the proportion of intervals or relative frequency of the behavior. Baseline rate usually refers to the rate of performance when no intervention is in effect to alter the behavior.

The actual formula for computing the *chance* level of agreement on occurrences is:

Chance agreement on occurrences

$$= \frac{0_1 \text{ occurrences} \times 0_2 \text{ occurrences}}{\text{total intervals}^2} \times 100$$

Where 0_1 occurrences = the number of intervals in which observer 1 scored the behavior as occurring,

0_2 occurrences = the number of intervals in which observer 2 scored the behavior as occurring, and

total intervals^2 = all intervals of observation squared

0_1 and 0_2 occurrences are likely to be high if the client performs the behavior frequently. In the above hypothetical example, both observers recorded 90 occurrences of the behavior. With such frequent recordings of occurrences, just on the basis of randomly marking this number of intervals, "chance" agreement would be high. In the above formula, chance would be 81 percent ([90 $\times$ 90/100^2] $\times$ 100). Merely because occurrence intervals are quite frequent, agreement would appear high. When investigators report agreement at this level, it may be important to know whether this level would have been expected any way merely as a function of chance.

Perhaps the problem of high agreement based on chance could be avoided by counting as agreements only those intervals in which observers agreed on *non*occurrences. The intervals in which they agreed on occurrences could be omitted. If only the number of intervals when both observers agreed on behavior not occurring were counted as agreements, the chance level of agreement would be lower. In fact, chance agreement on nonoccurrences would be calculated on a formula resembling the above:

Chance agreement on nonoccurrences

$$= \frac{0^1 \text{ nonoccurrences} \times 0_2 \text{ nonoccurrences}}{\text{total intervals}^2} \times 100$$

In the above example, both observers recorded nonoccurrences in ten of the one hundred intervals, making chance agreement on nonoccurrences 1 percent ([10 $\times$ 10]/100^2 $\times$ 100).[3] When agreements are defined as nonoccurrences

---

3. The level of agreement expected by chance is based on the proportion of intervals in which observers report the behavior as occurring or not occurring. Although chance agreement can be calculated by the formulas provided here, other sources provide probability functions in which chance agreement can be determined simply and directly (Hawkins and Dotson, 1975; Hopkins and Hermann, 1977).

that are scored at a low frequency, chance agreement is low. Hence, if the point-by-point ratio were computed and observers agreed 80 percent of the time on nonoccurrences, this would clearly mean they agreed well above the level expected by chance.

Defining agreements on the basis of nonoccurrences is not a general solution, since in many cases nonoccurrences may be relatively high (e.g., when the behavior rarely occurs). Moreover, as an experiment proceeds, it is likely that in different phases occurrences will be relatively high and nonoccurrences will be relatively low and that this pattern will be reversed. The question for investigators that has received considerable attention is how to compute agreement between observers over the course of an experiment and to take into account the changing level of agreement that would be expected by chance. Several alternative methods of addressing this question have been suggested.

Alternative Methods of Handling Expected ("Chance") Levels of Agreement

The above discussion suggests that agreement between observers may depend on the base rate of performance. If observers record behavior as occurring relatively frequently, agreement on occurrences will tend to be higher than if behavior is occurring relatively infrequently. The impact of base rates of performance on interpreting reliability has recently received considerable attention (e.g., Birkhimer and Brown, 1979a; 1979b; Hartmann, 1977; Hawkins and Dotson, 1975; Hopkins and Hermann, 1977). Several recommendations have been made to handle the problem of expected levels of agreement, only a few of which can be highlighted here.[4]

Variations of Occurrence and Nonoccurrence Agreement

The problem of base rates occurs when the intervals that are counted as agreements in a reliability check are the ones scored at a high rate. Typically, agreements are defined as instances in which both observers record the behavior as occurring. If occurrences are scored relatively often, the expected level of agreement on the basis of chance is relatively high. One solution is to vary the

4. Two series of articles on interobserver agreement and alternative methods of computing agreement based on estimates of chance appeared in separate issues of the *Journal of Applied Behavior Analysis* (1977, Vol. *10*, Issue 1, pp. 97–150; 1979, Vol. *12*, Issue 4, pp. 523–571).

definition of agreements in the point-by-point ratio to reduce the expected level of agreement based on "chance" (Bijou, Peterson, and Ault, 1968). Agreements on occurrences would be calculated only when the rate of behavior is low, i.e., when relatively few intervals are scored as occurrences of the response. This is somewhat different from the usual way in which agreements on occurrences are counted even when occurrences are scored frequently. Hence, with low rates of occurrences, point-by-point agreement on occurrences provides a stringent measure of how observers agree without a high level expected by chance. Conversely, when the occurrences of behavior are relatively high, agreement can be computed on intervals in which both observers record the behavior as not occurring. With a high rate of occurrences, agreement on nonoccurrences is not likely to be inflated by chance.

Although the recommendation is sound, the solution is somewhat cumbersome. First, over time in a given investigation, it is likely that the rates of occurrence of response will change at different points so that high and low rates occur in different phases. The definition of agreement would also change at different times. The primary interest in assessing agreement is determining whether observers see the behavior as occurring. Constantly changing the definition of agreements within a study handles the problem of chance agreement but does not provide a clear and direct measure of agreement on scoring the behavior.

Another problem with the proposed solution is that agreement estimates tend to fluctuate markedly when the intervals that define agreement are infrequent. For example, if one hundred intervals are observed and behavior occurs in only two intervals, the recommendation would be to compute agreement on occurrence intervals. Assume that one observer records two occurrences, the other records only one, and that they both agree on this one. Reliability will be based only on computing agreement for the two intervals, and will be 50 percent (agreements = 1, disagreements = 1, and overall reliability equals agreements divided by agreements plus disagreements). If the observer who provided the check on reliability scored 0, 1, or both occurrences in agreement with the primary observer, agreement would be 0, 50, or 100 percent, respectively. Thus, with a small number of intervals counted as agreements, reliability estimates fluctuate widely and are subject to misinterpretation in their own right.

Related solutions have been proposed. One is to report reliability separately for occurrence and nonoccurrence intervals throughout each phase of the investigation. Another proposal is to provide a weighted overall estimate of agreement that considers the relative number of occurrence to nonoccurrence intervals (e.g., Harris and Lahey, 1978; Taylor, 1980). Despite the merit of these suggestions, they have yet to be adopted in applied research.

Plotting Agreement Data

The problem with obtaining a high estimate of interobserver agreement (e.g., 90 percent) is that it may be a function of the rate of behavior and the method of defining agreements. Even if agreement is high, it is possible that observers disagree on many instances of the behavior. Agreement estimates may not adequately convey how discrepant the observers actually are in their estimates of behavior. One recommendation to handle the problem is to plot the data separately for both the primary observer and the secondary observer to check agreement (Hawkins and Dotson, 1975; Kratochwill and Wetzel, 1977). Usually, only the data for the primary observer are plotted. However, the data obtained from the secondary observer also can be plotted so that the similarity in the scores from the observers can be seen on the graphic display.

An interesting advantage of this recommendation is that one can determine whether the observers disagree to such an extent that the conclusions drawn from the data would differ because of the extent of the disagreement. For example, Figure 3-1 shows hypothetical data for baseline and intervention phases. The data are plotted for the primary observer for each day of observation (circles). The occasional reliability checks by a second observer are also plotted (squares). The data in the upper panel show that both observers were relatively close in their estimates of performance. If the data of the second observer were substituted for those of the first, the pattern of data showing superior performance during the intervention phase would not be altered.

In contrast, the lower panel shows marked discrepancies between the primary and secondary observer. The discrepancy is referred to as "marked" because of the impact that the differences would have on the conclusions reached about the changes in behavior. If the data of the second observer were used, it would not be clear that performances really improved during the intervention phase. The data for the second observer suggest that perhaps there was no change in performance over the two phases or, alternatively, that there is bias in the observations and that no clear conclusion can be reached.

In any case, plotting the data from both observers provides useful information about how closely the observers actually agreed in their totals for occurrences of the response. Independently of the numerical estimate of agreement, graphic display permits one to examine whether the scores from each observer would lead to different conclusions about the effects of an intervention, which is a very important reason for evaluating agreement in the first place. Plotting data from a second observer whose data are used to evaluate agreement provides an important source of information that could be hidden by agreement ratios potentially inflated by "chance." Alternative ways of plotting data from primary and secondary observers have been proposed (Birkhimer and Brown,

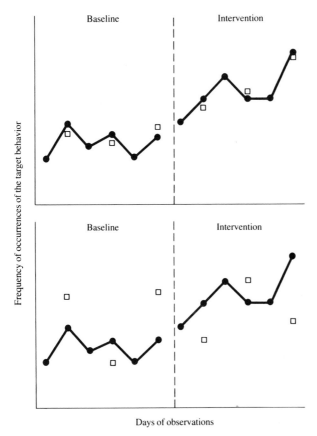

Figure 3-1. Hypothetical data showing observations from the primary observer (circles connected by lines) and the second observer, whose data are used to check agreement (squares). The *upper panel* shows close correspondence between observers; the conclusions about behavior change from baseline to intervention phases would not vary if the data from the second observer were substituted in place of the data from the primary observer. The *lower panel* shows marked discrepancies between observers; the conclusions about behavior change would be very different depending on which observer's data were used.

1979a; Yelton, 1979). Such methods have yet to be adopted but provide useful tools in interpreting agreement data and intervention effects.

Correlational Statistics

Another means of addressing the problem of chance agreement and the misleading interpretations that might result from high percentage agreement is to use correlational statistics (Hartmann, 1977; Hopkins and Hermann, 1977).

One correlational statistic that has been recommended is *kappa* (*k*) (Cohen, 1965). Kappa is especially suited for categorical data such as interval observation or discrete categorization when each response or interval is recorded as occurring or not.

Kappa provides an estimate of agreement between observers corrected for chance. When observers agree at the same level one would expect on the basis of chance, $k = 0$. If agreement surpasses the expected chance level, k exceeds 0 and approaches a maximum of $+1.00$.[5]

Kappa is computed by the following formula:

$$k = \frac{P_o - P_c}{1 - P_c}$$

where P_0 = the proportion of agreements between observers on occurrences and nonoccurrences (or agreements on occurrences and nonoccurrences divided by the total number of agreements and disagreements).

P_c = the proportion of expected agreements on the basis of chance.[6]

For example, two observers may observe a child for one hundred intervals. Observer 1 scores eighty intervals of occurrence of aggressive behavior and twenty intervals of nonoccurrence. Observer 2 scores seventy intervals of aggressive behavior and thirty intervals of nonoccurrence. Assume observers agree on seventy of the occurrence intervals and on twenty nonoccurrence intervals and disagree on the remaining ten intervals. Using the above formula, $P_o = .90$ and $P_c = .62$ with kappa $= .74$.

The advantage of kappa is that it corrects for chance based on the observed frequency of occurrence and nonoccurrence intervals. Other agreement measures are difficult to interpret because chance agreement may yield a high positive value (e.g., 80 percent) which gives the impression that high agreement has been obtained. For example, with the above data used in the computation of k, a point-by-point ratio agreement on occurrence and nonoccurrence intervals combined would yield 90 percent agreement. However, on the basis of

5. Kappa can also go from 0.00 to -1.00 in the unlikely event that agreement between observers is less than the level expected by chance.
6. P_c is computed by multiplying the number of occurrences for observer 1 times the number of occurrences for observer 2 plus the number of nonoccurrences for observer 1 times the number of nonoccurrences for observer 2. The sum of these is divided by the total number of intervals squared.

chance alone, the percent agreement would be 62. Kappa provides a measure of agreement over and above chance.[7]

General Comments

Most applied research papers continue to report agreement using a point-by-point ratio in its various forms. Relatively recently researchers have become sensitive to the fact that estimates of agreement may be misleading. Based on the observed frequency of performance, the expected level of agreement (chance) may be relatively high. The goal in developing observational codes is not merely demonstrating high agreement (e.g., 80 or 90 percent) but rather showing that agreement is relatively high and exceeds chance.

Several alternatives have been suggested to take into account chance or expected levels of agreement. Only a few of the solutions were highlighted here. Which of the solutions adequately resolves the problem without introducing new complexities remains a matter of considerable controversy. And, in the applied literature, investigators have not uniformly adopted one particular way of handling the problem. At this point, there is consensus on the problem that chance agreement can obscure estimates of reliability. Further, there is general agreement that in reporting reliability, it is useful to consider one of the many different ways of conveying or incorporating chance agreement. Hence, as a general guideline, it is probably useful to compute and report agreement expected on the basis of chance or to compute agreement in alternative formats (e.g., separately for occurrences and nonoccurrences) to provide additional data that convey how observers actually concur in their observations.

Sources of Artifact and Bias

The above discussion suggests that how agreement estimates are calculated and characteristics of the data (e.g., response frequency) may influence the quantitative estimates of agreement. Interpretation of agreement estimates also depends on knowing several features about the circumstances in which agreement is assessed. Sources of bias that can obscure interpretation of inter-

7. Kappa is not the only correlational statistic that can estimate agreement on categorical data (see Hartmann, 1977). For example, another estimate very similar to kappa is phi (Φ), which also extends from -1.00 through $+1.00$ and yields 0.00 when agreement is at the chance level. The advantage of phi is that a conversion table has been provided to convey levels of phi based on obtained agreement on occurrences and nonoccurrences (Lewin and Wakefield, 1979). Thus, investigators can convert their usual data into phi equivalents without computational difficulties.

observer agreement include reactivity of reliability assessment, observer drift, observer expectancies and experimenter feedback, and complexity of the observations (Kazdin, 1977a; Kent and Foster, 1977).

Reactivity of Reliability Assessment

Interobserver agreement is usually checked periodically during an investigation. Typically, observers are aware that their observations are being checked if for no other reason than another observer may be present, and both observers must coordinate their recording to observe the same person at the same time. Because observers are aware that reliability is being checked, the situation is potentially reactive. Reactivity refers to the possibility that behavior may change when people realize they are being monitored. Indeed, research has shown that observer awareness that reliability is being checked influences the observations they make. In a number of investigations, observers have been led to believe that agreement was being assessed on some occasions and not assessed on others (Kent, Kanowitz, O'Leary, and Cheiken, 1977; Kent, O'Leary, Diament, and Dietz, 1974; Reid, 1970; Romanczyk, Kent, Diament, and O'Leary, 1973). In fact, agreement was assessed even when they did not believe they were being checked. The general findings are consistent; observers show higher interobserver agreement when they are aware that reliability is being checked than when they are unaware.

It is not entirely clear why agreement is higher under conditions when observers are aware that reliability is being checked. When observers are aware of reliability checks, they may modify the behavioral definitions or codes slightly to concur with the other observer to whom their data are compared (Romanczyk et al., 1973). Also, observers may record slightly different behaviors when they believe they are being checked. For example, in observations of classroom behavior, Romanczyk et al. (1973) found that observers recorded much less disruptive student behavior when they were unaware, rather than aware, that interobserver agreement was assessed. Thus, interpretation of estimates of agreement depends very much on the conditions of reliability assessment. Estimates obtained when observers are unaware of agreement checks tend to be lower than those obtained when they are aware of these checks.

Awareness of assessing agreement can be handled in different ways. As a general rule, the conditions of reliability assessment should be similar to the conditions in which data are ordinarily obtained. If observers ordinarily believe their behaviors are not being monitored, these conditions should be maintained during reliability checks. In practice, it may be difficult to conduct agreement checks without observers being aware of the checks. Measuring interobserver agreement usually involves special arrangements that are not ordinarily in effect each day. For example, in most investigations two observers usually do not record the behavior of the same target subject at the same time unless agreement is being assessed. Hence, it may be difficult to conduct checks without alerting observers to this fact. An alternative might be to lead observers to believe that all of their observations are being monitored over the course of the investigation. This latter alternative would appear to be advantageous, given evidence that observers tend to be more accurate when they believe their agreement is being assessed (Reid, 1970; Taplin and Reid, 1973).

Observer Drift

Observers usually receive extensive instruction and feedback regarding accuracy in applying the definitions for recording behavior. Training is designed to ensure that observers adhere to the definitions of behavior and record behavior at a consistent level of accuracy. Once mastery is achieved and estimates of agreement are consistently high, it is assumed that observers continue to apply the same definition of behavior over time. However, evidence suggests that observers "drift" from the original definition of behavior (e.g., Kent et al., 1974; O'Leary & Kent, 1973; Reid, 1970; Reid and DeMaster, 1972; Taplin and Reid, 1973). *Observer drift* refers to the tendency of observers to change the manner in which they apply definitions of behavior over time.

The hazard of drift is that it is not easily detected. Interobserver agreement may remain high even though the observers are deviating from the original definitions of behavior. If observers consistently work together and communicate with each other, they may develop similar variations of the original definitions (Hawkins and Dobes, 1977; O'Leary and Kent, 1973). Thus, high levels of agreement can be maintained even if accuracy declines. In some reports, drift is detected by comparing interobserver agreement among a subgroup of observers who constantly work together with agreement across subgroups who have not worked with each other (Hawkins and Dobes, 1977; Kent et al., 1974, 1977). Over time, subgroups of observers may modify and apply the definitions of behavior differently, which can only be detected by comparing data from observers who have not worked together.

If observers modify the definitions of behavior over time, the data from different phases may not be comparable. For example, if disruptive behaviors in the classroom or at home are observed, the data from different days in the study may not reflect precisely the same behaviors, due to observer drift. And, as already noted, the differences in the definitions of behavior may occur even though observers continue to show high interobserver agreement.

Observer drift can be controlled in a variety of ways. First, observers can undergo continuous training over the course of the investigation. Videotapes of the clients can be shown in periodic retraining sessions where the codes are discussed among all observers. Observers can meet as a group, rate behavior in the situation, and receive feedback regarding the accuracy of their observations, i.e., adherence to the original codes. The feedback can convey the extent to which observers correctly invoke the definitions for scoring behavior. Feedback for accuracy in applying the definitions helps reduce drift from the original behavioral codes (DeMaster, Reid, and Twentyman, 1977).

Another solution, somewhat less practical, is to videotape all observations of the client and to have observers score the tapes in random order at the end of the investigation. Drift would not differentially bias data in different phases because tapes are rated in random order. Of course, this alternative is somewhat impractical because of the time and expense of taping the client's behavior for several observation sessions. Moreover, the investigator needs the data on a day-to-day basis to make decisions regarding when to implement or withdraw the intervention, a characteristic of single-case designs that will become clearer in subsequent chapters. Yet taped samples of behavior from selected occasions could be compared with actual observations obtained by observers in the setting to assess whether drift has occurred over time.

Drift might also be controlled by periodically bringing newly trained observers into the setting to assess interobserver agreement (Skindrud, 1973). Comparison of newly trained observers with observers who have continuously participated in the investigation can reveal whether the codes are applied differently over time. Presumably, new observers would adhere more closely to the original definitions than other observers who have had the opportunity to drift from the original definitions.

Observer Expectancies and Feedback

Another potential source of bias is the expectancies of observers regarding the client's behavior and the feedback observers receive from the experimenter in relation to that behavior. Several studies have shown that if observers are led to expect change (e.g., an increase or decrease in behavior), these expectancies do not usually bias observational data (Kent et al., 1974; O'Leary, Kent and Kanowitz, 1975; Skindrud, 1972). Yet expectancies can influence the observations when combined with feedback from the experimenter. For example, in one study observers were led to believe that an intervention (token reinforcement) would reduce disruptive classroom behavior (O'Leary et al., 1975). When observers reported data that showed a reduction in disruptive behavior, the investigator made positive comments (approval) to them about the data; if no change or an increase in disruptive behavior was scored, the investigator made negative comments. Instructions to expect change combined with feedback for scoring reductions led to decreases in the disruptive behavior. In fact, observers were only rating a videotape of classroom behavior in which no changes in the disruptive behaviors occurred over time. Thus, the expectancies and feedback about the effects of treatment affected the data.

It is reassuring that research suggests that expectancies alone are not likely to influence behavioral observations. However, it may be crucial to control the feedback that observers obtain about the data and whether the investigator's expectations are confirmed. Obviously, experimenters should not and probably do not provide feedback to observers for directional changes in client behavior. Any feedback provided to observers should be restricted to information about the accuracy of their observations, in order to prevent or minimize drift rather than information about changes in the client's behavior.

Complexity of the Observations

In the situations discussed up to this point, the assumption has been made that observers score only one behavior at a time. Often observers record several behaviors within a given observational period. For example, with interval assessment, the observers may score several different behaviors during a particular interval. Research has shown that complexity of the observations influences agreement and accuracy of the observations.

Complexity has been investigated in different ways. For example, complexity can refer to the *number of different responses* that are scored in a given period. Observational codes that consist of several categories of responses are more complex than those with fewer categories. As might be expected, observers have been found to be more accurate and show higher agreement when there are fewer categories of behavior to score (Mash and McElwee, 1974). Complexity can also refer to the *range of client behaviors that are performed.* Within a given scoring system, clients may perform many different behaviors over time or perform relatively few behaviors over time. The greater number of different behaviors that clients perform, the lower the interobserver agreement (House and House, 1979; Jones, Reid, and Patterson, 1974; Reid, 1974; Reid, Skindrud, Taplin, and Jones, 1973; Taplin and Reid, 1973). Thus, the greater the diversity of behavior and the number of different discriminations the observers must make, the lower interobserver agreement is likely to be. Conversely, the more similar and less diverse the behaviors clients perform over time, the greater the interobserver agreement.

The precise reasons why complexity of observations and interobserver agreement are inversely related are not entirely clear. It is reasonable to assume that with complex observational systems in which several behaviors must be scored, observers may have difficulty in making discriminations among all of the codes and definitions or are more likely to make errors. With much more information to process and code, errors in applying the codes and scoring would be expected to increase.

The complexity of the observations has important implications for interpreting estimates of interobserver agreement. Agreement for a given response may be influenced by the number of other types of responses that are included in the observational system and the number of different behaviors that clients perform. Thus, estimates of agreement for a particular behavior may mean different things depending on the nature of the observations that are obtained.

When several behaviors are observed simultaneously, observers need to be trained at higher levels of agreement on each of the codes than might be the case if only one or two behaviors were observed. If several different subjects are observed, the complexity of the observational system too may be increased relative to observation of one or two subjects. In training observers, the temptation is to provide relatively simplified conditions of assessment to ensure that observers understand each of the definitions and apply them consistently. When several codes, behaviors, or subjects are to be observed in the investigation, observers need to be trained to record behavior with the same level of complexity. High levels of interobserver agreement need to be established for the exact conditions under which observers will be required to perform.

Acceptable Levels of Agreement

The interpretation of estimates of interobserver agreement has become increasingly complex. In the past five to ten years, interpretation of agreement data has received considerable attention. Before that, agreement ratios were routinely computed using frequency and point-by-point agreement ratios without concern about their limitations. Few investigators were aware of the influence of such factors as base rates or the conditions associated with measuring agreement (e.g., observer awareness of agreement checks) that may contribute to estimates of agreement. Despite the complexity of the process of assessing agreement, the main question for the researchers still remains, what is an acceptable level of agreement?

The level of agreement that is acceptable is one that indicates to the researcher that the observers are sufficiently consistent in their recordings of behavior, that behaviors are adequately defined, and that the measure will be sensitive to changes in the client's performance over time. Traditionally, agreement was regarded as acceptable if it met or surpassed .80 or 80 percent, computed by frequency or point-by-point agreement ratios. Research has shown that many factors contribute to any particular estimate of agreement. High levels of agreement may not necessarily be acceptable if the formula for computing agreement or the conditions of evaluating agreement introduce potential biases or artifacts. Conversely, lower levels of agreement may be quite useful and acceptable if the conditions under which they were obtained minimize sources of bias and artifact. Hence, it is not only the quantitative estimate that needs to be evaluated, but also how that estimate was obtained and under what conditions.

In addition to the methods of estimating agreement and the conditions under which the estimates are obtained, the level of agreement that is acceptable depends on characteristics of the data. Agreement is a measure of the consistency of observers. Lack of consistency or disagreements introduce variability into the data. The extent to which inconsistencies interfere with drawing conclusions is a function of the data. For example, assume that the client's "real" behavior (free from any observer bias) shows relatively little variability over time. Also, assume that across baseline and intervention phases, dramatic changes in behavior occur. Under conditions of slight variability and marked changes, moderate inconsistencies in the data may not interfere with drawing conclusions about intervention effects. On the other hand, if the variability in the client's behavior is relatively large and the changes over time are not especially dramatic, a moderate amount of inconsistency among observers may hide the change. Hence, although high agreement between observers is always a goal, the level of agreement that is acceptable to detect systematic changes in the client's performance depends on the client's behavior and the effects of intervention.

In light of the large number of considerations embedded in the estimate of interobserver agreement, concrete guidelines that apply to all methods of computing agreement, conditions in which agreement is assessed, and patterns of data are difficult to provide. The traditional guideline of seeking agreement at or above .80 is not necessarily poor; however, attainment of this criterion is not necessarily meaningful or acceptable, given other conditions that could contribute to this estimate. Perhaps the major recommendation, given the current status of views of agreement, is to encourage investigators to consider alternative methods of estimating agreement (i.e., more than one method) and to specify carefully the conditions in which the checks on agreement are conducted. With added information, the investigator and those who read reports of applied research will be in a better position to evaluate the assessment procedures.

Summary and Conclusions

A crucial component of direct observation of behavior is to ensure that observers score behavior consistently. Consistent assessment is essential to ensure that minimal variation is introduced into the data by observers and to check on the adequacy of the response definition(s). Interobserver agreement is assessed periodically by having two or more persons simultaneously but independently observe the client and record behavior. The resulting scores are compared to evaluate consistency of the observations.

Several commonly used methods to assess agreement consist of *frequency ratio, point-by-point agreement ratio,* and *Pearson product-moment correlation.* These methods provide different information, including, respectively, correspondence of observers on the total frequency of behavior for a given observational session, the exact agreement of observers on specific occurrences of the behavior within a session, or the covariation of observer data across several sessions.

A major issue in evaluating agreement data pertains to the *base rate* of the client's performance. As the frequency of behavior or occurrences increases, the level of agreement on these occurrences between observers increases as a function of chance. Thus, if behavior is recorded as relatively frequent, agreement between the observers is likely to be high. Without calculating the expected or chance level of agreement, investigators may believe that high observer agreement is a function of the well-defined behaviors and high levels of consistency between observers. Point-by-point agreement ratios as usually calculated do not consider the chance level of agreement and may be misleading. Hence, alternative methods of calculating agreement have been proposed, based on the relative frequency of occurrences or nonoccurrences of the response, graphic displays of the data from the observer who serves to check reliability, and computation of correlational measures (e.g., kappa, phi). These latter methods and their variations have yet to be routinely incorporated into applied research, even though there is a consensus over the problem of chance agreement that they are designed to address.

Apart from the method of computing agreement, several sources of bias and artifact have been identified that may influence the agreement data. These include *reactivity of assessment, observer drift, expectancies of the observers and feedback from the experimenter,* and *complexity of the observations.* In general, observers tend to agree more and to be more accurate when they are aware, rather than unaware, that their observations are being checked. The definitions that observers apply to behavior may depart ("drift") from the original definitions they held at the beginning of the investigation. Under some conditions, observers' expectancies regarding changes in the client's behavior and feedback indicating that the experimenter's expectancies are confirmed may bias the observations. Finally, accuracy of observations and interobserver agreement tend to decrease as a function of the complexity of the observational system (e.g., number of different categories to be observed and number of different behaviors clients perform within a given observational system).

Research over the last several years has brought to light several complexities regarding the evaluation of interobserver agreement. Traditional guidelines about the levels of agreement that are acceptable have become less clear. It is important to keep in mind that the purpose of assessing agreement is to ensure that observers are consistent in their observations and that sufficient agreement exists to reflect change in the client's behavior over time. In conducting and reporting assessment of agreement, it may be advisable to consider alternative ways to estimate agreement and to specify the conditions in which agreement checks are conducted.

4

Experimentation, Valid Inferences, and Pre-Experimental Designs

Previous chapters have discussed requirements for assessing performance so that objective data can be obtained. In research and clinical practice, assessment provides the information used to infer that therapeutic change has occurred. Although assessment is essential, by itself it is insufficient to draw inferences about the basis of change. Experimentation is needed to examine specifically why change has occurred. Through experimentation, extraneous factors that might explain the results can be ruled out to provide an unambiguous evaluation of the intervention and its effects.

This chapter discusses the purposes of experimentation and the types of factors that must be ruled out if valid inferences are to be drawn. In addition, the chapter introduces pre-experimental single-case designs that approximate experimentation in terms of how they are designed and the information they yield. Examination of pre-experimental designs, their characteristics, strengths, and limitations, conveys the need for experimentation and sets the stage for single-case designs addressed in subsequent chapters.

Experimentation and Valid Inferences

The purpose of experimentation in general is to examine relationships between variables. The unique feature of experimentation is that it examines the direct influence of one variable (the independent variable) on another (the dependent variable). Experimentation usually evaluates the influence of a small number of variables under conditions that will permit unambiguous inferences to be drawn. Experiments help simplify the situation so that the influence of the variables of interest can be separated from the influence of other factors. Drawing valid inferences about the effects of an independent variable or intervention requires attention to a variety of factors that potentially obscure the findings.

Internal Validity

The task for experimentation is to examine the influence of a particular intervention in such a way that extraneous factors will not interfere with the conclusions that the investigator wishes to draw. Experiments help to reduce the plausibility that alternative influences could explain the results. The better the design of the experiment, the better it rules out alternative explanations of the results. In the ideal case, only one explanation of the results of an experiment would be possible, namely, that the independent variable accounted for change.

An experiment cannot determine with complete certainty that the independent variable accounted for change. However, if the experiment is carefully designed, the likelihood that the independent variable accounts for the results is high. When the results can be attributed with little or no ambiguity to the effects of the independent variable, the experiment is said to be internally valid. *Internal validity* refers to the extent to which an experiment rules out alternative explanations of the results. Factors or influences other than the independent variable that could explain the results are called *threats to internal validity*.

Threats to Internal Validity

Several types of threats to internal validity have been identified (e.g., Cook and Campbell, 1979; Kazdin, 1980c). It is important to discuss threats to internal validity because they convey the reasons that carefully designed experiments are needed. An experiment needs to be designed to make implausible the influences of all the threats. A summary of major threats that must be considered in the evaluation of most experiments is provided in Table 4-1. Even though the changes in performance may have resulted from the intervention or independent variable, the factors listed in Table 4-1 might also explain the results. If inferences are to be drawn about the independent variable, the threats to internal validity must be ruled out. To the extent that each threat is ruled out or made relatively implausible, the experiment is said to be internally valid.

History and *maturation,* as threats to internal validity, are relatively straightforward (see Table 4-1). Administration of the intervention may coincide with special or unique events in the client's life or with maturational pro-

Table 4-1. Major threats to internal validity

1. *History*	Any event (other than the intervention) occurring at the time of the experiment that could influence the results or account for the pattern of data otherwise attributed to the intervention. Historical events might include family crises, change in job, teacher, or spouse, power blackouts, or any other events.
2. *Maturation*	Any change over time that may result from processes within the subject. Such processes may include growing older, stronger, healthier, smarter, and more tired or bored.
3. *Testing*	Any change that may be attributed to the effects of repeated assessment. Testing constitutes an experience that, depending on the measure, may lead to systematic changes in performance.
4. *Instrumentation*	Any change that takes place in the measuring instrument or assessment procedure over time. Such changes may result from the use of human observers whose judgments about the client or criteria for scoring behavior may change over time.
5. *Statistical regression*	Any change from one assessment occasion to another that might be due to a reversion of scores toward the mean. If clients score at the extremes on one assessment occasion, their scores may change in the direction toward the mean on a second testing.
6. *Selection biases*	Any differences between groups that are due to the differential selection or assignment of subjects to groups. Groups may differ as a function of the initial selection criteria rather than as a function of the different conditions to which they have been assigned as part of the experiment.
7. *Attrition*	Any change in overall scores between groups or in a given group over time that may be attributed to the loss of some of the subjects. Subjects who drop out or who are lost, for whatever reason, may make the overall group data appear to have changed. The change may be a result from the loss of performance scores for some of the subjects.
8. *Diffusion of treatment*	The intervention to be evaluated is usually given to one group but not to another or given to a person at one time but not at another time. Diffusion of treatment can occur when the intervention is inadvertently provided to part or all of the control group or at the times when treatment should not be in effect. The efficacy of the intervention will be underestimated if experimental and control groups or conditions both receive the intervention that was supposed to be provided only to the experimental condition.

cesses within the person over time. The design must rule out the possibility that the pattern of results is likely to have resulted from either one of these threats. The potential influence of *instrumentation* also must be ruled out. It is possible that the data show changes over time not because of progress in the client's behavior but rather because the observers have gradually changed their criteria for scoring client performance. The instrument, or measuring device, has in some way changed. If it is possible that changes in the criteria observers invoke to score behavior, rather than actual changes in client performance, could account for the pattern of the results, instrumentation serves as a threat to internal validity.

Testing and *statistical regression* are threats that can more readily interfere with drawing valid inferences in between-group research than in single-case research. In much of group research, the assessment devices are administered on two occasions, before and after treatment. The change that occurs from the first to the second assessment occasion may be due to the intervening treatment. Alternatively, merely taking the test twice may have led to improvement. Group research often includes a no-treatment control group, which allows evaluation of the impact of the intervention over and above the influence of repeated testing.

Statistical regression refers to changes in extreme scores from one assessment occasion to another. When persons are selected on the basis of their extreme scores (e.g., those who score low on a screening measure of social interaction skills or high on a measure of hyperactivity), they can be expected on the average to show some changes in the opposite direction (toward the mean) at the second testing merely as a function of regression. If treatment has been provided, the investigator may believe that the improvements resulted from the treatment. However, the improvements may have occurred anyway as a function of *regression toward the mean,* i.e., the tendency of scores at the extremes to revert toward mean levels upon repeated testing.[1] The effects of regression must be separated from the effects of the intervention.

In group research, regression effects are usually ruled out by including a no-treatment group and by randomly assigning subjects to all groups. In this way, differential regression between groups would be ruled out and the effects of the

---

1. Regression toward the mean is a statistical phenomenon that is related to the correlation between initial test and retest scores. The lower the correlation, the greater the amount of error in the measure, and the greater the regression toward the mean. It is important to note further that regression does not mean that all extreme scores will revert toward the mean upon retesting or that any particular person will inevitably score in a less extreme fashion on the next occasion. The phenomenon refers to changes for segments of a sample (i.e., the extremes) as a whole and how those segments, on the average, will respond.

intervention can be separated from the effects of regression. In single-case research, inferences about behavior change are drawn on the basis of repeated assessment over time. Although fluctuations of performance from one day or session to the next may be based on regression toward the mean, this usually does not compete with drawing inferences about treatment. Regression cannot account for the usual pattern of data with assessment on several occasions over time and with the effects of treatment shown at different points throughout the assessment period.

Selection biases are also a problem of internal validity, primarily in group research in which subjects in one group may differ from subjects in another group. At the end of the experiment, the groups differ on the dependent measure, but this may be due to initial differences rather than to differences resulting from the intervention. Selection biases usually do not present problems in single-case experiments because inferences do not depend on comparisons of different persons. *Attrition* or loss of subjects over time is usually not a threat to internal validity in single-case research. Attrition can present a threat if a group of subjects is evaluated with one of the single-case experimental designs and average scores are used for the data analysis over time. If some subjects drop out, the group average may change (e.g., improve). The change may not result from any treatment effect but rather from the loss of scores that may have been particularly low or high in computing the average at different points in the experiment.

Diffusion of treatment is one of the more subtle threats to internal validity. When the investigator is comparing treatment and no treatment or two or more different treatments, it is important to ensure that the conditions remain distinct and include the intended intervention. Occasionally, the different conditions do not remain as distinct as intended. For example, the effects of parental praise on a child's behavior in the home might be evaluated in a single-case experimental design in which praise is given to the child in some phases and withdrawn in other phases. It is possible that when parents are instructed to cease the use of praise, they may continue anyway. The results may show little or no difference between treatment and "no-treatment" phases because the treatment was inadvertently administered to some extent in the no-treatment phase. The diffusion of treatment will interfere with drawing accurate inferences about the impact of treatment and hence constitutes a threat to internal validity.

It is important to identify major threats to internal validity as the basis for understanding the logic of experimentation in general. The reason for arranging the situation to conform to one of the many experimental designs is to rule out the threats that serve as plausible alternative hypotheses or explanations of the results. Single-case experiments can readily rule out the threats to internal validity. The specific designs accomplish this somewhat differently, as will be discussed in subsequent chapters.

External Validity

Although the purpose of experimentation is to demonstrate the relationship between independent and dependent variables, this is not the only task. The goal is also to demonstrate general relationships that extend beyond the unique circumstances and arrangements of any particular investigation. Internal validity refers to the extent to which an experiment demonstrates unambiguously that the intervention accounts for change. *External validity* addresses the broader question and refers to the extent to which the results of an experiment can be generalized or extended beyond the conditions of the experiment. In any experiment, questions can be raised about whether the results can be extended to other persons, settings, assessment devices, clinical problems, and so on, all of which are encompassed by external validity. Characteristics of the experiment that may limit the generality of the results are referred to as *threats to external validity*.

Threats to External Validity

Numerous threats to external validity can be delineated (Bracht and Glass, 1968; Cook and Campbell, 1979). A summary of the major threats is presented in Table 4-2. As with internal validity, threats to external validity constitute questions that can be raised about the findings. Generally, the questions ask if any features within the experiment might delimit generality of the results.

The factors that may limit the generality of the results of an experiment are not all known until subsequent research expands on the conditions under which the relationship was originally examined. For example, the manner in which instructions are given, the age of the subjects, the setting in which the intervention was implemented, characteristics of the trainers or therapists, and other factors may contribute to the generality of a given finding. Technically, the generality of experimental findings can be a function of virtually any characteristic of the experiment. Some characteristics that may limit extension of the findings can be identified in advance; these are summarized in Table 4-2.

An initial question of obvious importance is whether the findings can be *generalized across subjects*. Even though the findings may be internally valid, it is possible that the results might only extend to persons very much like those included in the investigation. Unique features of the population—its members'

Table 4-2. Major threats to external validity

1. Generality across subjects	The extent to which the results can be extended to subjects or clients whose characteristics may differ from those included in the investigation.
2. Generality across settings	The extent to which the results extend to other situations in which the client functions beyond those included in training.
3. Generality across response measures	The extent to which the results extend to behaviors not included in the program. These behaviors may be similar to those focused on or may be entirely different responses.
4. Generality across times	The extent to which the results extend beyond the times during the day that the intervention is in effect and to times after the intervention has been terminated (maintenance).
5. Generality across behavior change agents	The extent to which the intervention effects can be extended to other persons who can administer the intervention. The effects may be restricted to persons with special skills, training, or expertise.
6. Reactive experimental arrangements	The possibility that subjects may be influenced by their awareness that they are participating in an investigation or in a special program. People may behave differently depending on the reactivity of the intervention and program to which they are exposed.
7. Reactive assessment	The extent to which subjects are aware that their behavior is being assessed and that this awareness may influence how they respond. Persons who are aware of assessment may respond differently from how they would if they were unaware of the assessment.
8. Pretest sensitization	The possibility that assessing the subjects before treatment in some way sensitizes them to the intervention that follows. The administration of a pretest may sensitize subjects so that they are affected differently by the intervention from persons who had not received the initial assessment.
9. Multiple-treatment interference	When the same subjects are exposed to more than one treatment, the conclusions reached about a particular treatment may be restricted. Specifically, the results may only apply to other persons who experience both of the treatments in the same way or in the same order.

special experiences, intelligence, age, and receptivity to the particular sort of intervention under investigation—must be considered as potential qualifiers of the findings. For example, findings obtained with children might not apply to adolescents or adults, those obtained with "normals" might not apply to those with serious physical or psychiatric impairment; and those obtained with laboratory rats might not apply to other types of animals, including humans.

Generality across settings, responses, and time each include two sorts of features as potential threats to external validity. First, for those subjects included in the experiment, it is possible that the results will be restricted to the particular response focused on, the setting, or the time of the assessment. For example, altering the deportment of elementary school children may lead to changes in these behaviors in the classroom at a particular time when the program is in effect. One question is whether the results extend to other responses (e.g., academic tasks), or to the same responses outside of the classroom (e.g., misbehavior on the playground), and at different times (e.g., after school, on weekends at home).

Second, generality also raises the larger issue of whether the results would be obtained if the intervention initially had been applied to other responses, settings, or at other times. Would the same intervention achieve similar effects if other responses (e.g., completing homework, engaging in discussion), settings (e.g., at home), or times (e.g., after school) were included. Any one of the threats may provide qualifiers or restrictions on the generality of the results. For example, the same intervention might not be expected to lead to the same results no matter what the behavior or problem is to which it is applied. Hence, independently of other questions about generality, the extent to which the results may be restricted to particular responses may emerge in its own right.

Generality of behavior change agent is a special issue that warrants comment. As it is stated, the threat has special relevance for intervention research in which some persons (e.g., parents, teachers, hospital staff, peers, spouses) attempt to alter the behaviors of others (e.g., children, students, psychiatric patients). When an intervention is effective, it is possible to raise questions about the generality of the results across behavior change agents. For example, when parents are effective in altering behavior, could the results also be obtained by others carrying out the same procedures? Perhaps there are special characteristics of the behavior change agents that have helped achieve the intervention effects. The clients may be more responsive to a given intervention as a function of who is carrying it out.

Reactivity of the experimental arrangement refers to the possibility that subjects are aware that they are participating in an investigation and that this knowledge may bear on the generality of the results. The experimental situations may be reactive, i.e., alter the behavior of the subjects because they are aware that they are being evaluated. It is possible that the results would not be evident in other situations in which persons do not know that they are being evaluated. Perhaps the results depend on the fact that subjects were responding within the context of a special situation.

The *reactivity of assessment* warrants special mention even though it can also be subsumed under the experimental arrangement. If subjects are aware of the observations that are being conducted or when they are conducted, the generality of the results may be restricted. To what extent would the results be obtained if subjects were unaware that their behaviors were being assessed? Alternatively, to what extent do the results extend to other assessment situations in which subjects are unaware that they are being observed? Most assessment is conducted under conditions in which subjects are aware that their responses are being measured in some way. In such circumstances, it is possible to ask whether the results would be obtained if subjects were unaware of the assessment procedures.

Pretest sensitization is a special case of reactive assessment. When subjects are assessed before the intervention and are aware of that assessment, the possibility exists that they will be more responsive to the intervention because of this initial assessment. The assessment may have *sensitized* the subjects to what follows. For example, being weighed or continually monitoring one's own weight may help sensitize a person to various diet programs to which he or she is exposed through advertisements. The initial act of assessment may make a person more (or less) responsive to the advertisements. Pretest sensitization refers to reactive assessment given before the intervention. If there is no preintervention assessment or that assessment is unknown to the subjects, pretest sensitization does not emerge as a possible threat.

The final threat to external validity in Table 4-2 is *multiple-treatment interference*. This threat only arises when the same subject or subjects receive two or more treatments. In such an experiment, the results may be internally valid. However, the possibility exists that the particular sequence or order in which the interventions were given may have contributed to the results. For example, if two treatments are administered in succession, the second may be more (or less) effective or equally effective as the first. The results might be due to the fact that the intervention was second and followed this particular intervention. A different ordering of the treatments might have produced different results. Hence, the conclusions that were drawn may be restricted to the special way in which the multiple treatments were presented.

The major threats to external validity do not exhaust the factors that may limit the generality of the results of a given experiment. Any feature of the experiment might be proposed to limit the circumstances under which the relationship between the independent and dependent variables operate. Of course, merely because one of the threats to external validity is applicable to the experiment does not necessarily mean that the generality of the results is jeopardized. It only means that some caution should be exercised in extending the results. One or more conditions of the experiment *may* restrict generality;

only further investigation can attest to whether the potential threat actually limits the generality of the findings.

Priorities of Internal and External Validity

In the discussion of research in general, internal validity is usually regarded as a priority over external validity. Obviously, one must first have an unambiguously demonstrated finding before one can raise questions about its generality. In the abstract, this priority cannot be refuted. However, the priorities of internal versus external validity in any given instance depend to some extent on the purposes of the research.

Internal validity is clearly given greater priority in basic research. Special experimental arrangements are designed not only to rule out threats to internal validity but also to maximize the likelihood of demonstrating a particular relationship between independent and dependent variables. Events in the experiment are carefully controlled and conditions are arranged for purposes of the demonstration. Whether the conditions represent events ordinarily evident in everyday life is not necessarily crucial. The purpose of such experiments is to show what *can* happen when the situation is arranged in a particular way.

For example, laboratory experiments may show that a particular beverage (e.g., a soft drink) causes cancer in animals fed high doses of the drink. Many circumstances of the experiment may be arranged to maximize the chances of demonstrating a relationship between beverage consumption and cancer. The animals' diets, activities, and environment may be carefully controlled. The findings may have important theoretical implications for how, where, and why cancers develop. Of course, the major question for applied purposes is whether cancers actually develop this way outside of the laboratory. For example, do the findings extend from mice and rats to humans, to lower doses of the suspected ingredients, to diets that may include many other potentially neutralizing substances (e.g., water, vitamins, and minerals), and so on? These latter questions all pertain to the external validity of the findings.

In clinical or applied research, internal validity is no less important than in basic research. However, questions of external validity may be equally important as internal validity, if not more important. In many instances, applied research does not permit the luxury of waiting for subsequent studies to show whether the results can be extended to other conditions. Single-case research is often conducted in schools, hospitals, clinics, the home, and other applied settings. The generality of the results obtained in any particular application may serve as the crucial question. For example, a hyperactive child may be treated in a hospital. The intervention may lead to change within the hospital during the periods in which the intervention is implemented and as reflected on a particular assessment device. The main question of interest from the clinical perspective is whether the results carry over to the other settings than the hospital, to other behaviors than the specific ones measured, to different times, and so on.

In experimentation in general, internal validity as noted above is given priority to answer the basic question, i.e., was the intervention responsible for change? In applied work there is some obligation to consider external validity within the design itself. The possibility exists that the results will be restricted to special circumstances of the experiment. For example, research on social skills training often measures the social behaviors of adults or children in simulated role-playing interactions. Behavior changes are demonstrated in these situations that suggest that therapeutic effects have been achieved with treatment. Unfortunately, recent research has demonstrated that how persons perform in role-playing situations may have little relationship to how they perform in actual social situations in which the same behaviors can be observed (Bellack et al., 1979; Bellack, Hersen, and Turner, 1978). Hence, the external validity of the results on one dimension (generality of responses) is critical.

Similarly, most investigations of treatment assess performance under conditions in which subjects are aware of the assessment procedures. However, the main interest is in how clients usually behave in ordinary situations when they do not believe that their behavior is being assessed. It is quite possible that findings obtained in the restricted assessment conditions of experimentation, even in applied experimentation, may not carry over to nonreactive assessment conditions of ordinary life (see Kazdin, 1979c).

The issues raised by external validity represent major questions for research in applied work. For example, traditionally the major research question of psychotherapy outcome is to determine what treatments work with what clients, clinical problems, and therapists. This formulation of the question conveys how pivotal external validity is. Considerations of the generality of treatment effects across clients, problems, and therapists are all aspects of external validity.

In single-case research, and indeed in between-group research as well, individual investigations primarily address concerns of internal validity. The investigation is arranged to rule out extraneous factors other than the intervention that might account for the results. External validity is primarily addressed in subsequent investigations that alter some of the conditions of the original study. These replications of the original investigation evaluate whether the effects of the intervention can be found across different subjects, settings, target behaviors, behavior-change agents, and so on. Single-case designs in applied research focus on intervention effects that, it is hoped, will have wide generality. Hence, replication of findings to evaluate generality is extremely important. (Both generality of findings and replication research in single-case investigations are addressed later in Chapter 11.)

Pre-Experimental Single-Case Designs

Whether a particular demonstration qualifies as an experiment is usually determined by the extent to which it can rule out threats to internal validity. Difficulties arise in the delineation of some demonstrations, as will be evident later, because ruling out threats to internal validity is not an all-or-none matter. By design, experiments constitute a special arrangement in which threats to internal validity are made implausible. The investigator is able to control important features of the investigation, such as the assignment of subjects to conditions, the implementation and withdrawal of the intervention, and other factors that are required to rule out extraneous factors that could explain the results.

Pre-experimental designs refer to demonstrations that do not completely rule out the influence of extraneous factors. Pre-experiments are often distinguished from "true experiments" (Campbell and Stanley, 1963), yet they are not dichotomous. Whether a particular threat to internal validity has been ruled out is a matter of degree. In some instances, pre-experimental designs can rule out specific threats to internal validity. It is useful to examine pre-experimental designs in relation to single-case experimentation. Because of their inherent limitations, pre-experimental designs convey the need for experimentation and why particular designs, described in subsequent chapters, are executed in one fashion rather than another.

Uncontrolled Case Studies

Case studies are considered pre-experimental designs in the sense that they do not allow internally valid conclusions to be reached. The threats to internal validity are usually not addressed in case studies in such a way as to provide conclusions about particular events (e.g., family trauma, treatment) and their effects (e.g., later delinquency, improvement). Case studies are especially important from the standpoint of design because they point to problems about drawing valid inferences. Also, in some instances, because of the way in which cases are conducted, valid inferences can be drawn even though the demonstration is pre-experimental (Kazdin, 1981).

Case studies have been defined in many different ways. Traditionally, the case study has consisted of the intensive investigation of an individual client. Case reports often include detailed descriptions of individual clients. The descriptions may rely heavily on anecdotal accounts of a therapist who draws inferences about factors that contributed to the client's plight and changes over the course of treatment. The intensive study of the individual has occupied an important role in clinical psychology, psychiatry, education, medicine, and other areas in which dramatic cases have suggested important findings. In the context of treatment, individual case studies have provided influential demonstrations such as the cases of Little Hans, Anna O., and Little Albert, as discussed in Chapter 1. In the usual case report, evaluation of the client is unsystematic and excludes virtually all of the procedures that are normally used in experimentation to rule out threats to internal validity.

In general, the case study has been defined to consist of uncontrolled reports in which one individual and his or her treatment are carefully reported and inferences are drawn about the basis of therapeutic change. Aside from the focus on the individual, the case study has also come to refer to a methodological approach in which a person or group is studied in such a fashion that unambiguous inferences cannot be drawn about the factors that contribute to performance (Campbell and Stanley, 1963; Paul, 1969). Thus, even if several persons are studied, the approach may be that of a case study. Often cases are treated on an individual basis but the information is aggregated across cases, as, for example, in reports about the efficacy of various treatments (e.g., Lazarus, 1963; Wolpe, 1958).

Case studies, whether of a single person, a group of persons, or an accumulation of several persons, are regarded as "pre-experimental" because of their inadequacies in assessment and design. Specifically, the demonstrations often rely on unsystematic assessment in which the therapist merely provides his or her opinion about the results (anecdotal reports) rather than systematic and objective measures. Also, controls often do not exist over how and when treatment is applied, so that some of the factors that could rule out threats to internal validity cannot be utilized.

Distinctions Among Uncontrolled Case Studies

By definition, case studies do not provide conclusions as clear as those available from experimentation. However, uncontrolled case studies can differ considerably from one another and vary in the extent to which valid conclusions might be reached (Kazdin, 1981). Under some circumstances, uncontrolled case studies may be able to provide information that closely approaches that which can be obtained from experimentation. Consider some of the ways in which case studies may differ from one another.

Type of Data. Case studies may vary in the type of data or information that is used as a basis for claiming that change has been achieved. At one extreme, *anecdotal information* may be used, which includes reports by the client or therapist that change has been achieved. At the other extreme, case studies can include *objective information,* such as self-report inventories, ratings by other persons, and direct measures of overt behavior. Objective measures have their own problems (e.g., reactivity, response biases) but still provide a stronger basis for determining whether change has occurred. If objective information is available, at least the therapist has a better basis for claiming that change has been achieved. The data that are available do not allow one to infer the basis for the change. Objective data serve as a prerequisite because they provide information that change has in fact occurred.

Assessment Occasions. Another dimension that can distinguish case studies is the *number and timing of the assessment occasions.* The occasions in which objective information is collected have extremely important implications for drawing inferences about the effects of the intervention. Major options consist of collecting information on a *one- or two-shot basis* (e.g., posttreatment only or pre- and posttreatment) or *continuously over time* (e.g., every day or a few times per week for an extended period). When information is collected on one or two occasions, there are special difficulties in explaining the basis of the changes. Threats to internal validity (e.g., testing, instrumentation, statistical regression) are especially difficult to rule out. With continuous assessment over time, these threats are much less plausible especially if continuous assessment begins before treatment and continues over the course of treatment. Continuous assessment allows one to examine the pattern to the data and whether the pattern appears to have been altered at the point in which the intervention was introduced. If a case study includes continuous assessment on several occasions over time, some of the threats to internal validity related to assessment can be ruled out.

Past and Future Projections of Performance. The extent to which claims can be made about performance in the past and likely performance in the future can distinguish cases. Past and future projections refer to the course of a particular behavior or problem. For some behaviors or problems, an extended *history* may be evident indicating no change. If performance changes when treatment is applied, the likelihood that treatment caused the change is increased. Problems that have a short history or that tend to occur for brief periods or in episodes may have changed anyway without the treatment. Problems with an extended history of stable performance are likely to have continued unless some special event (e.g., treatment) altered its course. Thus, the history of the problem may dictate the likelihood that extraneous events, other than treatment, could plausibly account for the change.

Projections of what performance would be like in the *future* might be obtained from knowledge of the nature of the problem. For example, the problem may be one that would not improve without intervention (e.g., terminal illness). Knowing the likely outcome increases the inferences that can be drawn about the impact of an intervention that alters this course. The patient's improvement attests to the efficacy of the treatment as the critical variable because change in the problem controverts the expected prediction.

Projections of future performance may derive from continuous assessment over time. If a particular problem is very stable, as indicated by continuous assessment before treatment, the likely prediction is that it will remain at that level in the future. If an intervention is applied and performance departs from the predicted level, this suggests that the intervention rather than other factors (e.g., history and maturation, repeated testing) may have been responsible for the change.

Type of Effect. Cases also differ in terms of the type of effects or changes that are evident as treatment is applied. The *immediacy and magnitude of change* contribute to the inferences that can be drawn about the role of treatment. Usually, the more immediate the therapeutic change after the onset of treatment, the stronger a case can be made that the treatment was responsible for change. An immediate change with the onset of treatment may make it more plausible that the treatment rather than other events (e.g., history and maturation) led to change. On the other hand, gradual changes or changes that begin well after treatment has been applied are more difficult to interpret because of the intervening experiences between the onset of treatment and therapeutic change.

Aside from the immediacy of change, the magnitude of the change is important as well. When marked changes in behavior are achieved, this suggests that only a special event, probably the treatment, could be responsible. Of course, the magnitude and immediacy of change, when combined, increase the confidence one can place in according treatment a causal role. Rapid and dramatic changes provide a strong basis for attributing the effects to treatment. Gradual and relatively small changes might more easily be discounted by random fluctuations of performance, normal cycles of behavior, or developmental changes.

Number and Heterogeneity of Subjects. The *number of subjects* included in an uncontrolled case report can influence the confidence that can be placed in any inferences drawn about treatment. Demonstrations with several cases rather than with one case provide a stronger basis for inferring the effects of treatment. The more cases that improve with treatment, the more unlikely that any particular extraneous event was responsible for change. Extraneous events probably varied among the cases, and the common experience, namely, treatment, may be the most plausible reason for the therapeutic changes.

The *heterogeneity of the cases* or diversity of the types of persons may also contribute to inferences about the cause of therapeutic change. If change is demonstrated among several clients who differ in subject and demographic variables (e.g., age, gender, race, social class, clinical problems), the inferences that can be made about treatment are stronger than if this diversity does not exist. Essentially, with a heterogeneous set of clients, the likelihood that a particular threat to internal validity (e.g., history, maturation) could explain the results is reduced.

Drawing Inferences from Case Studies

The above dimensions do not exhaust all the factors distinguishing case studies that might be relevant for drawing inferences about the role of treatment. Any particular uncontrolled case report can be evaluated on each of the dimensions. Although the case study may be pre-experimental, the extent to which inferences can be drawn and threats to internal validity ruled out is determined by where it falls on the above dimensions.

Of course, it would be impossible to present all the types of case studies that could be distinguished based on the above dimensions. An indefinite number could be generated, based on where the case lies on each continuum. Yet it is important to look at a few types of uncontrolled cases based on the above dimension and to examine how internal validity is or is not adequately addressed.

Table 4-3 illustrates a few types of uncontrolled case studies that differ on some of the dimensions mentioned above. Also, the extent to which each type of case rules out the specific threats to internal validity is presented. For each type of case the collection of objective data was included because, as noted earlier, the absence of objective or quantifiable data usually precludes drawing conclusions about whether change occurred.

Case Study Type I: With Pre- and Postassessment. A case study in which a client is treated may utilize pre- and posttreatment assessment. The inferences

Table 4-3. Selected types of hypothetical cases and the threats to internal validity they address

Type of case study	Type I	Type II	Type III
Characteristics of case present (+) or absent (−)			
Objective data	+	+	+
Continuous assessment	−	+	+
Stability of problem	−	−	+
Immediate and marked effects	−	+	−
Multiple cases	−	−	+
Major threats to internal validity ruled out (+) or not ruled out(−)			
History	−	?	+
Maturation	−	?	+
Testing	−	+	+
Instrumentation	−	+	+
Statistical regression	−	+	+

Note: In the table, a "+" indicates that the threat to internal validity is probably controlled, a "−" indicates that the threat remains a problem, and a "?" indicates that the threat may remain uncontrolled.

In preparation of the table, selected threats (see Table 4-1) were omitted because they arise primarily in the comparison of different groups in experiments. They are not usually a problem for a case study, which, of course, does not rely on group comparisons.

that can be drawn from a case with such assessment are not necessarily increased by the assessment alone. Whether specific threats to internal validity are ruled out depends on characteristics of the case with respect to the other dimensions. Table 4-3 illustrates a case with pre- and postassessment but without other characteristics that would help rule out threats to internal validity.

If changes occur in the case from pre- to posttreatment assessment, one cannot draw valid inferences about whether the treatment led to change. It is quite possible that events occurring in time (history), processes of change within the individual (maturation), repeated exposure to assessment (testing), changes in the scoring criteria (instrumentation), or reversion of the score to the mean (regression) rather than treatment led to change. The case included objective assessment, so that there is a firmer basis for claiming that changes were made than if only anecdotal reports were provided. Yet threats to internal validity were not ruled out, so the basis for change remains a matter of surmise.

Case Study Type II: With Repeated Assessment and Marked Changes. If the case study includes assessment on several occasions before and after treatment and the changes associated with the intervention are relatively marked, the inferences that can be drawn about treatment are vastly improved. Table 4-3 illustrates the characteristics of such a case, along with the extent to which specific threats to internal validity are addressed.

The fact that continuous assessment is included is important in ruling out the specific threats to internal validity related to assessment. First, the changes that coincide with treatment are not likely to result from exposure to repeated testing or changes in the instrument. When continuous assessment is utilized, changes due to testing or instrumentation would have been evident before treatment began. Similarly, regression to the mean from one data point to another, a special problem with assessment conducted at only two points in time, is eliminated. Repeated observation over time shows a *pattern* in the data. Extreme scores may be a problem for any particular assessment occasion in relation to the immediately prior occasion. However, these changes cannot account for the pattern of performance for an extended period.

Aside from continuous assessment, this case illustration includes relatively marked treatment effects, i.e., changes that are relatively immediate and large. These types of changes produced in treatment help rule out the influence of history and maturation as plausible rival hypotheses. Maturation in particular may be relatively implausible because maturational changes are not likely to be abrupt and large. Nevertheless, a "?" was placed in the table because maturation cannot be ruled out completely. In this case example, information on the stability of the problem in the past and future was not included. Hence, it is not known whether the clinical problem might ordinarily change on its own and whether maturational influences are plausible. Some problems that are episodic in nature conceivably could show marked changes that have little to do with treatment. With immediate and large changes in behavior, history is also unlikely to account for the results. Yet a "?" was placed in the table here too. Without knowledge of the stability of the problem over time, one cannot be confident about the impact of extraneous events.

For this case overall, much more can be said about the impact of treatment than in the previous case. Continuous assessment and marked changes help to rule out specific rival hypotheses. In a given instance, history and maturation may be ruled out too, although these are likely to depend on other dimensions in the table that specifically were not included in this case.

Case Study Type III: With Multiple Cases, Continuous Assessment, and Stability Information. Several cases rather than only one may be studied where each includes continuous assessment. The cases may be treated one at a time and accumulated into a final summary statement of treatment effects or treated as a single group at the same time. In this illustration, assessment information is available on repeated occasions before and after treatment. Also, the stability of the problem is known in this example. Stability refers to the dimension of past–future projections and denotes that other research suggests that the problem does not usually change over time. When the problem is known to be highly stable or to follow a particular course without treatment, the investigator has an implicit prediction of the effects of no treatment. The results can be compared with this predicted level of performance.

As is evident in Table 4-3, several threats to internal validity are addressed by a case report meeting the specified characteristics. History and maturation are not likely to interfere with drawing conclusions about the causal role of treatment because several different cases are included. All cases are not likely to have a single historical event or maturational process in common that could account for the results. Knowledge about the stability of the problem in the future also helps to rule out the influence of history and maturation. If the problem is known to be stable over time, this means that ordinary historical events and maturational processes do not provide a strong enough influence in their own right. Because of the use of multiple subjects and the knowledge about the stability of the problem, history and maturation probably are implausible explanations of therapeutic change.

The threats to internal validity related to testing are handled largely by continuous assessment over time. Repeated testing, changes in the instrument, and reversion of scores toward the mean may influence performance from one occasion to another. Yet problems associated with testing are not likely to influence the pattern of data over a large number of occasions. Also, information about the stability of the problem helps to further make implausible changes due to testing. The fact that the problem is known to be stable means that it probably would not change merely as a function of repeated assessment.

In general, the case study of the type illustrated in this example provides a strong basis for drawing valid inferences about the impact of treatment. The manner in which the multiple case report is designed does not constitute an experiment, as usually conceived, because each case represents an uncontrolled demonstration. However, characteristics of the type of case study can rule out specific threats to internal validity in a manner approaching that of true experiments.

Examples of Pre-Experimental Designs

The above discussion suggests that some types of case studies may permit inferences to be drawn about the basis of treatment, depending on how the study is conducted. The point can be conveyed more concretely by briefly examining illustrations of pre-experimental designs that include several of the features that would permit exclusion of various threats to internal validity. Each illustration presented below includes objective information and continuous assessment over time. Hence, it is important to bear in mind that meeting these conditions already distinguishes the reports from the vast majority of case studies or pre-experimental designs. Reports with these characteristics were selected because these dimensions facilitate ruling out threats to internal validity, as discussed earlier. Although none of the illustrations qualifies as a true experiment, they differ in the extent to which specific threats can be made implausible.

In the first illustration, treatment was applied to decrease the weight of an obese fifty-five-year-old woman (180 lb., 5 ft. 5 in.) (Martin and Sachs, 1973). The woman had been advised to lose weight, a recommendation of some urgency because she had recently had a heart attack. The woman was treated as an outpatient. The treatment consisted of developing a contract or agreement with the therapist based on adherence to a variety of rules and recommendations that would alter her eating habits. Several rules were developed pertaining to rewarding herself for resisting tempting foods, self-recording what was eaten after meals and snacks, weighing herself frequently each day, chewing foods slowly, and others. The patient had been weighed before treatment, and therapy began with weekly assessment for a four and one-half week period.

The results of the program, which appear in Figure 4-1, indicate that the woman's initial weight of 180 was followed by a gradual decline in weight over the next few weeks before treatment was terminated. For present purposes, what can be said about the impact of treatment? Actually, statements about the effects of the treatment in accounting for the changes would be tentative at best. To begin with, the stability of her pretreatment weight is unclear. The first data point indicated that the woman was 180 lb. before treatment. Perhaps this weight would have declined over the next few weeks even without a special weight-reduction program. The absence of clear information regarding the stability of the woman's weight before treatment makes evaluation of her subsequent loss rather difficult. The fact that the decline is gradual and modest introduces further ambiguity. The weight loss is clear, but it would be difficult to argue strongly that the intervention rather than historical events, maturational processes, or repeated assessment could not have led to the same results.

The next illustration of a pre-experimental design provides a slightly more convincing demonstration that treatment may have led to the results. This case included a twenty-eight-year-old woman with a fifteen-year history of an itchy inflamed rash on her neck (Dobes, 1977). The rash included oozing lesions and scar tissue, which were exacerbated by her constant scratching. A program was

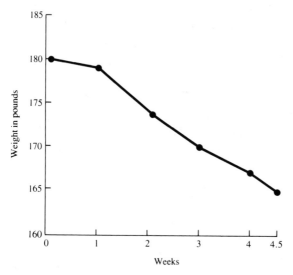

Figure 4–1. Weight in pounds per week. The line represents the connecting of the weights, respectively, on the zero, seventh, fourteenth, twenty-first, twenty-eighth, and thirty-first day of the weight loss program. (*Source:* Martin and Sachs, 1973.)

designed to decrease scratching. Instances of scratching were recorded each day by the client on a wrist counter she wore. Before treatment, her initial rate of scratching was observed daily. After six days, the program was begun. The client was instructed to graph her scratching and to try to decrease her frequency of scratching each day by at least two or three instances. If she had obtained her weekly goal in reducing her scratching, she and her husband would go out to dinner. The results of the program appear in Figure 4-2, which shows her daily rate of scratching across baseline and intervention phases.

The results suggest that the intervention may have been responsible for change. The inference is aided by continuous assessment over time before and during the intervention phase. The problem appeared at a fairly stable level before the intervention, which helps to suggest that it may not have changed without the intervention. A few features of the demonstration may detract from the confidence one might place in according treatment a causal role. The gradual and slow decline of the behavior was intentionally programmed in treatment, so the client reduced scratching when she had mastered the previous level. The gradual decline evident in the figure might also have resulted from other influences, such as increased attention from her husband (historical event) or boredom with continuing the assessment procedure (maturation). Also, the fact that the patient was responsible for collecting the observations

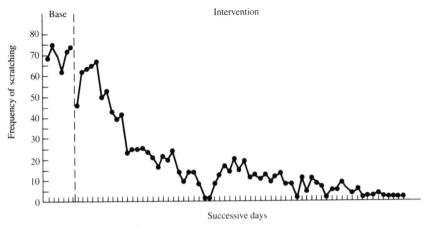

Figure 4–2. Frequency of scratching over the course of baseline and behavioral intervention phases. (*Source:* Dobes, 1977.)

raises concerns about whether accuracy of scoring changed (instrumentation) over time rather than the actual rate of scratching. Yet the data can be taken as presented without undue methodological skepticism. As such, the intervention appears to have led to change, but the pre-experimental nature of the design and the pattern of results make it difficult to rule out threats to internal validity with great confidence.

In the next illustration, the effects of the intervention appeared even clearer than in the previous example. In this report, an extremely aggressive 4½-year-old boy served as the focus (Firestone, 1976). The boy had been expelled from nursery school in the previous year for his aggressive behavior and was on the verge of expulsion again. Several behaviors including physical aggression (kicking, striking, or pulling others and destroying property) were observed for approximately two hours each day in his nursery school class. After a few days of baseline, a time out from reinforcement procedure was used to suppress aggressive acts. The procedure consisted of placing the child in a chair in a corner of the classroom in which there were no toys or other rewarding activities. He was to remain in the chair until he was quiet for two minutes.

The effects of the procedure in suppressing aggressive acts are illustrated in Figure 4-3. The first few baseline days suggest a relatively consistent rate of aggressive acts. When the time out procedure was implemented, behavior sharply declined, after which it remained at a very stable rate. Can the effects be attributed to the intervention? The few days of observation in baseline suggest a stable pattern, and the onset of the intervention was associated with

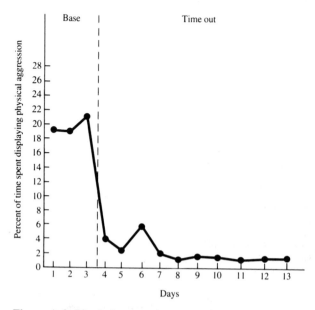

Figure 4–3. Physical aggression over the course of baseline and time out from rein-forcement conditions. (*Source:* Firestone, 1976.)

rapid and marked effects. It is unlikely that history, maturation, or other threats could readily account for the results. Within the limits of pre-experimental designs, the results are relatively clear.

Among the previous examples, the likelihood that the intervention accounted for change was increasingly plausible in light of characteristics of the report. In this final illustration of pre-experimental designs, the effects of the intervention are extremely clear. The purpose of this report was to investigate a new method of treating bedwetting (enuresis) among children (Azrin, Hontos, and Besalel-Azrin, 1979). Forty-four children, ranging in age from three to fifteen years, were included. Their families collected data on the number of nighttime bedwetting accidents for seven days before treatment. After baseline, the training procedure was implemented: the child was required to practice getting up from bed at night, remaking the bed after he or she wet, and changing clothes. Other procedures were included as well, such as waking the child early at night in the beginning of training, developing increased bladder capacity by reinforcing increases in urine volume, and so on. The parents and children practiced some of the procedures in the training session, but the intervention was essentially carried out at home when the child wet his or her bed.

The effects of training are illustrated in Figure 4-4, which shows bedwetting during the pretraining (baseline) and training periods. The demonstration is a pre-experimental design, but several of the conditions discussed earlier in the chapter were included to help rule out threats to internal validity. The data suggest that the problem was relatively stable for the group as a whole during the baseline period. Also, the changes in performance at the onset of treatment were immediate and marked. Finally, several subjects were included who probably were not very homogeneous (encompassing young children through teenagers). In light of these characteristics of the demonstration, it is not very plausible that the changes could be accounted for by history, maturation, repeated assessment, changes in the assessment procedures, or statistical regression.

The above demonstration is technically regarded as a pre-experimental design. As a general rule, the mere presentation of two phases, baseline and treatment, does not readily permit inferences to be drawn about the effects of the intervention. Such a design usually cannot rule out the threats to internal validity. These threats can be ruled out in the above demonstration because of

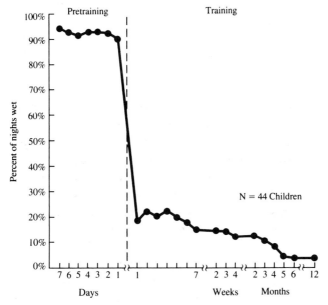

Figure 4-4. Bedwetting by forty-four enuretic children after office instruction in an operant learning method. Each data point designates the percentage of nights on which bedwetting occurred. The data prior to the dotted line are for a seven-day period prior to training. The data are presented daily for the first week, weekly for the first month, and monthly for the first six months and for the twelfth month. (*Source:* Azrin, Hontos, and Besalel-Azrin, 1979.)

a variety of circumstances (e.g., highly stable performance, rapid and marked changes). Yet these circumstances cannot be depended on in planning the investigation from the outset. Investigations that assess behavior before and during treatment usually do not allow inferences to be drawn about treatment. The experiment needs to be planned in such a way that inferences can be drawn about the effects of treatment even if the results are not ideal. True experiments provide the necessary arrangements to draw unambiguous inferences.

Pre-Experimental and Single-Case Experimental Designs

Most of the pre-experimental designs or case studies that are reported do not provide sufficient information to rule out major threats to internal validity. Some of the examples presented in the previous discussion are exceptions. Even though they are pre-experimental designs, they include several features that make threats to internal validity implausible. When objective assessment is conducted, continuous data are obtained, stable data before or after treatment are provided, marked effects are evident, and several subjects are used, it is difficult to explain the results by referring to the usual threats to internal validity. The results do not necessarily mean that the intervention led to change; even true experiments do not provide certainty that extraneous influences are completely ruled out. Hence, when case studies include several features that can rule out threats to internal validity, they do not depart very much from true experiments.

The differences are a matter of degree rather than a clear qualitative distinction. The difficulty is that the vast majority of case reports make no attempt to rule out threats to internal validity and, consequently, can be easily distinguished from experimentation. When case studies include methods to rule out various threats to internal validity, they constitute the exception. On the other hand, true experiments by definition include methods to rule out threats to internal validity. Although some carefully evaluated cases approximate and closely resemble experimentation, the differences remain. Experimentation provides a greater degree of control over the situation to minimize the likelihood that threats to internal validity can explain the results.

Single-case experimentation includes several of the features discussed earlier that can improve the inferences that can be drawn from pre-experimental designs. The use of *objective information, continuous assessment of performance* over time, and the *reliance on stable levels* of performance before and after treatment, are routinely part of the requirements of the designs. However, single-case experiments go beyond these characteristics and apply the intervention in very special ways to rule out threats to internal validity. The ways in which the situation is arranged vary as a function of the specific experimental designs. Several strategies are employed, based on the manner in which treatment is applied, withdrawn, and withheld. The explicit application of treatment under the control of the investigator is a major characteristic that reduces the plausibility of alternative rival hypotheses for the results.

Summary and Conclusions

The purpose of experimentation is to arrange the situation in such a way that extraneous influences that might affect the results do not interfere with drawing causal inferences about the impact of the intervention. The *internal validity* of an experiment refers to the extent to which the experiment rules out alternative explanations of the results. The factors or influences other than the intervention that could explain the results are called *threats to internal validity*. Major threats include the influence of history, maturation, testing, instrumentation, statistical regression, selection biases, attrition, and diffusion of treatment.

Apart from internal validity, the goal of experimentation is to demonstrate relationships that can extend beyond the unique circumstances of a particular experiment. *External validity* addresses questions of the extent to which the results of an investigation can be generalized or extended beyond the conditions of the experiment. In applied research, considerations of external validity are especially critical because the purpose of undertaking the intervention may be to produce changes that are not restricted to conditions peculiar to the experiment. Several characteristics of the experiment may limit the generality of the results. These characteristics are referred to as threats to external validity and include generality across subjects, settings, responses, time, behavior-change agents, reactivity of experimental arrangements and the assessment procedures, pretest sensitization, and multiple-treatment interference.

Experimentation provides the most powerful tool for establishing internally valid relationships. In *true experiments,* each of the threats is made implausible by virtue of the way in which the intervention is applied. *Pre-experimental* designs refer to methods of investigation that usually do not allow confidence in drawing conclusions about intervention effects.

The uncontrolled case study conveys the problems that may arise when interventions are evaluated with pre-experimental designs. In case studies, interventions are applied and evaluated unsystematically and threats to internal validity may be plausible interpretations of the results. In some instances, even uncontrolled case studies may permit one to rule out rival interpretations. The extent to which pre-experimental designs can yield valid inferences depends on such dimensions as the type of data that are obtained, the number of assessment occasions, whether information is available about past and future projections of performance, the types of effects that are achieved by the intervention, and the number and heterogeneity of the subjects. When several of these conditions are met, pre-experimental designs can rule out selected threats to internal validity.

The difficulty with pre-experimental designs is that, as a rule, they cannot rule out threats to internal validity. Experimentation provides an arrangement in which threats can be ruled out. The manner in which this arrangement is accomplished varies as a function of alternative experimental designs, which are treated in the chapters that follow.

5
Introduction to Single-Case Research and ABAB Designs

The previous chapter discussed the threats to validity that need to be ruled out or made implausible if changes in behavior are to be attributed to the intervention. It is interesting to note that in some circumstances, pre-experimental designs are capable of ruling out selected threats to internal validity. The conclusions that can be reached from case studies and other pre-experimental designs are greatly enhanced when objective measures are used, when performance is assessed on several occasions over time, when information is available regarding the stability of performance over time, and when marked changes in behavior are associated with the intervention. Pre-experimental designs that include these features can closely approximate single-case designs in terms of the inferences that can be drawn.

Single-case designs also include the characteristics listed above that address threats to internal validity. The designs go beyond pre-experimental designs by arranging the administration of the intervention to reduce further the plausibility of alternative threats to internal validity. The intervention is presented in such a way that it would be extremely implausible to explain the pattern of results by referring to extraneous factors.

The underlying rationale of single-case experimental designs is similar to that of traditional between-group experimentation. All experiments compare the effects of different conditions (independent variables) on performance. In traditional between-group experimentation, the comparison is made between groups of subjects who are treated differently. On a random basis, some subjects are designated to receive a particular intervention and others are not. The effect of the intervention is evaluated by comparing the performance of the different groups. In single-case research, inferences are usually made about the effects of the intervention by comparing different conditions presented to the same subject over time. Experimentation with the single case has special requirements that must be met if inferences are to be drawn about the effects of the intervention. It is useful to highlight basic requirements before specific designs are presented.

General Requirements of Single-Case Designs
Continuous Assessment

Perhaps the most fundamental design requirement of single-case experimentation is the reliance on repeated observations of performance over time. The client's performance is observed on several occasions, usually before the intervention is applied and continuously over the period while the intervention is in effect. Typically, observations are conducted on a daily basis or at least on multiple occasions each week.

Continuous assessment is a basic requirement because single-case designs examine the effects of interventions on performance over time. Continuous assessment allows the investigator to examine the pattern and stability of performance before treatment is initiated. The pretreatment information over an extended period provides a picture of what performance is like without the intervention. When the intervention eventually is implemented, the observations are continued and the investigator can examine whether behavior changes coincide with the intervention.

The role of continuous assessment in single-case research can be illustrated by examining a basic difference of between-group and single-case research. In both types of research, as already noted, the effects of a particular intervention on performance are examined. In the most basic case, the intervention is examined by comparing performance when the intervention is presented versus performance when it is withheld. In treatment research, this is the basic comparison of treatment versus no treatment, a question raised to evaluate whether a particular intervention improves performance. In between-group research, the question is addressed by giving the intervention to some persons (treatment group) but not to others (no treatment group). One or two observations (e.g., pre- and posttreatment assessment) are obtained for several different persons. In single-case research, the effects of the intervention are examined by observing the influence of treatment and no treatment on the performance of the same person(s). Instead of one or two observations of several persons, several observations are obtained for one or a few persons. Continuous assessment provides the several observations over time needed to make the comparison of interest with the individual subject.

Baseline Assessment

Each of the single-case experimental designs usually begins with observing behavior for several days before the intervention is implemented. This initial period of observation, referred to as the *baseline phase,* provides information about the level of behavior before a special intervention begins. The baseline phase serves different functions. First, data collected during the baseline phase describe the existing level of performance. The *descriptive function* of baseline provides information about the extent of the client's problem. Second, the data serve as the basis for predicting the level of performance for the immediate future if the intervention is not provided. Even though the descriptive function of the baseline phase is important for indicating the extent of the client's problem, from the standpoint of single-case designs, the *predictive function* is central.

To evaluate the impact of an intervention in single-case research, it is important to have an idea of what performance would be like in the future without the intervention. Of course, a description of present performance does not necessarily provide a statement of what performance would be like in the future. Performance might change even without treatment. The only way to be certain of future performance without the intervention would be to continue baseline observations without implementing the intervention. However, the purpose is to implement and evaluate the intervention and to see if behavior improves in some way.

Baseline data are gathered to help predict performance in the immediate future before treatment is implemented. Baseline performance is observed for several days to provide a sufficient basis for making a prediction of future performance. The prediction is achieved by *projecting or extrapolating* into the future a continuation of baseline performance.

A hypothetical example can be used to illustrate how observations during the baseline phase are used to predict future performance and how this prediction is pivotal to drawing inferences about the effects of the intervention. Figure 5-1 illustrates a hypothetical case in which observations were collected on a hypochondriacal patient's frequency of complaining. As evident in the figure, observations during the baseline (pretreatment) phase were obtained for ten days. The hypothetical baseline data suggest a reasonably consistent pattern of complaints each day in the hospital.

The baseline level can be used to project the likely level of performance in

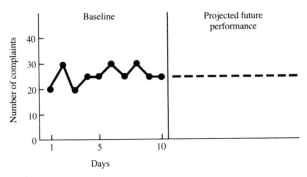

Figure 5-1. Hypothetical example of baseline observations of frequency of complaining. Data in baseline (solid line) are used to predict the likely rate of performance in the future (dashed line).

the immediate future if conditions continue as they are. The projected (dashed) line suggests the approximate level of future performance. This projected level is essential for single-case experimentation because it serves as a criterion to evaluate whether the intervention leads to change. Presumably, if treatment is effective, performance will differ from the projected level of baseline. For example, if a program is designed to reduce a hypochondriac's complaints, and is successful in doing so, the level of complaints should decrease well below the projected level of baseline. In any case, continuous assessment in the beginning of single-case experimental designs consists of observation of baseline or pretreatment performance. As the individual single-case designs are described later, the importance of initial baseline assessment will become especially clear.

Stability of Performance

Since baseline performance is used to predict how the client will behave in the future, it is important that the data are stable. A *stable rate* of performance is characterized by the absence of a trend (or slope) in the data and relatively little variability in performance. The notions of trend and variability raise separate issues, even though they both relate to stability.

Trend in the Data. A trend refers to the tendency for performance to decrease or increase systematically or consistently over time. One of three simple data patterns might be evident during baseline observations. First, baseline data may show no trend or slope. In this case, performance is best represented by a horizontal line indicating that it is not increasing or decreasing over time. As a hypothetical example, observations may be obtained on the disruptive and inappropriate classroom behaviors of a hyperactive child. The upper panel of Figure 5-2 shows baseline performance with no trend. The absence of trend in baseline provides a relatively clear basis for evaluating subsequent intervention effects. Improvements in performance are likely to be reflected in a trend that departs from the horizontal line of baseline performance.

If behavior does show a trend during baseline, behavior would be increasing or decreasing over time. The trend during baseline may or may not present problems for evaluating intervention effects, depending on the direction of the trend in relation to the desired change in behavior. Performance may be changing in the direction *opposite* from that which treatment is designed to achieve. For example, a hyperactive child may show an increase in disruptive and inappropriate behavior during baseline observations. The middle panel of Figure 5-2 shows how baseline data might appear; over the period of observations the client's behavior is becoming worse, i.e., more disruptive. Because the intervention will attempt to alter behavior in the opposite direction, this initial trend is not likely to interfere with evaluating intervention effects.

In contrast, the baseline trend may be in the *same direction* that the intervention is likely to produce. Essentially, the baseline phase may show improvements in behavior. For example, the behavior of a hyperactive child may improve over the course of baseline as disruptive and inappropriate behavior decrease, as shown in the lower panel of Figure 5-2. Because the intervention attempts to improve performance, it may be difficult to evaluate the effect of the subsequent intervention. The projected level of performance for baseline is toward improvement. A very strong intervention effect of treatment would be needed to show clearly that treatment surpassed this projected level from baseline.

If baseline is showing an improvement, one might raise the question of why an intervention should be provided at all. Yet even when behavior is improving during baseline, it may not be improving quickly enough. For example, an autistic child may show a gradual decrease in headbanging during baseline observations. The reduction may be so gradual that serious self-injury might be inflicted unless the behavior is treated quickly. Hence, even though behavior is changing in the desired direction, additional changes may be needed.

Occasionally, a trend may exist in the data and still not interfere with evaluating treatments. Also, when trends do exist, several design options and data evaluation procedures can help clarify the effects of the intervention (see Chapters 9 and 10, respectively). For present purposes, it is important to convey that the one feature of a stable baseline is little or no trend, and that the absence of trend provides a clear basis for evaluating intervention effects. Presumably,

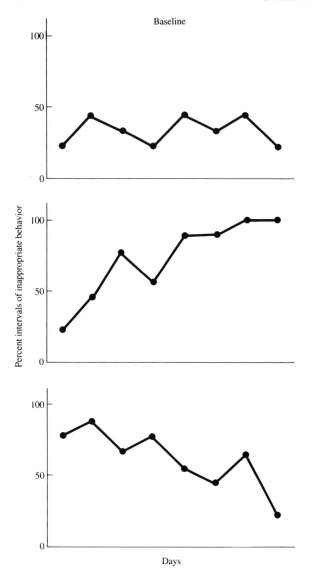

Figure 5–2. Hypothetical data for disruptive behavior of a hyperactive child. *Upper panel* shows a stable rate of performance with no systematic trend over time. *Middle panel* shows a systematic trend with behavior becoming worse over time. *Lower panel* shows a systematic trend with behavior becoming better over time. This latter pattern of data (lower panel) is the most likely one to interfere with evaluation of interventions, because the change is in the same direction of change anticipated with treatment.

when the intervention is implemented, a trend toward improvement in behavior will be evident. This is readily detected with an initial baseline that does not already show a trend toward improvement.

Variability in the Data. In addition to trend, stability of the data refers to the fluctuation or variability in the subject's performance over time. Excessive variability in the data during baseline or other phases can interfere with drawing conclusions about treatment. As a general rule, the greater the variability in the data, the more difficult it is to draw conclusions about the effects of the intervention.

Excessive variability is a relative notion. Whether the variability is excessive and interferes with drawing conclusions about the intervention depends on many factors, such as the initial level of behavior during the baseline phase and the magnitude of behavior change when the intervention is implemented. In the extreme case, baseline performance may fluctuate daily from extremely high to extremely low levels (e.g., 0 to 100 percent). Such a pattern of performance is illustrated in Figure 5-3 (upper panel), in which hypothetical baseline data are provided. With such extreme fluctuations in performance, it is difficult to predict any particular level of future performance.

Alternatively, baseline data may show relatively little variability. A typical example is represented in the hypothetical data in the lower panel of Figure 5-3. Performance fluctuates but the extent of the fluctuation is small compared with the upper panel. With relatively slight fluctuations, the projected pattern of future performance is relatively clear and hence intervention effects will be less difficult to evaluate.

Ideally, baseline data will show little variability. Occasionally relatively large variability may exist in the data. Several options are available to minimize the impact of such variability on drawing conclusions about intervention effects (see Chapter 10). However, the evaluation of intervention effects is greatly facilitated by relatively consistent performance during baseline.

ABAB Designs

The discussion to this point has highlighted the basic requirements of single-case designs. In particular, assessing performance continuously over time and obtaining stable rates of performance are pivotal to the logic of the designs. Precisely how these features are essential for demonstrating intervention effects can be conveyed by discussing ABAB designs, which are the most basic experimental designs in single-case research. ABAB designs consist of a family of procedures in which observations of performance are made over time for a

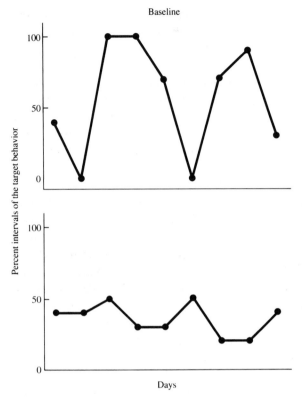

Figure 5-3. Baseline data showing relatively large variability *(upper panel)* and relatively small variability *(lower panel)*. Intervention effects are more readily evaluated with little variability in the data.

given client (or group of clients). Over the course of the investigation, changes are made in the experimental conditions to which the client is exposed.

Basic Characteristics of the Designs
Description and Underlying Rationale

The ABAB design examines the effects of an intervention by alternating the baseline condition (A phase), when no intervention is in effect, with the intervention condition (B phase). The A and B phases are repeated again to complete the four phases. The effects of the intervention are clear if performance improves during the first intervention phase, reverts to or approaches original baseline levels of performance when treatment is withdrawn, and improves when treatment is reinstated in the second intervention phase.

The simple description of the ABAB design does not convey the underlying rationale that accounts for its experimental utility. It is the rationale that is crucial to convey because it underlies all of the variations of the ABAB designs. The initial phase begins with baseline observations when behavior is observed under conditions before treatment is implemented. This phase is continued until the rate of the response appears to be stable or until it is evident that the response does not improve over time. As noted earlier, baseline observations serve two purposes, namely, to *describe* the current level of behavior and to *predict* what behavior would be like in the future if no intervention were implemented. The description of behavior before treatment is obviously necessary to give the investigator an idea of the nature of the problem. From the standpoint of the design, the crucial feature of baseline is the prediction of behavior in the future. A stable rate of behavior is needed to project into the future what behavior would probably be like. Figure 5-4 shows hypothetical data for an ABAB design. During baseline, the level of behavior is assessed (solid line), and this line is projected to predict the level of behavior into the future (dashed line). When a projection can be made with some degree of confidence, the intervention (B) phase is implemented.

The intervention phase has similar purposes to the baseline phase, namely, to describe current performance and to predict performance in the future if

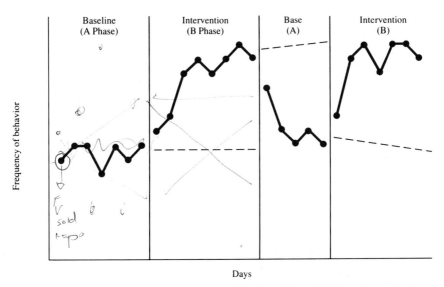

Figure 5-4. Hypothetical data for an ABAB design. The solid lines in each phase present the actual data. The dashed lines indicate the projection or predicted level of performance from the previous phase.

conditions were unchanged. However, there is an added purpose of the intervention phase. In the baseline phase a prediction was made about future performance. In the intervention phase, the investigator can test whether performance during the intervention phase (phase B, solid line) actually departs from the projected level of baseline (phase B, dashed line). In effect, baseline observations were used to make a prediction about performance. During the first intervention phase, data can test the prediction. Do the data during the intervention phase depart from the projected level of baseline? If the answer is yes, this shows that there is a change in performance. In Figure 5-4, it is clear that performance changed during the first intervention phase. At this point in the design, it is not entirely clear that the intervention was responsible for change. Other factors, such as history and maturation, might be proposed to account for change and cannot be convincingly ruled out. As a *pre*-experimental design, the demonstration could end with the first two (AB) phases. However, single-case experiments that meet the requirements of the ABAB design extend to three, four, or more phases to provide more certainty about the role of the intervention in changing behavior.

In the third phase, the intervention is usually withdrawn and the conditions of baseline are restored. This second A phase has several purposes. The two purposes common to the other phases are included, namely, to describe current performance and to predict what performance would be like in the future. A third purpose is similar to that of the intervention phase, namely, to test the level of performance predicted from the previous phase. One purpose of the intervention phase was to make a prediction of what performance would be like in the future if the conditions remain unchanged (see dashed line, second A phase). The second A phase tests to see whether this level of performance in fact occurred. By comparing the solid and dashed lines in the second A phase, it is clear that the predicted and obtained levels of performance differ. Thus, the change that occurs suggests that something altered performance from its projected course.

There is one final and unique purpose of the second A phase that is rarely discussed. The *first* A phase made a prediction of what performance would be like in the future (the dashed line in the first B phase). This was the first prediction in the design, and like any prediction, it may be incorrect. The second A phase restores the conditions of baseline and can test the first prediction. If behavior had continued without an intervention, would it have continued at the same level as the original baseline or would it have changed markedly? The second A phase examines whether performance would have been at or near the level predicted originally. A comparison of the solid line of the second A phase with the dashed line of the first B phase, in Figure 5-4, shows that the lines really are no different. Thus, performance predicted by the original baseline phase was generally accurate. Performance would have remained at this level without the intervention.

In the final phase of the ABAB design, the intervention is reinstated again. This phase serves the same purposes as the previous phase, namely to describe performance, to test whether performance departs from the projected level of the previous phase, and to test whether performance is the same as predicted from the previous intervention phase. (If additional phases were added to the design, the purpose of the second B phase would of course be to predict future performance.)

In short, the logic of the ABAB design and its variations consists of making and testing predictions about performance under different conditions. Essentially, data in the separate phases provide information about present performance, predict the probable level of future performance, and test the extent to which predictions of performance from previous phases were accurate. By repeatedly altering experimental conditions in the design, there are several different opportunities to compare phases and to test whether performance is altered by the intervention. If behavior changes when the intervention is introduced, reverts to or near baseline levels after the intervention is withdrawn, and again improves when treatment is reinstated, the pattern of results suggests rather strongly that the intervention was responsible for change. Various threats to internal validity, outlined earlier, might have accounted for change in one of the phases. However, any particular threat or set of threats does not usually provide a plausible explanation for the pattern of data. The most parsimonious explanation is that the intervention and its withdrawal accounted for changes.

Illustrations

The ABAB design and its underlying rationale are nicely illustrated in an investigation that evaluated the effects of teacher behavior on the performance of an educably retarded male adolescent who attended a special education class (Deitz, 1977). The client frequently talked out loud, which was disruptive to the class. To decrease this behavior, a reinforcement program was devised in which the client could earn extra time with the teacher for decreasing the number of times he spoke out. The student was told that if he emitted few (three or fewer) instances of talking out within a fifty-five-minute period, the teacher would spend extra time working with him. Thus, the client would receive reinforcing consequences if he showed a low rate of disruptive behavior (a schedule referred to as *differential reinforcement of low rates, or a DRL schedule*). As

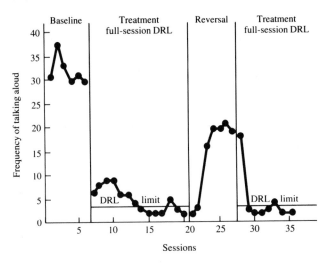

Figure 5–5. The frequency of talking aloud per fifty-five-minute session of an educably retarded male. During treatment, the teacher spent fifteen minutes working with him if he talked aloud three times or fewer. (*Source:* Deitz, 1977.)

evident in Figure 5-5, the intervention was evaluated in an ABAB design. Instances of talking out decreased when the intervention was applied and increased toward baseline levels when the program was withdrawn. Finally, when the intervention was reinstated, behavior again improved. Overall, the data follow the pattern described earlier and, hence, clearly demonstrate the contribution of the intervention to behavior change.

In another example, Zlutnick et al. (1975) reduced the seizures of several children. Seizure activity often includes suddenly tensing or flexing the muscles, staring into space, jerking or shaking, grimacing, dizziness, falling to the ground, and losing consciousness. The treatment was based on interrupting the activity that immediately preceded the seizure. For example, one seven-year-old boy had seizures that began with a fixed stare, followed by body rigidity, violent shaking, and falling to the floor. Because the seizure was always preceded by a fixed stare, an attempt was made to interrupt the behaviors leading up to a seizure. The intervention was conducted in a special education classroom, where the staff was instructed to interrupt the preseizure activity. The procedure consisted of going over to the child and shouting "no," and grasping him and shaking him once when the stare began. This relatively simple intervention was evaluated in an ABAB design, as shown in Figure 5-6. The intervention markedly reduced seizures. For the week of the reversal phase, during which the interruption procedure was no longer used, seizures returned to their

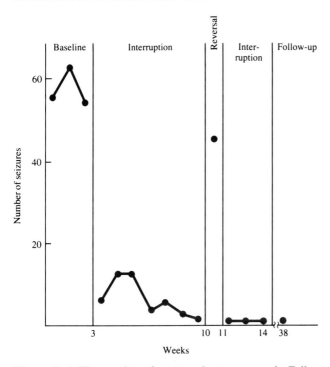

Figure 5–6. The number of motor seizures per week. Follow-up data represent the number of seizures for the six-month period after the intervention was withdrawn. (*Source:* Zlutnick, Mayville, and Moffat, 1975.)

high baseline level. The intervention was again implemented, which effectively eliminated the seizures. At the end of a six-month follow-up, only one seizure had been observed. Overall, the effects of the intervention were clearly demonstrated in the design.

Both of the above examples illustrate basic applications of the ABAB design. And both convey clear effects of the interventions because behavior changed as a function of altering phases over the course of the investigation. Of course, several other variations of the ABAB design are available, many of which are highlighted below.

Design Variations

An extremely large number of variations of the ABAB designs have been reported. Essentially, the designs may vary as a function of several factors, including the procedures that are implemented to "reverse" behavior in the second A phase, the order of the phases, the number of phases, and the number of different interventions included in the design. Although the underlying rationale for all of the variations is the same, it is important to illustrate major design options.

"Reversal" Phase

A characteristic of the ABAB design is that the intervention is terminated or withdrawn during the second A or reversal phase to determine whether behavior change can be attributed to the intervention. Withdrawing the intervention (e.g., reinforcement procedure, drug) and thereby returning to baseline conditions is frequently used to achieve this reversal of performance. *Returning to baseline conditions* is only one way to show a relationship between performance and treatment (see Goetz, Holmberg, and LeBlanc, 1975; Lindsay and Stoffelmayr, 1976).

A second alternative is to *administer consequences noncontingently*. For example, during an intervention (B) phase, parents may deliver praise to alter their child's performance. Instead of withdrawing praise to return to baseline conditions (A phase), parents may continue to deliver praise but deliver it noncontingently, or independently of the child's behavior. This strategy is selected to show that it is not the event (e.g., praise) per se that leads to behavior change but rather the relationship between the event and behavior.

For example, Twardosz and Baer (1973) trained two severely retarded adolescent boys with limited speech to ask questions. The boys received praise and tokens for asking questions in special treatment sessions where speech was developed. After behavior change was demonstrated, noncontingent reinforcement was provided to each subject. Tokens and praise were given at the beginning of the session before any responses had occurred and, of course, did not depend on performance of the target behavior. As expected, noncontingent reinforcement led to a return of behavior to baseline levels.

Aside from administering consequences at the beginning of a session, noncontingent delivery can be accomplished in other ways. For example, in some studies, reinforcers are provided on the basis of elapsed time so that at the end of an interval (e.g., fifteen minutes), persons receive the reinforcing consequences. The reinforcers are noncontingent in this case, because they are delivered independently of performance at the end of the interval. Noncontingent reinforcement is more likely to lead to a return to baseline levels of performance if reinforcers are delivered at the beginning of the session than during or after the session. Over the course of the session, it is likely that the desired behaviors will occur on some occasions and be reinforced accidentally. Hence, in some studies noncontingent reinforcement during the course of treatment may improve behavior (Kazdin, 1973; Lindsay and Stoffelmayr, 1976).

A third variation of the reversal phase is to continue contingent consequences but to alter the behaviors that are associated with the consequences. For example, if the intervention consists of reinforcing a particular behavior, the reversal phase can consist of reinforcing all behaviors except the one that was reinforced during the intervention phase. The procedure for administering reinforcement for all behaviors except a specific response is called *differential reinforcement of other behavior* (or DRO schedule). During a reversal phase using a DRO schedule, all behaviors would be reinforced except the one that was reinforced during the intervention phase. For example, in a classroom, praise on a DRO schedule might be delivered whenever children were *not* studying. This strategy for showing a reversal of behavior is used to demonstrate that the relationship between the target behavior and the consequences rather than mere administration of the consequences accounts for behavior change.

As an illustration, Rowbury, Baer, and Baer (1976) provided behavior-problem preschool children with praise and tokens that could be exchanged for play time. These reinforcers were delivered for completing standard preacademic tasks, such as fitting puzzle pieces and matching forms, colors, and sizes. During the reversal (or second A) phase, a DRO schedule was used. Tokens were given for just sitting down or for starting the task rather than for completing the task. Under the DRO schedule, children completed fewer tasks than they had completed during the intervention. Hence, DRO served a purpose similar to a return to baseline or noncontingent delivery of consequences.

A DRO schedule differs from the previous noncontingent delivery of consequences. During the DRO, reinforcement *is* contingent on behavior but on behaviors different from the one reinforced during the experimental phase. The reason for using a DRO is to show that the effects of a contingency can change rapidly. Behavior approaches the original baseline levels more quickly when "other behavior" is reinforced directly than when noncontingent reinforcement is administered, even though both are quite useful for the purposes of ABAB designs (Goetz et al., 1975).

Order of the Phases

The ABAB version suggests that observing behavior under baseline conditions (A phase) is the first step in the design. However, in many circumstances, the design may begin with the intervention (or B) phase. The intervention may need to be implemented immediately because of the severity of the behavior (e.g., self-destructive behavior, stabbing one's peers). In cases where clinical considerations dictate immediate interventions, it may be unreasonable to insist on collecting baseline data. (Of course, return to baseline phases might not be possible either, a problem discussed later.)

Second, in many cases, baseline levels of performance are obvious because the behavior may never have occurred. For example, when behavior has never been performed (e.g., self-care skills among some retarded persons, exercise among many of us, and table manners of a Hun), treatment may begin without baseline. When a behavior is known to be performed at a zero rate over an extended period, beginning with a baseline phase may serve no useful purpose. The design would still require a reversal of treatment conditions at some point.

In each of the above cases, the design may begin with the intervention phase and continue as a BABA design. The logic of the design and the methodological functions of the alternating phases are unchanged. Drawing inferences about the impact of treatment depends on the pattern of results discussed earlier. For example, in one investigation a BABA design was used to evaluate the effects of token reinforcement delivered to two retarded men who engaged in little social interaction (Kazdin and Polster, 1973). The program, conducted in a sheltered workshop, consisted of providing tokens to each man when he conversed with another person. Conversing was defined as a verbal exchange in which the client and peer made informative comments to each other (e.g., about news, television, sports) rather than just general greetings and replies (e.g., "Hi, how are you?" "Fine."). Because social behaviors were considered by staff to be consistently low during the periods before the program, staff wished to begin an intervention immediately. Hence, the reinforcement program was begun in the first phase and evaluated in a BABA design, as illustrated for one of the clients in Figure 5-7. Social interaction steadily increased in the first phase (reinforcement) and ceased almost completely when the program was withdrawn (reversal). When reinforcement was reinstated, social interaction was again high. The pattern of the first three phases suggested that the intervention was responsible for change. Hence, in the second reinforcement phase, the consequences were given intermittently to help maintain behavior when the program was ultimately discontinued. Behavior tended to be maintained in the final reversal phase even though the program was withdrawn.

Number of Phases

Perhaps the most basic dimension that distinguishes variations of the ABAB design is the number of phases. The ABAB design with four phases elaborated earlier has been a very commonly used version. Several other options are avail-

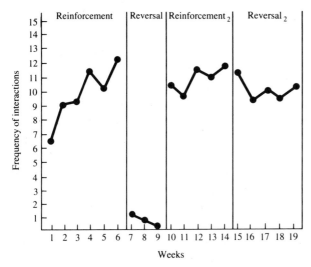

Figure 5-7. Mean frequency of interactions per day as a function of a social and token reinforcement program evaluated in a BABA design. (*Source:* Kazdin and Polster, 1973.)

able. As a minimum, the design must include *at least three phases,* such as the ABA (baseline, intervention, baseline) or BAB (intervention, baseline, intervention). There is general agreement that when fewer than three phases are used, drawing conclusions about the causal relationship between the intervention and behavior change is very tenuous. That is, the threats to internal validity become increasingly plausible as rival explanations of the results. Several phases may be included, as in an ABABAB design in which the intervention effect is repeatedly demonstrated or, as discussed below, in which different interventions are included.

Number of Different Interventions

Another way in which ABAB designs can vary pertains to the number of different interventions that are included in the design. As usually discussed, the design consists of a single intervention that is implemented at different phases in the investigation. Occasionally, investigators may include separate interventions (B and C phases) in the same design. Separate interventions may be needed in situations where the first one does not alter behavior or does not achieve a sufficient change for the desired result. Alternatively, the investigator may wish to examine the relative effectiveness of two separate interventions.

The interventions (B,C) may be administered at different points in the design as represented by ABCBCA or ABCABC designs.

An illustration of a design with more than one intervention was provided by Foxx and Shapiro (1978), who were interested in decreasing disruptive behaviors of retarded boys in a special education class. The behaviors included hitting others, throwing objects, yelling, leaving one's seat, and similar activities. After baseline observations, a reinforcement program was implemented in which children received food and social reinforcement when they were working quietly and studying. Although this decreased disruptive behavior, the effects were minimal. Hence, a time out from reinforcement procedure was added in the next phase in which the reinforcement procedure was continued. In addition, for incidents of misbehavior, the child lost the opportunity to earn food and social reinforcement. Specifically, when misbehavior occurred, the child had to remove a ribbon he wore around the neck. The loss of the ribbon meant that he could not receive reinforcing consequences. The effect of the time-out ribbon procedure and the design in which the effects were demonstrated appear in Figure 5-8. As evident from the figure, an ABCBC design was used. The

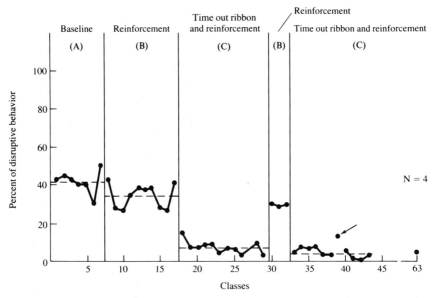

Figure 5–8. The mean percent of time spent in disruptive behavior by four subjects. The horizontal dashed lines indicate the mean for each condition. The arrow marks a one-day reversal in which the time out contingency was suspended. A follow-up assessment of the teacher-conducted program occurred on day sixty-three. (*Source:* Foxx and Shapiro, 1978.)

effects of the time out procedure (C phases) were dramatic. It is worth noting that the investigation did not include a return to baseline condition but meets the requirements of the design. The reinforcement and time out procedures were alternated to fulfill the design requirements.

General Comments

The above dimensions represent ways in which ABAB designs vary. It is important to mention the dimensions that distinguish ABAB design variations rather than to mention each of the individual design options. Indeed, in principle it would not be possible to mention each version because an infinite number of ABAB design variations exist, based on the number of phases, interventions, ordering of phases, and types of reversal phases that are included. The specific design variation that the investigator selects is partially determined by purposes of the project, the results evident during the course of treatment (e.g., no behavior change with the first intervention), and the exigencies or constraints of the situation (e.g., limited time in which to complete the investigation).

Problems and Limitations

The defining characteristic of the ABAB designs and their variations consists of alternating phases in such a way that performance is expected to improve at some points and to return to or to approach baseline rates at other points. The need to show a "reversal" of behavior is pivotal if causal inferences are to be drawn about the impact of the intervention. Several problems arise with the designs as a result of this requirement.

Absence of a "Reversal" of Behavior

It is quite possible that behavior will not revert toward baseline levels once the intervention is withdrawn or altered. Indeed, in several demonstrations using ABAB designs, removing treatment has had no clear effect on performance and no reversal of behavior was obtained (Kazdin, 1980a). In such cases, it is not clear that the intervention was responsible for change. Extraneous factors associated with the intervention may have led to change. These factors (e.g., changes in home or school situation, illness or improvement from an illness, better sleep at night) may have coincidentally occurred when the intervention was implemented and remained in effect after the intervention was withdrawn. History and maturation may be plausible explanations of the results.

Alternatively, the intervention may have led to change initially but behavior may have come under the control of other influences. For example, in one investigation, teacher praise was used to increase the interaction of socially withdrawn children (Baer, Rowbury, and Goetz, 1976). After student social behavior increased over time, eventually the interactions of the children's peers rather than teacher praise were the controlling factor that sustained performance. Consequently, withdrawing teacher praise did not lead to reductions of student interaction.

Another situation in which a reversal of behavior may not be found is when punishment is used to suppress behavior. Occasionally, when behavior is completely suppressed with punishment, it may not return to baseline levels after treatment is withdrawn. In one report, for example, electric shock was used to decrease the coughing of a fourteen-year-old boy who had not responded to medical treatment nor to attempts to ignore coughing (Creer, Chai and Hoffman, 1977). The cough was so disruptive and distracting to others that the boy had been expelled from school until his cough could be controlled. After baseline observations, treatment was administered. Treatment began by applying a mild electric shock to the child's forearm for coughing. Application of only one shock after the first cough completely eliminated the behavior. The boy immediately returned to school and did not suffer further episodes of coughing up to 2½ years after treatment.

Essentially, cessation of the punishment procedure (return to baseline) did not lead to a return of the behavior. From the standpoint of design, there was no reversal of behavior. In this particular case, it is highly plausible that treatment accounted for elimination of behavior, given the extended history of the problem, the lack of effects of alternative treatments and the rapidity of behavior change. On the other hand, in the general case, merely showing a change in performance without a return to baseline levels of performance at some point in the design is insufficient for drawing conclusions about the impact of treatment.

Behaviors may not revert to baseline levels of performance for another reason. Most intervention programs evaluated in ABAB designs consist of altering the behavior of persons (parents, teachers, staff) who will influence the client's target behavior. After behavior change in the client has been achieved, it may be difficult to convince behavior change agents to alter their performance to approximate their behavior during the original baseline. It may not be a matter of convincing behavior change agents; their behavior may be permanently altered in some fashion. For example, parents or teachers might be told to stop administering praise or to administer praise noncontingently. Yet this may not be carried out. In such cases, the program remains in effect and baseline conditions cannot be reinstated. The intervention may have been responsible for change, but this cannot be demonstrated if the behavior change agents cannot or do not alter their behavior to restore baseline conditions.

The above discussion emphasizes various factors that contribute to the failure of behavior to revert to baseline or preintervention levels. Strictly speaking, it is difficult to evaluate intervention effects in ABAB designs without showing that behavior reverts to or approaches baseline levels. Of course, there are many situations in which behaviors might be reversed, but questions can be raised about even attempting to do this, as discussed below.

Undesirability of "Reversing" Behavior

Certainly a major issue in evaluating ABAB designs is whether reversal phases should be used at all. If behavior could be returned to baseline levels as part of the design, is such a change ethical? Attempting to return behavior to baseline is tantamount to making the client worse. In many cases, it is obvious that a withdrawal of treatment is clearly not in the interest of the client; a reversal of behavior would be difficult if not impossible to defend ethically. For example, autistic and retarded children sometimes injure themselves severely by hitting their heads for extended periods of time. If a program decreased this behavior, it would be ethically unacceptable to show that headbanging would return in a phase if treatment were withdrawn. Extensive physical damage to the child might result. Even in situations where the behavior is not dangerous, it may be difficult to justify suspension of the program on ethical grounds.

A phase in which treatment is withdrawn is essentially designed to make the person's behavior worse in some way. Whether behavior should be made worse and when such a goal would be justified are difficult issues to resolve. In a clinical situation, the consequences of making the client worse need to be weighed carefully for the client and those in contact with the client.

It is not only the client's behavior that may suffer in returning to baseline conditions. As noted earlier, behavior change agents may be required to alter their behavior after they have learned the techniques that can be used to improve the client. For example, parents who may have relied heavily on reprimands and corporal punishment may have learned how to achieve behavior change in their child with positive reinforcement during the intervention phase. Reintroducing the conditions of baseline means suspending skills that one would like to develop further in their behavior. Ethical questions are raised regarding the changes in behavior change agents as well as in the client.

Withdrawal of treatment can be and often is used as part of ABAB designs. In many cases the reversal phase can be relatively brief, even for only one or a few days. Yet, the problems of reversing behavior may still arise. Occasionally, researchers and clinicians note that if ethical questions are not raised by reversing behavior toward baseline, perhaps this is a sign that the behavior focused on is *not* very important. This particular statement can be challenged, but the sentiment it expresses is important. Careful consideration must be given to the consequences of reverting to baseline for the client and those who are responsible for his or her care.

Evaluation of the Design

The ABAB design and its variations can provide convincing evidence that an intervention was responsible for change. Indeed, when the data pattern shows that performance changes consistently as the phases are altered, the evidence is dramatic. Nevertheless, there are limitations peculiar to ABAB designs, particularly when they are considered for use in applied and clinical settings.

In ABAB designs, the methodological and clinical priorities of the investigator may compete. The investigator has an explicit hope that behavior will revert toward baseline levels when the intervention is withdrawn. Such a reversal is required to demonstrate an effect of the intervention. The clinician, on the other hand, hopes that the behavior will be maintained after treatment is withdrawn. Indeed, the intended purpose of most interventions or treatments is to attain a permanent change even after the intervention is withdrawn. The interests in achieving a reversal and not achieving a reversal are obviously contradictory.

Of course, showing a reversal in behavior is not always a problem in applied settings. Reversal phases often are very brief, lasting for a day or two. For example, in one investigation in a classroom setting, a reward system for appropriate classroom behavior was completely withdrawn as part of the reversal phase in an ABAB design (Broden, Hall, Dunlap, and Clark, 1970). In the first few hours of the day, disruptive behavior had returned to such a high level that the intervention was reinstated on that same day. Thus, the return-to-baseline phase was less than one day. On some occasions, reversal phases are very brief and concerns about temporarily suspending the program may be partially alleviated. However, short reversal phases are usually possible only when behavior shows rapid reversals, i.e., becomes worse relatively quickly after the intervention is withdrawn. To have behaviors become worse even for short periods is usually undesirable. The goal of the treatment is to achieve changes that are maintained rather than quickly lost as soon as the intervention is withdrawn.

It is possible to include a reversal in the design to show that the intervention was responsible for change and still attempt to maintain behavior. After experimental control has been demonstrated in a return-to-baseline phase, procedures can be included to maintain performance after all treatment has been withdrawn. Thus, the ABAB design and its variations are not necessarily incompatible with achieving maintenance of behavior. Nevertheless, the usual requirement of returning behavior to baseline levels or implementing a less effective intervention when a more effective one seems to be available, raises potential problems for clinical applications of the design. Hence, in many situations, the investigator may wish to select one of the many other alternative designs that do not require undoing the apparent benefits of treatment even if only for a short period.

Summary and Conclusions

With ABAB designs, the effect of an intervention is usually demonstrated by alternating intervention and baseline conditions in separate phases over time. Variations of the basic design have been used that differ as a function of several dimensions. The designs may vary in the procedures that are used to cause behavior to return to or approach baseline levels. *Withdrawal of the intervention* or reinstatement of baseline conditions, *noncontingent consequences,* or *contingent consequences for other behaviors* than the one associated with the consequences during the intervention phase are three options commonly used in reversal phases. Design variations are also determined by the order in which the baseline and intervention phases are presented, the number of phases, and the number of different interventions that are presented in the design. Given the different dimensions, an infinite number of ABAB design options are available. However, the underlying rationale and the manner in which intervention effects are demonstrated remain the same.

ABAB designs represent methodologically powerful experimental tools for demonstrating intervention effects. When the pattern of the data reveals shifts in performance as a function of alteration of the phases, the evidence for intervention effects is very dramatic. For research in clinical and other applied settings, the central feature of the designs may raise special problems. Specifically, the designs require that phases be alternated so that performance improves at some points and reverts toward baseline levels at other points. In some cases, a reversal of behavior does not occur, which creates problems in drawing inferences about the intervention. In other cases, it may be undesirable to withdraw or alter treatment, and serious ethical questions may be raised. When the requirements of the design compete with clinical priorities, other designs may be more appropriate for demonstrating intervention effects.

6

Multiple-Baseline Designs

With multiple-baseline designs, intervention effects are evaluated by a method quite different from that described for ABAB designs. The effects are demonstrated by introducing the intervention to different baselines (e.g., behaviors or persons) at different points in time. If each baseline changes when the intervention is introduced, the effects can be attributed to the intervention rather than to extraneous events. Once the intervention is implemented to alter a particular behavior, it need not be withdrawn. Thus, within the design, there is no need to return behavior to or near baseline levels of performance. Hence, multiple-baseline designs do not share the practical, clinical, or ethical concerns raised in ABAB designs by temporarily withdrawing the intervention.

Basic Characteristics of the Designs
Description and Underlying Rationale

In the multiple-baseline design, inferences are based on examining performance across several different baselines. The manner in which inferences are drawn is illustrated by discussing the *multiple-baseline design across behaviors*. This is a commonly used variation in which the different baselines refer to several different behaviors of a particular person or group of persons.

Baseline data are gathered on two or more behaviors. Consider a hypothetical example in which three separate behaviors are observed, as portrayed in Figure 6-1. The data gathered on each of the behaviors serve the purposes common to each single-case design. That is, the baseline data for each behavior describe the current level of performance and predict future performance. After performance is stable for all of the behaviors, the intervention is applied to the first behavior. Data continue to be gathered for each behavior. If the intervention is effective, one would expect changes in the behavior to which the intervention is applied. On the other hand, the behaviors that have yet to receive the intervention should remain at baseline levels. After all, no intervention was implemented to alter these behaviors. When the first behavior changes and the others remain at their baseline levels, this suggests that the intervention probably was responsible for the change. However, the data are not entirely clear at this point. So, after performance stabilizes across all behaviors, the intervention is applied to the second behavior. At this point both the first and second behavior are receiving the intervention, and data continue to be gath-

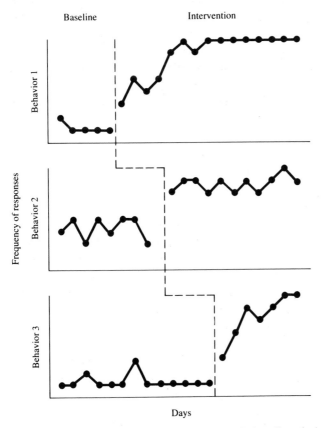

Figure 6–1. Hypothetical data for a multiple-baseline design across behaviors in which the intervention was introduced to three behaviors at different points in time.

ered for all behaviors. As evident in Figure 6-1, the second behavior in this hypothetical example also improved when the intervention was introduced. Finally, after continuing observation of all behaviors, the intervention is applied to the final behavior, which changed when the intervention was introduced.

The multiple-baseline design demonstrates the effect of an intervention by showing that behavior changes when and only when the intervention is applied. The pattern of data in Figure 6-1 argues strongly that the intervention, rather than some extraneous event, was responsible for change. Extraneous factors might have influenced performance. For example, it is possible that some event at home, school, or work coincided with the onset of the intervention and altered behavior. Yet one would not expect this to affect only one of the behaviors and at the exact point that the intervention was applied. A coincidence of this sort is possible, so the intervention is applied at different points in time to two or more behaviors. The pattern of results illustrates that whenever the intervention is applied, behavior changes. The repeated demonstration that behavior changes in response to applications of the intervention usually makes implausible the influence of extraneous factors.

As in the ABAB designs, the multiple-baseline designs are based on testing of predictions. Each time the intervention is introduced, a test is made between the level of performance during the intervention and the projected level of the previous baseline. Essentially, each behavior is a "mini" AB experiment that tests a prediction of the projected baseline performance and whether performance continues at the same level after treatment is applied. The predicting and testing of predictions over time for a single baseline is similar for ABAB and multiple-baseline designs.

A unique feature of multiple-baseline designs is the testing of predictions across different behaviors. Essentially, the different behaviors in the design serve as control conditions to evaluate what changes can be expected without the application of treatment. At any point in which the intervention is applied to one behavior and not to remaining behaviors, a comparison exists between treatment and no-treatment conditions. The behavior that receives treatment should change, i.e., show a clear departure from the level of performance predicted by baseline. Yet it is important to examine whether other baselines that have yet to receive treatment show any changes during the same period. The comparison of performance across the behaviors at the same points in time is critical to the multiple-baseline design. The baselines that do not receive treatment show the likely fluctuations of performance if no changes occur in the environment. When only the treated behavior changes, this suggests that normal fluctuations in performance would not account for the change. The repeated demonstration of changes in specific behaviors when the intervention is applied provides a convincing demonstration that the intervention was responsible for change.

Illustrations

Multiple-baseline designs across behaviors have been used frequently. The design was illustrated nicely in an investigation designed to treat four elementary school children who were considered by their teachers to be excessively shy, passive, unassertive, and overly conforming (Bornstein, Bellack, and Hersen, 1977). Training focused on specific skills that would enable the children to communicate more effectively and in general to be more assertive. The children were deficient in such behaviors as making eye contact with others while speaking, talking too softly, and not making appropriate requests of others. Baseline observations were obtained on separate behaviors as each child interacted with two other people in a role-playing situation. After baseline observations, training was implemented across each of the behaviors. Training included guidance for the appropriate response, feedback, and repeated rehearsal of the correct behavior.

The effects of the training program were examined in separate multiple-baseline designs. The results for Jane, an eight-year-old girl, are presented in Figure 6-2. The three behaviors that were trained included improving eye contact, increasing loudness of speech, and increasing the requests that the child made of other people. Training focused on each of the behaviors at different points in time. Each behavior changed when and only when the training procedures were introduced. The last behavior graphed at the bottom of the figure represented an overall rating of Jane's assertiveness and was not trained directly. Presumably, if the other behaviors were changed, the authors reasoned that overall assertiveness ratings of the child would improve. The specific behaviors and overall assertiveness did improve and were maintained when Jane was observed two and four weeks after treatment.

The requirements of the multiple-baseline design were clearly met in this report. If all three behaviors had changed when only the first one was included in training, it would have been unclear whether training was responsible for the change. In that case, an extraneous event might have influenced all behaviors simultaneously. Yet the specific effects obtained in this report clearly demonstrate the influence of training.

A multiple-baseline design across behaviors was also used in a program for hospitalized children with chronic asthma (Renne and Creer, 1976). The purpose of the program was to train children to use an apparatus that delivers medication to the respiratory passages through inhalation. Two boys and two

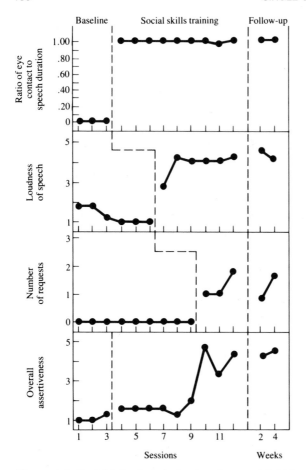

Figure 6–2. Social behaviors during baseline, social skills training, and follow-up for Jane. (*Source:* Bornstein, Bellack, and Hersen, 1977.)

girls (ages seven through twelve) had failed to use the apparatus correctly despite repeated instruction and hence were not receiving the medication. To inhale the medication through the apparatus, several behaviors had to be performed, including facing the apparatus when the mouthpiece was inserted into the child's mouth, holding the correct facial posture without moving the lips, cheeks, or nostrils (which would allow escape of the medication into the air), and correct breathing by moving the abdominal wall to pull the medicated air deep into the lungs.

To teach the children the requisite skills, each child was seen individually.

The three behaviors were trained one at a time by providing instructions, feed-back, and rewards for correct performance. Children earned tickets that could be saved and later exchanged for a surprise gift (choice of an item costing two dollars or less on a shopping trip). The effects of the incentive system in devel-oping the requisite behaviors are illustrated in Figure 6-3, where the data for the children are averaged for each of the behaviors. The program was very effective in reducing the inappropriate behaviors. At each point that the reward system was introduced for the appropriate behavior, the inappropriate behavior decreased. Thus, the data followed the expected pattern of results for the mul-

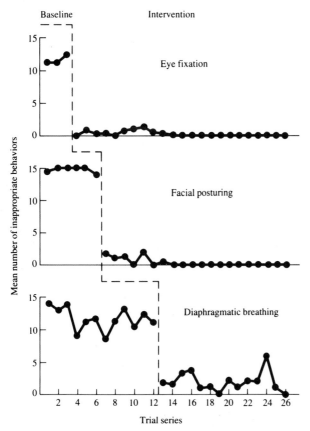

Figure 6–3. The mean number of inappropriate events recorded by the experimenters over a twenty-six-trial series for four subjects on three target responses: eye fixation, facial posturing, and diaphragmatic breathing. The maximum number of inappro-priate responses per trial was fifteen for each behavior. (*Source:* Renne and Creer, 1976.)

tiple-baseline design. Because the children used the inhalation apparatus correctly after training, greater relief from asthma symptoms was obtained, and fewer administrations of the medication were needed than before training.

Design Variations

The underlying rationale of the design has been discussed by elaborating the multiple-baseline design across behaviors. Yet the design can vary on the basis of what is assessed. The several baselines need not refer to different behaviors of a particular person or group of persons. Alternatives include observations across different individuals or across different situations, settings, or times. In addition, multiple-baseline designs may vary along other dimensions, such as the number of baselines and the manner in which a particular intervention is applied to these baselines.

Multiple-Baseline Design Across Individuals

In this variation of the design, baseline data are gathered for a particular behavior performed by two or more persons. The multiple baselines refer to the *number of persons* whose behaviors are observed. The design begins with observations of baseline performance of the same behavior for each person. After the behavior of each person has reached a stable rate, the intervention is applied to only one of them while baseline conditions are continued for the other(s). The behavior of the person exposed to the intervention would be expected to change; the behaviors of the others would be expected to continue at their baseline levels. When behaviors stabilize for all persons, the intervention is extended to another person. This procedure is continued until all of the persons for whom baseline data were collected receive the intervention. The effect of the intervention is demonstrated when a change in each person's performance is obtained at the point when the intervention is introduced and not before.

The multiple-baseline design across individuals was used to evaluate a program designed to train parents to develop appropriate mealtime behaviors in their children (McMahon and Forehand, 1978). Three normal preschool children from different families participated, based on the parents' interest in changing such behaviors as playing with food, throwing or stealing food, leaving the table before the meal, and other inappropriate behaviors. At an initial consultation in the parents' homes, the procedures were explained and parents received a brief brochure describing how to provide attention and praise for appropriate mealtime behavior and how to punish inappropriate behaviors (with time out from reinforcement). With only brief contact with the therapist and the written guidelines, the parents implemented the program. The effects were evaluated by observing the eating behaviors of children in their homes.

As evident in Figure 6-4, the program was implemented across the children at different points in time. The program led to reductions in each child's inappropriate eating behaviors. The effects are relatively clear because changes were associated with the implementation of the intervention. Interestingly, the

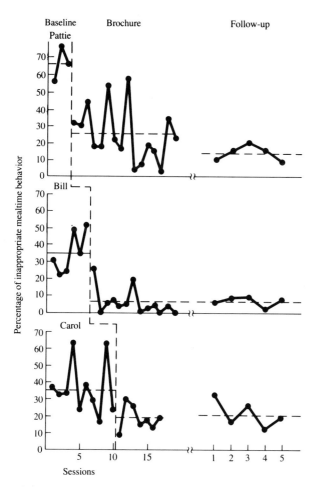

Figure 6–4. Percentage of intervals scored as inappropriate mealtime behavior. (Broken horizontal line in each phase indicates the mean percentage of intervals scored as inappropriate mealtime behavior across sessions for that phase.) (*Source:* McMahon and Forehand, 1978.)

effects of the program were maintained at a follow-up assessment approximately six weeks after the intervention.

The multiple-baseline design across individuals is especially suited to situations in which a particular behavior or set of behaviors in need of change is constant among different persons. The design is often used in group settings such as the classroom or a psychiatric ward, where the performance of a particular target behavior may be a priority for all group members. As with other variations of the design, no reversal or experimental conditions are required to demonstrate the effects of the intervention.

Multiple-Baseline Design Across Situations, Settings, and Time

In this variation of the design, baseline data are gathered for a particular behavior performed by one or more persons. The multiple baselines refer to the *different situations, settings, or time periods* of the day in which observations are obtained. The design begins with observations of baseline performance in each of the situations. After the behavior is stable in each situation, the intervention is applied to alter behavior in one of the situations while baseline conditions are continued for the others. Performance in the situation to which the intervention has been applied should show a change; performance in the other situations should not. When behavior stabilizes in all of the situations, the intervention is extended to performance in the other situations. This procedure is continued until performance in all of the situations for which baseline data were collected receive the intervention.

An interesting example of a multiple-baseline design across situations was reported by Kandel, Ayllon, and Rosenbaum (1977), who treated a severely withdrawn boy who was enrolled in a special school for emotionally disturbed and handicapped children. The boy, named Bobby, was diagnosed as autistic and suffering from brain dysfunction. At school he was always physically isolated, talked to himself, and spent his free playtime alone. A program was designed to improve his social interaction during the two separate freeplay situations at school. The situations included activity on the playground and juice time, when the children assembled each day in a courtyard outside of class.

Baseline data on the occurrences of social interaction with peers were gathered in each situation. On the final day of baseline, the investigators encouraged other children to interact with Bobby, which proved very upsetting to him and was not pursued further. The treatment after baseline consisted of training the child directly in the situation with his peers, an intervention referred to as *systematic exposure.*

Treatment began on the playground, where the trainer modeled appropriate social interaction for the child and then brought two other children to interact with him. The two children also encouraged Bobby to participate in additional activities on the playground and helped keep him from leaving the activity. Toys were used as the focus of some of the interactions in training sessions. Also, rewards (candy) were given to the two children who helped with training. The exposure procedure was first implemented on the playground then extended in the same fashion to the other free-play period.

The training program was evaluated in a multiple-baseline design across the two settings. As evident in Figure 6-5, social interaction improved in each setting as soon as training was introduced. The marked and rapid changes make the effects of the intervention very clear. Follow-up, conducted three weeks later when the program was no longer in effect, showed that the behaviors were maintained. The nine-month follow-up (upper portion of figures) was obtained after Bobby had been attending a regular school where free time was observed. Apparently, he maintained high levels of social interaction in the regular school.

When a particular behavior needs to be altered in two or more situations, the multiple-baseline design across situations or settings is especially useful. The intervention is first implemented in one situation and, if effective, is extended gradually to other situations as well. The intervention is extended until all situations in which baseline data were gathered are included.

Number of Baselines

A major dimension that distinguishes variations of the multiple-baseline design is the number of baselines (i.e., behaviors, persons, or situations) that are included. As noted earlier, observations must be obtained on a minimum of two baselines. Typically, three or more are used. The number of baselines contributes to the strength of the demonstration. Other things being equal, demonstration that the intervention was responsible for change is clearer the larger the number of baselines that show the predicted pattern of performance.

In a multiple-baseline design, it is possible that one of the baselines may not change when the intervention is introduced. If only two baselines were included and one of them did not change, the results cannot be attributed to the intervention because the requisite pattern of data was not obtained. On the other hand, if several (e.g., five) baselines were included in the design and one of them did not change, the effects of the intervention may still be very clear. The remaining baselines may show that whenever the intervention was introduced, performance changed, with the one exception. The clear pattern of performance for most of the behaviors still strongly suggests that the intervention

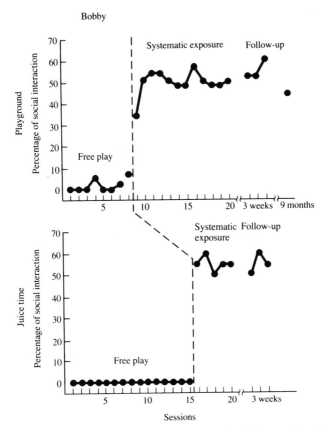

Figure 6–5. Bobby's social interaction on the playground and in the courtyard at juice time, two settings in which the intervention was introduced. (*Source:* Kandel, Ayllon, and Rosenbaum, 1977.)

was responsible for change. The problem of inconsistent effects of the intervention across different baselines will be addressed later in the chapter. At this point it is important only to note that the inclusion of several baselines beyond the minimum of two or three may clarify the effects of the intervention. Indeed, in several studies, baseline data are obtained and intervention effects are evident across several (e.g., eight or nine) behaviors, persons, or situations (e.g., Clark, Boyd, and Macrae, 1975; Wells, Forehand, Hickey, and Green, 1977).

Although the use of several baselines in a multiple-baseline design can provide an exceptionally clear and convincing demonstration, the use of a minimum number is often sufficient. For example, the case of the severely withdrawn child described earlier was evaluated in a multiple-baseline design across only two situations (see Figure 6-5). Hence, two baselines may serve the purposes of enabling inferences to be drawn about the role of the intervention on behavior change. The data pattern may need to be especially clear when only two baseline behaviors, persons, or situations serve as the basis for evaluating the intervention.

The adequacy of the demonstration that the intervention was responsible for change is not merely a function of the number of baselines assessed. Other factors, such as the stability of the behaviors during the baseline phases and the magnitude and rapidity of change once the intervention is applied also determine the ease with which inferences can be drawn about the role of the intervention. Thus, in many situations, the use of two behaviors is quite adequate.

Partial Applications of Treatment

Multiple-baseline designs vary in the manner in which treatment is applied to the various baselines. For the variations discussed thus far, a particular intervention is applied to the different behaviors at different points in time. Several variations of the designs depart from this procedure. In some circumstances, the intervention may be applied to the first behavior (individuals or situations) and produce little or no change. It may not be useful to continue applying this intervention to other behaviors. The intervention may not achieve enough change in the first behavior to warrant further use. Hence, a second intervention may be applied following sort of an ABC design for the first behavior. If the second intervention (C) produces change, it is applied to other behaviors in the usual fashion of the multiple-baseline design. The design is different only in the fact that the first intervention was not applied to all of the behaviors, persons, or situations.

For example, Switzer, Deal, and Bailey (1977) used a group-based program to reduce stealing in three different second-grade classrooms. Students frequently stole things from one another (e.g., money, pens) as well as from the teacher. Stealing was measured by placing various items such as money, magic markers, and gum around the room each day and measuring the number of items that subsequently were missing. The initial intervention consisted of lecturing the students by telling them the virtues of honesty and how they should be "good boys and girls." Figure 6-6 shows that this procedure was not very effective when it was introduced across the first two classes in a multiple-baseline design.

Because lecturing had no effect on stealing, a second intervention was implemented. This consisted of a group program in which the teacher told the stu-

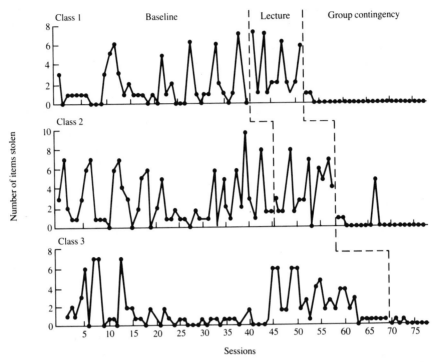

Figure 6–6. The number of items stolen per day in each of the three second-grade classrooms. (*Source:* Switzer, Deal, and Bailey, 1977.)

dents that the class could earn an extra ten minutes of free time if nothing was missing from the classroom. The group incentive program was introduced in a multiple-baseline fashion to each of the classrooms. As evident in Figure 6-6, the opportunity to earn extra recess reduced the amount of classroom stealing, particularly for the first two classes. The effect for the third class is not as dramatic because stealing near the end of the baseline phase tended to be low.

For present purposes, the important point to note is that the third class did not receive all of the treatments. Evidence from the first two classes indicated that lectures did not accomplish very much. Hence, there was no point in providing lectures in the third class. Thus, multiple-baseline designs do not always consist of applying only one treatment to each baseline. If an initial treatment does not appear to be effective, some other intervention(s) can be tried. The intervention that eventually alters performance is extended to the different behaviors, persons, or situations.

Another variation of the design that involves partial application of treatment is the case in which one of the baselines never receives treatment. Essentially, the final baseline (behavior, person, or situation) is observed over the course of the investigation but never receives the intervention. In some instances, the baseline consists of a behavior that is desirable and for which no change is sought.

In one investigation, for example, an aversive procedure was used to alter sexual deviation in an adult male who was in a psychiatric hospital (Hayes, Brownell, and Barlow, 1978). The patient's history included attempted rape, exhibitionism, and fantasies involving sadistic acts. Treatment consisted of having the patient imagine aversive consequences (such as being caught by the police) associated with imagination of exhibitionistic or sadistic acts. Over the course of treatment, sexual arousal was measured directly by the client's degree of erection (penile blood volume) as he viewed slides of exhibitionist, sadistic, and heterosexual scenes. For example, heterosexual slides displayed pictures of nude females and sadistic slides displayed nude females tied or chained.

The effects of the imagery-based procedure were evaluated in a multiple-baseline design in which treatment was used to suppress sexual arousal to exhibitionist and sadistic scenes. Of course, there was no attempt to suppress arousal to heterosexual (socially appropriate) scenes. Arousal was already relatively high, and it was hoped that this would remain after successful treatment. Hence, the intervention was introduced only to the two "deviant" types of scenes.

As shown in Figure 6-7, psychophysiological arousal decreased for exhibitionist and sadistic scenes when treatment was introduced. The demonstration is very clear because of the rapid and relatively large effects of treatment and because an untreated response did not change. The demonstration is unambiguous even though the minimum number of baselines that received treatment was included. The extra baseline (which did not receive treatment) was a useful addition to the design, showing that changes would not occur merely with the passage of time during the investigation.

General Comments

The above discussion highlights major variations of the multiple-baseline design. Perhaps the major source of diversity is whether the multiple baselines refer to the behaviors of a particular person, to different persons, or to performance in different situations. As might be expected, numerous variations of multiple-baseline designs exist. The variations usually involve combinations of the dimensions discussed above. Variations also occasionally involve compo-

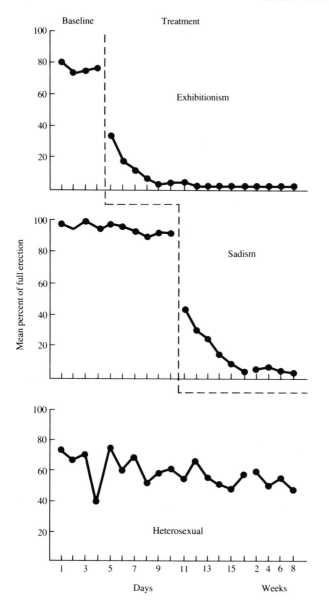

Figure 6–7. Percentage of full erection to exhibitionistic, sadistic, and heterosexual stimuli during baseline, treatment, and follow-up phases. (*Source:* Hayes, Brownell, and Barlow, 1978.)

nents of ABAB designs; these will be addressed in Chapter 9, in which combined designs are discussed.

Problems and Limitations

Several sources of ambiguity can arise in drawing inferences about intervention effects using multiple-baseline designs. Ambiguities can result from the interdependence of the behaviors, persons, or situations that serve as the baselines or from inconsistent effects of the intervention on the different baselines. Finally, both practical and methodological problems may arise when the intervention is withheld from one or more of the behaviors, persons, or situations for a protracted period of time.

Interdependence of the Baselines

The critical requirement for demonstrating unambiguous effects of the intervention in a multiple-baseline design is that each baseline (behavior, person, or situation) changes only when the intervention is introduced and not before. Sometimes the baselines may be interdependent, so that change in one of the baselines carries over to another baseline even though the intervention has not been extended to that latter baseline. This effect can interfere with drawing conclusions about the intervention in each version of the multiple-baseline design.

In the design *across behaviors,* changing the first behavior may be associated with changes in one of the other behaviors. Indeed, several studies have reported that altering one behavior is associated with changes in other behaviors that are not treated (e.g., Jackson and Calhoun, 1977; Wahler, 1975). In situations where generalization across responses occurs, the multiple-baseline design across behaviors may not show a clear relationship between the intervention and behavior change.

In the multiple-baseline design *across individuals,* it is possible that altering the behavior of one person influences other persons who have yet to receive the intervention. For example, investigations in situations where one person can observe the performance of others, such as classmates at school or siblings at home, changes in the behavior of one person occasionally result in changes in other persons (Kazdin, 1979d). Interventions based on reinforcement or punishment occasionally have produced vicarious effects, i.e., behavior changes among persons who merely observe others receive consequences. Here too, it may not be possible to attribute the changes to the intervention if changes occur for persons who have yet to receive the intervention. Similarly, in the multiple-baseline design across *situations,* settings, or time, altering the behavior of the person in one situation may lead to generalization of performance across other situations (e.g., Kazdin, 1973). The specific effect of the intervention may not be clear.

In each of the above cases, intervention effects extended beyond the specific baseline to which the intervention was applied. In such instances, the effects are ambiguous. It is possible that extraneous events coincided with the application of the intervention and led to general changes in performance. Alternatively, it is possible that the intervention accounted for the changes in several behaviors, persons, or situations even though it was only applied to one. The problem is not that the intervention failed to produce the change; it may have. Rather, the problem lies in unambiguously inferring that the intervention was the causal agent.

Although the interdependence of the baselines is a potential problem in each of the multiple-baseline designs, few demonstrations have been reported that show this problem. Of course, the problem may be infrequent because such studies are rarely reported and published (since, by definition, the effects of the intervention were unclear). When changes do occur across more than one of the baselines, this does not necessarily mean that the demonstration is ambiguous. The specific effect of the demonstration may be clear for a few but not all of the baselines. The ambiguity may be erased by rapid and marked treatment effects for those baselines that do show the treatment effect. The investigator may also introduce features of other designs, such as a return to baseline phase for one or more of the behaviors, to show that the intervention was responsible for change, a topic discussed later.

Inconsistent Effects of the Intervention

Another potential problem of multiple-baseline designs is that the intervention may produce inconsistent effects on the behaviors, persons, or situations to which it is introduced. Certainly one form of inconsistent effect occurs when some behaviors improve before the intervention is introduced, as discussed above. For the present discussion, "inconsistent effects" refers to the fact that some behaviors are altered when the intervention is introduced and others are not. The problem is that each behavior did not change at the point the intervention was introduced.

The inconsistent effects of an intervention in a multiple-baseline design raise obvious problems. In the most serious case, the design might include only two behaviors, the minimum number of baselines required. The intervention is introduced to both behaviors at different points in time, but only one of these changes. The results are usually too ambiguous to meet the requirements of the design. Stated another way, extraneous factors other than the intervention might well account for behavior changes, so the internal validity of the investigation has not been achieved.

Alternatively, if several behaviors are included in the design and one or two do not change when the intervention is introduced, this may be an entirely different matter. The effects of the intervention may still be quite clear from the two, three, or more behaviors that did change when the intervention was introduced. The behaviors that did not change are exceptions. Of course, the fact that some behaviors changed and others did not raises questions about the generality or strength of the intervention. But the internal validity of the demonstration, namely, that the intervention was responsible for change, is not at issue. In short, the pattern of the data need not be perfect to permit the inference that the intervention was responsible for change. If several of the baselines show the intended effect, an exception may not necessarily interfere with drawing causal inferences about the role of the intervention.

Prolonged Baselines

Multiple-baseline designs depend on withholding the intervention from each baseline (behavior, person, or situation) for a period of time. The intervention is applied to the first behavior while it is temporarily withheld from the second, third, and other behaviors. Eventually, of course, the intervention is extended to each of the baselines. If several behaviors (or persons, or situations) are included in the design, the possibility exists that several days or weeks might elapse before the final behavior receives treatment. Several issues arise when the intervention is withheld, either completely or for extended periods.

Obviously, clinical and ethical considerations may militate against withholding treatment. If the treatment appears to improve behavior when it is applied initially, perhaps it should be extended immediately to other behaviors. Withholding treatment may be unethical, especially if there is a hint in the data from the initial baselines that treatment influences behavior. Of course, the ethical issue here is not unique to multiple-baseline or single-case designs but can be raised in virtually any area of experimentation in which a treatment of unknown effectiveness is under evaluation (see Perkoff, 1980). Whether it is ethical to withhold a "treatment" may depend on some assurances that the treatment is helpful and is responsible for change. These latter questions, of course, are the basis of using experimental designs to evaluate treatment.

Although some justification may exist for temporarily withholding treatment for purposes of evaluation, concerns increase when the period of withholding treatment is protracted. If the final behaviors in the design will not receive the intervention for several days or weeks, this may be unacceptable in light of clinical considerations. As discussed below, there are ways to retain the multiple-baseline design so that the final behaviors receive the intervention with relatively little delay.

Aside from ethical and clinical considerations, methodological problems may arise when baseline phases are prolonged for one or more of the behaviors. As noted earlier, the multiple-baseline design depends on showing that performance changes when and only when the intervention is introduced. When baseline phases are extended for a prolonged period, performance may sometimes improve slightly even before the intervention is applied. Several reasons may account for the improvement. First, the interdependence of the various behaviors that are included in the design may be responsible for changes in a behavior that has yet to receive the intervention. Indeed, as more and more behaviors receive the intervention in the design, the likelihood may increase that other behaviors yet to receive treatment will show the indirect or generalized benefits of the treatment. Second, over an extended period, clients may have increased opportunities to develop the desired behaviors either through direct practice or the observation of others. For example, if persons are measured each day on their social behavior, play skills, or compliance to instructions, improvements may eventually appear in baseline phases for behaviors (or persons) who have yet to receive the intervention. The prolonged baseline assessment may provide some opportunities through repeated practice or modeling to improve in performance. In any case, when some behaviors (or persons, or situations) show improvements before the intervention is introduced, the requirements of the multiple-baseline design may not be met.

The problem that may arise with an extended baseline was evident in a program that trained severely and profoundly retarded persons (ages nine through twenty-two) to follow instructions during a play activity (Kazdin and Erickson, 1975). The residents were placed into small play groups of three to five persons. The groups were seen separately each day for a period of play. During the playtime, residents within a group were individually instructed to complete a sequence of behaviors related to playing ball. After baseline observations, a training program was implemented in which individual residents received instructions, food reinforcement, and assistance from a staff member. Training was implemented in a multiple-baseline design across each of the groups of residents. As evident in Figure 6-8, instruction-following for each of the groups improved at the point that the intervention was implemented. The demonstration is generally clear, especially for groups A and B. For groups C and D, performance tended to improve over the course of the baseline phase. In group

D, it is not clear that training helped very much. As it turns out, during the baseline phase, two of the three residents in group D occasionally performed the play activity correctly. Over time, their performance improved and became more consistent. By the end of baseline, the third resident in the group had not changed, but the other two performed the behaviors at high levels. When training was finally implemented, only one of the residents in group D profited from it. Thus, the overall effect of treatment for group D is unclear. If the duration of the baseline phase for this group had not been so long, the effect would probably have been much easier to evaluate.

The above results suggest that prolonged baselines may be associated with improvements. This should not be taken to imply that one need only gather

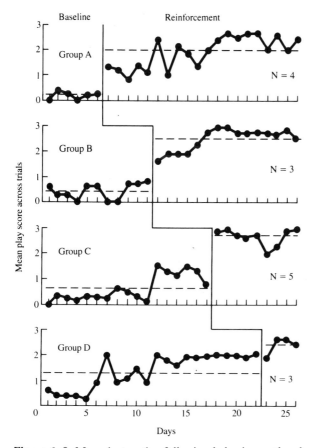

Figure 6–8. Mean instruction-following behavior on the play activity for groups during baseline and reinforcement phases. (*Source:* Kazdin and Erickson, 1975.)

baseline data on a behavior for a protracted period and change will occur. Rather, a problem may arise in a multiple-baseline design because the final behavior(s) or period(s) do not receive the intervention while several other events are taking place that may help improve overall performance. If treatment is delayed, the influence of early applications of treatment may extend to other behaviors or persons still awaiting the intervention.

Extended baseline assessment of behavior in a multiple-baseline design need not necessarily lead to improvements. Occasionally, undesirable behaviors may emerge with extended baseline assessment, which can obscure the effects of the intervention. For example, Horner and Keilitz (1975) trained mentally retarded children and adolescents to brush their teeth. The effects of this training were evaluated in a multiple-baseline design across subjects. Baseline observations provided several opportunities to observe toothbrushing. For the subject with the longest baseline phase, several competing behaviors emerged (e.g., eating toothpaste, playing in water) and were performed with increased frequency over the extended baseline period. Training was not only required to improve the target skills but also to reduce competing behaviors that ordinarily would not have been evident without repeated and extended assessment (Horner and Baer, 1978). The intervention was effective in this instance with the subject who had performed competing behaviors. However, in other demonstrations, interventions that might otherwise be effective may not alter behavior because of competing behaviors that develop through extended assessment. In such cases, the competing behaviors could interfere with demonstrating the benefits of the intervention.

Decrements in performance with extended baselines may also result from other factors. For example, repeated testing may be associated with boredom. Indeed, requiring the subject to complete a task for assessment purposes may be difficult for an extended baseline. The likelihood of competing effects or boredom varies as a function of the assessment strategy. If observations are part of routine activities (e.g,, in ordinary classroom settings), these problems may not arise. On the other hand, if the subject is required to perform special tasks under laboratory-like conditions, repetition of a particular activity (e.g., role-playing tests of social interaction) may become tedious.

Actually, the ethical, clinical, and methodological problems that may result from prolonged baselines can usually be avoided. To begin with, multiple-baseline designs usually do not include a large number of behaviors (e.g., six or more), so that the delays in applying the intervention to the final behavior are not great. Even if several baselines are used, the problems of prolonged baselines can be avoided in a number of ways. First, when several behaviors are observed, few data points may be needed for the baseline phases for some of the behaviors. For example, if six behaviors are observed, baseline phases for the first few behaviors may last only one or a few days. Also, the delay or lag period between implementing treatment for one behavior and implementing the same treatment for the next behavior need not be very long. A lag of a few days may be all that is necessary, so that the total period of the baseline phase before the final behavior receives treatment may not be particularly long.

Also, when several behaviors are included in the multiple-baseline design, treatment can be introduced for two behaviors at the same point in time. The demonstration still takes advantage of the multiple-baseline design, but it does not require implementing the treatment for only one behavior at a time. For example, a hypothetical multiple-baseline design is presented in Figure 6-9 in which six behaviors are observed. A multiple-baseline design might apply a particular treatment to each of the behaviors, one at a time (see left panel of figure). It might take several days before the final behavior could be included in treatment. Alternatively, the treatment could be extended to each of the behaviors two at a time (see right panel of the figure). This variation of the design does not decrease the strength of the demonstration, because the intervention is still introduced at two (or more) different points in time. The obvious advantage is that the final behavior is treated much sooner in this version of the design than in the version in which each behavior is treated separately. In short, delays in applying the intervention to the final behavior (or person, or

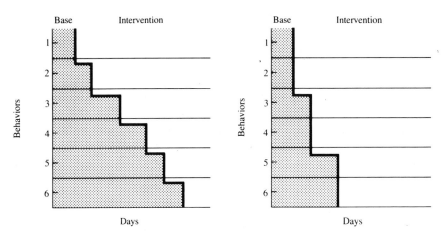

Figure 6-9. Hypothetical example of multiple-baseline design across six behaviors. *Left panel* shows design in which the intervention is introduced to each behavior, one at a time. *Right panel* shows design in which the intervention is introduced to two behaviors at a time. The shaded area conveys the different durations of baseline phases in each version of the design.

situation) can be reduced by applying the treatment to more than one behavior at a time.

Another way to avoid the problem of prolonged baseline assessment is to observe behavior on an intermittent rather than on a continuous basis. Observations could be made once a week rather than daily. Of course, in single-case research, behaviors are usually assessed daily or at each session in order to reveal the pattern of performance over time. Under some conditions, it may be useful to assess performance only occasionally (Horner and Baer, 1978). Specifically, if the baseline phase is likely to be extended, if the observations are likely to be reactive, i.e., influence the behavior that is assessed, and if the investigator has some reason to believe that behaviors are likely to be especially stable, the investigator may assess behavior only occasionally.

The periodic or intermittent assessment of behavior when contingencies are not in effect for that behavior is referred to as probes or *probe assessment*. Probes provide an estimate of what daily performance would be like. For example, hypothetical data are presented in Figure 6-10, which illustrate a multiple-baseline design across behaviors. Instead of assessing behavior every day, probes are illustrated in two of the baseline phases. The probes provide a sample of data and avoid the problem of extended assessment.

Certainly an advantage of probe assessment is the reduction in cost in terms of the time the observer must spend collecting baseline data. Of course, the risks of occasional assessment must be considered as well. It is possible that probe assessment will not reflect a clear pattern in the data, which is required to make decisions about when to implement the intervention and to infer that the intervention was responsible for change. Research has shown that assessment once every two or three days closely approximates data from daily observations (Bijou, Peterson, Harris, Allen, and Johnston, 1969). However, probes conducted on a highly intermittent basis (e.g., once every week or two) may not accurately represent performance. Thus, if probes are to be used to reduce the number of assessment occasions, the investigator needs to have an a priori presumption that performance is stable. The clearest instance of stability would be if behavior never occurs or reflects a complex skill that is not likely to change over time without special training.[1]

Evaluation of the Design

Multiple-baseline designs have a number of advantages that make them experimentally as well as clinically useful. To begin with, the designs do not depend

---

1. Probes can be used for other purposes, such as the assessment of maintenance of behavior and transfer of behavior to other situations or settings (see Chapter 9).

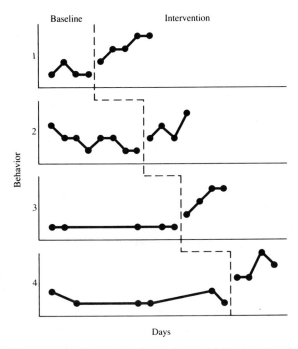

Figure 6–10. Hypothetical data for a multiple-baseline design across behaviors. Daily observations were conducted and are plotted for the first and second behaviors. Probes (intermittent assessment) were conducted for baseline of the third and fourth behaviors.

on withdrawing treatment to show that behavior change is a function of the intervention. Hence, there is no need to reduce or temporarily suspend treatment effects for purposes of the design. This characteristic makes multiple-baseline designs a highly preferred alternative to ABAB designs and their variations in many applied situations.

Another feature of the designs also is quite suited to practical and clinical considerations. The designs require applying the intervention to one behavior (person or situation) at a time. If behavior is altered, the intervention is extended to the other behaviors to complete the demonstration. The *gradual* application of the intervention across the different behaviors has practical and clinical benefits.

In many applied settings, parents, teachers, hospital staff, and other behavior change agents are responsible for applying the intervention. Considerable skill may be required to apply treatment effectively. A benefit of the multiple-baseline design is first implementing treatment on a small scale (one behavior) before it is extended to other behaviors. Behavior change agents can proceed gradually and only increase the scope of the treatment after having mastered the initial application. Where behavior change agents are learning new skills in applying an intervention, the gradual application can be very useful. Essentially, application of treatment by the behavior change agents follows a shaping model in which the task requirements of the behavior are gradually increased. This approach may be preferred by behavior change agents who might otherwise be overwhelmed by trying to alter several behaviors, persons, or situations simultaneously.

A related advantage is that the application to only one behavior at a time permits a test of the effectiveness of the procedure. Before the intervention is applied widely, the preliminary effects on the first behavior can be examined. If treatment effects are not sufficiently strong or if the procedure is not implemented correctly, it is useful to learn this early before applying the procedure widely across all behaviors, persons, or situations of interest.

In specific variations of the multiple-baseline design, the gradual manner in which treatment is extended also can be useful for the clients. For example, in the multiple-baseline design across behaviors or situations, the intervention is first applied to only one behavior or to behavior in only one situation. Gradually, other behaviors and situations are incorporated into the program. This follows a shaping model for the client, since early in the program changes are only required for one behavior or in one situation. As the client improves, increased demands are placed on performance. Overall, the manner in which treatment is implemented to meet the methodological requirements of the multiple-baseline design may be quite harmonious with practical and clinical considerations regarding how behavior change agents and clients perform. Designs in which methodological and clinical considerations are compatible are especially useful in applied settings.

Summary and Conclusions

Multiple-baseline designs demonstrate the effects of an intervention by presenting the intervention to each of several different baselines at different points in time. A clear effect is evident if performance changes when and only when the intervention is applied. Several variations of the design exist, depending primarily on whether the multiple-baseline data are collected across behaviors, persons, or situations, settings, and time. The designs may also vary as a function of the number of baselines and the manner in which treatment is applied. The designs require a minimum of two baselines. The strength of the demonstration that the intervention rather than extraneous events was responsible for change is a function of the number of behaviors to which treatment is applied, the stability of baseline performance for each of the behaviors, and the magnitude and rapidity of the changes in behavior once treatment is applied

Sources of ambiguity may make it difficult to draw inferences about the effects of the intervention. First, problems may arise when different baselines are interdependent so that implementation of treatment for one behavior (or person, or situation) leads to changes in other behaviors (or persons, or situations) as well, even though these latter behaviors have not received treatment. Another problem may arise in the designs if the intervention appears to alter some behaviors but does not alter other behaviors when the intervention is applied. If several behaviors are included in the design, a failure of one of the behaviors to change may not raise a problem. The effects may still be quite clear from the several behaviors that did change when the intervention was introduced.

A final problem that may arise with multiple-baseline designs pertains to withholding treatment for a prolonged period while the investigator is waiting to apply the intervention to the final behavior, person, or situation. Clinical and ethical considerations may create difficulties in withholding treatment for a protracted period. Also, it is possible that extended baselines will introduce ambiguity into the demonstration. In cases in which persons are retested on several occasions or have the opportunity to observe the desired behavior among other subjects, extended baseline assessment may lead to systematic improvements or decrements in behavior. Thus, demonstration of the effects of the intervention on extended baselines may be difficult. Prolonged baselines can be avoided by utilizing short baseline phases or brief lags before applying treatment to the next baseline, and by implementing the intervention across two or more behaviors (or persons, or situations) simultaneously in the design. Thus, the intervention need not be withheld even for the final behaviors in the multiple-baseline design. Multiple-baseline designs are quite popular, in part because they do not require reversals of performance. Also, the designs are consistent with many of the demands of applied settings in which treatment is implemented on a small scale first before being extended widely.

7

Changing-Criterion Designs

With a changing-criterion design, the effect of the intervention is demonstrated by showing that behavior changes gradually over the course of the intervention phase. The behavior improves in increments to match a criterion for performance that is specified as part of the intervention. For example, if reinforcement is provided to a child for practicing a musical instrument, a criterion (e.g., amount of time spent practicing) is specified to the child as the requirement for earning the reinforcing consequences. The required level of performance in a changing-criterion design is altered repeatedly over the course of the intervention to improve performance over time. The effects of the intervention are shown when performance repeatedly changes to meet the criterion.

Although the design resembles other single-case experimental designs, it has important distinguishing characteristics. Unlike the ABAB designs, the changing-criterion design does not require withdrawing or temporarily suspending the intervention to demonstrate a functional relationship between the intervention and behavior. Unlike multiple-baseline designs, the intervention is not applied to one behavior, and then eventually to others. In a multiple-baseline design, the intervention is withheld temporarily from the various baselines (behaviors) to which it is eventually applied. The changing-criterion design neither withdraws nor withholds treatment as part of the demonstration. Notwithstanding the desirable features of the changing-criterion design, it has been used less often than the other designs. Part of the reason may be that the design has been formally described as a distinct design relatively recently (Hall, 1971;

Hall and Fox, 1977; Hartmann and Hall, 1976) and may be restricted in the types of behaviors to which it can be applied, as discussed below.

Basic Characteristics of the Design
Description and Underlying Rationale

The changing-criterion design begins with a baseline phase in which observations of a single behavior are made for one or more persons. After the baseline (or A) phase, the intervention (or B) phase is begun. The unique feature of a changing-criterion design is the use of several *subphases* within the intervention phase. During the intervention phase, a criterion is set for performance. For example, in programs based on the use of reinforcing consequences, the client is instructed that he or she will receive the consequences if a certain level of performance is achieved. If performance meets or surpasses the criterion, the consequence is provided.

As an illustration, a person may be interested in doing more exercise. Baseline may reveal that the person never exercises. The intervention phase may begin by setting a criterion such as ten minutes of exercise per day. If the criterion is met or exceeded (ten or more minutes of exercise), the client may earn a reinforcing consequence (e.g., special privilege at home, money toward purchasing a desired item). Whether the criterion is met is determined each day. Only if performance meets or surpasses the criterion will the consequence be earned. If performance consistently meets the criterion for several days, the criterion is increased slightly (e.g., 20 minutes of exercise). As performance stabilizes at this new level, the criterion is again shifted upward to another level. The criterion continues to be altered in this manner until the desired level of performance (e.g., exercise) is met.

A hypothetical example of the changing-criterion design is illustrated in Figure 7-1, which shows that baseline phase is followed by an intervention phase. Within the intervention phase, several subphases are delineated (by vertical dashed lines). In each subphase a different criterion for performance is specified (dashed horizontal line within each subphase). As performance stabilizes and consistently meets the criterion, the criterion is made more stringent, and criterion changes are made repeatedly over the course of the design.

The underlying rationale of the changing-criterion resembles that of designs discussed previously. As in the ABAB and multiple-baseline designs, the baseline phase serves to describe current performance and to predict performance in the future. The subphases continue to make and to test predictions. In each subphase, a criterion or performance standard is set. If the intervention is responsible for change, performance would be expected to follow the shifts in

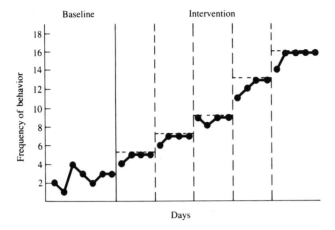

Figure 7–1. Hypothetical example of a changing-criterion design in which several sub-phases are presented during the intervention phase. The subphases differ in the criterion (dashed line) for performance that is required of the subject.

the criterion. The changing criteria reflect what performance would be like if the intervention exerts control over behavior. If behavior fluctuates randomly (no systematic pattern) or tends to increase or decrease due to extraneous factors, then performance would not follow the criteria over the course of the intervention phase. In such instances, the intervention cannot be accorded a causal role in accounting for performance. On the other hand, if performance corresponds closely to the changes in the criterion, then the intervention can be considered to be responsible for change.

Illustrations

An illustration of the design was provided in a program for persons who consumed excessive amounts of caffeine in their daily diets (Foxx and Rubinoff, 1979). Caffeine consumed in large quantities is potentially harmful and is associated with a variety of symptoms, including irritability, palpitations, and gastrointestinal disturbances, and has been linked to cardiovascular disorders and cancer as well. An intervention was used to decrease consumption of caffeine. The intervention consisted of having the subjects deposit a sum of money (twenty dollars) which would be returned in small portions if they fell below the criterion for the maximum level of caffeine that could be consumed on a given day. The subjects signed a contract that specified how they would earn back or lose their twenty dollars. Each day, subjects recorded their total caffeine consumption on the basis of a list of beverages that provided their caffeine equivalence (in milligrams).

The program was implemented and evaluated for three subjects in separate changing-criterion designs. The effects of the program for one subject, who was a female schoolteacher, are illustrated in Figure 7-2. As evident from the figure, her average daily caffeine consumption was about 1000 mg., a relatively high rate that equals approximately eight cups of brewed coffee. When the intervention was initiated, she was required to reduce her daily consumption by about 100 mg. less than baseline. When performance was consistently below the criterion (solid line), the criterion was reduced by approximately 100 mg. again. This change in the criterion continued over four subphases while the intervention was in effect. In each subphase, the reinforcer (money) was earned only if caffeine consumption fell at or below the criterion level. The figure shows that performance consistently fell below the criterion. The subject's performance shows a steplike function in which caffeine consumption decreased in each subphase while the intervention was in effect. At the end of the inter-

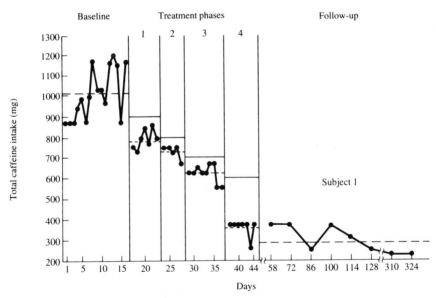

Figure 7-2. Subject's daily caffeine intake (mg) during baseline, treatment, and follow-up. The criterion level for each treatment phase was 102 mg of caffeine less than the previous treatment phase. Solid horizontal lines indicate the criterion level for each phase. Broken horizontal lines indicate the mean for each condition. (*Source:* Foxx and Rubinoff, 1979.)

vention phase, the program was terminated. Assessment over a ten-month follow-up period indicated that the subject maintained her low rate of caffeine consumption.

A changing-criterion design was also used in a program to improve the academic performance of two disruptive elementary school boys who refused to complete assignments or who completed them at low rates (Hall and Fox, 1977, Exp. 2). Each student was given a worksheet with math problems and worked on them before recess. After baseline observations of the number of problems completed correctly, a program was implemented in which each child was told that he could go to recess and play basketball if he completed a certain number of problems correctly. If he failed to complete the problems, he remained in the room at recess until they were completed correctly. The criterion for the first subphase of the intervention phase was computed by calculating the mean for baseline and setting the criterion at the next highest whole number (or problem).

The effects of the program for one of the children are illustrated in Figure 7-3, which shows that the criterion level of performance (numbers at top of each subphase) was consistently met in each subphase. In the final phase, text-

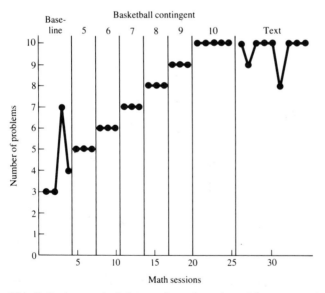

Fig. 7–3. A record of the number of math problems correctly solved by Dennis, a "behavior disordered" boy during baseline, recess, and the opportunity-to-play-basketball contingent on changing levels of performance and return-to-textbook phases. (*Source:* Etzel, LeBlanc, and Baer, 1977.)

book problems were substituted for the ones included in previous phases and the criterion level of performance remained in effect. The results show that performance closely corresponded to the criterion shifts with only two exceptions in the final phase.

Design Variations

The changing-criterion design has been used relatively infrequently and hence most applications closely follow the basic design illustrated above. Features of the basic design can vary, including the number of changes that are made in the criterion, the duration of the subphases at each criterion, and the amount of change when the criterion is altered. These dimensions vary among all changing-criterion designs and do not represent clear distinctions in different versions of the design. One dimension that is a fundamental variation of the design pertains to the directionality of the changes made in the criterion.

Directionality of Change

The basic changing-criterion design includes several subphases while the intervention is in effect. In the subphases, the criterion is altered on several different occasions. The criterion is usually made more stringent over the course of treatment. For example, the criterion may be altered to decrease cigarette smoking or to increase the amount of time spent exercising or studying. The effects of treatment are evaluated by examining a change in behavior in a particular direction over time. The expected changes are unidirectional, i.e., either an increase *or* decrease in behavior.

Difficulties may arise in evaluating unidirectional changes over the course of the intervention phase in a changing-criterion design. Behavior may improve systematically as a function of extraneous factors rather than the intervention. Improvements attributed to extraneous factors may be difficult to distinguish from intervention effects unless performance closely follows the criterion that is set in each subphase. The experimental control exerted by the intervention can be more readily detected by altering the criterion so that there are *bidirectional* changes in performance, i.e., both increases and decreases in behavior.

In this variation of the design, the criterion is made increasingly more stringent in the usual fashion. However, during one of the subphases, the criterion is temporarily made *less* stringent. For example, the criterion may be raised throughout the intervention phase. During one subphase, the criterion is lowered slightly to a previous criterion level. This subphase constitutes sort of a "mini" reversal phase. Treatment is not withdrawn but rather the criterion is altered so that the direction of the expected change in behavior is opposite from the changes in the previous phase. If the intervention is responsible for change, one would expect performance to follow the criterion rather than to continue in the same direction.

The use of a changing-criterion design with bidirectional changes was illustrated by Hall and Fox (1977, Exp. 2), who altered the academic performance of two boys. One of the cases was provided earlier (Figure 7-3), which described a program designed to improve completion of math problems. As noted in that example, baseline observations recorded the number of math problems completed correctly from a worksheet. After baseline, a program was implemented in which each child could earn recess and the opportunity to play basketball if he met the criterion. The criterion referred to the number of math problems he was required to complete within the session. If he failed to complete the criterion number of problems, he did not earn the reinforcer for that session. In each subphase of the intervention phase, the criterion requirement was increased by one problem. The shift in the criterion was made after three consecutive days of performing at the criterion level.

The effects of the program on math performance for the second boy are illustrated in Figure 7-4. The figure shows that performance closely followed the criterion (number at top) in each subphase. Of special interest is the second to the last subphase. During this subphase, the criterion level was *reduced* (made less stringent) by one math problem rather than raised by this amount, as in all of the previous subphases. Performance fell slightly to match this less stringent criterion. All of the subphases show a remarkably close correspondence between the criterion and performance. The demonstration is particularly strong by showing changes in both directions, i.e., bidirectional changes, as a function of the changing criteria.

In the above example, the demonstration of bidirectional phases was not really needed because of the close correspondence between performance and each criterion change during the subphases. Thus, there was little ambiguity about the effect of the intervention. In changing-criterion designs where behavior does not show this close correspondence, a bidirectional change may be particularly useful. When performance does not closely correspond to the criteria, the influence of the intervention may be difficult to detect. Adding a phase in which behavior changes in opposite directions to follow a criterion reduces the ambiguity about the influence of treatment. Bidirectional changes are much less plausibly explained by extraneous factors than are unidirectional changes.

The use of a "mini" reversal phase in the design is helpful because of the

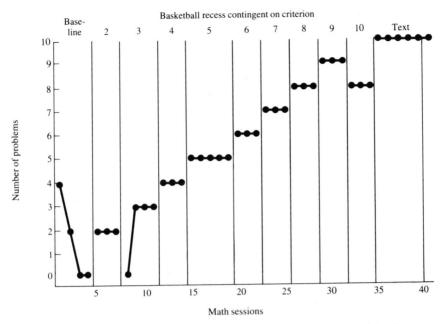

Fig. 7–4. A record of the number of math problems correctly solved by Steve, a "behavior disordered" boy, during baseline, and recess and opportunity-to-play-basketball contingent on changing levels of performance and return to textbook phases. (Subphase 10 illustrates the reduction in the criterion level to achieve bidirectional change.) (*Source:* Etzel, LeBlanc, and Baer, 1977.)

bidirectional change it allows. The strength of this variation of the design is based on the underlying rationale of the ABAB designs. The "mini" reversal usually does not raise all of the objections that characterize reversal phases of ABAB design. The "mini" reversal does not consist of completely withdrawing treatment to achieve baseline performance. Rather, the intervention remains in effect, and the expected level of performance still represents an improvement over baseline. The amount of improvement is decreased slightly to show that behavior change depends on the criterion that is set. Of course, in a given case, the treatment goal may be to approach the terminal behavior as soon as possible. Examination of bidirectional changes or a "mini" reversal might be clinically untenable.

General Comments

Few variations of the changing-criterion design have been developed. The major source of variation distinguished in the present discussion has been whether the designs seek unidirectional or bidirectional changes. This dimension is important to distinguish because the underlying rationale of designs that seek bidirectional changes differs slightly from the rationale of the basic design in which only unidirectional changes are sought. When bidirectional changes are sought, the design borrows features of ABAB designs. Specifically, the effects of the intervention are inferred from showing that alterations of the intervention lead to directional changes in performance.

Of course, changing-criterion designs can vary along several other dimensions, such as the number of times the criterion is changed, the duration of the phases in which the criterion is altered, and the magnitude of the criterion change, as already noted. Variation among these dimensions does not constitute special versions of the changing-criterion design, because they do not alter fundamental characteristics of the design. In any given demonstration, the ways in which the intervention and changing criteria are implemented represent important design considerations and hence are discussed later in the chapter.

Problems and Limitations

The unique feature of the changing-criterion design is the intervention phase, in which performance is expected to change in response to different criteria. Ambiguity may arise in drawing inferences about the intervention if performance does not follow the shifts of the criterion. Actually, several different problems regarding the relationship between performance and the changes in criteria can be identified.

Correspondence of the Criterion and Behavior

The strength of the demonstration depends on showing a close correspondence between the criterion and behavior over the course of the intervention phase. In some of the examples in this chapter (e.g., Figure 7-4), behavior fell exactly at the criterion levels on virtually all occasions of the intervention phase. In such instances, there is little ambiguity regarding the impact of the intervention. Typically, it is likely that the level of behavior will not fall exactly at the criterion. When correspondence is not exact, it may be difficult to evaluate whether the intervention accounts for the change. Currently, no clearly accepted measure is available to evaluate the extent to which the criterion level and behavior correspond. Hence, a potential problem in changing-criterion designs is deciding when the criterion and performance correspond closely enough to allow the inference that treatment was responsible for change.[1]

In some cases in which correspondence is not close, authors refer to the fact that mean levels of performance across subphases show a stepwise relationship. Even though actual performance does not follow the criterion closely, in fact, the average rate of performance within each subphase may change with each change in the criterion. Alternatively, investigators may note that performance fell at or near the criterion in each subphase on all or most of the occasions. Hence, even though performance levels did not fall exactly at the criterion level, it is clear that the criterion was associated with a shift or new level of performance. As yet, consistent procedures for evaluating correspondence between behavior and the criterion have not been adopted.

The ambiguities that arise when the criterion and performance levels do not closely correspond may be partially resolved by examining bidirectional rather than unidirectional changes in the intervention phase. When bidirectional changes are made, the criterion may be more stringent and less stringent at different points during the intervention phase. It is easier to evaluate the impact of the intervention when looking for changes in different directions (decrease followed by an increase in performance) than when looking for a point-by-point correspondence between the criterion and performance. Hence, when ambiguity exists in any particular case about the correspondence between the changing criterion and behavior, a "mini" reversal over one of the subphases of the design may be very useful, as outlined earlier.

Rapid Changes in Performance

The lack of correspondence between behavior and the criterion is a general problem of the design. Although several factors may contribute to the lack of correspondence, one in particular warrants special comment. When the inter-

---

1. One suggestion to evaluate the correspondence between performance and the criterion over the course of the intervention phase is to compute a Pearson product-moment correlation (see Hall and Fox, 1977). The criterion level and actual performance would be paired each day to calculate a correlation. Unfortunately, a product-moment correlation may provide little or no information about the extent to which the criterion is matched. Actual performance may *never* match the changing criterion during the intervention phase and the correlation could still be perfect ($r = 1.00$). The correlation could result from the fact that the differences between the criterion and performance were constant and always in the same direction. The product-moment correlation provides information about the extent to which the two data points (criterion and actual performance) covary over assessment occasions and not whether one matches the other in absolute value.

vention is first implemented, behavior may change rapidly. Improvements may occur that greatly exceed the initial criterion set for performance.

The changing-criterion design depends on gradual changes in performance. A terminal goal (e.g., zero cigarettes smoked per day) is reached gradually over the course of several subphases. In fact, the design is recommended for use in situations in which behavior needs to be *shaped,* i.e., altered gradually toward a terminal goal (Hall and Fox, 1977). In shaping, successive approximations of the final behavior are rewarded. Stated another way, increasingly stringent requirements are set over time to move behavior toward a particular end point. In a changing-criterion design, shaping is the underlying rationale behind starting out with a relatively small criterion and progressing over several different criterion levels. Even though a criterion may only require a small increment in behavior (e.g., minutes of studying), it is possible that performance changes rapidly and greatly exceeds that criterion. In such cases, it may be difficult to evaluate intervention effects.

The effects of rapid changes in behavior that exceed criterion performance can be seen in a program designed to alter the disruptive behavior of high school students (Deitz and Repp, 1973). These investigators were interested in decreasing the frequency that students engaged in social conversations rather than academic discussions in class. During their lessons, students frequently talked about things other than their work. Baseline observations were recorded daily to assess the rate of inappropriate verbalizations. After baseline, the intervention began, in which students received a reward for lowering their rate of inappropriate talking. (Reinforcing a low rate of behavior is referred to as differential reinforcement of low rates [or DRL schedule].) The reinforcer consisted of a free day (Friday), which the students could use as they wished. The free day was earned only if inappropriate verbalizations did not exceed the daily criterion on any of the previous days during that week. The criterion was altered each week. In the first week the reinforcer was earned only if five or fewer inappropriate verbalizations occurred in class each day; in the next three weeks the daily criterion was shifted to three, two, and zero verbalizations, respectively. If inappropriate verbalizations exceeded the criterion in effect for that day, Friday would not be earned as a free-activity day.

The results of the program and the extent to which performance met the requirements of the changing-criterion design can be seen in Figure 7-5. The figure shows that performance during the intervention phase always equaled or fell below the criterion level (horizontal line). This is the clearest in the final treatment phase, in which the daily criterion was zero (no inappropriate verbalizations) and the responses never occurred. However, close examination of the changing-criterion phases shows that performance did not follow each criterion shift. The first subphase was associated with a rapid decrease in performance, well below the criterion. This level of performance did not change in the second subphase, even though the criterion was lowered. In short, the rapid shift in performance well below criterion levels in the first two subphases makes the role of the intervention somewhat unclear. Verbalizations did not seem to follow the criterion closely. Thus with the baseline and intervention phase alone, a strong case cannot be made that the intervention was responsible for change. The investigators included a final phase, in which the original baseline conditions were reinstated. Of course, this return-to-baseline or reversal phase is a feature of the ABAB design and is usually not included in a changing-criterion design. The reversal of performance evident in the last phase makes the role of the intervention much clearer. (The combination of features from different designs such as the changing-criterion and ABAB designs are discussed in Chapter 9.)

Without drawing from features of other designs, difficulties may arise in according the intervention a causal role in behavior change if rapid shifts in performance are evident. If the criterion level is quickly and markedly sur-

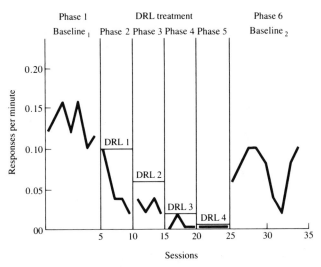

Figure 7-5. Inappropriate verbalizations of a class of high school students. Baseline₁—before the intervention. DRL Treatment—separate phases in which a decreasingly lower rate of verbalizations was required to earn the reinforcer. The limit for the four phases was 5 or fewer during the session, 3 or fewer, 2 or fewer, or 0 responses, respectively. Baseline₂—withdrawal of treatment. (*Source:* Deitz and Repp, 1973.)

passed, this raises the possibility that extraneous influences may have coincided with the onset of the intervention. The extraneous influences may account for the directional changes in behavior that depart from criterion levels that are set.

In practice, one might expect that criterion levels will often be surpassed. Usually, the client receives a reward if performance is at or surpasses the criterion level. If the behavior is not easy for the client to monitor, it may be difficult for him or her to perform the behavior at the exact point that the criterion is met. The response pattern that tends to exceed the criterion level slightly will guarantee earning of the consequence. To the extent that the criterion is consistently exceeded, ambiguity in drawing inferences about the intervention may result.

Number of Criterion Shifts

An important feature of the changing-criterion design is the number of times that the criterion is changed. The minimum number of shifts in the criterion (subphases) is two. Only if two or more subphases are included can one assess the extent to which performance matches different criteria. With only one criterion level over the entire intervention phase, it would be difficult to show that the intervention was responsible for change, unless features from other designs (e.g., reversal phase) were included. Although the minimum number of criterion shifts is two, typically several subphases are included, as illustrated in the examples of the design presented earlier.

Several different criterion shifts are desirable. Yet a large number of shifts does not necessarily lead to a clearer demonstration. The purpose of the design is to show that performance follows shifts in the criterion. This overall objective may be served by several criterion shifts, but too many shifts may introduce rather than resolve ambiguities. Each time the criterion is shifted, it is important to keep that criterion in effect to show that performance corresponds and stabilizes at this level. Without a stable rate of performance at or near the level of the criterion, it may be difficult to claim that the criterion and performance correspond.

An example of a changing-criterion design with several shifts in the criterion was reported in an investigation that reduced the cigarette smoking of a twenty-four-year-old male (Friedman and Axelrod, 1973). During baseline, the client observed his own rate of cigarette smoking with a wrist counter. (His fiancé also independently counted smoking to assess reliability.) During the intervention phase, the client was instructed to set a criterion level of smoking each day that he thought he could follow. When he was able to smoke only the number of cigarettes specified by the self-imposed criterion, he was instructed to lower the criterion further.

The results are presented in Figure 7-6, in which the reduction and eventual termination of smoking are evident. In the intervention phase, several different criterion levels (short horizontal lines with the criterion number as superscript) were used. Twenty-five different criterion levels were included in the intervention phase. Although it is quite obvious that smoking decreased, performance did not clearly follow the criteria that were set. The criterion levels were not really followed closely until day forty (criterion set at eight), after which close correspondence is evident.

The demonstration is reasonably clear because of the close correspondence of smoking with the criterion late in the intervention phase. However, the results might have been much clearer if a given criterion level were in effect for a longer period of time to see if that level really influenced performance. Then the next criterion level could be implemented to see if performance shifted to that level and stabilized. The large number of criterion shifts may have competed with demonstrating a clear effect.

Magnitude of Criterion Shifts

Another important design consideration is the magnitude of the criterion shift that is made over the subphases when the intervention is in effect. The basic design specifies that the criterion is changed at several different points. Yet no clear guidelines are inherent in the design that convey how much the criterion should be changed at any given point. The particular clinical problem and the client's performance determine the amount of change made in the criterion over the course of the intervention phase. The client's ability to meet initial criterion levels and relatively small shifts in the criterion may signal the investigator that larger shifts (i.e., more stringent criteria) might be attempted. Alternatively, failure of the client to meet the constantly changing criteria may suggest that smaller changes might be required if the client is to earn the consequences.

Even deciding the criterion that should be set at the inception of the intervention phase may pose questions. For example, if decreasing the consumption of cigarettes is the target focus, the intervention phase may begin by setting the criterion slightly below baseline levels. The lowest or near lowest baseline data point might serve as the first criterion for the intervention phase. Alternatively, the investigator might specify that a 10 or 15 percent reduction of the

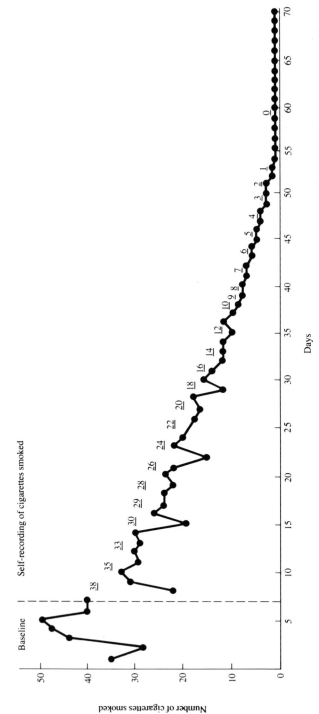

Figure 7-6. The number of cigarettes smoked each day during each of two experimental conditions. Baseline—the client kept a record of the number of cigarettes smoked during a seven-day period. Self-recording of cigarettes smoked—the client recorded the number of cigarettes smoked daily and attempted not to smoke more than at criterion level. The client set the original criterion and lowered the criteria at his own discretion. (The horizontal lines represent the criteria.) (*Source:* Friedman and Axelrod, 1973.)

mean baseline level would be the first criterion. In either case, it is important to set a criterion that the client can meet. The appropriate place to begin, i.e., the initial criterion, may need to be negotiated with the client.

As performance meets the criterion, the client may need to be consulted again to decide the next criterion level. At each step, the client may be consulted to help decide the criterion level that represents the next subphase of the design. In many cases, of course, the client may not be able to negotiate the procedures and changes in the criterion (e.g., severely and profoundly retarded, young children, some psychiatric patients).

With or without the aid of the client, the investigator needs to decide the steps or changes in the criterion. Three general guidelines can be provided. First, the investigator usually should proceed gradually in changing the criterion to maximize the likelihood that the client can meet each criterion. Abrupt and large shifts in the criterion may mean that relatively stringent performance demands are placed on the client. The client may be less likely to meet stringent criterion levels than more graduated criterion levels. Thus, the magnitude of the change in the criterion should be relatively modest to maximize the likelihood that client can successfully meet that level.

Second, the investigator should change the criteria over the course of the intervention phase so that correspondence between the criteria and behavior can be detected. The change in the criterion must be large enough so that one can discern that performance changes when the criterion is altered. The investigator may make very small changes in the criterion. However, if variability in performance is relatively large, it may be difficult to discern that the performance followed the criterion. Hence, there is a general relationship between the variability in the client's performance and the amount of change in the criterion that may need to be made. The more variability in day-to-day performance during the intervention phase, the greater the change needed in the criterion from subphase to subphase to reflect change.

The relationship between variability in performance and the changes in the criteria necessary to reflect change is illustrated in two hypothetical changing-criterion designs displayed in Figure 7-7. The upper panel shows that subject variability is relatively high during the intervention phase, and it is relatively difficult to detect that the performance follows the changing criterion. The lower panel shows that subject variability is relatively small during the intervention phase and follows the criterion closely. In fact, for the lower panel, smaller changes in the criteria probably would have been adequate and the correspondence between performance and criteria would have been clear. In contrast, the upper panel shows that much larger shifts in the criterion would

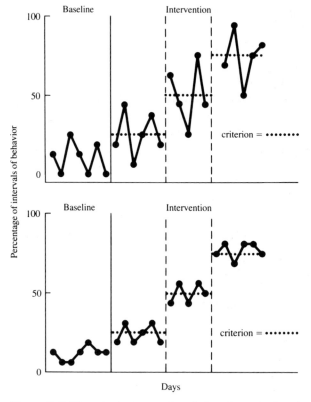

Figure 7-7. Hypothetical examples of changing-criterion designs. *Upper panel* shows data with relatively high variability (fluctuations). *Lower panel* shows relatively low variability. Greater variability makes it more difficult to show that performance matches or is influenced by the changing criterion. In both of the above graphs, the mean level of performance increased with each subphase during the intervention phase. The influence of the criterion is clearer in the lower panel because the data points hover more closely to the criterion in each subphase.

be needed to demonstrate unambiguously that performance changed systematically.

It is important to bear in mind that changes in the criterion need not be in equal steps over the course of the intervention. In the beginning, smaller changes in the criteria may be needed to maximize opportunities for the client's success in earning the consequence. As progress is made, the client may be able to make larger steps in reducing or increasing the behavior. The level and stability of performance at any particular criterion level determine how long that criterion is in effect and the magnitude of the change made in the criterion at that particular point.

General Comments

Many of the ambiguities that can arise in the changing-criterion design pertain to the correspondence between the criteria and the behavior. Some of the potential problems of the lack of correspondence can be anticipated and possibly circumvented by the investigator as a function of how and when the criteria are changed. The purpose of changing the criteria from the standpoint of the design is to provide several subphases during the intervention phase. In each subphase, it is important to be able to assess the extent to which performance meets the criterion. Across all subphases, it is crucial to be able to evaluate the extent to which the criteria have been followed in general. These specific and overall judgments can be facilitated by keeping individual subphases in effect until performance stabilizes. Also, the magnitude of the criterion shifts should be made so that the association between performance and the criterion can be detected. The criterion should be changed so that a performance at the new criterion level will clearly depart from performance of the previous criterion level. Finally, a change in the intervention phase to a previous criterion level will often be very helpful in determining the relationship between the intervention and behavior change.

Evaluation of the Design

The changing-criterion design has several features that make it clinically useful as well as methodologically sound. The design does not require withdrawing treatment, as in the ABAB design. The multiple problems related to reverting behavior toward baseline levels are avoided. Also, the design does not require withholding treatment from some of the different behaviors, persons, or situations in need of the intervention, as is the case with variations of the multiple-baseline design. A convincing demonstration of the effect of the intervention is provided if the level of performance in the intervention phase matches the criterion as that criterion is changed.

The most salient feature of the design is the gradual approximation of the final level of the desired performance. Repeatedly changing the criterion means that the goal of the program is approached gradually. A large number of behaviors in treatment may be approached in this gradual fashion. Increased demands are placed on the client (i.e., more stringent criteria) only after the client has shown mastery of performance at an easier level. The gradual approximation of a final behavior, referred to as shaping, consists of setting increasingly more stringent performance standards. If the requirements are too stringent and the client does not perform the behavior, the requirements are reduced. In shaping, the investigator may shift criteria for reinforcement often and may occasionally make large criterion shifts to see if progress can be made more quickly. If client performance does not meet the criterion, the criterion is quickly shifted back to a less demanding level. In short, shaping allows considerable flexibility in altering the criterion for reinforcement from day to day or session to session as a function of the actual or apparent progress that the client is making.

In utilizing the changing criterion-design, slightly less flexibility exists in constantly changing the requirements for performance and reinforcement. The design depends on showing that performance clearly corresponds to the criterion level and continues to do so as the criterion is altered. If the criterion is shifted abruptly and the performance never meets the criterion, a less stringent criterion can be set. However, constant shifts in the criterion in the design without showing that performance meets these standards may not provide a clear demonstration. For this reason it may be useful to make gradual changes in the criterion to maximize the chances that the client can respond successfully, i.e., meet the criterion.

Summary and Conclusions

The changing-criterion design demonstrates the effect of an intervention by showing that performance changes at several different points during the intervention phase as the criterion is altered. A clear effect is evident if performance closely follows the changing criterion. In most uses of the design, the criterion for performance is made increasingly more stringent over the course of the intervention phase. Hence, behavior continues to change in the same direction. In one variation of the design, the criterion may be made slightly less stringent at some point in the intervention phase to determine whether the direction of performance changes. The use of a *"mini" reversal* phase to show that behavior increases and decreases depending on the criterion can clarify the demonstration when close correspondence between performance and the criterion level is not achieved.

An important issue in evaluating the changing-criterion design is deciding when correspondence between the criterion and performance has been achieved. Unless there is a close point-by-point correspondence between the criterion level and performance, it may be difficult to infer that the intervention was responsible for change. Typically, investigators have inferred a causal relationship if performance follows a stepwise function so that changes in the criterion are followed by changes in performance, even if performance does not exactly meet the criterion level.

Drawing inferences may be especially difficult when performance changes rapidly as soon as the intervention is implemented. The design depends on showing gradual changes in performance as the terminal goal is approached. If performance greatly exceeds the criterion level, the intervention may still be responsible for change. Yet because the underlying rationale of the design depends on showing a close relationship between performance and criterion levels, conclusions about the impact of treatment will be difficult to infer.

Certainly a noteworthy feature of the design is that it is based on gradual changes in behavior. The design is consistent with shaping procedures where few performance requirements are made initially, and these requirements are gradually increased as the client masters earlier criterion levels. In many clinical situations, the investigator may wish to change client performance gradually. For behaviors involving complex skills or where improvements require relatively large departures from how the client usually behaves, gradual approximations may be especially useful. Hence, the changing-criterion design may be well suited to a variety of clinical problems, clients, and settings.

8

Multiple-Treatment Designs

The designs discussed in previous chapters usually restrict themselves to the evaluation of a single intervention or treatment. Occasionally, some of the designs have utilized more than one intervention, as in variations of ABAB (e.g., ABCABC) or multiple-baseline designs. In such designs, difficulties arise when the investigator is interested in comparing two or more interventions within the same subject. If two or more treatments are applied to the same subject in ABAB or multiple-baseline designs, they are given in separate phases so that one comes before the other at some point in the design. The *sequence* in which the interventions appear partially restricts the conclusions that can be reached about the relative effects of alternative treatments. In an ABCABC design, for example, the effects of C may be better (or worse), because it followed B. The effects of the two interventions (B and C) may be very different if they were each administered by themselves without one being preceded by the other.

In clinical research, the investigator is often interested in comparing alternative treatments for a single subject. The purpose is to make claims about the relative effectiveness of alternative treatments independently of the sequence problem highlighted above. Different design options are available that allow comparison of multiple treatments within a single subject and serve as the basis of the present chapter.

Basic Characteristics of the Designs

Alternative single-case designs have been proposed to evaluate the effects of multiple treatments. Although different designs can be distinguished, they share some overall characteristics regarding the manner in which separate treatments are compared. In each of the designs, a single behavior of one or more persons is observed. As with other designs, baseline observations of the target behavior are obtained. After baseline, the intervention phase is implemented, in which the behavior is subjected to two or more interventions. These interventions are implemented in the same intervention phase.

Although two or more interventions are implemented in the same phase, both are not in effect at the same time. For example, two procedures such as praise and token reinforcement might be compared to determine their separate effects in altering classroom behavior. Both interventions would not be implemented at the same moment. This would not permit evaluation of the separate effects of the interventions. Even though they are administered in the same phase, the interventions have to be administered separately in some way so that they can be evaluated. In a manner of speaking, the interventions must "take turns" in terms of when they are applied. The variations of multiple-treatment designs depend primarily on the precise manner in which the different interventions are scheduled so they can be evaluated.

Major Design Variations

Multiple-Schedule Design

Description and Underlying Rationale. The multiple-schedule design consists of implementation of two or more interventions designed to alter a single behavior. The interventions are implemented in the same phase. The unique and defining feature of the multiple-schedule design is that the *separate interventions are associated or consistently paired with distinct stimulus conditions.* The major purpose of the design is to show that the client performs differently under the different treatment conditions and that the different stimuli exert control over behavior.

The multiple-schedule design has been used primarily in laboratory research with infrahuman subjects in which the effects of different reinforcement schedules have been examined. Different reinforcement schedules are administered at different times during an intervention phase. Each schedule is associated with a distinct stimulus (e.g., light that is on or off). After the stimulus has been associated with its respective intervention, a clear discrimination is evident in performance. When one stimulus is presented, one pattern of performance is obtained. When the other stimulus is presented, a different pattern of performance is obtained. The difference in performance among the stimulus conditions is a function of the different interventions. The design is used to demonstrate that the client or organism can discriminate in response to the different stimulus conditions.

The underlying rationale unique to this design pertains to the differences in responding that are evident under the different stimulus conditions. If the client makes a discrimination in performance between the different stimulus conditions, the data should show clearly different performance levels. On any given day, the different stimulus conditions and treatments are implemented. Yet performance may vary markedly depending on the precise condition in effect at that time. When performance differs sharply as a function of the different conditions in effect, a functional relationship can be drawn between the stimulus conditions and performance.

If the stimulus conditions and interventions do not differentially influence performance, one would expect an unsystematic pattern across the different conditions during the intervention phase. If extraneous events rather than the treatment conditions were influencing performance sytematically, one might see a general improvement or decrement over time. However, such a pattern would be evident in performance under each of the different stimulus conditions. A different pattern of responding would not be evident under the different stimulus conditions.

Illustrations. The multiple-schedule design has been used infrequently in applied research. The design emphasizes the control that certain stimulus conditions exert after being paried with various interventions. Although it is often important to identify the control that stimuli can exert over performance, most applied investigations are concerned with identifying the effects of different treatments independently of the particular stimuli with which they are associated. Nevertheless, a few demonstrations have utilized multiple-schedule designs to demonstrate how persons in clinical and other applied settings discriminate among stimulus conditions.

An illustration of the design in the context of treatment was reported by Agras, Leitenberg, Barlow, and Thomson (1969) who evaluated the effects of social reinforcement for treating a hospitalized fifty-year-old woman who feared enclosed places (claustrophobia). The woman was unable to remain in a room with the door closed, could not go into an elevator, movie theater, church, or drive in a car very long. To measure fear of enclosed places, the woman was asked to sit in a small windowless room until she felt uncomfortable. The time the patient remained in the room was measured four times each day. After baseline observations, one of two therapists worked with the patient to help her practice remaining in the room for longer periods of time. Each day both therapists worked with the patient for two sessions each. One therapist provided praise when the patient was able to increase the amount of time that she remained in the room on the practice trials. The other therapist maintained a pleasant relationship but did not provide contingent praise. Essentially, the different therapists were associated with different interventions (contingent praise versus no praise) in a multiple-schedule design. The question is whether the patient would make a discrimination of the different therapist-intervention combinations.

The results are illustrated in Figure 8-1, which shows the average amount of time the patient spent in the small room each day with each of the therapists. At the beginning of the intervention phase, the patient showed slightly higher performance with the therapist who provided reinforcement (RT in the figure) than with the therapist who did not (NRT). The therapists changed roles so

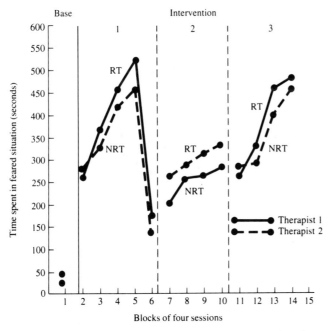

Figure 8-1. The effects of reinforcing and nonreinforcing therapists on the modification of claustrophobic behavior. One therapist provided reinforcement (reinforcing therapist or RT) while the other did not (nonreinforcing therapist or NRT). The therapists eventually switched these contingencies. (*Source:* Agras, Leitenberg, Barlow, and Thomson, 1969.)

that the one who provided contingent praise stopped doing this and the other one began to deliver praise. As evident in the second subphase of the intervention phase, when the therapists changed roles, the patient made a discrimination. The therapist who provided praise continued to evoke superior patient performance. Finally, in the third panel of the intervention phase, the therapists returned to their initial roles and again the patient made the discrimination.

The above results indicated that the patient remained in the small room for longer periods of time whenever practicing with the therapist who provided reinforcement. A clear discrimination was made in relation to the different therapists. The effects were not particularly strong but were generally consistent.

As evident in the above illustration, multiple-schedule designs can demonstrate that behavior is under the control of different stimuli. The stimuli exert differential influences on performance because of the specific interventions with which they are paired. Although multiple-schedule designs are used relatively infrequently for applied questions, their relevance and potential utility have been underestimated. The applied relevance of the type of effects demonstrated in multiple-schedule designs is evident from an interesting example several years ago demonstrating the different influences that adults can exert over child behavior (Redd, 1969). In this investigation, three adults altered the behaviors of two institutionalized severely retarded boys. The purpose was to evaluate the impact of different reinforcement schedules on the cooperative play of each of these children with their peers during a play period.

During baseline, no adults were in the playroom, but data were gathered on cooperative play. After baseline, adults came into the room one at a time and administered reinforcers (praise and candy) according to different schedules. One adult always gave the reinforcers contingently so that only instances of cooperative behavior were reinforced. Another adult came in at a different time and gave the reinforcers noncontingently, so that cooperative behavior specifically was not being reinforced. A third adult came in at yet a different time and dispensed the reinforcers on a "mixed" schedule so that they were contingent on some occasions and noncontingent on other occasions.

The three adults each had their own particular schedule for administering the consequences. After the procedure had continued for several sessions, the stimulus control exerted by the adults was evident. Specifically, when the adult who administered contingent reinforcement entered the room, the cooperative behavior of the children increased. When the adult who administered noncontingent reinforcement entered the room at a different time, cooperative behavior did not increase. Finally, when the adult who administered the mixed schedule entered the room, cooperative play increased only slightly.

The demonstration relied on a multiple-schedule design by virtue of consistently associating particular stimulus conditions (three adults) with the interventions (different reinforcement schedules). After repeated association of the adults with their respective schedules, the children discriminated in their performance. The results indicated that children learned to react to adults in a manner consistent with how the adults had reinforced their behavior.

Simultaneous-Treatment Design

Description and Underlying Rationale. In the multiple-schedule design, separate interventions are applied under different stimulus conditions. Typically, each intervention is associated with a particular stimulus to show that performance varies systematically as a function of the stimulus that is presented. As noted earlier, in applied research the usual priority is to evaluate the relative impact of two or more treatments free from the influence of any particular stimulus condition. There usually is no strong interest in associating separate treatments with unique stimuli.

Multiple treatments can be readily compared in single-case research without associating the treatments with a particular stimulus. Indeed, in the example noted earlier (Agras et al., 1969), the investigators used a multiple-schedule design by associating two therapists with different interventions (praise versus no praise). The investigators were also interested in showing that the different interventions led to different results, no matter who administered them. Hence, the interventions that therapists administered were changed at different points in the design. When different treatment conditions are varied or alternated across different stimulus conditions, the design usually is distinguished from a multiple-schedule design (Kazdin and Hartmann, 1978; Kratochwill, 1978). The distinction is not always clear in particular instances of the design. Usually multiple-schedule design is reserved for instances in which the interventions are purposely paired with particular stimuli so that stimulus control is demonstrated.

The comparison of different treatments in single-case research is more common in designs in which the interventions are balanced or purposely varied across the different stimulus conditions. Treatments are administered across different stimulus conditions (e.g., times of the day, therapists, settings), but the interventions are balanced across each of the conditions (Browning, 1967; Browning and Stover, 1971). At the end of the intervention phase, one can examine the effects of the interventions on a particular target behavior that is not confounded by or uniquely associated with a particular stimulus condition.

The design in which multiple treatments are compared without being associated with a particular stimulus has received a large number of labels, including multi-element treatment design (Ulman and Sulzer-Azaroff, 1975), simultaneous-treatment design (Browning, 1967; McCullough, Cornell, McDaniel, and Mueller, 1974), concurrent schedule design (Hersen and Barlow, 1976), and alternating-treatments design (Barlow and Hayes, 1979). For present purposes, the term simultaneous-treatment design will be used. Other terms and the special variations to which they occasionally refer will be noted as well.

The underlying rationale of the design is similar to that of the multiple-schedule design. After baseline observations, two or more interventions are implemented in the same phase to alter a particular behavior. The distinguishing feature is that the different conditions are distributed or varied across stimulus conditions in such a way that the influence of the different treatments can be separated from the influence associated with the different stimulus conditions.

In the simultaneous-treatment design, the different conditions are administered in an alternating fashion, and thus some authors have referred to the procedure as an *alternating conditions* (Ulman and Sulzer-Azaroff, 1975) or *alternating-treatments* design (Barlow and Hayes, 1979). The different conditions are administered in the same phase, usually on the same day, and thus the design has also been referred to as a *simultaneous-treatment* (Kazdin and Hartmann, 1978) or *concurrent schedule* design (Hersen and Barlow, 1976).[1]

The design begins with baseline observation of the target response. The observations are usually obtained daily under two or more conditions, such as two times per day (e.g., morning or afternoon) or in two different locations (e.g., classroom and playground). During the baseline phase, the target behavior is observed daily under each of the conditions or settings. After baseline

---

1. Although it may be only of academic interest, none of the currently proposed terms for this design quite accurately describes its unique features. "Simultaneous-treatment" design incorrectly implies that the interventions are implemented simultaneously. If this were true, the effectiveness of the separate interventions could not be independently evaluated. "Alternating treatments" design incorrectly suggests that the interventions must be treatments or active interventions. As discussed later in the chapter, "no treatment" or baseline can be used as one of the conditions that is alternated. Also, alternating treatments is sufficiently broad to encompass multiple-schedule designs in which treatments also are alternated. "Concurrent schedule" design implies that the interventions are restricted to reinforcement schedules, which is rarely the case in applied work. For additional comments on the confusion of terminology in this design and attempts to resolve it, other sources can be consulted (Barlow and Hayes, 1979; Kratochwill, 1978).

observations, the intervention phase is begun. In the usual case, two different interventions are compared. Both interventions are implemented each day. However, the interventions are administered under the different stimulus conditions. The interventions are administered an equal number of times across each of the conditions of administration so that, unlike the multiple-schedule design, the interventions are not uniquely associated with a particular stimulus. The intervention phase is continued until the response stabilizes under the separate interventions.

The crucial feature of the design is the unique intervention phase, in which separate interventions are administered concurrently. Hence, it is worthwhile to detail how the interventions are varied during this phase. Consider as a hypothetical example a design in which two interventions (I_1 and I_2) are to be compared. The interventions are to be implemented daily but across two separate sessions or time periods (T_1 and T_2). The interventions are balanced across the intervention. *Balancing* refers to the fact that each intervention is administered under each of the conditions an equal number of times. On any given day, the interventions are administered under separate conditions.

Table 8-1 illustrates different ways in which the interventions might be administered on a daily basis. As evident from the Table 8-1A, each intervention is administered each day, and the time period in which a particular intervention is in effect is alternated daily. In Table 8-1A, the alternating pattern is accomplished by simply having one intervention administered first on one day, second on the next, first in the next day, and so on. The alternating pattern

Table 8-1. The administration of two interventions (I_1 and I_2) balanced across two time periods (T_1 and T_2)

A.
Alternating order every other day during the intervention phase

		Days					
Time periods	1	2	3	4	5	6	... n
T_1	I_1	I_2	I_1	I_2	I_1	I_2	
T_2	I_2	I_1	I_2	I_1	I_2	I_1	

B.
Alternating in a random order during the intervention phase

		Days					
Time periods	1	2	3	4	5	6	... n
T_1	I_1	I_2	I_2	I_1	I_2	I_1	
T_2	I_2	I_1	I_1	I_2	I_1	I_2	

could be randomly determined, with the restriction that throughout the intervention phase each intervention appears equally often in the first and second time period. This randomly ordered procedure is illustrated in Table 8-1B.

The table refers to the schedule of administering the different interventions during the first intervention phase. If one of the interventions is more (or most) effective than the other(s), the design usually concludes with a final phase in which that intervention is administered across all conditions. That is, the more (or most) effective intervention is applied across all time periods or situations included in the design.

A hypothetical example of the data plotted from a simple version of the simultaneous-treatment design is illustrated in Figure 8-2. In the example, observations were made daily for two time periods. The data are plotted in baseline separately for these periods. During the intervention phase, two separate interventions were implemented and were balanced across the time periods. In this phase, data are plotted according to the interventions so that the differential effects of the interventions can be seen. Because intervention 1 was more effective than intervention 2, it was implemented across both time periods in the final phase. This last phase provides an opportunity to see if behavior improves in the periods in which the less effective intervention had been administered. Hence, in this last phase, data are plotted according to the

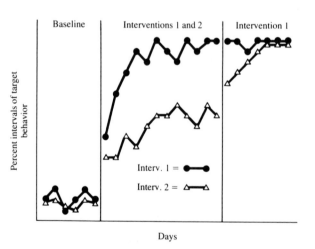

Figure 8–2. Hypothetical example of a simultaneous-treatment design. In baseline the observations are plotted across the two different time periods. In the first intervention phase, both interventions are administered and balanced across the time periods. The data are plotted according to the different interventions. In the final phase, the more effective intervention (Intervention 1) was implemented across both time periods.

different time periods as they were balanced across the interventions, even though both receive the more effective procedure. As evident in the figure, performance improved in those time periods that previously had been associated with the less effective intervention.

Illustrations. A simultaneous-treatment design was used to evaluate the effects of alternative ways of earning reinforcers among children in a special education classroom (Kazdin and Geesey, 1977). Baseline data were obtained for two educably retarded boys who were selected because of their high rates of disruptive behavior. Observations were made of attentive behavior during two periods in the morning, when academic tasks were assigned by the teacher. After the baseline phase, the intervention was implemented, which consisted of two variations of a token reinforcement program. Each child·was told that he could earn tokens (marks on a card) for working attentively and that these tokens could be exchanged for various prizes and rewards (e.g., extra recess). The two variations of reinforcement consisted of the manner in which the reinforcers would be dispensed. The programs differed according to whether the tokens could be exchanged for rewards that only the subject would receive (self-exchange) or whether they could be exchanged for rewards for the subject and the entire class (class-exchange). Thus, the child could earn for himself or for everyone. Tokens were earned during the two observation periods each day. Different-colored cards were used to record the tokens in each period to separate the self- and the class-reward programs. When a predetermined number of tokens was earned on a card, the child selected from a lottery jar which of the available rewards was earned. This reward was given to the child or to everyone in class depending on which card had earned the reinforcers. Each program was implemented daily in one of the two observation periods. The programs were alternated daily so that one appeared during the first period on one day and during the second period on the next, and so on.

The results for Max, a seven-year-old boy, can be seen in Figure 8-3. The data are plotted in two ways to show the overall effect of the program (upper panel) and the different effects of the separate interventions (lower panel). The upper portion of the figure shows that attentive behavior improved during the first and second token reinforcement phases. Of greater interest is the lower portion, in which the data are plotted separately across time periods. During the first intervention phase, data are plotted according to whether the self-exchange or class-exchange was in effect. The results indicated that Max was more attentive when he was working for rewards for the entire class rather than just for himself. Hence, in the third and final phase, the class-exchange period was implemented daily across both time periods. He no longer earned

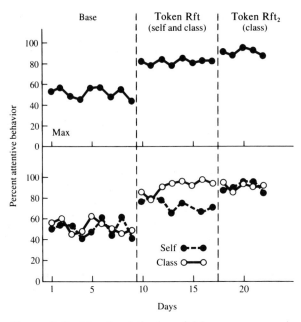

Figure 8-3. Attentive behavior of Max across experimental conditions. Baseline (base)—no experimental intervention. Token reinforcement (token rft)—implementation of the token program where tokens earned could purchase events for himself (self) or the entire class (class). Second phase of token reinforcement (token rft₂)— implementation of the class exchange intervention across both time periods. The *upper panel* presents the overall data collapsed across time periods and interventions. The *lower panel* presents the data according to the time periods across which the interventions were balanced, although the interventions were presented only in the last two phases. (*Source:* Kazdin and Geesey, 1977.)

for himself alone, since this proved to be the less effective intervention. In the final phase, attentive behavior was consistently high across both time periods. This last phase suggests further that the class exchange method was indeed the more effective intervention, because it raised the level of performance for the time periods previously devoted to self-exchange.

Other Multiple-Treatment Design Options

The multiple-schedule and simultaneous-treatment designs discussed here constitute the more commonly used multiple-treatment designs. A few other options are available that warrant brief mention, even though they are infrequently used in applied research.

Simultaneous Availability of All Conditions. As noted above, in the usual simultaneous-treatment or alternating-treatments design, the interventions are scheduled at different periods each day. The pattern of performance in effect during each of the different treatments is used as a basis to infer the effectiveness of the alternative interventions. Almost always, the treatments are scheduled at entirely different times during the day. It is possible to make each of the alternative treatments available at the same time. The different interventions are available but are in some way selected by the client.

In the only clear demonstration of this variation, Browning (1967) compared the effects of three procedures (praise and attention, verbal admonishment, and ignoring) to reduce the bragging of a nine-year-old hospitalized boy. One of the boy's problem behaviors was extensive bragging that entailed untrue and grandiose stories about himself. After baseline observations, the staff implemented the above procedures in a simultaneous-treatment design. The different treatments were balanced across three groups of staff members (two persons in each group). Each week, the staff members associated with a particular intervention were rotated so that all the staff eventually administered each of the interventions.

The unique feature of the design is that during the day, all of the staff were available to the child. The specific consequence the child received for bragging depended on the staff members with whom he was in contact. The boy had access to and could seek out the staff members of his choosing. And the staff provided the different consequences to the child according to the interventions to which they had been assigned for that week. The measure of treatment effects was the frequency and duration of bragging directed at the various staff members. The results indicated that bragging incidents tended to diminish in duration in the presence of staff members who ignored the behavior relative to those who administered the attention or admonishment.

This design variation is slightly different from the previous ones because all treatments were available simultaneously. The intervention that was implemented was determined by the child who approached particular staff members. As Barlow and Hayes (1979) pointed out, this variation of the design is useful for measuring a client's preference for a particular intervention. The client can seek those staff members who perform a particular intervention. Since all staff members are equally available, the extent to which those who administer a particular intervention are sought out may be of interest in its own right.

The variation of the design in which all interventions are actually available at the same time and the client selects the persons with whom he or she interacts has been rarely used. Methodologically, this variation is best suited to measure preferences for a particular condition, which is somewhat different from the usual question of interest, namely, the effectiveness of alternative conditions. Nevertheless, some authors have felt that this design is important to distinguish as a distinct variation (Barlow and Hayes, 1979).

Randomization Design. Multiple-treatment designs for single subjects alternate the interventions or conditions in various ways during the intervention phase. The designs discussed above resemble a randomization design (Edgington, 1969, 1980), which refers to a way of presenting alternative treatments. The design developed largely through concern with the requirements for statistical evaluation of alternative treatments rather than from the mainstream of single-case experimental research (see Edgington, 1969).

The randomization design, as applied to one subject or a group of subjects, refers to presentation of alternative interventions in a random order. For example, baseline (A) and treatment (B) conditions could be presented to subjects on a daily basis in the following order ABBABABABAAB. Each day a different condition is presented, usually with the restriction that each is presented an equal number of times. Because the condition administered on any particular day is randomly determined, the results are amenable to several statistical tests (Edgington, 1969; Kazdin, 1976).

Features of the randomization design are included in versions of a simultaneous-treatment design. For example, in the intervention phase of a simultaneous-treatment design, the alternative interventions must be balanced across stimulus conditions (e.g., time periods). When the order that the treatments are applied is determined randomly (see Table 8-1B), the phase meets the requirements of a randomization design. Essentially, a randomization design consists of one way of ordering the treatments in the intervention phase of a multiple-treatment design.

Technically, the design can be used without an initial baseline if two treatments (B,C) or baseline with one or more treatments (A,B,C) are compared. If a sufficient number of occasions is presented, differential effects of the interventions can be detected. Of course, without the initial baseline that is typical of single-case experimental designs, information is lost about the initial level of performance. However, this initial information in a particular case may be unnecessary or impractical to obtain.

Randomization designs have not been reported very frequently in applied work. If used in applied work, the design shares the problems evident in other multiple-treatment designs, discussed later in the chapter (see also Kazdin, 1980b). As noted earlier, the randomization design has usually been proposed for purposes of statistical evaluation of single-case data (Edgington, 1980). Hence, the topic will re-emerge in Chapter 10, in which data evaluation is explicitly addressed.

Additional Design Variations

Aside from delineating multiple-schedule and simultaneous-treatment designs, other variations of multiple-treatment designs can be distinguished. Major variations include comparison of alternative intervention and no treatment (continuation of baseline) during the intervention phase and the alternative ways of evaluating the interventions based on the final phase of the design.

Conditions Included in the Design

The primary purpose of employing a multiple-treatment design is to evaluate the relative effectiveness of alternative interventions. Thus, variations discussed to this point have emphasized the comparison of different interventions that are implemented to alter behavior. Not all of the conditions compared in the intervention phase need be active treatments. In some variations, one of the conditions included in the intervention phase is a continuation of baseline conditions, i.e., no intervention.

A major purpose of the initial baseline phase of multiple treatment, and other single-case experimental designs, is to project what performance would be like in the future if no treatment were implemented. In a multiple-treatment design, it is possible to implement one or more interventions *and* to continue baseline conditions, all in the same phase. In addition to projecting what baseline would be like in the future, it is possible to assess baseline levels of performance concurrently with the intervention(s). If performance changes under those time periods in which the interventions are in effect but remains at the original baseline level during the periods in which baseline conditions are continued, this provides a dramatic demonstration that behavior changes resulted from the intervention. Because the baseline conditions are continued in the intervention phase, the investigator has a direct measure of performance without the intervention. Any extraneous influences that might be confounded with the onset of the intervention phase should affect the baseline conditions that have been continued. By continuing baseline in the intervention phase, greater assurances are provided that the intervention accounts for change. Moreover, the investigator can judge the magnitude of the changes due to the intervention by directly comparing performance during the intervention phase under baseline and intervention conditions that are assessed concurrently.

An example of a simultaneous-treatment design in which baseline constituted one of the alternating conditions was provided by Ollendick, Shapiro, and Barrett (1981), who reduced the frequency of stereotyped repetitive movements among hospitalized retarded children. Three children, ages seven to eight years old, exhibited stereotypic behaviors such as repetitive hand gestures

and hair twirling. Observations of the children were made in a classroom setting while each child performed various visual-motor tasks (e.g., puzzles).
Behavior was observed each day for three sessions, after which the intervention
phase was implemented.

During the intervention phase, three conditions were compared, including
two active interventions and a continuation of baseline conditions. One treatment procedure consisted of physically restraining the child's hands on the
table for thirty seconds so he or she could not perform the repetitive behaviors.
The second treatment consisted of physically guiding the child to engage in the
appropriate use of the task materials. Instead of merely restraining the child,
this procedure was designed to develop appropriate alternative behaviors the
children could perform with their hands. The final condition during the intervention phase was a continuation of baseline. Physical restraint, positive practice, and continuation of baseline were implemented each day across the three
different time periods.

Figure 8-4 illustrates the results for one child who engaged in hand-posturing gestures. As evident from the first intervention phase, both physical
restraint and positive practice led to reductions in performance; positive practice was more effective. The extent of the reduction is especially clear in light

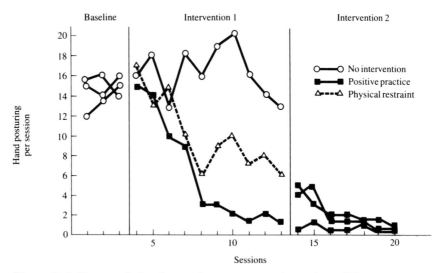

Figure 8-4. Stereotypic hand-posturing across experimental conditions. The three
separate lines in each phase represent three separate time periods each session. Only
in the initial intervention phase were the three separate conditions in effect, balanced
across the time periods. In the second intervention phase, positive practice was in
effect for all three periods. (*Source:* Ollendick, Shapiro, and Barrett, 1981.)

of the continuation of baseline as a third condition during the intervention phase. When baseline (no-treatment) conditions were in effect during the intervention phase, performance remained at the approximate level of the original baseline phase. In the final phase, positive practice was applied to all of the time periods each day. Positive practice, which had proved to be the most effective condition in the previous phase, led to dramatic reductions in performance when implemented across all time periods. Thus, the strength of this intervention is especially clear from the design.

The continuation of baseline in the intervention phase allows direct assessment of what performance is like without treatment. Of course, since inclusion of baseline constitutes another condition in the intervention phase, it does introduce a new complexity to the design. As discussed later in the chapter, increasing the number of conditions compared in the intervention phase raises potential problems. Yet if performance during the initial baseline phase is unstable or shows a trend that the investigator believes may interfere with the evaluation of the interventions, it may be especially useful to continue baseline as one of the conditions in the design.

Final Phase of the Design

The simultaneous-treatment design is usually defined by a baseline phase followed by an intervention phase in which behavior is exposed to two or more interventions. The designs usually include a third and final phase that contributes to the strength of the demonstration. The final phase of the simultaneous-treatment design is particularly interesting, because precisely what is done in this phase usually adds a feature of some other single-case design.

In the usual case, the intervention phase may compare two or more conditions (e.g., two or more treatments, or one intervention and a continuation of baseline). If one of the two conditions is shown to be more effective than the other during the first intervention phase, it is often implemented on all occasions and under all stimulus conditions in the final phase of the design. When the final phase of the simultaneous-treatment design consists of applying the more (or most) effective intervention across all of the stimulus conditions, the design bears some resemblance to a multiple-baseline design.

Essentially, the design includes two intervention phases, one in which two (or more) interventions are compared and one in which the more (most) effective one is applied. The "multiple baselines" do not refer to different behaviors or settings but rather to the different time periods each day in which the observations are obtained. The more (most) effective intervention is applied to one time period during the first intervention phase. In the second intervention phase, the more (most) effective intervention is extended to all of the time periods. Thus, the more (most) effective intervention is introduced to the time periods at different points in the design (first intervention phase, then second intervention phase).

Of course, the design is not exactly like a multiple-baseline design because the more (or most) effective intervention is introduced to time periods that may not have continued under baseline conditions. Rather, less effective interventions have been applied to these time periods during the first intervention phase. On the other hand, when the simultaneous-treatment design compares one intervention with a continuation of baseline, then the two intervention phases correspond closely to a multiple-baseline design. The intervention is introduced to one of the daily time periods in the first intervention phase while the other time period continues in baseline conditions. In the second intervention phase, the intervention is extended to all time periods in exactly the manner of a multiple-baseline design.

Occasionally, the final phase of the simultaneous-treatment design consists of withdrawing all of the treatments. Thus, a reversal phase is included, and the logic of the design follows that of ABAB designs discussed earlier (e.g., Kazdin and Geesey, 1977, 1980). Of course, an attractive feature of the simultaneous-treatment design is the ability to demonstrate an experimental effect without withdrawing treatment. Hence, the reversal phase is not commonly used as the final phase of the design.

General Comments

Multiple-treatment designs can vary along more dimensions than the conditions that are implemented in the first and second intervention phases, as discussed above. For example, designs differ in the number of interventions or conditions that are compared and the number of stimulus conditions across which the interventions are balanced. However important these dimensions are, they do not alter basic features of the designs. The full range of variations of the designs becomes clearer as we turn to the problems that may emerge in multiple-treatment designs and how these problems can be addressed.

Problems and Considerations

Multiple-treatment designs provide a unique contribution to evaluation because of the manner in which separate conditions can be compared. Among single-case experimental designs, those in which multiple treatments are compared are relatively complex. Hence, several considerations are raised by their use in terms of the types of interventions and behaviors that are investigated, the extent to which interventions can be discriminated by the clients, the number of interventions and stimulus conditions that are used, and the possibility that multiple-treatment interference may contribute to the results.

Type of Intervention and Behavior

Multiple-schedule and simultaneous-treatment designs depend on showing changes for a given behavior across daily sessions or time periods. If two (or more) interventions are alternated on a given day, behavior must be able to shift rapidly to demonstrate differential effects of the interventions. The need for behavior to change rapidly dictates both the types of interventions and the behaviors that can be studied in multiple-treatment designs.

Interventions suitable for multiple-treatment designs may need to show rapid effects initially and to have little or no carryover effects when terminated. Consider the initial requirement of rapid start-up effects. Because two (or more) interventions are usually implemented on the same day, it is important that the intervention not take too long within a given session to begin to show its effects. For example, if each intervention is administered in one of two one-hour time periods each day, relatively little time exists to show a change in behavior before the intervention is terminated for that day. Not all treatments may produce effects relatively quickly. This problem is obvious in some forms of medication used to treat clinical problems in adults and children (e.g., depression), in which days or weeks may be required before therapeutic effects can be observed.

In most behavioral programs, in which intervention effects are based on reinforcement and punishment, the effects of the intervention may be evident within a relatively short period. If several opportunities (occurrences of the behavior) exist to apply the consequences within a given time period, intervention effects may be relatively rapid. Some interventions, such as extinction where consequences are not provided, may take considerable time to show an effect. The slow "start-up" time for intervention effects depends on characteristics of the treatment (e.g., extinction burst, gradual decline of behavior) that might preclude demonstrating a treatment effect in a short time period (see Kazdin, 1980a). Of course, it is premature to suggest that some treatments would not demonstrate an effect in any given design variation. However, when treatments are alternated within a single day, as is often the case in multiple-treatment designs, the initial start-up time necessary for treatment to demonstrate an effect is important.

Another requirement is that interventions must have little or no carryover effects after they are terminated. If the effects of the first intervention linger after it is no longer presented, the intervention that follows would be confounded by the previous one. For example, it might be difficult to compare medication and behavioral procedures in a simultaneous-treatment design. It might be impossible to administer both treatments on the same day because of the carryover that most medications have. The effects of the medication, if administered in the morning, might continue into the period later that day in which the other treatment was implemented. Because of the continued effects of the medication, the separate influence of the other intervention could not be evaluated.

Pharmacological interventions are not the only ones that can have carryover effects. Interventions based on environmental contingencies also may have carryover effects and thus may obscure evaluation of the separate effects of the interventions. (This will be discussed below in the section on multiple-treatment interference.) In any case, if two or more treatments are to be compared, it is important to be able to terminate each of the interventions quickly so that they can be alternated over time. If treatments cannot be removed quickly, they will be difficult to compare with each other in a simultaneous-treatment design.

Apart from the interventions, the behaviors studied in multiple-treatment designs must be susceptible to rapid changes. Behaviors that depend upon improvements over an extended period may not be able to shift rapidly in response to session-by-session changes in the intervention. For example, it would be difficult to evaluate alternative interventions for reducing weight of obese persons. Changes in the measure (weight in pounds) would not vary to a significant degree unless an effective treatment were continued without interruption over an extended period. Constantly alternating the interventions on a daily basis might not affect weight at all. On the other hand, alternative measures (e.g., calories consumed at different times during the day) may well permit use of the design.

Aside from being able to change rapidly, the frequency of the behavior may also be a determinant of the extent to which interventions can show changes in multiple-treatment designs. For example, if the purpose of the interventions is to decrease the occurrence of low-frequency behaviors (e.g., severe aggressive acts), it may be difficult to show a differential effect of the interventions. If punishment procedures are compared, too few opportunities may exist for the intervention to be applied in any particular session. Indeed, the behavior may not even occur in some of the sessions. Thus, even though a session may be devoted to a particular punishment technique, the technique may not actually be applied. Such a session cannot fairly be represented as one in which this particular treatment was employed.

High frequency of occurrences also may present problems for reflecting differences among interventions. If there is an upper limit to the number of responses because of a limited set of discrete opportunities for the behavior, it may be difficult to show differential improvements. For example, a child may receive two different reinforcement programs to improve academic performance. Each day, the child receives a worksheet with twenty problems at two different times as the basis for assessing change. During each time period, there are only twenty opportunities for correct responding. If baseline performance is 50 percent correct (ten problems), this means that the differences between treatments can only be detected, on the average, in response to the ten other problems. If each intervention is moderately effective, there is likely to be a ceiling effect, i.e., absence of differences because of the restricted upper limit to the measure. Perhaps the interventions would have differed in effectiveness if the measure were not restricted to a limited number of response opportunities.

In general, differential effectiveness of the intervention is likely to depend on several opportunities for the behavior to occur. If two or more active interventions are compared that are likely to change behavior, the differences in their effects on performance are relatively smaller than those evident if one intervention is simply compared to a continuation of baseline. In order for the design to be sensitive to relatively less marked differences between or among treatments, the frequency of the behavior must be such that differences could be shown. Low frequency of behavior may present problems if it means that there are few opportunities to apply the procedures being compared. High frequency of behavior may be a problem if the range of responses is restricted by an upper limit that impedes demonstration of differences among effective interventions.

Discriminability of Treatment

When multiple treatments are administered to one client in the same phase, the client must be able to make at least two sorts of discriminations. First, the client must be able to discriminate whether the treatment agents or time periods are associated with a particular intervention. In the multiple-schedule design, this discrimination may not be very difficult because the interventions are constantly associated with a particular stimulus. In the simultaneous-treatment design, the client must be able to discern that the specific interventions constantly vary across the different stimulus conditions. In the beginning of the intervention phase, the client may inadvertently associate a particular intervention with a particular stimulus condition (e.g., time period, staff member, or setting). If the interventions are to show different effects on performance, it will be important for the client to respond to the interventions that are in effect independently of who administers them.

Second, the client must be able to distinguish the separate interventions. Since the design is aimed at showing that the interventions can produce different effects, the client must be able to tell which intervention is in effect at any particular time. Discriminating the different interventions may depend on the procedures themselves.

The ease of making a discrimination of course depends on the *similarity of the procedures* that are compared. If two very different procedures are compared, the clients are more likely to be able to discriminate which intervention is in effect than if subtle variations of the same procedure are compared. For example, if the investigation compared the effects of five versus fifteen minutes of isolation as a punishment technique, it might be difficult to discriminate which intervention was in effect. Although the interventions might produce different effects if they were administered to separate groups of subjects or to the same subject in different phases over time, they may not produce a difference or produce smaller differences when alternated daily, in part because the client cannot discriminate consistently which one is in effect at any particular point in time.

The discriminability of the different interventions may depend on the *frequency* with which each intervention is actually invoked, as alluded to earlier. The more frequently the intervention is applied during a given time period, the more likely the client will be able to discriminate which intervention is in effect. If in a given time interval the intervention is applied rarely, the procedures are not likely to show a difference across the observation periods. In some special circumstances where the goal of treatment is to reduce the frequency of behavior, the number of times the intervention is applied may decrease over time. As behavior decreases in frequency, the different treatments will be applied less often, and the client may be less able to tell which treatment is in effect. For example, if reprimands and isolation are compared as two procedures to decrease behavior, each procedure might show some effect within the first few days of treatment. As the behaviors decrease in frequency, so will the opportunities to administer the interventions. The client may have increased difficulty in determining at any point which of the different interventions is in effect.

To ensure that clients can discriminate which intervention is in effect at any particular point in time, investigators often provide daily instructions before each of the treatments that is administered in a simultaneous-treatment design (e.g., Johnson and Bailey, 1977; Kazdin and Geesey, 1977, 1980; Kazdin and Mascitelli, 1980). The instructions tell the client explicitly which condition will be in effect at a particular point in time. As a general guideline, instructions might be very valuable to enhance the discrimination of the different treatments, especially if there are several different treatments, if the balancing of treatments across conditions is complex, or if the interventions are only in effect for brief periods during the day.[2]

Number of Interventions and Stimulus Conditions

A central feature of the simultaneous-treatment design is balancing the conditions of administration with the separate interventions so that the intervention effects can be evaluated separately from the effects of the conditions. Theoretically, any number of different interventions can be compared during the intervention phase. In practice, only a few interventions usually can be compared. The problem is that as the number of interventions increases, so does the number of sessions or days needed to balance interventions across the conditions of administration. If several interventions are compared, an extraordinarily large number of days would be required to balance the interventions across all of the conditions. As a general rule, two or three interventions or conditions are optimal for avoiding the complexities of balancing the interventions across the conditions of administration. Indeed, most multiple-treatment designs have compared two or three interventions.

The difficulty of balancing interventions also depends on the number of stimulus conditions included in the design. In the usual variation, the two interventions are varied across two levels (e.g., morning or afternoon) of one stimulus dimension (e.g., time periods). In some variations, the interventions may be varied across two stimulus dimensions (e.g., time periods and staff members). Thus, two interventions (I_1 and I_2) might be balanced across two time periods (T_1 and T_2) and two staff members (S_1 and S_2). The interventions must be paired equally often across all time period and staff combinations (T_1S_1, T_1S_2,

---

2. Interestingly, if instructions precede each intervention to convey to the clients exactly which procedure is in effect, the distinction between multiple-schedule and simultaneous-treatment becomes blurred (Kazdin and Hartmann, 1978). In effect, the instructions become stimuli that are consistently associated with particular interventions. However, the blurred distinction need not become an issue. In the simultaneous-treatment design, an attempt is made to balance the interventions across diverse stimulus conditions (with the exception of instructions), and in the multiple-schedule design the balance is not usually attempted. Indeed, in the latter design, the purpose is to show that particular stimuli come to exert control over behavior because of their constant association with particular treatments.

T_2S_1, T_2S_2) during the intervention phase. As the number of dimensions or stimulus conditions increases, longer periods are needed to ensure that balancing is complete. The number of interventions and stimulus conditions included in the design may be limited by practical constraints or the duration of the intervention phase. In general, most simultaneous-treatment designs balance the interventions across two levels of a particular dimension (e.g., time periods). Some variations have included more levels of a particular dimension (e.g., three time periods) or two or more separate dimensions (e.g., time periods and staff) (e.g., Bittle and Hake, 1977; Browning, 1967; Kazdin, 1977d; Ollendick et al., 1981). From a practical standpoint, the investigation can be simplified by balancing interventions across only two levels of one dimension.

Multiple-Treatment Interference

Multiple treatment refers to the effect of administering more than one treatment to the same subject(s). When more than one treatment is provided, the possibility exists that the effect of one treatment may be influenced by the effect of another treatment (Campbell and Stanley, 1963). Drawing unambiguous conclusions may be difficult if treatments interfere with each other in this way. In any design in which two or more treatments are provided to the same subject, multiple-treatment interference may limit the conclusions that can be drawn.

Multiple-treatment interference may result from many different ways of administering treatments. For example, if two treatments are examined in an ABAB design (e.g., ABCBC), multiple-treatment interference may result from the sequence in which the treatments are administered. The effects of the different interventions (B,C) may be due to the sequence in which they appeared. It is not possible to evaluate the effects of C alone, because it was preceded by B, which may have influenced all subsequent performance. Occasionally, investigators include a reversal phase in ABAB designs with multiple treatments (e.g., ABAC), with the belief that recovery of baseline levels of performance removes the possibility of multiple-treatment interference. However, intervening reversal phases (e.g., ABACABAC) do not alter the possible influence of sequence effects. Even though baseline levels of performance are recovered, it is still possible that the effects of C are determined in part by the previous history of condition B. Behavior may be more (or less) easily altered by the second intervention because of the intervention that preceded it. An intervening reversal (or A) phase does not eliminate that possibility.

In multiple-schedule and simultaneous-treatment designs, multiple-treatment interference refers to the possibility that the effect of any intervention may be influenced by the other intervention(s) to which it is juxtaposed. Thus, the effects obtained for a given intervention may differ from what they would be if the intervention were administered by itself in a separate phase without the juxtaposition of other treatments. For example, in a classroom program, an investigator may wish to compare the effects of disapproval for disruptive behavior with praise for on-task behavior. Both interventions might be administered each day in a multiple-schedule or simultaneous-treatment design. The possibility exists that the effects of disapproval or praise during one period of the day may be influenced by the other intervention at another period of the day. In general, the results of a particular intervention in a multiple-treatment design may be determined in part by the other intervention(s) to which it is compared.

The extent to which alternative treatments can lead to multiple-treatment interference has not been thoroughly investigated. In one investigation, the effects of alternating different treatments were examined in a classroom of mentally retarded children ages nine through twelve (Shapiro, Kazdin, and McGonigle, 1982). The investigators examined whether performance under a particular intervention would be influenced by another condition implemented at a different time period each day. After baseline observations, token reinforcement for attentive classroom behavior was implemented for one of two time periods each day. This intervention remained constant and in effect for the remainder of the investigation but was alternated across the daily time periods. In some phases, token reinforcement was alternated on a daily basis with baseline conditions and in other phases with response cost (withdrawing tokens for inappropriate behavior). The level of performance during the token reinforcement periods tended to change as a function of the other condition with which it was compared on a given day. Specifically, on-task behavior during the token reinforcement periods tended to be higher when token reinforcement was compared with continuation of baseline than when it was compared with response cost. Moreover, performance was much more variable in the token reinforcement periods (i.e., it showed significantly greater fluctuations) when the condition to which it compared was response cost than when the other condition was a continuation of baseline. Thus, the procedure juxtaposed in the design influenced different facets of performance.

Another variation of multiple-treatment interference was reported by Johnson and Bailey (1977), who were interested in increasing participation in activities among mentally retarded women in a halfway house. The program was designed to increase participation in leisure activities (e.g., painting, playing cards, working on puzzles or with clay, and rug making). Two procedures were compared, which consisted of merely making the requisite materials available for the activities, or making the materials available and also providing a reward (e.g., cosmetics, stationery) for participation. The two interventions were alternated in two sessions (time periods) each night in the manner described earlier for a simultaneous-treatment design.

Although both procedures improved participation over baseline, the reward procedure led to the greater changes. Interestingly, the effect of making materials available depended on whether it was presented during the first or second time period. The procedure was markedly more effective when it was presented first rather than when it was presented as the second intervention on a given day. Stated another way, making materials available was more effective in increasing participation when it preceded the reward period rather than when it followed the reward period. Thus, there was a definite effect of the sequence or order in which this condition appeared. Interestingly, the effect of the reward procedure did not depend on the time period in which it appeared.

The above examples illustrate different ways in which multiple-treatment interference may operate in designs that balance interventions across alternating time periods. The effects of one intervention may be due in part to the other condition with which it is compared and the order in which it appears daily in the sequence. In general, conclusions about differences between or among treatments in one of the multiple-treatment designs must be qualified by the possibility of multiple-treatment interference in dictating the pattern of results.

Evaluation of the Designs

Multiple-treatment designs have several advantages that make them especially useful for applied research. To begin with, the designs do not depend on a reversal of conditions, as do the ABAB designs. Hence, problems of behavior failing to reverse or the undesirability of reversing behavior are avoided. Similarly, the designs do not depend on temporarily withholding treatment, as is the case in multiple-baseline designs in which the intervention is applied to one behavior (or person, or situation) at a time, while the remaining behaviors can continue in extended baseline phases. In multiple-treatment designs, the interventions are applied and continued throughout the investigation. The strength of the demonstration depends on showing that treatments produce differential effects across the time periods or situations in which performance is observed.

A second advantage of the design is particularly noteworthy. Most of the single-case experimental designs depend heavily on obtaining baseline data that are relatively stable and show no trend in the therapeutic direction. If baseline data show improvements, special difficulties usually arise in evaluating the impact of subsequent interventions. In multiple-treatment designs, interventions can be implemented and evaluated even when baseline data show initial trends (Ulman and Sulzer-Azaroff, 1975). The designs rely on comparing performance associated with the alternating conditions. The differences can still be detected when superimposed on any existing trend in the data.

A third main advantage of the design is that it can compare alternative treatments for a given individual within a relatively short period. If two or more interventions were compared in an ABAB or multiple-baseline design, the interventions must follow one another in separate phases. Providing each intervention in a separate phase greatly extends the duration of the investigation. In the multiple-treatment designs, the interventions can be compared in the same phase, so that within a relatively short period one can assess if two or more interventions have different impact. The phase in which both interventions are compared need not necessarily be longer than intervention phases of other single-case designs. Yet only one intervention phase is needed in the simultaneous-treatment design to compare separate interventions. In clinical situations, when time is at a premium, the need to identify the more or most effective interventon among available alternatives can be extremely important.

Of course, in discussing the comparison of two or more treatments in a single-case design, the topic of multiple-treatment interference cannot be ignored. When two or more treatments are compared in sequence, as in an ABAB design, the possibility exists that the effects of one intervention are partially attributable to the sequence in which it appeared. In a multiple-treatment design, these sequence effects are not a problem, because separate phases with different interventions do not follow each other. However, multiple-treatment interference may take another form.

As discussed earlier, the effects of one treatment may be due in part to the other condition to which it is juxtaposed (Shapiro et al., 1982). Hence, in all of the single-case experimental designs in which two or more treatments are given to the same subject, multiple-treatment interference remains an issue, even though it may take different forms. The advantage of the multiple-treatment designs is not in the elimination of multiple-treatment interference. Rather, the advantage stems from the efficiency in comparing alternative treatments in a single phase. As soon as one intervention emerges as more effective than another, it can be implemented across all time periods and staff.

There is yet another advantage of multiple-treatment designs that has not been addressed. In the simultaneous-treatment design, the interventions are balanced across various stimulus conditions (e.g., time periods or staff). The data are usually plotted according to the interventions so that one can determine which among the alternatives is the most effective. It is possible to plot the data in another way to examine the impact of the stimulus conditions on client behavior. For example, if the intervention is balanced across two staff members or groups of staff members (e.g., morning and afternoon nursing shift, teacher and teacher aide), the data can be plotted to examine the differential effectiveness of the staff who administer the program. In many situations, it may be valuable to identify whether some staff are having greater effects on client performance than others independently of the particular intervention they are administering. Because the staff members are balanced across the interventions, the separate effects of the staff and interventions can be plotted. If the data are plotted according to the staff who administer the interventions in the different periods each day, one can identify staff who might warrant additional training. Alternatively, it may be of interest to evaluate whether the client's performance systematically changes as a function of the time period in which observations are made. The data can be plotted by time period to determine whether a particular intervention is more effective at one time than another. In any case, the manner in which interventions are balanced across conditions permits examination of additional questions about the factors that may influence client performance than usually available in single-case designs.

Summary and Conclusions

Multiple-treatment designs are used to compare the effectiveness of alternative interventions or conditions that are administered to the same subject or group of subjects. The designs demonstrate an effect of the alternative interventions by presenting each of them in a single intervention phase after an initial baseline phase. The manner in which the separate interventions are administered during the intervention phase serves as the basis for distinguishing various multiple-treatment designs.

In the *multiple-schedule design,* two or more interventions are usually administered in the intervention phase. Each intervention is consistently associated with a particular stimulus (e.g., adult, setting, time). The purpose of the design is to demonstrate that a particular stimulus, because of its consistent association with one of the interventions, exerts stimulus control over performance.

In the *simultaneous-treatment design* (also referred to as *alternating treatments* or *concurrent schedule design*), two or more interventions or conditions also are administered in the same intervention phase. Each of the interventions is balanced across the various stimulus conditions (e.g., staff, setting, and time) so that the effects of the interventions can be separated from these conditions of administration. When one of the interventions emerges as the more (or most) effective during the intervention phase, a final phase is usually included in the design in which that intervention is implemented across all stimulus conditions or occasions. Simultaneous-treatment designs usually evaluate two or more interventions. However, the interventions can be compared with no treatment or a continuation of baseline conditions.

Several considerations are relevant for evaluating whether a multiple-treatment design will be appropriate in any given situation. First, because the designs depend on showing rapid changes in performance for a given behavior, special restrictions may be placed on the types of interventions and behavior that can be included. Second, because multiple treatments are often administered in close proximity (e.g., on the same day), it is important to ensure that the interventions will be discriminable to the clients so that they know when each is in effect. Third, the number of interventions and stimulus conditions employed in the investigation may have distinct practical limits. The requirements for balancing the interventions across stimulus conditions become more demanding as the number of interventions and stimulus conditions increase.

Finally, a major issue of designs in which two or more conditions are provided to the same subjects is *multiple-treatment interference*. Multiple-treatment designs avoid the effects of following one intervention by another in separate phases (i.e., sequence effects), which is a potential problem when two or more treatments are evaluated in ABAB designs. However, multiple-treatment designs juxtapose alternative treatments in a way that still may influence the inferences that can be drawn about the treatment. The possibility remains that the effect of a particular intervention may result in part from the manner in which it is juxtaposed and the particular intervention to which it is contrasted. The extent to which multiple-treatment interference influences the results of the designs described in this chapter has not been well studied.

Multiple-treatment designs have several advantages. The intervention need not be withdrawn or withheld from the clients as part of the methodological requirements of the design. Also, the effects of alternative treatments can be compared relatively quickly (i.e., in a single phase), so that the more (or most) effective intervention can be applied. Also, because the designs depend on differential effects of alternative conditions on behavior, trends during the initial baseline phase need not impede initiating the interventions. Finally, when the interventions are balanced across stimulus conditions (e.g., staff), the separate effects of the interventions and these conditions can be examined. In general, the designs are often quite suitable to the clinical demand of identifying effective interventions for a given client.

9

Additional Design Options

Variations of the designs discussed to this point constitute the majority of evaluation strategies used in single-case research. Several other options are available that represent combinations of various single-case designs, the use of special design features to address questions about the maintenance or generalization of behavior, or the use of between-group design strategies. This chapter discusses several design options, the rationales for their use, and the benefits of alternative strategies for applied research.

Combined Designs

Description and Underlying Rationale

Previous chapters have discussed several different designs. Although the designs are most often used in their "pure" forms, as described already, features from two or more designs are frequently combined. Combined designs are those that include features from two or more designs within the same investigation.

The purpose of using combined designs is to increase the strength of the experimental demonstration. The clarity of the results can be enhanced by showing that the intervention effects meet the requirements of more than one design. For example, an intervention may be evaluated in a multiple-baseline design across subjects. The intervention is introduced to subjects at different points in time and shows the expected pattern of results. The investigator may include a reversal phase for one or more of the subjects to show that behavior reverts to or near the original baseline level. Demonstration of the impact of the intervention may be especially persuasive, because requirements of multiple-baseline and ABAB designs were met.

The use of combined designs would seem to be an example of methodological overkill. That is, the design may include more features than necessary for clearly demonstrating an experimental effect. Yet combined designs are not merely used for experimental elegance. Rather, the designs address genuine problems that are anticipated or actually emerge within an investigation.

The investigator may anticipate a problem that could compete with drawing valid inferences about intervention effects. For example, the investigator may select a multiple-baseline design (e.g., across behaviors) and believe that altering one of the baselines might well influence other baselines. A combined design may be selected. If baselines are likely to be interdependent, which the investigator may have good reason to suspect, he or she may want to plan some other feature in the design to reduce ambiguities if requirements of the multiple-baseline design were not met. A reversal phase might be planned in the event that the effects of the intervention across the multiple baselines are not clear. Alternatively, a phase may be included to apply the intervention so that performance meets a changing criterion. The criterion level could change once or twice during an intervention phase to incorporate components of a changing-criterion design.

Combined designs do not necessarily result from plans the investigator makes in advance of the investigation. Unexpected ambiguities often emerge over the course of the investigation. Ambiguity refers to the possibility that the extraneous events rather than the intervention may have led to change. The investigator decides whether a feature from some other design might be added to clarify the demonstration.

An important feature of single-case designs in general is that the investigator alters the design in light of the emerging pattern of data. Indeed, basic decisions are made after viewing the data (e.g., when to change from one phase to another). Combined designs often reflect the fact that the investigator is reacting to the data by invoking elements of different designs to resolve the ambiguity of the demonstration.

Variations

In each design discussed in previous chapters, the intervention is introduced and experimentally evaluated in a unique way. For example, ABAB designs include replication of at least one of the phases (usually baseline) at different points in the design; multiple-baseline designs introduce the intervention at different points in time; changing-criterion designs constantly change the performance standards during the intervention, and so on with other designs.

Combined designs incorporate features from different designs. Because of the different basic designs and their many variations, it is not possible to illustrate all of the combined designs that can be conceived. However, it is useful to illustrate combined designs that tend to be used relatively frequently and other designs that, although used less frequently, illustrate the range of options available to the investigator.

Perhaps the most commonly used combined design integrates features of ABAB and multiple-baseline designs. An excellent example combining features of an ABAB design and a multiple-baseline design across behaviors was reported in an investigation designed to help an eighty-two-year-old man who had suffered a massive heart attack (Dapcich-Miura and Hovel, 1979). After leaving the hospital, the patient was instructed to increase his physical activity, to eat foods high in potassium (e.g., orange juice and bananas), and to take medication.[1] A reinforcement program was implemented in which he received tokens (poker chips) each time he walked around the block, drank juice, and took his medication. The tokens could be saved and exchanged for selecting the dinner menu at home or for going out to a restaurant of his choice.

The results, illustrated in Figure 9-1, show that the reinforcement program was gradually extended to each of the behaviors over time in the usual multiple-baseline design. Also, baseline conditions were temporarily reinstated to follow an ABAB design. The results are quite clear. The data met the experimental criteria for each of the designs. With such clear effects of the multiple-baseline portion of the design, one might wonder why a reversal phase was implemented at all. Actually, the investigators were interested in evaluating whether the behaviors would be maintained without the intervention. Temporarily withdrawing the intervention resulted in immediate losses of the desired behaviors.

In another illustration, features of an ABAB design and multiple-baseline design across settings were used to evaluate treatment for hyperventilation in a mentally retarded hospitalized adolescent (Singh, Dawson, and Gregory, 1980). Hyperventilation is a respiratory disorder characterized by prolonged and deep breathing and is often associated with anxiety, tension, muscle spasms, and seizures. Treatment focuses on decreasing deep breathing to resume normal respiration of oxygen and carbon dioxide. In this investigation,

---

1. A diet high in potassium was encouraged because the patient's medication probably included diuretics (medications that increase the flow of urine). With such medication, potassium often is lost from the body and has to be consumed in extra quantities.

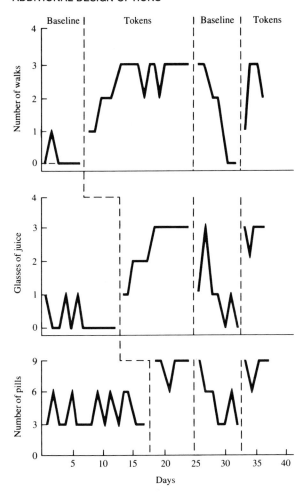

Figure 9-1. Number of adherence behaviors (walking, orange juice drinking, and pill taking) per day under baseline and token reinforcement conditions. (*Source:* Dapcich-Miura and Hovel, 1979.)

instances of deep breathing were followed by opening a vial of aromatic ammonia and holding it under the resident's nose for 3 sec. This punishment procedure was implemented across four settings of the hospital (classroom, dining room, bathroom, and day room) in a multiple-baseline design. After the intervention had been applied to each setting, a return-to-baseline condition was included followed by reinstating punishment across each of the settings. In the final phase, several staff members in the total ward environment were

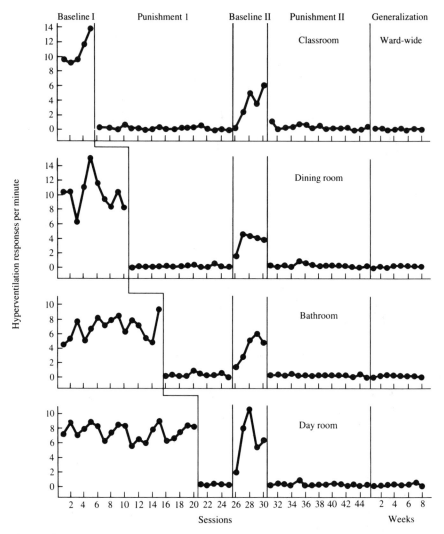

Figure 9–2. Number of hyperventilation responses per minute across experimental phases and settings. (*Source:* Singh, Dawson, and Gregory, 1980.)

brought into the program so that the gains would generalize throughout the setting. As shown in Figure 9-2, the program was highly effective in eliminating hyperventilation. The results were remarkably clear and requirements of both ABAB and multiple-baseline designs were met.

When ABAB and multiple-baseline designs are combined, there is no need to extend the reversal or return-to-baseline phase across all of the behaviors, persons, or situations. For example, Favell, McGimsey, and Jones (1980) evaluated an intervention designed to induce retarded persons (ages nine through twenty-one) to eat more slowly. Large percentages of institutionalized retarded persons have been found to eat markedly faster than normals. Rapid eating is not only socially unacceptable but may present health problems (e.g., vomiting or aspiration). To develop slower eating, the investigators provided praise and a bite of a favorite food to residents who paused between bites. Verbal and physical prompts were used initially by stating "wait" and by manually guiding the persons to wait. These prompts were removed and reinforcement was given less frequently as eating rates became stable.

A multiple-baseline design across two subjects illustrates the effects of the intervention, as shown in Figure 9-3. A reversal phase was used with the first subject, which further demonstrated the effects of the intervention. The design is interesting to note because the reversal phase was only employed for one of the baselines (subjects). Because multiple-baseline designs are often selected to circumvent use of return-to-baseline phases, the partial application of a

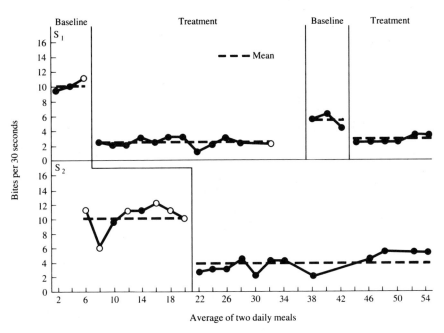

Figure 9-3. Rate of eating for subjects 1 and 2 across baseline and treatment conditions. (Solid data points represent data from two daily meals; open data points represent data from a single meal.) (*Source:* Favell, McGimsey, and Jones, 1980.)

reversal phase in a combined design may be more useful than the withdrawal of the intervention across all of the behaviors, persons, or situations.

Although features of ABAB and multiple-baseline designs are commonly combined, other design combinations have been used as well. In the usual case, reversal phases are added to other designs, as noted in the chapters on the changing-criterion and multiple-treatment designs. The utility of combining diverse design features is evident in an example of a combined ABAB and changing-criterion design that was used to evaluate a program to reduce noise in a college dormitory (Meyers et al., 1976). Automated recordings of noise levels (in decibels) were obtained through microphones placed in the dormitory. After baseline observations of noise level, instructions and feedback were provided to the residents to help them decrease their noise. Feedback included providing a publicly displayed scoreboard showing the number of times in which the noise level exceeded the desired level. Also, a bell sounded for each instance of noise beyond the criterion level so residents knew immediately when noise was too high.

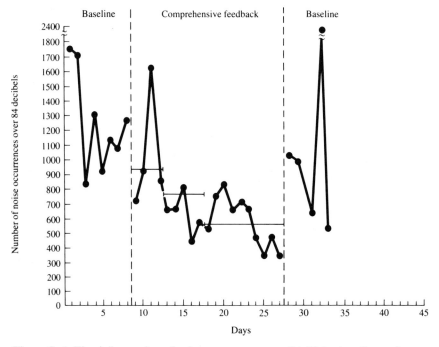

Figure 9–4. The daily number of noise occurrences over 84 dB for baseline and treatment conditions. The solid horizontal lines indicate weekly treatment criteria. (*Source:* Meyers, Artz, and Craighead, 1976.)

As shown in Figure 9-4, several days of baseline were followed by the intervention phase, in which the criterion for defining excessive noise was gradually decreased in the manner of a changing-criterion design. In the final phase, baseline conditions were reinstated following procedures for an ABAB design. Although noise level decreased during the intervention phase, the level did not clearly match the changing criterion. When the intervention was withdrawn in the final phase, noise tended to revert toward baseline levels. The addition of the reversal phase proved to be crucial for drawing inferences about the effects of the feedback program. Without the final phase of the design, there would have been ambiguity about the role of the intervention in altering noise level.

Problems and Considerations

The above examples by no means exhaust the combinations of single-case experimental designs that have been reported. The examples represent the more commonly used combinations. More complex combinations have been reported in which, for example, variations of multiple-treatment and multiple-baseline or ABAB designs are combined into a single demonstration (e.g., Bittle and Hake, 1977; Johnson and Bailey, 1977). As combined designs incorporate features from several design variations, it is difficult to illustrate the different design components in a single graphical display of the data. Although highly complex design variations and combinations can be generated, it is important to emphasize that the combinations are not an exercise in methodology. The combined designs are intended to provide alternatives to address weaknesses that might result from using variations of one of the usual designs without combined features.

The use of combined designs can greatly enhance the clarity of intervention effects in single-case designs. Features of different designs complement each other, so that the weaknesses of any particular design are not likely to interfere with drawing valid inferences. For example, it would not be a problem if behavior does not perfectly match a criterion in a changing-criterion design if that design also includes components of a multiple-baseline or ABAB design; nor would it be a problem if each behavior did not show a change when and only when the intervention was introduced in a multiple-baseline design if functional control were clearly shown through the use of a return-to-baseline phase. Thus, within a single demonstration, combined designs provide different opportunities for showing that the intervention is responsible for the change.

Most combined designs consist of adding a reversal or return-to-baseline phase to another type of design. A reversal phase can clarify the conclusions that are drawn from multiple-baseline, changing-criterion, and multiple-treatment designs. Interestingly, when the basic design is an ABAB design, components from other designs are often difficult to add to form a combined design if they are not planned in advance. In an ABAB design, components of multiple-baseline or multiple-treatment designs may be difficult to include, because special features ordinarily included in other designs (e.g., different baselines or observation periods) are required. On the other hand, it may be possible to use changing criteria during the intervention phase of an ABAB design to help demonstrate functional control over behavior.

The advantages of combined designs bear some costs. The problems evident in the constituent designs often extend to the combined designs as well. For example, in a commonly used combined design, multiple-baseline and ABAB components are combined. Some of the problems of both designs may be evident. The investigator has to contend with the disadvantages of reversal phases and with the possibility of extended baseline phases for behaviors that are the last to receive the intervention. These potential problems do not interfere with drawing inferences about the intervention, because in one way or another a causal relationship can be demonstrated. However, practical and clinical considerations may introduce difficulties in meeting criteria for both of the designs. Indeed, such considerations often dictate the selection of one design (e.g., multiple baseline) over another (e.g., ABAB). Given the range of options available within a particular type of design and the combinations of different designs, it is not possible to state flatly what disadvantages or advantages will merge in a combined design. It is important that the investigator be aware of both the advantages and limitations that may emerge when combined designs are considered, so that they can be weighed in advance.

Designs to Examine Transfer of Training and Response Maintenance

The discussions of designs in previous chapters have focused primarily on techniques to evaluate whether an intervention was responsible for change. Typically, the effects of an intervention are replicated in some way in the design to demonstrate that the intervention rather than extraneous factors produced the results. As applied behavior analysis has evolved, techniques designed to alter behavior have been fairly well documented. Increasingly, efforts have shifted from investigations that merely demonstrate change to investigations that explore the generalization of changes across situations and settings (transfer of training) and over time (response maintenance).[2] The investigation of transfer

2. Several procedures have been developed to promote transfer of training and response maintenance and are described in other sources (e.g., Kazdin, 1980a; Marholin, Siegel, and Phillips, 1976; Stokes and Baer, 1977).

of training and response maintenance can be facilitated by several design options. Design variations based on the use of probe techniques and withdrawal of treatment after behavior change has been demonstrated are discussed below.

Probe Designs

Probes were introduced earlier and defined as the assessment of behavior on selected occasions when no contingencies are in effect for that behavior. Probes are commonly used to determine whether a behavior not focused on directly has changed over the course of the investigation. Because the contingencies are not in effect for behaviors assessed by probes, the data from probe assessment address the generality of behavior across responses and situations.

Probes have been used to evaluate different facets of generality. Typically, the investigator trains a particular response and examines whether the response occurs under slightly different conditions from those included in training. For example, Nutter and Reid (1978) trained mentally retarded women to select clothing combinations that were color coordinated. Developing appropriate dressing is a relevant response, because it may facilitate the integration of mentally retarded persons into ordinary community life. Normative data were collected to identify popular color combinations in the actual dress of women in ordinary community settings. Once the color combinations were identified, the mentally retarded women were trained. Training consisted of providing instructions, modeling, practice, feedback, and praise as the women worked with a wooden doll that could be dressed in different clothing. Although training focused on dressing dolls in color-coordinated outfits, the interest, of course, was in altering how the residents actually selected clothing for their own dress. Hence generalization probes were conducted periodically in which residents selected clothing outfits from a large pool of clothing.

Color-coordination training, introduced in a multiple-baseline design across subjects, led to clear effects, shown in Figure 9-5. The selection of popular color combinations for dressing the dolls increased during training (closed circles). Of greater interest are the probe data (open circles), which show the actual selection of clothing outfits by the residents. Selection of color-coordinated outfits tended to be low during baseline and much higher during the training phase. Given the pattern of data, it seems evident that the effects of training extended to actual clothing selection. The probes were quite valuable in evaluating the generality of training for selecting clothes for ordinary dressing, which was not directly trained.

The use of probes to assess generality across situations was illustrated in a study designed to develop pedestrian skills among adolescents and adults who

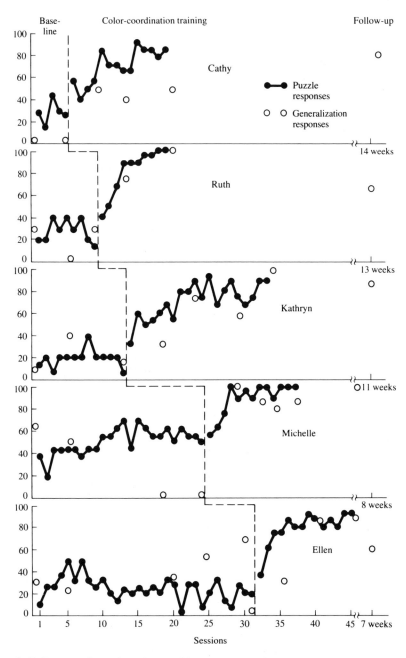

Figure 9–5. Percent of popular color combinations selected by each participant during baseline, test, and generalization sessions. Test sessions followed color-coordination training sessions and were identical to baseline sessions. The follow-up sessions occurred at the specified intervals after color-coordination training ended. (*Source:* Nutter and Reid, 1978.)

were physically handicapped and mentally retarded (Page, Iwata, and Neef, 1976). The skills included several behaviors required to cross different types of intersections safely. Training was conducted in a classroom setting where instruction, practice with a doll, social reinforcement, feedback, and modeling were used to develop the skills. Assessment of correct performance was conducted in the classroom only when the participants met criterion levels for specific skills. On these assessment occasions, performance was measured in the classroom (class probes) and on actual performance at city intersections (street probes). Of special interest here, for the measure of generality across settings, are the data on performance in the city intersections where training was not implemented.

The data are plotted separately for each of the five subjects in Figure 9-6. It is clear from the multiple-baseline design that improvements were evident both in the classroom and in the naturalistic setting. Probe assessment in different conditions provided valuable data about the effects of training beyond the training situation.

The use of probes represents a relatively economical way of evaluating the generality of responses across a variety of conditions. The use is economical, because assessment is conducted only on some occasions rather than on a continuous basis. An important feature of probe assessment is that it provides a preview of what can be expected beyond the conditions of training. Often training is conducted in one setting (e.g., classroom) with the hope that it will carry over to other settings (e.g., playground, home). The use of probes can provide ongoing, albeit only occasional, assessment of performance across settings and provide information on the extent to which generalization occurs. If generalization does occur, this should be evident in probe assessment. If generalization does not occur, the investigator can then implement procedures designed to promote generality and to evaluate their effects through changes on the probe assessment.

Withdrawal Designs

In many behavioral programs, the intervention is withdrawn abruptly, either during an ABAB design or after the investigation is terminated. As might be expected, under such circumstances behaviors typically revert to or near baseline levels. Marked changes in the environmental contingencies might be expected to alter behavior. However, the rapidity of the return of behavior to baseline levels may in part be a function of the manner in which the contingencies are withdrawn.

Recently, design variations have been suggested that evaluate the gradual

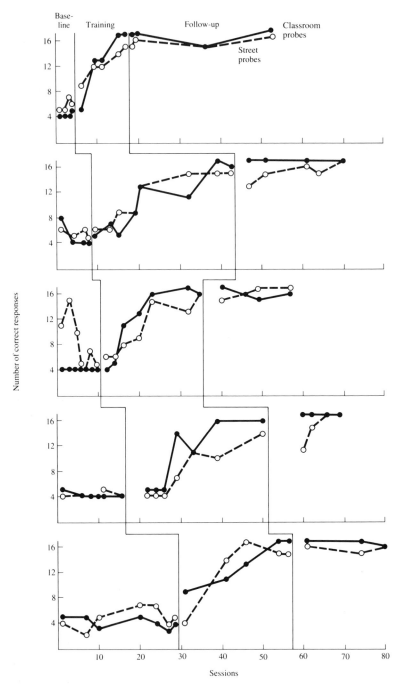

Figure 9-6. Number of correct responses of 17 possible for classroom and street probes during baseline, training, and follow-up conditions. (*Source:* Page, Iwata, and Neef, 1976.)

withdrawal of interventions on response maintenance (Rusch and Kazdin, 1981). The designs are referred to as *withdrawal designs* because the intervention is withdrawn in diverse ways to sustain performance.[3] Withdrawal designs are used to assess whether responses are maintained under different conditions rather than to demonstrate the initial effects of an intervention in altering behavior. Hence, features of withdrawal designs can be added to other designs discussed in previous chapters. After the intervention effects have been demonstrated unambiguously, withdrawal procedures can be added to evaluate response maintenance.

Sequential-Withdrawal Design. Interventions often consist of several components rather than a single procedure. For example, a training program designed to develop social skills may consist of instructions, practice, reinforcement, feedback, modeling, and other ingredients, all combined into a single "package." After the investigator has demonstrated control of this package on behavior, he or she may want to study maintenance of the behavior. A sequential-withdrawal design consists of *gradually withdrawing different components of a treatment package to see if behavior is maintained.* The different components are withdrawn in consecutive phases so that the effects of altering the original package on performance can be evaluated until all of the components of the package have been eliminated. Of course, if the entire intervention package were abruptly withdrawn, behavior would probably revert to baseline levels. The gradual withdrawal of components of the intervention permits monitoring of response maintenance before the intervention is completely terminated.

An example of a sequential-withdrawal design was provided by Rusch, Connis, and Sowers (1979), who implemented a training program consisting of prompts, praise, tokens, and response cost (fines) to increase the amount of time a mildly retarded adult spent engaging in appropriate work activities. The adult worked in a restaurant setting utilized for vocational training, and she performed several tasks (e.g., setting up and cleaning tables and stocking supplies such as cups, milk, and sugar).

In the first of several phases, various components of the package in combination were shown to influence behavior (attending to the tasks of the job) in an ABAB design. After a high level of attending to the tasks had been achieved, the different components of the intervention were gradually withdrawn (i.e., faded). The results of the program (see Figure 9-7) show the initial

---

3. The term "withdrawal" design has occasionally been used to refer to variations of ABAB designs in which the intervention is "withdrawn" and baseline conditions are reinstated (Leitenberg, 1973). In the present use, procedures are withdrawn, but there is no necessary connection between ABAB designs and the procedures described here.

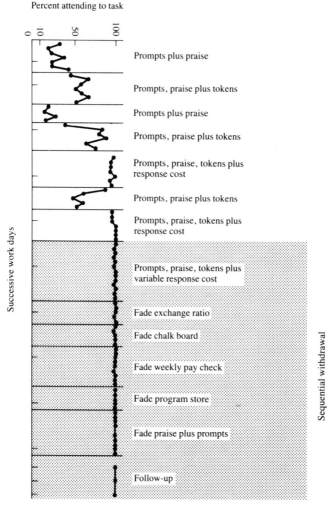

Figure 9–7. Sequential-withdrawal design to evaluate maintenance of behavior. (*Source:* Rusch, Connis, and Sowers, 1979.)

ABAB portion of the design followed by the sequential withdrawal period (shaded area). During the withdrawal phases, separate portions of the program were gradually withdrawn in sequence until all components had been withdrawn. By the last phase and follow-up assessment, the contingencies were completely withdrawn and behavior was maintained at a high level.

The above study suggests that sequentially withdrawing portions of treatment helped maintain behavior. Of course, it is possible that the behavior would have been maintained even if the intervention were abruptly withdrawn. To evaluate this possibility, it may be useful to withdraw the package completely early in the investigation in one or two phases to see if behavior returns to or near baseline levels. If the behaviors revert to baseline levels, the program can be reinstated to return behavior to its previous high level. At this point, the components of the package can be sequentially withdrawn. If behavior is maintained, the investigator has some confidence that the withdrawal procedure may have contributed to maintenance.

Partial-Withdrawal Design. Another strategy to evaluate maintenance consists of withdrawing a component of the intervention package or the total package from one of the several different baselines (behaviors, persons, or situations) of a multiple-baseline design. The design bears some resemblance to the sequential design that gradually withdraws different components of a package for a particular person (or baseline). The partial-withdrawal design *withdraws the intervention gradually across different persons or baselines.* In the design, the intervention is first withdrawn from only one of the behaviors (or baselines) included in the design. If withdrawing the intervention does not lead to a loss of the behavior, then the intervention can be withdrawn from other behaviors (or baselines) as well.

The partial-withdrawal design is relatively straightforward and can be easily illustrated with a brief hypothetical example. An intervention such as training social interaction skills among withdrawn children might be introduced in a multiple-baseline design across children. Observation of social interactions in a classroom situation may reveal that the interactions increase for each child when the intervention is introduced. Having demonstrated the effects of the program, a partial-withdrawal phase might be introduced for one of the children. This phase amounts to a reversal phase for one of the subjects to test in a preliminary fashion whether behavior will be maintained. If behavior is maintained, the intervention is withdrawn from the other children. If, on the other hand, the behavior is not maintained for the first child, this provides a preview of the likely results for the other children for whom the program has yet to be withdrawn. The investigator then knows that additional procedures must be implemented to avoid loss of the behaviors.

The partial-withdrawal phase indicates whether behaviors are likely to be maintained if the intervention package or components of the package are withdrawn from all the subjects or behaviors. Of course, one cannot be certain that the pattern evident for one of the baselines necessarily reflects how the other baselines respond. For example, a partial withdrawal may consist of withdrawing the entire intervention from one of the baselines. Even if behavior is maintained, this does not necessarily mean that other behaviors included in the investigation would be maintained. Behaviors may be differentially maintained after an intervention is withdrawn as a function of other features of the situation (e.g., ordinary support systems for the behavior, opportunities to perform the behaviors). Similarly, in a multiple-baseline design across persons, the maintenance or loss of behaviors evident in a partial withdrawal for one person may not necessarily reflect the pattern of data for the other persons included in the design. Keeping these cautions in mind, partial-withdrawal designs may be useful in tentatively identifying whether the removal of a portion of treatment from one baseline is likely to be associated with losses of that behavior and by extrapolation of other behaviors as well.

Combined Sequential and Partial-Withdrawal Design. The sequential and partial-withdrawal procedures can be useful in combination. Components of a treatment package can be withdrawn gradually or consecutively across phases for a given baseline (i.e., sequential withdrawal), and the procedure for withdrawing the intervention can be attempted for one baseline at a time (i.e., partial withdrawal).

An example of the combined use of sequential and partial-withdrawal procedures was provided in an investigation designed to teach mentally retarded adults how to tell time (Sowers, Rusch, Connis, and Cummings, 1980). Training consisted of three ingredients: providing preinstructions or prompts to show the adults where the hands of the clock should be at different times, instructional feedback or information that the subject was responding correctly or incorrectly in telling time, and a time card that showed clocks with the correct times the persons needed to remember. The effects of training were evaluated on punctuality, i.e., minutes early and late from breaks and lunch in the vocational setting. The subjects decided on the basis of the clock whether to leave or to return and received feedback as a function of their performance. The training package was evaluated in a multiple-baseline design across subjects. The data for two participants, presented in Figure 9-8, show that punctuality improved for each participant when the intervention package was introduced.

The investigators wished to explore the maintenance of this behavior and included both sequential and partial-withdrawal procedures. The sequential-withdrawal feature of the design can be seen with both subjects in which components of the overall package were withdrawn in consecutive phases. For example, after the second phase for Chris, the preinstruction procedure was withdrawn from the package; in the next phase feedback was withdrawn. The partial-withdrawal portion of the design consisted of withdrawing the components of treatment for one subject at a time. Initially, the components were withdrawn for Chris before being withdrawn from David. Interestingly, when

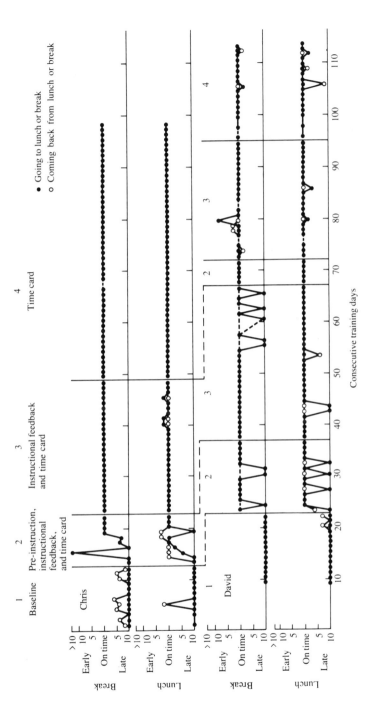

Figure 9–8. Number of minutes each trainee went to and returned from lunch and break, early and late. (*Source:* Sowers, Rusch, Connis, and Cummings, 1980.)

preinstruction was withdrawn from David, punctuality decreased (phase 3 for David). So, the investigators reinstated the original training package. Later, when phase 3 was reinstated, punctuality did not decrease. In the final phase for both Chris and David, behavior was maintained even though only the time card procedure was in effect.

In another example of combined sequential and partial-withdrawal design, Vogelsberg and Rusch (1979) trained three severely handicapped persons, ages seventeen through twenty-one, to cross intersections safely. Training included instructions, practice, and feedback to develop a variety of behaviors, including approaching the intersection, looking for cars, and walking across the street. The sequential-withdrawal aspect of the investigation consisted of removing portions of the training package in a graduated fashion. First, instructions and practice were withdrawn to see if behaviors would be maintained with feedback alone. Next, feedback was removed so that the program had essentially been eliminated.

The partial-withdrawal feature of the investigation consisted of gradually fading the package for one subject before proceeding to others. When instructions and practice were withdrawn from the first subject, behaviors were maintained so the components were withdrawn from other subjects as well; their behaviors were also maintained. When feedback was withdrawn, again for only one of the subjects, one of the critical behaviors (looking for cars before crossing) was not maintained. These results suggested that important behaviors might be lost from the repertoires of other subjects as well, so feedback was not withdrawn. To avoid loss of the skills, feedback was reintroduced for the first subject and training for all subjects was supplemented with additional procedures (e.g., rehearsal of entire sequence of street-crossing skills) to develop sustained performance.

The advantage of the combined sequential and partial-withdrawal design is that it offers separate opportunities to preview the extent to which behaviors are likely to be maintained before the intervention or components of the intervention are completely withdrawn. The sequential-withdrawal portion examines gradual withdrawal of components for an individual subject or for one baseline (e.g., behaviors or situations). The partial-withdrawal portion ensures that components are not removed from all the baselines until the data from the first baseline are examined. Thus, the investigator proceeds cautiously before removing a component of the package that might be crucial to sustain performance.

General Comments. Withdrawal designs are useful for examining response maintenance after the effectiveness of the intervention has been demontrated.

The designs evaluate factors that contribute to response maintenance. Response maintenance is a difficult area of research, because investigations require continued participation of the subject after the intervention has been terminated, administration of follow-up assessment under conditions (e.g., the natural environment) where opportunities to observe performance are less convenient, assessment over a period of sufficient duration to be of clinical or applied relevance, and demonstration that behavior would not have been maintained or would have not been maintained as well without special efforts to implement maintenance procedures. These are difficult issues to address in any research and are not resolved by withdrawal designs. The different withdrawal designs do provide techniques to explore the means through which interventions can be terminated without loss of performance. Presumably, through such designs research can begin to explore alternative ways of terminating interventions without loss of the desired behaviors.

Between-Group Designs

Traditionally, research in psychology and other social sciences has emphasized between-group designs, in which the effects of an intervention (or any independent variable) are evaluated by comparing different groups. In the simplest case, one group receives an intervention and another group does not. More typically, several groups are compared that differ in specific conditions to which they are exposed. If the groups are equivalent before receiving different conditions, subsequent differences between or among the groups serve as the basis for drawing conclusions about the intervention(s). Traditional between-group designs, their variations, and unique methodological features and problems have been described in numerous sources (e.g., Campbell and Stanley, 1963; Kazdin, 1980c; Neale and Liebert, 1980; Underwood and Shaughnessy, 1975) and cannot be elaborated here. Between-group research methodology is often used in combination with single-case methodology. Hence it is useful to discuss the contribution of between-group methodology to single-case designs.

Description and Underlying Rationale

For many researchers, questions might be raised about the contribution that between-group methodology can make to single-case experimental research. The questions are legitimate, given repeated statements about the limitations of between-group research and the advantages of single-case research in surmounting these limitations (e.g., Hersen and Barlow, 1976; Sidman, 1960). Actually, between-group designs often provide important information that is not easily obtained or is not obtained in the same way as it is in single-case designs. Between-group methodology provides alternative ways to gather information of applied interest and provides an important way to replicate findings obtained from research using the subjects as their own controls.[4]

Consider some of the salient contributions that between-group research can make to applied research. First, between-group comparisons are especially useful when the investigator is interested in comparing two or more treatments. Difficulties occasionally arise in comparing different treatments within the same subject. Difficulties are obvious if the investigator is interested in comparing interventions with theoretically discrepant or conflicting rationales. One treatment would appear to contradict or undermine the rationale of the other treatment, and the credibility of the second treatment would be in question. Even if two treatments are applied that appear to be consistent, their juxtaposition in different phases for the same subject may be difficult. As already discussed in detail, when two or more treatments are given to the same subjects, the possibility of multiple-treatment interference exists, i.e., the effects of one treatment may be influenced by other treatment(s) the subject received. Multiple-treatment interference is a concern if treatments are implemented in different phases (e.g., as in variations of ABAB designs) or are implemented in the same phase (e.g., as in simultaneous-treatment designs). Comparisons of treatments in between-group designs provide an evaluation of each intervention without the possible influence of the other.

A second contribution of between-group methodology to applied research is to provide information about the magnitude of change between groups that do and do not receive the intervention. Often the investigator is not only interested in demonstrating that change has occurred but also in measuring the magnitude of change in relation to persons who have yet to receive the intervention. Essentially, a no-treatment group provides an estimate of performance that serves as a baseline against which the performance of the treatment group is compared.

At first glance, it would seem that the data from an ABAB design for a single subject or group of subjects provide the necessary information about what performance is like with and without treatment. The initial phase of an ABAB design presents information without the influence of treatment. However, initial levels of behavior may not remain constant over the course of treat-

---

4. Although the topic cannot be taken up here in any length, it is important to note that for several areas of research within psychology, the results for selected independent variables differ, depending on whether the variables are studied between groups or within subjects (e.g., Behar and Adams, 1966; Grice and Hunter, 1964; Hiss and Thomas, 1963; Lawson, 1957; Schrier, 1958).

ment. Pretreatment performance provides a true estimate of untreated behavior only if there is some guarantee that performance would not change over time. Yet for many areas of applied research, including even severe clinical problems, performance may systematically change (improve or become worse) over time. Hence, initial baseline data may be outdated because it does not provide a concurrent estimate of untreated performance.

Perhaps one could look to the return-to-baseline phase in the ABAB design to estimate concurrent performance uninfluenced by intervention effects. Yet reversal phases may not necessarily provide an estimate of what performance is like without treatment. Reversal phases provide information about what performance is like after treatment is withdrawn which may be very different from what performance is like when treatment has not been provided at all. Alternating baseline and intervention phases may influence the level of performance during the return-to-baseline phases. If the investigator is interested in discussing the magnitude of changes produced by treatment relative to no treatment, a comparison of subjects who have not received the intervention would be useful and appropriate. (This logic applies as well when the investigator is interested in evaluating the magnitude of changes produced by one active intervention relative to another intervention.)

A third use of between-group methodology for applied research arises when large-scale applications of interventions are investigated. With large-scale investigations, several settings and locations may be employed to evaluate a particular intervention or to compare competing interventions. Because of the magnitude of the project (e.g., several schools, cities, hospitals), some of the central characteristics of single-case methodology may not be feasible. For example, in large-scale applications across schools, resources may not permit such luxuries as continuous assessment on a daily basis over time. By virtue of costs of assessment, observers, and travel to and from schools, assessment may be made at a few points in time (e.g., pretreatment, posttreatment, and follow-up). In such cases, between-group research may be the more feasible strategy because of its requirement for fewer resources for assessment.

Finally, an important contribution of between-group research is to examine the separate and combined effects of different variables in a single experiment, i.e., interaction effects. The investigator may be interested in studying two or more variables simultaneously. For example, the investigator may wish to examine the effects of feedback and reinforcement alone and in combination. Two levels of feedback (feedback versus no feedback) and two levels of reinforcement (contingent praise versus no praise) may be combined to produce four different combinations of the variables. It is extremely difficult and cumbersome to begin to investigate these different conditions in single-case methodology, in large part because of the difficulties of sequence and multiple-treatment interference effects.

The problems of studying interactions among variables are compounded when one is interested in studying several variables simultaneously and in studying interactions between subject variables (e.g., characteristics of the subjects, trainers) and interventions. In single-case research it is difficult to explore interactions of the interventions with other variables to ask questions about generality of intervention effects, i.e., the extent to which intervention effects extend across other variables.[5]

Between-group research can readily address interaction effects in designs (factorial designs) that simultaneously examine one or more independent variables. Also, the interactions of subject variables with intervention effects, especially important in relation to studying generality, can be readily investigated. The contribution of between-group research to the generality of experimental findings is taken up again in Chapter 11.

The above discussion does not exhaust the contributions of between-group research to questions of interest in applied research.[6] Between-group methodology does not always or necessarily conflict with single-case methodology. To be sure, there are important differences in between-group and single-case research that have been noted repeatedly, such as the focus on groups versus individuals, the use of statistics versus visual inspection to evaluate data, the use of one- or two-shot assessment versus continuous assessment over time, and so on (see Kazdin, 1980c; Sidman, 1960). However, many investigations

5. Some authors have suggested that interactions can be readily investigated in single-case research by looking at cases of several subjects who receive different combinations of the conditions of interest (Hersen and Barlow, 1976). Accumulating several subjects who receive different conditions is a partial attempt to approach separate groups of subjects as in between-group research. However, the result is unsatisfactory unless in the end the individual and combined effects of the different conditions can be separated from one another and from potential confounds. Apart from merely accumulating a sufficient number of cases to approximate between-group research, main effects and interactions need to be distinguished from multiple-treatment interference effects and unique subject characteristics, which in some way have to be evaluated separately from the experimental conditions of interest. Single-case research does not permit separation of these multiple influences in any straightforward way.

6. An important contribution of between-group research not detailed here pertains to the evaluation of "naturalistic interventions" that are not under the control of the experimenter. Between-group comparisons are exceedingly important to address questions about differences between or among groups that are distinguished on the basis of circumstances out of the experimenter's control. Such research can address such important applied questions as: Do certain sorts of lifestyles affect mortality? Does the consumption of cigarettes, alcohol, or coffee contribute to certain diseases? Do some family characteristics predispose children to psychiatric disorders? Does television viewing have an impact on children? Under conditions that require greater specification, the answer to each of the questions is yes.

obscure the usual boundaries of one type of research by including characteristics of both methodologies. The basic design features of between-group and single-case research can be combined. In a sense, between-group and single-case methodology, when used together, represent combined designs with unique advantages.

Illustrations

The contribution of between-group research to applied questions and the combination of between-group and single-case methodologies can be illustrated by examples from the applied literature. A frequent interest in applied research is the comparison of different interventions. In single-case design, the administration of two or more interventions to the same persons may yield ambiguous results because of the possibility of multiple-treatment interference. Between-group research can ameliorate this problem, because groups each receive only one treatment. Also, for the investigator interested in comparing the long-term effects of treatments, a between-group design usually represents the only viable option.

An excellent example of the contribution of between-group designs to applied research was provided in a study spanning several years that compared the effectiveness of alternative treatments for hospitalized psychiatric patients (Paul and Lentz, 1977). In this investigation, a social learning procedure was compared with milieu therapy and routine hospitalization. The main interest was in comparing the social learning procedure, which emphasized social and token reinforcement for adaptive behaviors in the hospital, with milieu therapy, which emphasized group processes and activities and staff expectations for patient improvements.

The treatments were implemented in separate psychiatric wards and were evaluated on multiple measures including direct behavioral assessment conducted on a continuous basis. The primary design was a between-group comparison with repeated assessment over time. Interestingly, during a portion of the design, baseline conditions were reinstated for a brief period to evaluate the impact of treatment. Among the many measures used to evaluate the program were daily recordings of specific discrete behaviors. Three categories of behaviors selected here for illustrative purposes include interpersonal skills (e.g., measures of social interaction, participation in meetings), instrumental role behavior (e.g., performing as expected in such areas as attending activities, working on a task in job training), and self-care skills (e.g., several behaviors related to appropriate personal appearance, meal behavior, bathing). The weekly summaries of these areas of performance over the course of the inves-

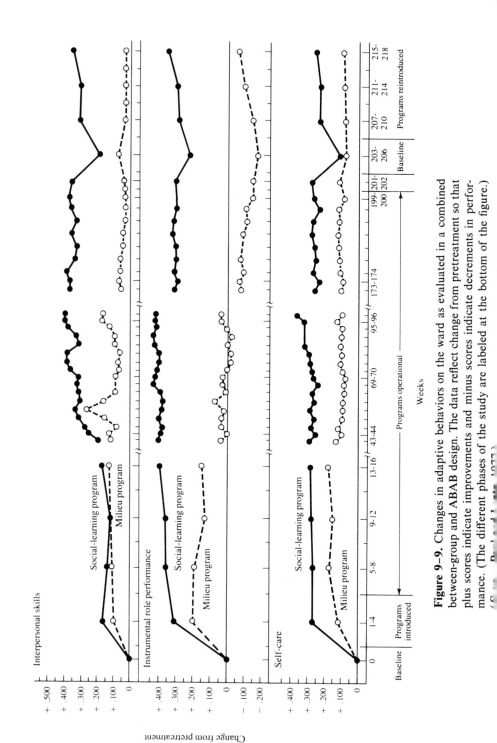

Figure 9–9. Changes in adaptive behaviors on the ward as evaluated in a combined between-group and ABAB design. The data reflect change from pretreatment so that plus scores indicate improvements and minus scores indicate decrements in performance. (The different phases of the study are labeled at the bottom of the figure.)

tigation are presented in Figure 9-9. In general, the results showed that the social learning program was superior to the milieu program. Although the return-to-baseline period (weeks 203 to 206) was brief and associated with a single assessment, performance tended to decrease for the social learning program during this period and improve when baseline was terminated.

The crucial feature of the Paul and Lentz (1977) investigation was the between-group comparison; the return-to-baseline phase was an ancillary part of the demonstration. The investigation points to the unique contribution of between-group research, because the effects of two treatments were compared over an extended period, indeed even beyond the period illustrated in the figure. When the investigator is interested in comparing the long-term effects of two or more treatments, all of the treatments cannot be given to the same subjects. Groups of subjects must receive one of the treatments and be assessed over time.

The above investigation illustrates large-scale outcome research over an extended period of time. Between-group methodology can contribute important information in smaller-scale studies, especially when combined with single-case methodology. One use of between-group methodology is to employ a no-treatment group to evaluate changes made over an extended period without intervening treatments. For example, in one investigation the effects of a reinforcement program were evaluated for increasing the punctuality of workers in an industrial setting (Hermann, de Montes, Dominguez, Montes, and Hopkins, 1973). Of twelve persons who were frequently tardy for work, six were assigned to a treatment group and the other six to a control group. The treatment group received slips of paper for coming to work on time, which were exchangeable for small monetary incentives at the end of a week. The control group received no treatment.

Figure 9-10 shows that the intervention was applied to the treatment group (lower panel) in an ABAB fashion and produced marked effects in reducing tardiness. The demonstration would have been quite sufficient with the treatment group alone, given the pattern of results over the different phases. However, the control condition provided additional information. Specifically, comparing treatment with control group levels of tardiness assessed the magnitude of improvement due to the intervention. The baseline phases alternated with the incentive condition for the treatment group would not necessarily show the level of tardiness that would have occurred if treatment had never been introduced. The control group provides a better estimate of the level of tardiness over time, which, interestingly enough, increased over the course of the project.

In another combination of between-group and single-case methodologies, a behavioral program was applied to alter the disruptive behaviors of a high

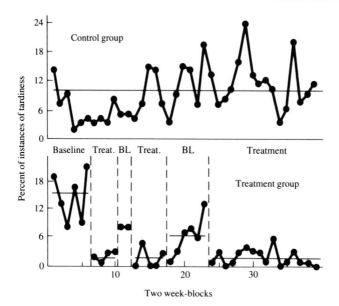

Figure 9–10. Tardiness of industrial workers. Control group—no intervention throughout the study. Treatment group—baseline (BL), in which no intervention was implemented and treatment, in which money was contingent upon punctuality. Horizontal lines represent the means for each condition. (*Source:* Hermann, de Montes, Dominguez, Montes, and Hopkins, 1973.)

school classroom (McAllister, Stachowiak, Baer, and Conderman, 1969). The program was introduced in a multiple-baseline design across two behaviors. The program consisted of providing praise for the appropriate behavior (e.g., remaining quiet) and disapproval for inappropriate behavior (e.g., turning around). A no-treatment control classroom similar in age, student IQ, and socioeconomic status was also observed over time.

The results of the program, plotted in Figure 9-11, show that inappropriate talking and turning around changed in the experimental classroom when and only when the intervention was introduced. The effects are relatively clear across the two baselines. The data become especially convincing when one examines the data from the control classroom that was observed but never received the program. This between-group feature shows clearly that the target behaviors would not have changed without the intervention. The control group provides convincing data about the stability of the behaviors over time without the intervention and adds to the clarity of the demonstration.

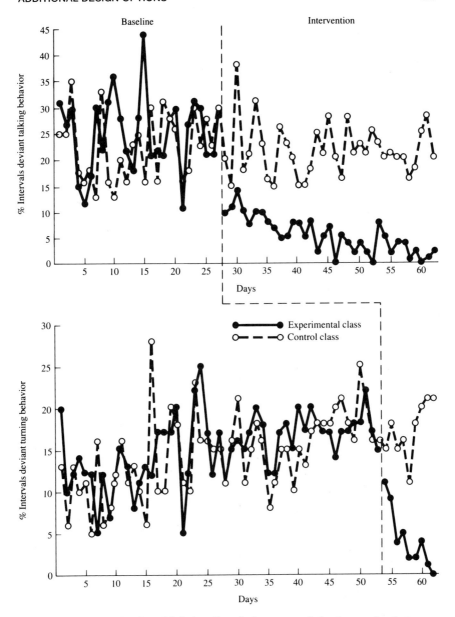

Figure 9–11. Combined multiple-baseline design across behaviors and a between-group design. The intervention was introduced to different behaviors of one class at different points in time. The intervention was never introduced to the control class. (*Source:* McAllister, Stachowiak, Baer, and Conderman, 1969.)

General Comments

Between-group designs are often criticized by proponents of single-case research. Conversely, advocates of between-group research rarely acknowledge that single-case research can make a contribution to science. Both positions are difficult to defend for several reasons. First, alternative design methodologies are differentially suited to different research questions. Between-group designs appear to be particularly appropriate for larger-scale investigations, for comparative studies, and for the evaluation of interaction effects (e.g., subject × intervention). Second, the effects of particular variables in experimentation occasionally depend on the manner in which they are studied. Hence, to understand the variables, it is important to evaluate their effects in different types of designs. Third, applied circumstances often make single-case designs the only possible option. For example, clinically rare problems might not be experimentally investigated if they were not investigated at the level of the single case (e.g., Barlow, Reynolds, and Agras, 1973; Rekers and Lovaas, 1974).

Overall, the issue of research is not a question of the superiority of one type of design over another. Different methodologies are means of addressing the overall goal, namely, understanding the influence of the variety of variables that affect behavior. Alternative design and data evaluation strategies are not in competition but rather address particular questions in service of the overall goal.

Summary and Conclusions

Although single-case designs are often implemented in the manner described in previous chapters, elements from different designs are frequently combined. *Combined designs* can increase the strength of the experimental demonstration. The use of combined designs may be planned in advance or decided on the basis of the emerging data. If the conditions of a particular design fail to be met or are not met convincingly, components from other designs may be introduced to reduce the ambiguity of the demonstration.

Apart from combined designs, special features may be added to existing designs to evaluate aspects of generality of intervention effects across responses, situations, and settings. *Probe assessment* was discussed as a valuable tool to explore generality across responses and settings. With probes, assessment is conducted for responses other than those included in training or for the target response in settings where training has not taken place. Periodically, assessment can provide information about the extent to which training effects extend to other areas of performance.

Withdrawal designs were discussed in the context of evaluating response maintenance. Withdrawal designs refer to different procedures in which components of the intervention are gradually withdrawn from a particular subject or behavior *(sequential withdrawal)* or across several subjects or behaviors *(partial withdrawal)*. The gradual withdrawal of components of the intervention provides a preview of the likelihood that behavior will be maintained after treatment is terminated.

Finally, the contribution of *between-group designs* to questions of applied research was discussed. Between-group designs alone and in concert with single-case designs can provide information that would not otherwise be readily obtained. Large-scale investigations of interventions, comparative outcome studies, and evaluation of interactions among intervention and subject variables are especially well suited to between-group designs. Features of between-group designs often are included in single-case research to provide information about the magnitude of change relative to a group that has not received the intervention.

In general, the present chapter discussed some of the complexities in combining alternative design strategies and adding elements from different methodologies to address applied questions. The combinations of various design strategies convey the diverse alternatives available in single-case research beyond the individual design variations discussed in previous chapters. Part of the strength of single-case research is the flexibility of designs available and the opportunities for improvisation based on the data during the investigation itself.

10
Data Evaluation

Previous chapters have discussed fundamental issues about assessment and design for single-case research. Discussions of assessment and alternative designs presented ways of measuring performance and of arranging the experiment so that one can infer a functional relationship between the intervention and behavior change. Assuming that the target behavior has been adequately assessed and the intervention was included in an appropriate experimental design, one important matter remains: evaluating the data that are obtained. Data evaluation consists of the methods used to draw conclusions about behavior change.

In applied investigations, experimental and therapeutic criteria are used to evaluate data (Risley, 1970). The *experimental criterion* refers to the ways in which data are evaluated to determine whether the intervention has had an effect. Evaluating whether an intervention had an effect is usually done by visually inspecting a graphic display of the data. Occasionally, statistical tests are used in place of visual inspection to evaluate the reliability of the findings.

The *therapeutic criterion* refers to whether the effects of the intervention are important or of clinical or applied significance. It is possible that experimentally reliable effects would be produced but that these effects would not have made an important change in the clients' lives. Applied research has dual requirements for data evaluation by invoking both experimental and applied criteria. This chapter details these criteria and how they are applied to single-case experimental data.[1]

Visual Inspection

The experimental criterion refers to a comparison of performance during the intervention with what it would be if the intervention had not been implemented. The criterion is not unqiue to single-case or applied research but is a characteristic of experimentation in general. The purpose of the experimental criterion is to decide whether a veridical change has been demonstrated and whether that change can be attributed to the intervention. In traditional between-group research, the experimental criterion is met primarily by comparing performance between or among groups and examining the differences statistically. Groups receive different conditions (e.g., treatment versus no treatment) and statistical tests are used to evaluate whether performance after treatment is sufficiently different to attain conventional levels of statistical significance. In single-case research, statistical tests are occasionally used to evaluate the data, although this practice remains the exception rather than the rule.

In single-case research, the experimental criterion is met by examining the effects of the intervention at different points over time. The effects of the intervention are replicated (reproduced) at different points so that a judgment can be made based on the overall pattern of data. The manner in which intervention effects are replicated depends on the specific design. The underlying rationale of each design, outlined in previous chapters, conveys the ways in which baseline performance is used to predict future performance, and subsequent applications of the intervention test whether the predicted level is violated. For example, in the ABAB design the intervention effect is replicated over time for a single subject or group of subjects. The effect of the intervention is clear when systematic changes in behavior occur during each phase in which the intervention is presented or withdrawn. Similarly, in a multiple-baseline design, the intervention effect is replicated across the dimension for which multiple-baseline data have been gathered. The experimental criterion is met by determining whether performance shifts at each point that the intervention is introduced.

The manner in which a decision is reached about whether the data pattern

1. The primary method of data evaluation for single-case research is based on visual inspection. Recently, use of statistical methods has increased. This chapter presents the underlying rationales, methods, and problems of these and other data evaluation procedures. Additional information, computational details, and examples of applications of visual inspection and statistical analyses are provided in Appendix A and B, respectively.

reflects a systematic intervention effect is referred to as *visual inspection*. Visual inspection refers to reaching a judgment about the reliability or consistency of intervention effects by visually examining the graphed data. Visual examination of the data would seem to be subject to a tremendous amount of bias and subjectivity. If data evaluation is based on visually examining the pattern of the data, intervention effects (like beauty) might be in the eyes of the beholder. To be sure, several problems can emerge with visual inspection, and these will be highlighted below. However, it is important to convey the underlying rationale of visual inspection and how the method is carried out.

Description and Underlying Rationale

In single-case research, data are graphically displayed over the course of baseline and intervention phases, as illustrated in the figures presented throughout the previous chapters. The data are plotted graphically to facilitate a judgment about whether the requirements of the design have been met, i.e., if the data show the pattern required to infer a causal relationship. (Appendix A discusses alternative ways of presenting data for visual inspection.)

Visual inspection can be used in part because of the sorts of intervention effects that are sought in applied research. The underlying rationale of the experimental and applied analysis of behavior is that investigators should seek variables that attain potent effects and that such effects should be obvious from merely inspecting the data (Baer, 1977; Michael, 1974; Sidman, 1960). Visual inspection is regarded as a relatively *un*refined and *in*sensitive criterion for deciding whether the intervention has produced a reliable change. The unsophisticated features of the method are regarded as a virtue. Because the criterion is somewhat crude, only those interventions that produce very marked effects will lead the scientific community to agree that the intervention produced a change. Weak results will not be regarded as meeting the stringent criteria of visual inspection. Hence, visual inspection will serve as a filter or screening device to allow only clear and potent interventions to be interpreted as producing reliable effects.

In traditional research, statistical evaluation is usually used to decide whether the data are reliable and whether a consistent effect has been achieved. Statistical evaluation often is more sensitive than visual inspection in detecting intervention effects. Intervention effects may be statistically significant even if they are relatively weak. The same effect might not be detected by visual inspection. The insensitivity of visual inspection for detecting weak effects has often been viewed as an advantage rather than a disadvantage because it encourages investigators to look for potent interventions or to develop weak interventions to the point that large effects are produced (Parsonson and Baer, 1978).

Criteria for Visual Inspection

The criteria used to decide whether intervention effects are consistent and reliable have rarely been made explicit (Parsonson and Baer, 1978). Part of the reason has been the frequent statement that the visual analysis depends on achieving very dramatic intervention effects. In cases where intervention effects are very strong, one need not carefully scrutinize or enumerate the criteria that underlie the judgment that the effects are veridical. Several situations arise in applied research in which intervention effects are likely to be so dramatic that visual inspection is easily invoked. For example, whenever the behavior of interest is not present in the client's behavior during the baseline phase (e.g., social interaction, exercise, reading) and increases to a very high rate during the intervention phase, a judgment about the effects of the intervention is easily made. Similarly, when the behavior of interest occurs frequently during the baseline phase (e.g., reports of hallucinations, aggressive acts, cigarette smoking) and stops completely during the intervention phase, the magnitude of change usually permits clear judgments based on visual inspection.

In cases in which behavior is at the opposite extremes of the assessment range before and during treatment, the ease of invoking visual inspection can be readily understood. For example, if the behavior never occurs during baseline, there is unparalleled stability in the data. Both the mean and standard deviation equal zero. Even a minor increase in the target behavior during the intervention phase would be easily detected. Of course, in most situations, the data do not show a change from one extreme of the assessment scale to the other, and the guidelines for making judgments by visual inspection need to be considered more deliberately.

Visual inspection depends on many characteristics of the data, but especially those that pertain to the magnitude of the changes across phases and the rate of these changes. The two characteristics related to magnitude are changes in *mean* and *level*. The two characteristics related to rate are changes in *trend* and *latency* of the change. It is important to examine each of these characteristics separately even though in any applied set of data they act in concert.

Changes in means across phases refer to shifts in the *average rate* of performance. Consistent changes in means across phases can serve as a basis for deciding whether the data pattern meets the requirements of the design. A hypothetical example showing changes in means across the intervention phase is illustrated in an ABAB design in Figure 10-1. As evident in the figure, per-

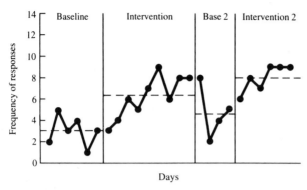

Figure 10–1. Hypothetical example of performance in an ABAB design with means in each phase represented with dashed lines.

formance on the average (horizontal dashed line in each phase) changed in response to the different baseline and intervention phases. Visual inspection of this pattern suggests that the intervention led to consistent changes.

Changes in level are a little less familiar but very important in allowing a decision through visual inspection as to whether the intervention produced reliable effects. Changes in level refer to the *shift or discontinuity of performance from the end of one phase to the beginning of the next phase.* A change in level is independent of the change in mean. When one asks about what happened immediately after the intervention was implemented or withdrawn, the implicit concern is over the level of performance. Figure 10-2 shows change in

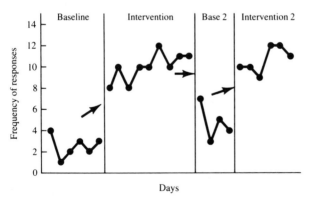

Figure 10–2. Hypothetical example of performance in an ABAB design. The arrows point to the changes in level or discontinuities associated with a change from one phase to another.

level across phases in ABAB design. The figure shows that whenever the phase was altered, behavior assumed a new rate, i.e., it shifted up or down rather quickly.

It so happens that a change in level in this latter example would also be accompanied by a change in mean across the phases. However, level and mean changes do not necessarily go together. It is possible that a rapid change in level occurs but that the mean remains the same across phase or that the mean changes but no abrupt shift in level has occurred.

Changes in trend are of obvious importance in applying visual inspection. Trend or slope refer to the tendency for the data to show systematic increases or decreases over time. The alteration of phases within the design may show that the direction of behavior changes as the intervention is applied or withdrawn. Figure 10-3 illustrates a hypothetical example in which trends have changed over the course of the phase in an ABAB design. The initial baseline trend is reversed by the intervention, reinstated when the intervention is withdrawn, and again reversed in the final phase. A change in trend would still be an important criterion even if there were no trend in baseline. A change from no trend (horizontal line) during baseline to a trend (increase or decrease in behavior) during the intervention phase would also constitute a change in trend.

Finally, the *latency of the change* that occurs when phases are altered is an important characteristic of the data for invoking visual inspection. Latency

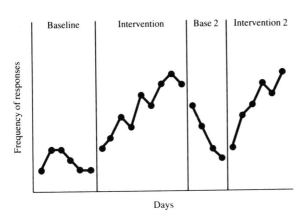

Figure 10–3. Hypothetical example of performance in an ABAB design with changes in trend across phases. Baseline shows a relatively stable or possibly decreasing trend. When the intervention is introduced, an accelerating trend is evident. This trend is reversed when the intervention is withdrawn (Base 2) and is reinstated when the intervention is reintroduced.

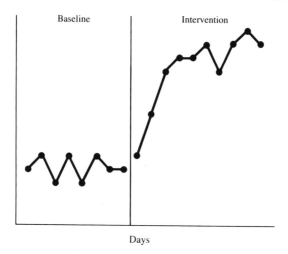

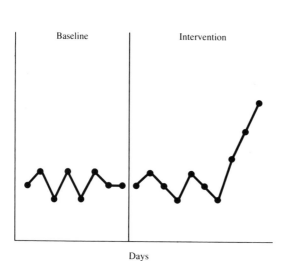

Figure 10–4. Hypothetical examples of first AB phases as part of larger ABAB designs. *Upper panel* shows that when the intervention was introduced, behavior changed rapidly. *Lower panel* shows that when the intervention was introduced, behavior change was delayed. The changes in both upper and lower panels are reasonably clear. Yet as a general rule, as the latency between the onset of the intervention and behavior change increases, questions are more likely to arise about whether the intervention or extraneous factors accounted for change.

refers to the period between the onset or termination of one condition (e.g., intervention, return to baseline) and changes in performance. The more closely in time that the change occurs after the experimental conditions have been altered, the clearer the intervention effect. A hypothetical example is provided in Figure 10-4, showing only the first two phases of separate ABAB designs. In the top panel, implementation of the intervention after baseline was associated with a rapid change in performance. The change would also be evident from changes in mean and trend. In the bottom panel, the intervention did not immediately lead to change. The time between the onset of the intervention and behavior change was longer than in the top panel, and it is slightly less clear that the intervention may have led to the change.[2]

Changes in means, levels, and trends, and variations in the latency of change across phases frequently accompany each other. Yet they are separate characteristics of the data and can occur alone or in combination.[3] Visual inspection is conducted by judging the extent to which changes in these characteristics are evident across phases and whether the changes are consistent with the requirements of the particular design.

Changes in the means, levels, and trends across phases are not the only dimensions that are invoked for visual inspection. There are many other factors, which might be called background characteristics, upon which visual inspection heavily depends. Whether a particular effect will be considered reliable through visual inspection depends on the variability of performance within a particular phase, the duration of the phase, and the consistency of the effect across phases or baselines, depending on the particular design. Other factors, such as the reliability of the assessment data, may also be relevant, because this information specifies the extent to which fluctuations in the data may be due to unreliable recording (e.g., Birkimer and Brown, 1979b). Data that present minimal variability, show consistent patterns over relatively extended phases, show that the changes in means, levels, or trends are replic-

2. As a general rule, the shorter the period between the onset of the intervention and behavior change, the easier it is to infer that the intervention led to change. The rationale is that as the time between the intervention and behavior increases, the more likely that intervening influences may have accounted for behavior change. Of course, the importance of the latency of the change after the onset of the intervention depends on the type of intervention and behavior studied. For example, one would not expect rapid changes in applying behavioral procedures to treat obesity. Weight reduction usually reflects gradual changes after treatment begins. Similarly, some medications do not produce rapid effects. Change depends on the buildup of therapeutic doses.

3. Data patterns that can be generated on the basis of changes in means, levels, and trend can be relatively complex. For further discussion, the reader is referred elsewhere (Glass, Willson, and Gottman, 1975; Jones et al., 1977; Kazdin, 1976; Parsonson and Baer, 1978).

able across phases for a given subject or across several subjects, are more easily interpreted than data in which one or more of these characteristics are not obtained.

In practice, changes in mean, level, and trend, and latency of change go together, thereby making visual inspection more easy to invoke than one might expect. For example, data across phases may not overlap. *Nonoverlapping data* refers to the finding that the values of the data points during the baseline phase do not approach any of the values of the data points attained during the intervention phase.

As an illustration, consider the results of a program designed to reduce the thumbsucking of a nine-year-old boy who suffered both dental and speech impairments related to excessive thumbsucking (Ross, 1975). A relatively simple intervention was implemented, namely, turning off the TV when he sucked his thumb while watching, and this intervention was evaluated in an ABAB design. As shown in Figure 10-5, the effects of the intervention were quite strong. The data do not overlap from one phase to another. In terms of specific characteristics of the data that are relied on for visual inspection, several statements could be made. First of all, the data across phases are characterized by dramatic shifts in *level*. Any time the phase was introduced, there was an abrupt discontinuity or shift in the data. The magnitude of the shift is important for concluding that the intervention led to change. Also, the *latency* of the shift in performance, another important characteristic of the data, facilitates drawing conclusions about the data. The changes occurred immediately after the A or B conditions were changed. Some changes in *trend* are evident. The

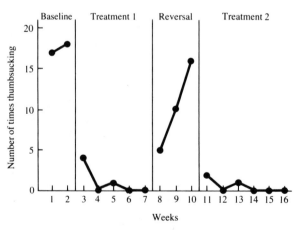

Figure 10–5. Thumbsucking frequency during television viewing (21 observations/ week). (*Source:* Ross, 1975.)

baseline phase suggests an increasing trend (increasing frequency of thumb-sucking), although too few data points are included to be confident of a consistent trend. In the reversal phase, there also seems to be a trend toward the baseline level. The trends in baseline and reversal phases, although tentative, are quite different from the trends in the two intervention phases. Finally, and most obviously, the *means,* if plotted for each phase, would show changes from phase to phase. Overall, each criterion discussed earlier can be applied to these data and in combination make obvious the strength of the intervention effect.

It is important to note that invoking the criteria for visual inspection requires judgments about the pattern of data in the entire design and not merely changes across one or two phases. Unambiguous effects require that the criteria mentioned above be met throughout the design. To the extent that the criteria are not consistently met, conclusions about the reliability of intervention effects become tentative. For example, changes in an ABAB design may show non-overlapping data points for the first AB phases but no clear differences across the second AB phases. The absence of a consistent pattern of data that meets the criteria mentioned above limits the conclusions that can be drawn.

Problems and Considerations

Visual inspection has been quite useful in identifying reliable intervention effects both in experimental and applied research. When intervention effects are potent, the need for statistical analysis is obviated. Intervention effects can be extremely clear from graphic displays of the data in which persons can judge for themselves whether the criteria discussed above have been met.

The use of visual inspection as the primary basis for evaluating data in single-case designs has raised major concerns. Perhaps the major issue pertains to the lack of concrete decision rules for determining whether a particular demonstration shows or fails to show a reliable effect. The process of visual inspection would seem to permit, if not actively encourage, subjectivity and inconsistency in the evaluation of intervention effects. In fact, a few studies have examined the extent to which persons consistently judge through visual inspection whether a particular intervention demonstrated an effect (DeProspero and Cohen, 1979; Gottman and Glass, 1978; Jones, Weinrott, and Vaught, 1978). The results have shown that judges, even when experts in the field, often disagree about particular data patterns and whether the effects were reliable.

One of the difficulties of visual inspection is that the full range of factors that contribute to judgments about the data and the manner in which these factors are integrated for a decision are unclear. DeProspero and Cohen (1979) found that the extent of agreement among judges using visual inspection was a complex function of changes in means, levels, and trends as well as the various background variables mentioned earlier, such as variability, stability, and replication of effects within or across subjects. All of these criteria, and perhaps others yet to be made explicit, are combined to reach a final judgment about the effects of the intervention. In cases in which the effects of the intervention are not dramatic, it is no surprise that judges disagree. The disagreement among judges using visual inspection has been used as an argument to favor statistical analysis of the data as a supplement to or replacement of visual inspection. The attractive feature of statistical analysis is that once the statistic is decided, the result that is achieved is usually consistent across investigators. And the final result (statistical significance) is not altered by the judgment of the investigator.

Another criticism levied against visual inspection is that it regards as significant only those effects that are very marked. Many interventions might prove to be consistent in the effects they produce but are relatively weak. Such effects might not be detected by visual inspection and would be overlooked. As noted by Baer (1977), to develop a technology of behavior change, it is important to select as significant those variables that consistently produce effects. Variables that pass the stringent criteria of visual inspection are likely to be powerful and consistent.

Overlooking weak but reliable effects can have unfortunate consequences. The possibility exists that interventions when first developed may have weak effects. It would be unfortunate if these interventions were prematurely discarded before they could be developed further. Interventions with reliable but weak effects might eventually achieve potent effects if investigators developed them further. Insofar as the stringent criteria of visual inspection discourage the pursuit of interventions that do not have potent effects, it may be a detriment to developing a technology of behavior change. On the other hand, the stringent criteria may encourage investigators to develop interventions to the point that they do produce marked changes before making claims about their demonstrated efficacy.

A final problem with visual inspection is that it requires a particular pattern of data in baseline and subsequent phases so that the results can be interpreted. Visual inspection criteria are more readily invoked when data show little or no trend or trend in directions opposite from the trend expected in the following phase and slight variability. However, trends and variability in the data may not always meet the idealized data requirements. In such cases visual inspection may be difficult to invoke. Other criteria, such as statistical analyses, may be of use in these situations.

Statistical Evaluation

Visual inspection constitues the criterion used most frequently to evaluate data from single-case experiments. The reason for this pertains to the historical development of the designs and the larger methodological approach of which they are a part, namely, the experimental analysis of behavior (Kazdin, 1978c). Systematic investigation of the single subject began in laboratory research with infrahuman subjects. The careful control afforded by laboratory conditions helped to meet major requirements of the design, including minimal variability and stable rates of performance. Potent variables were examined (e.g., schedules of reinforcement) with effects that could be easily detected against the highly stable baseline levels. The lawfulness and regularity of behavior in relation to selected variables obviated the need for statistical tests.

As the single-case experimental approach was extended to human behavior, applications began to encompass a variety of populations, behaviors, and settings. The need to investigate and identify potent variables has not changed. However, the complexity of the situations in which applied investigations are conducted occasionally has made evaluations of intervention effects more difficult. Control over and standardization of the assessment of responses, extraneous factors that can influence performance, and characteristics of the organisms (humans) themselves are reduced, compared with laboratory conditions. Hence, the potential sources of variation that may make interventions more difficult to evaluate are increased in applied research. In selected situations, the criteria for invoking visual inspection are not met, and alternative analyses have been proposed.

Recently, statistical analyses for single-case data have received increased attention. Statistical analyses have been proposed as a supplement to or replacement of visual inspection to permit inferences about the reliability or consistency of the changes. Statistical tests for single-case research have been associated with two major sources of controversy. First, several authors have debated whether statistical tests should be used at all (see Baer, 1977; Michael, 1974). The major objection is that statistical tests are likely to detect subtle and minor changes in performance and to identify as significant the effects of variables that ordinarily would be rejected through visual inspection. If the goal of applied research is to identify potent variables, a more stringent criterion than statistical analysis, namely visual inspection, is needed.[4] A related

---

4. Baer (1977) has noted that statistical analyses and visual inspection are not fundamentally different with respect to their underlying rationale. Both methods of data evaluation attempt to avoid committing what have been referred to in statistics as Type 1 and Type 2 errors.

objection is that statistically significant effects may not be of applied or clinical importance. Statistical analyses may detract from the goals of single-case research, namely, to discover variables that not only produce reliable effects but also result in therapeutically important outcomes.

The second source of controversy over the use of statistical analyses pertains to specific types of analyses and whether they are appropriate for single-case research. Development of statistical tests for single-case research has lagged behind development of analyses for between-group research. Various analyses that have been suggested are controversial because data from single-case research occasionally violate some of the assumptions on which various statistical tests depend. Hence, debate and controversy over particular tests have occupied much of the literature (see Hartmann, 1974; Kazdin, 1976; Kratochwill et al., 1974).

Reasons for Using Statistical Tests

The use of statistical analyses for single-case data has been suggested primarily to supplement rather than to replace visual inspection. When the data meet the criteria for visual inspection outlined earlier, there is little need to corroborate the results with statistical tests. In many situations, however, the ideal data patterns may not emerge, and statistical tests may provide important advantages. Consider a few of the circumstances in which statistical analyses may be especially valuable.

Unstable Baselines. Visual inspection depends on having stable baseline phases in which no trend in the direction of the expected change is evident. Evaluation of intervention effects is extremely difficult when baseline performance is sys-

---

Type 1 error refers to concluding that the intervention (or variable) produced a veridical effect when, in fact, the results are attributed to chance. Type 2 error refers to concluding that the intervention did *not* produce a veridical effect when, in fact, it did. Researchers typically give higher priority to avoiding a Type 1 error, concluding that a variable has an effect when the findings may have occurred by chance. In statistical analyses the probability of committing a Type 1 error can be specified (by the level of confidence of the statistical test or α). With visual inspection, the probability of a Type 1 error is not known. Hence, to avoid chance effects, the investigator looks for highly consistent effects that can be readily seen. By minimizing the probability of a Type 1 error, the probability of a Type 2 error is increased. Investigators relying on visual inspection are more likely to commit more Type 2 errors than are those relying on statistical analyses. Thus, reliance on visual inspection will overlook or discount many reliable but weak effects. From the standpoint of developing an effective technology of behavior change, Baer (1977) has argued that minimizing Type 1 errors will lead to identification of a few variables whose effects are consistent and potent across a wide range of conditions.

tematically improving. In this case, the intervention may be needed to accelerate the rate of improvement. For example, the self-destructive behavior of an autistic child might be decreasing gradually, but an intervention might still be necessary to speed up the process. Visual inspection may be difficult to apply with initial improvements during baseline. On the other hand, statistical analyses (mentioned later in the chapter) allow for evaluation of the intervention by taking into account this initial trend in baseline. Statistical analyses can examine whether a reliable intervention effect has occurred over and above what would be expected by continuation of the initial trend. Hence, statistical analyses can provide information that may be difficult to obtain through inspection.

Investigation of New Research Areas. Applied research has stressed the need to investigate interventions that produce marked effects on behavior. Visual inspection is easily applied when behavior changes are large and consistent across phases. In many instances, especially in new areas of research, intervention effects may be relatively weak. The investigator working in a new area is likely to be unfamiliar with the intervention and the conditions that maximize its efficacy. Consequently, the effects may be relatively weak. As the investigator learns more about the intervention, he or she can change the procedure to improve its efficacy.

In the initial stages of research, it may be important to identify promising interventions that warrant further scrutiny. Visual inspection may be too stringent a criterion that would reject interventions that produce reliable but weak effects. Such interventions should not be abandoned because they do not achieve large changes initially. These interventions may be developed further through subsequent research and eventually produce large effects that could be detected through visual inspection. Even if such variables would not eventually produce strong effects in their own right, they may be important because they can enhance or contribute to the effectiveness of other procedures. Hence, statistical analyses may serve a useful purpose in identifying variables that warrant further investigation.

Increased Intrasubject Variability. Single-case experimental designs have been used in a variety of applied settings such as psychiatric hospitals, institutions for mentally retarded persons, classrooms, day-care centers, and others. In such settings, investigators have frequently been able to control several features of the environment, including behavior of the staff and events occurring during the day other than the intervention, that may influence performance and implementation of the intervention. For example, in a classroom study, the investigator may carefully monitor the intervention so that it is implemented with little or no variation over time. Also, teacher interactions with the children may be carefully monitored and controlled. Students may receive the same or similar tasks while the observations are in effect. Because extraneous factors are held relatively constant for purposes of experimental control, variability in subject performance can be held to a minimum. As noted earlier, visual inspection is more easily applied to single-case data when variability is small. Hence, the careful experimental control over interventions in applied settings has facilitated the use of visual inspection.

Over the years, single-case research has been extended to several community or open field settings where such behaviors as littering, energy consumption, use of public transportation, and recycling of wastes have been altered (Glenwick and Jason, 1980; Kazdin, 1977c; Martin and Osborne, 1980). In such cases, control over the environment and potential influences on behavior are reduced and variability in subject performance may be relatively large. With larger variability, visual inspection may be more difficult to apply than in well-controlled settings. Statistical evaluation may be of greater use in examining whether reliable changes have been obtained.

Small Changes May Be Important. The rationale underlying visual inspection has been the search for large changes in the performance of individual subjects. Over the years, single-case designs and the interventions typically evaluated by these designs have been extended to a wide range of problems. For selected problems, it is not always the case that the merit of the intervention effects can be evaluated on the basis of the magnitude of change in an individual subject's performance. Small changes in the behavior of individual subjects or in the behaviors of large groups of subjects often are very important. For example, interventions have been applied to reduce crime in selected communities (e.g., Schnelle et al., 1975, 1978). In such applications, the intervention may not need to produce large changes to make an important contribution. Small but reliable changes may be very noteworthy given the significance of the focus. For instance, a small reduction in violent crimes (e.g., murder, rape) in a community would be important. Visual inspection may not detect small changes that are reliable. Statistical analyses may help determine whether the intervention had a reliable, even though undramatic, effect on behavior.

Similarly, in many "single-case" designs, several persons are investigated and large changes in any individual person's behavior may not be crucial for the success of the intervention. For example, an intervention designed to reduce energy consumption (e.g., use of one's personal car) may show relatively weak effects on the behavior of individual subjects. The results may not be dramatic by visual inspection criteria. However, small changes, when accrued over several different persons and an extended period of time, may be very important. This is another instance in which small changes in individual performance may be important because of the larger changes these would signal for an entire group. To the extent that statistical analyses can contribute to data evaluation in these circumstances, they may provide an important contribution.

Tests for Single-Case Research

Statistical tests for single-case research have been applied with increased frequency over the last several years, although their use still remains the exception rather than the rule. Several tests are available, but because of their infrequent use, they remain somewhat esoteric. The different tests are quite diverse in their assumptions, applicability to various designs, computations, and the demands they place on the investigator.

Several of the available statistical tests are listed in Table 10-1, along with their general characteristics. The present discussion highlights some of these tests, their uses, and issues that they raise for single-case experimentation. (The actual details of the tests and their underlying rationale and computation are too complex to include here. Examples of the alternative statistical tests and their application to single-case data are provided in Appendix B.)

Conventional t *and* F *Tests.* The need for special or esoteric statistics for single-case research is not immediately apparent from the designs. In each of the designs, two or more phases are compared to evaluate whether changes are statistically significant. For example, in an ABAB design, comparisons are made over baseline (A) and intervention (B) phases. An obvious test that would seem to be suitable would be a simple *t* test comparing changes from A to B phases, or an analysis of variance comparing ABAB phases. As noted in Table 10-1, these tests would compare whether differences in means are statistically reliable between, or among, the different phases. The advantage of *t* and *F* tests is that they are widely familiar to investigators whose training has been primarily with between-group research designs.

When several subjects exist in one or more groups, such tests (correlated *t* tests or repeated measures analysis of variance) can be performed. For single-case data, *t* and *F* tests may be inappropriate because a critical assumption of these tests is violated. In time-series data for a single subject, adjacent data points over time are often correlated. That is, data on day one are likely to predict data on day two; day two may predict day three, and so on. When the data are significantly correlated, the data are said to be *serially dependent*.

Table 10-1. Overview of selected statistics for single-case experimental designs

Test	Especially suited for	Test evaluates	How accomplished	Special requirements	Key references
t and *F*	Detecting change from one phase to another in which data for a single subject do not show serial dependency; ABAB, multiple-baseline and other designs in which separate phases can be identified.	Whether there is a significant change in mean from one phase to the next.	Conventional *t* and *F* tests are applied to the data.	Observations in separate phases, equal number of observations if data will be matched in some ways across phases to make comparisons. Evidence should be included that serial dependency does not exist before proceeding with the analysis.	Jones et al. (1977) Kratochwill et al. (1977)
Time-series analysis	Detecting change from one phase to another in which the data for a single subject show serial dependency.	Whether there is a significant change in level and/or trend between the adjacent phases.	Separate *t* tests are computed for changes in level and trend; the *t* tests take into account the degree of serial dependency, as reflected in autocorrelation.	Several data points or observations (e.g., 50) are recommended to determine the precise time-series analysis model that fits the data. The exact number of data points is a matter of debate (see text). Moreover, the consequences of departing from large numbers of data points are not well studied.	Glass et al. (1975) Hartmann et al. (1980) Jones et al. (1977)
Randomization tests	Situations in which treatment can be implemented and withdrawn repeatedly over the course of the design; ABAB designs in which A and B phases are alternated frequently (e.g., every day, few days, or week).	Whether performance under one of the conditions (e.g., B days) departs from performance under the other condition with which it is compared (e.g., A days).	The probability of obtaining a difference between the two or more conditions as large as the one obtained is computed. The probability is the proportion of the possible combinations of the data that would be as likely to provide a difference as large or larger than the one obtained.	Experimental conditions must be randomly assigned to occasions over time, usually on a daily or weekly basis; which condition will be in effect at any particular point must be assigned randomly.	Edgington (1969, 1980)

R_a test of rank	Multiple-baseline designs in which the influence of the intervention on different behaviors, persons, or situations is examined.	Whether performance changes at each point that the intervention is introduced relative to baselines that have yet to receive the intervention.	Each baseline (e.g., behavior) serves as an AB experiment. All baselines are ranked in terms of the magnitude of the behavior at each point that the intervention is introduced to a new baseline. The ranks refer to the position of the behavior that has received the intervention relative to the others that have not. If implementation of the intervention is associated with behavior change, the sum of ranks of the different baselines should reflect this change.	The underlying rationale of the test depends on applying the intervention to the different baselines in a random order. Also, a minimum requirement to detect a significant difference at the $p < .05$ level is 4 baselines (e.g., behaviors).	Kazdin (1976) Revusky (1967)
Split-middle technique	Examining trends in two or more phases as in ABAB, multiple-baseline, or other designs.	The rate of change in behavior over the course of different phases is examined by plotting linear trend lines that best fit the data.	A line is plotted that divides or "splits" the data at the median level in each phase. This line expresses the rate of change over the course of the phase. The technique is usually advocated as a method to describe data across phases. Statistical evaluation has been recommended by projecting the linear trend line of baseline into the intervention phase. A binomial test is applied to see whether the number of data points in the intervention phase fall above (or below) the projected line of the baseline.	Several observations are needed in two or more separate phases to compute trends. Observations should be equally spaced intervals in each phase.	White (1972, 1974)

Note: Details regarding the application of these tests for single-case data are provided in Appendix B.

One of the assumptions of t and F tests is that the data points are independent (i.e., have uncorrelated error terms). When serial dependency exists, the independence-of-error assumption is violated, and t and F tests do not follow the distribution from which statistical inferences are usually made.

General agreement exists that the use of conventional t and F tests is inappropriate if *serial dependency* exists in the data for a single subject. Serial dependency is measured by evaluating whether the data are correlated over time. The correlation is computed by pairing adjacent data points (days one and two, days two and three, days three and four, etc.), and computing a correlation coefficient. The correlation is referred to as *autocorrelation* and is a measure of serial dependency.[5] If serial dependency exists, conventional t and F tests should not be applied.

The extent to which single-case data show serial dependency is not entirely clear. Some investigators have suggested that dependency is relatively common (e.g., Jones et al., 1978); others have suggested that it is infrequent (e.g., Kennedy, 1976). The discrepancy has resulted in part from disagreements about the precise way in which autocorrelations are computed and, specifically, whether data from different phases (e.g., baseline, intervention) should be combined or treated separately in deriving autocorrelations. Other analyses than conventional t and F tests have increased in use because of the problem of serial dependency for single-case designs. The most popular alternative test is time-series analysis, which is discussed briefly below (see also Appendix B).

Time-Series Analysis. Time-series analysis is a statistical method that compares data over time for separate phases for an individual subject or group of subjects (see Glass et al., 1975; Hartmann et al., 1980; Jones et al., 1977). The analysis can be used in single-case designs in which the purpose is to compare alternative phases such as baseline and intervention phases. The test examines whether there is a statistically significant change in level and trend from one phase to the next. As noted in the discussion of visual inspection, a change in level refers to any discontinuity in the data at the point that the intervention is introduced. A change in trend refers to whether there is a difference in the rate of increase or decrease from one phase to the next. Figure 10-6 illustrates how changes in level and trend might appear graphically in a few data patterns (see Jones et al., 1977; Kazdin, 1976).

---

5. As a measure of serial dependency, the autocorrelation is suitable as discussed here. However, serial dependency is more complex than the simple correlation of adjacent data points. For a more extended discussion of serial dependency and autocorrelations, other sources should be consulted (Glass et al., 1975; Gottman and Glass, 1978; Hartmann, Gottman, Jones, Gardner, Kazdin, and Vaught, 1980; Kazdin, 1976).

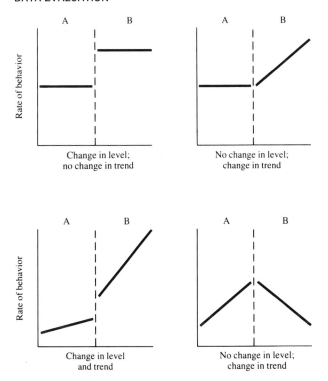

Figure 10-6. Examples of selected patterns of data over two (AB) phases illustrating changes in level and/or trend.

In time-series analysis, separate t tests are computed to evaluate changes in level and trend. The statistic is provided between AB phases to determine whether level and/or trend have changed significantly. The actual statistical analysis is not a simple formula that can be easily applied in a cookbook fashion. Several variations of time-series analysis exist that depend on various features of the data. Time-series analysis can be applied to any single-case design in which there is a change in conditions across phases. For example, in ABAB designs, separate comparisons can be made for each set of adjacent phases (e.g., A_1B_1, A_2B_2, B_1A_2). In multiple-baseline designs, baseline (A) and treatment (B) phases may be implemented across different responses, persons, or situations. Time-series can evaluate each of the baselines to assess whether there is a change in level or trend. Several investigations using single-case designs have reported the use of time-series analysis (e.g., McSweeney, 1978; Schnelle et al., 1975).

The analysis does make some demands on the investigator that may dictate the utility of the statistic in any particular instance. To begin with, the design depends on having a sufficient number of data points. The data points are needed to determine the existence and pattern of serial dependency in the data and to derive the appropriate time-series analysis model for the data. The actual number of data points needed within each phase has been debated, and estimates have ranged from 20 through 100 (e.g., Box and Jenkins, 1970; Glass et al., 1975; Hartmann et al., 1980; Jones et al., 1977). In many single-case experiments, phases are relatively brief. For example, in an ABAB design, the second A phases may be relatively brief because of the problems associated with returning behavior to baseline levels. Similarly, in a multiple-baseline design, the initial baseline phases for some of the behaviors may be brief so that the intervention will not be withheld for a very long time. In these instances, too few data points may be available to apply time-series analysis.

Time-series analysis is especially useful when the idealized data requirements suited for visual inspection are not met. When there is a trend in the therapeutic direction in baseline, when variability is large, or when treatment effects are neither rapid nor marked, time-series analysis may be especially useful. Also, the analysis is especially useful when the investigator is interested in drawing conclusions about changes in either level or trend rather than changes in overall means. The analysis provides evaluations of these separate features of the data that might not be easily detected through visual inspection or conventional comparisons of means across phases.

General Comments. Several statistical analyses are available beyond conventional *t* and *F* tests and time-series analyses, highlighted above. Table 10-1 previously illustrated some of the more frequently discussed options, including ranking test, randomization tests, and split-middle technique. The tests vary considerably in the manner in which they are applied and the demands they place on the investigator. As noted earlier, the tests and their application to single-case data are illustrated in Appendix B.

Problems and Considerations

Statistical analyses can add to the evaluation of single-case data, particularly in circumstances in which the criteria for visual inspection are not met. In evaluating the utility of statistical analyses, several issues need to be borne in mind. Perhaps the most important pertains to the demands that the statistical tests may place on the investigator.

Single-case experimental designs place various constraints on the intervention and its implementation. Treatment may need to be withdrawn (e.g.,

ABAB design) or temporarily withheld (e.g., from behaviors or persons in a multiple-baseline design). The constraints placed on the investigator may be increased by attempting to structure the design so that selected statistical tests can be applied. Depending on the specific statistical test used, the investigator may have to vary aspects of treatment that compete with clinical or design priorities.

For example, time-series analysis requires several data points during baseline and intervention phases. Conducting protracted baseline or reversal phases to meet the requirements of time-series analysis can raise many problems. In other statistical analyses, the intervention needs to be introduced across different baselines of a multiple-baseline design in a random order (e.g., R_n) or treatment and no-treatment phases need to be alternated on a daily or weekly basis (e.g., randomization tests). Yet a variety of considerations often make these arrangements impractical. For example, the intervention may need to be applied to baselines as a function of the severity of the behaviors and persons in the design or for the convenience of the staff. Also, treatments cannot be alternated randomly across occasions because of the exigencies of implementing treatments in applied settings. In general, the demands placed on the investigator may be increased by the use of various statistical tests. In any given instance, one must evaluate whether use of the tests would compete with clinical or design considerations.

Another consideration pertains to the relationship of experimental design and statistical tests for single-case research. Statistical tests provide an important tool for evaluating whether changes in a particular demonstration are likely to be accounted for by chance. Statistical significance provides evidence that the change in behavior is reliable, but it does not provide information about what may have accounted for the change. For example, a time-series analysis could be applied to an AB design and could show a significant change. However, the design requirements would not argue strongly that the intervention rather than extraneous factors accounted for change. Hence, it is important to bear in mind that the use of statistical analyses does not gainsay the importance of the experimental designs discussed earlier.

Clinical or Applied Significance of Behavior Change

The nonstatistical and statistical data evaluation methods address the experimental criterion for single-case research. Both general methods consider whether the changes in performance are reliable and consistent with the requirements of the particular experimental design. As noted earlier, a therapeutic or applied criterion is also invoked to evaluate the intervention. This criterion refers to the clinical or applied significance of the changes in behavior or whether the intervention makes a difference in the everyday functioning of the client (Risley, 1970). Clinically significant changes refer to concerns about the magnitude of intervention effects.

In many instances, the criterion for deciding whether a clinically significant change has been achieved may be obvious. For example, an intervention may be applied to decrease an autistic child's self-destructive behavior, such as head-banging. Baseline observations may reveal an average of 100 instances of head-banging per hour. The intervention may reduce this to fifty instances per hour. Although this effect may be replicated over time and may meet visual inspection and statistical criteria, the intervention has not satisfied the therapeutic criterion. The change may be clear but not clinically important. Self-injurious behavior should probably be considered maladaptive if it occurs at all. Thus, without a virtual or complete elimination of self-injurious behavior, the clinical value of the treatment may be challenged. Essentially complete elimination would probably be needed to produce a clinically important change.

The ease of evaluating the importance of clinical change in the above example stems from the fact that self-destructive behavior is maladaptive whenever it occurs. For most behaviors focused on in applied research, the overall rate rather than its presence or absence dictates whether it is socially acceptable. This makes evaluation of the clinical significance of intervention effects more difficult. Other criteria must be invoked to decide whether the magnitude of change is important.

Social Validation

Until recently, the way in which the therapeutic criterion could be met has been unspecified in applied research. General statements that the changes in behavior should make a difference provide no clear guidelines for judging intervention effects. Recently, Wolf (1978) has introduced the notion of *social validation,* which encompasses ways of evaluating whether intervention effects produce changes of clinical or applied importance. Social validation refers generally to consideration of social criteria for evaluating the focus of treatment, the procedures that are used, and the effects that these treatments have on performance. For present purposes, the features related to evaluating the outcomes of treatment are especially relevant.

The social validation of intervention effects can be accomplished in two ways, which have been referred to as the social comparison and subjective evaluation methods (Kazdin, 1977b). With the *social comparison* method, the behavior of the client before and after treatment is compared with the behavior of nondeviant ("normal") peers. The question asked by this comparison is whether the client's behavior after treatment is distinguishable from the behavior of his or her peers who are functioning adequately in the environment. Presumably, if the client's behavior warrants treatment, that behavior should initially deviate from "normal" levels of performance. If treatment produces a clinically important change, at least with many clinical problems, the client's behavior should be brought within normative levels. With the *subjective evaluation* method, the client's behavior is evaluated by persons who are likely to have contact with him or her in everyday life and who evaluate whether distinct improvements in performance can be seen. The question addressed by this method is whether behavior changes have led to qualitative differences in how the client is viewed by others.[6]

Social Comparison. The essential feature of social comparison is to identify the client's peers, i.e., persons who are similar to the client in such variables as age, gender and socioeconomic class, but who differ in performance of the target behavior. The peer group should be identified as persons who are functioning adequately and hence whose behaviors do not warrant intervention. Presumably, a clinically important change would be evident if the intervention brought the clients to within the level of their peers whose behaviors are considered to be adequate.

For example, O'Brien and Azrin (1972) developed appropriate eating behaviors among hospitalized mentally retarded persons who seldom used utensils, constantly spilled food on themselves, stole food from others, and ate food previously spilled on the floor. The intervention consisted of the use of prompts, praise, and food reinforcement for appropriate eating behaviors. Although training increased appropriate eating behaviors, one can still ask whether the improvements really were very important and whether resident behavior approached the eating skills of persons who are regarded as "normal." To address these questions, the investigators compared the group that received training with the eating habits of "normals." Customers in a local restaurant were watched by observers, who recorded their eating behavior. Their level of inappropriate eating behaviors is illustrated by the dashed line in Figure 10-7. As evident in the figure, after training, the level of inappropriate mealtime

---

6. As the reader may recall, social comparison and subject evaluation were introduced earlier (Chapter 2) as a means for identifying the appropriate target focus. The methods represent different points in the assessment process, namely, to help identify what the important behaviors are for a person's adequate social functioning and to evaluate whether the amount of change in those behaviors is sufficient to achieve the desired end.

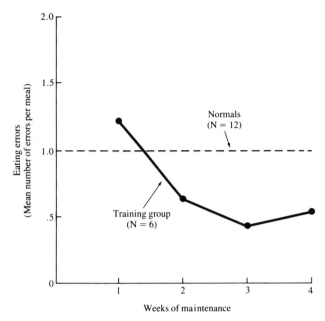

Figure 10-7. The mean number of improper responses per meal performed by the training group of retardates and the mean number of improper responses performed by normals. (*Sources:* O'Brien and Azrin, 1972.)

behaviors among the retarded residents was even lower than the normal rate of inappropriate eating in a restaurant. These results suggest that the magnitude of changes achieved with training brought behavior of the residents to acceptable levels of persons functioning in everyday life.

Several investigators have used the social comparison method to evaluate the clinical importance of behavior change (see Kazdin, 1977b). For example, research has shown that before treatment, conduct-problem children differ from their nonproblem peers on a variety of disruptive and unruly behaviors, including aggressive acts, teasing, whining, and yelling. After treatment, the disruptive behavior of these children has been brought into the range that appears to be normal and acceptable for their same-age peer group (Kent and O'Leary, 1976; Patterson, 1974; Walker and Hops, 1976). Similarly, the social behaviors of withdrawn or highly aggressive children have been brought into the normative level of their peers (e.g., Matson, Kazdin, Esveldt-Dawson, 1980; O'Connor, 1969). Treatments for altering the interpersonal problems of adults have also evaluated outcome by showing that treated persons approach, achieve, or surpass the performance of others who consider themselves to be functioning especially well in their interpersonal relations (e.g., Kazdin, 1979b; McFall and Marston, 1970).

Subjective Evaluation. Subjective evaluation as a means of validating the effects of treatment consists of global evaluations of behavior. The behaviors that have been altered are observed by persons who interact with the client or who are in a special position (e.g., through expertise) to judge those behaviors. Global evaluations are made to provide an overall appraisal of the client's performance after treatment. It is possible that systematic changes in behavior are demonstrated, but that persons in everyday life cannot see a "real" difference in performance. If the client has made a clinically significant change, this should be obvious to persons who are in a position to judge the client. Hence, judgments by persons in everyday contact with the client add a crucial dimension for evaluating the clinical significance of the change.

Subjective evaluation has been used in several studies at Achievement Place, a home-style living facility for predelinquent youths. For example, in one project, four delinquent girls were trained to engage in appropriate conversational skills (Maloney et al., 1976). Conversational skills improved when the girls received rewards for answering questions and for engaging in nonverbal behaviors (e.g., facial orientation) related to conversation. To evaluate whether the changes in specific behaviors could be readily seen in conversation, videotapes of pre- and posttraining sessions were evaluated by other persons with whom the clients might normally interact, including a social worker, probation officer, teacher, counselor, and student. The tapes were rated in random order so that the judges could not tell which were pre- and posttreatment sessions. The judges rated posttraining sessions as reflecting more appropriate conversation than the pretraining session. Thus, training produced a change in performance that could be seen by persons unfamiliar with the training or the concrete behaviors focused on.

In another project at Achievement Place, predelinquent boys were trained to interact appropriately with police (Werner et al., 1975). Questionnaire and checklist information from police were used to identify important behaviors in suspect-police interactions. These behaviors included facing the officer, responding politely, and showing cooperation, understanding, and interest in reforming. These behaviors increased markedly in three boys who received training based on modeling, practice, and feedback. To determine whether the changes made a difference in performance, police, parents of adjudicated youths, and college students evaluated videotapes of youth and police in role-play interactions after training. Trained boys were rated much more favorably on such measures as suspiciousness, cooperativeness, politeness, and appropriate interaction than were predelinquent boys who had not been trained. These data suggest that the changes in several specific behaviors made during training could be detected in overall performance.

Subjective evaluations have been used in several studies to examine the applied significance of behavior changes. For example, research in the classroom has shown that developing specific responses in composition writing (e.g., use of adjectives, adverbs, varied sentence beginnings) leads to increases in rating of the interest value and creativity of the compositions by teachers and college students (e.g., Brigham, Graubard, and Stans, 1972; Van Houten, Morrison, Jarvis, and McDonald, 1974). Programs with adults have developed public speaking skills by training concrete behaviors such as looking at and scanning the audience and making gestures while speaking (Fawcett and Miller, 1975). Aside from improvements in specific behaviors, ratings completed by the audience have shown improvements in speaker enthusiasm, sincerity, knowledge, and overall performance after training. Thus, the specific behaviors focused on and the magnitude of change seem to be clinically important.

Combined Validational Procedures. Social comparison and subjective evaluation provide different but complementary methods of examining the clinical significance of behavior change. Hence, they can be used together to provide an even stronger basis for making claims that important changes have been achieved. For example, Minkin et al. (1976) developed conversational skills in predelinquent girls at Achievement Place. Specific conversational behaviors included asking questions, providing feedback or responding to the other person in the conversation, and talking for a specific perod of time. These behaviors were trained using instructions, modeling, practice, feedback, and monetary rewards. Subjective evaluation was attained by having adult judges rate videotapes of pre- and posttraining conversation (in random order). Global ratings indicated that conversational ability was much higher for the posttraining conversations. Thus, the subjective evaluations suggested that the changes in behavior achieved during training were readily detected in overall conversation. In addition, posttraining ratings of conversation were obtained for nondelinquent female students who provided normative information. Ratings of conversational skills of the delinquent girls fell within the range of the ratings of the nondelinquent peers. Thus, both subjective evaluations and normative information on conversational ability uniformly attested to the importance of the changes achieved in training.

Problems and Considerations

Social validation of behavior change represents an important advance in evaluating interventions. Both social comparison and subjective evaluation methods add important information about the effects of treatment. Yet each method raises a number of questions pertaining to interpretation of the data.

Social Comparison. Obtaining normative data for purposes of comparison introduces potential problems. To begin with, for many behaviors it is possible that bringing clients into the normal range is not an appropriate goal. The normative level itself may be worthy of change. For example, children in most classrooms who are not identified as problem readers probably could accelerate their level of performance. Perhaps normative levels should not be identified as an ideal in training others, but themselves may be worth changing. For a number of other behaviors, including the use of cigarettes, drugs, alcohol, or the consumption of energy in one's home, the normative level (or what most people do) may be a questionable goal. Often one might argue against using the normative level as a standard for evaluating treatment. Of course, most persons seen in treatment, rehabilitation, and special education settings are well below the behavior of others who are functioning adequately in everyday life, at least in terms of some important behaviors. In such cases, bringing these persons within the normative range would represent an important contribution. For example, bringing the community, academic, social, or self-care performance of retarded persons to within the normative range would be an important accomplishment. In general, the normative level may be a very useful criterion, but in particular instances it might be questioned as the ideal toward which treatment should strive.

Another problem for the social comparison method is identifying a normative group for the clients seen in training. To whom should the severely mentally retarded, chronic psychiatric patients, prisoners, delinquents, or others be compared in evaluating the effects of intervention programs? Developing normative levels of performance might be an unrealistic ideal in treatment, if that level refers to the performance of persons normally functioning in the community. Also, what variables would define a normative population? It is unclear how to select persons as subjects for a normative group. One's peers might be defined to include persons similar to the clients in gender, background, socioeconomic standing, intelligence, marital status, and so on. Considering or failing to consider these variables may alter the level of performance that is defined as normative.

For example, in one investigation normative data were gathered on the social behaviors of preschool children in a classroom situation (Greenwood, Walker, Todd, and Hops, 1976). Child social behavior varied as a function of age and gender of the child and previous preschool experience. Younger children, females, and children with no previous school experience showed less social interaction. Thus, the level of social interaction used for the social comparison method may vary as a function of several factors.

Obviously, the normative group to which the target client's performance is compared can influence how intervention effects are evaluated. For example, Stahl, Thomson, Leitenberg, and Hasazi (1974) developed social behaviors such as eye contact and talking among three psychiatric patients. To evaluate the results of training, patients were compared with their peers. The results differed according to the characteristics of the comparison group. For instance, one patient's verbalizations increased to a level very close to (within 9 percent of) other hospitalized patients with similar education who were not considered verbally deficient. Yet the patient's verbalization was still considerably below (about 30 percent) the level of intelligent normally functioning persons. Thus, the clinical significance of treatment would be viewed quite differently depending on the normative standard used for comparison.

Even if a normative group can be agreed on, exactly what range of their behaviors would define an acceptable normative level? Among persons whose behaviors are not identified as problematic, there will be a range of acceptable behaviors. It is relatively simple to identify deviant behavior that departs markedly from the behavior of "normal" peers. But as behavior becomes slightly less deviant, it is difficult to identify the point at which behavior is within the normative range. A subjective judgment is required to assess the point at which the person has entered into the normal range of performance.

In general, in using normative data, it is important to recognize the relativity of norms and the variables that contribute to normative standards. Changes in the group defined as a normative sample can lead to different conclusions about the clinical importance of intervention effects. Hence, when social comparison is used to validate intervention effects, it is especially important to specify the characteristics of this group very carefully to permit interpretation of the normative data.

Subjective Evaluation. The subjective evaluation method as a means of examining the clinical importance of intervention effects also raises critical issues. The greatest concern is the problem of relying on the opinions of others to determine whether treatment effects are important. Subjective evaluations of performance are much more readily susceptible to biases on the part of judges (raters) than are overt behavioral measures (Kent et al., 1974). Thus, one must interpret subjective evaluations cautiously. Subjective evaluations will often reflect change when the overt behaviors to which the evaluations refer do not (Kazdin, 1973; Schnelle, 1974). Subjective evaluations may reflect improvements because judges expect changes over the course of treatment or view the clients differently rather than any changes in actual behaviors.

Another issue raised by subjective evaluation is whether improvements in global ratings or performance necessarily reflect a clinically important change. Assume that a client's behaviors have changed and that these changes are reflected in global ratings by persons who are in contact with the client (e.g., parents, teachers). However, this provides no information about the adequacy of the change in relation to the client's functioning. The improvements may still be insufficient to alleviate completely the problem for which the client was placed into treatment.

A way to ensure that subjective evaluation of behavior reflects an important change is to provide these evaluations for the clients and for a normative sample as well (e.g., Minkin et al., 1976). This anchors the subjective evaluation scores to a normative criterion. The investigator can evaluate improvement in terms of absolute changes in ratings from pre- to posttraining for the clients and also the relative standing of the clients after training and their "normal" peers. Subjective evaluation of behavior of the target clients without some information from normative ratings may be inadequate as a criterion for evaluating the clinical importance of behavior change. Subjective evaluations leave unspecified the level of performance that is needed.

Despite the potential obstacles that may be present with subjective evaluation, it introduces an important criterion for evaluating intervention effects. The possibility exists in assessment and treatment that the behaviors focused on are not very important and the changes achieved with treatment have little or no impact on how persons are evaluated by others in everyday situations. Persons in everyday life are frequently responsible for identifying problem behaviors and making referrals to professionals for treatment. Thus, their evaluation of behavior is quite relevant as a criterion in its own right to determine whether important changes have been made.

Summary and Conclusions

Data from single-case experiments are evaluated according to experimental and therapeutic criteria. The *experimental criterion* refers to judgments about whether behavior change has occurred and whether the change can be attributed to the intervention. The *therapeutic criterion* refers to whether the effects of the intervention are important or of clinical or applied significance.

In single-case experiments, visual inspection is usually used to evaluate whether the experimental criterion has been met. Data from the experiment are graphed and judgments are made about whether change has occurred and whether the data pattern meets the requirements of the design. Several characteristics of the data contribute to judging through visual inspection whether behavior has changed. *Changes in the mean* (average) performance across phases, *changes in the level* of performance (shift at the point that the phase is changed), *changes in trend* (differences in the direction and rate of change across phases), and *latency of change* (rapidity of change at the point that the intervention is introduced or withdrawn) all contribute to judging whether a reliable effect has occurred. Invoking these criteria is greatly facilitated by stable baselines and minimal day-to-day variability, which allow the changes in the data to be detected.

The primary basis for using visual inspection is that it serves as a filter that may allow only especially potent interventions to be agreed on as significant. Yet objections have been raised about the use of visual inspection in situations where intervention effects are not spectacular. Judges occasionally disagree about whether reliable effects were obtained. Also, the decision rules for inferring that a change has been demonstrated are not always explicit or consistently invoked for visual inspection.

Statistical analyses have been suggested as a way of addressing the experimental criterion of single-case research to supplement visual inspection. Two sources of controversy have been voiced about the use of statistics, namely, whether they should be used at all and, if used, which statistical tests are appropriate. Statistical tests seem to be especially useful when several of the desired characteristics of the data required for visual inspection are not met. For example, when baselines are unstable and show systematic trend in a therapeutic direction, selected statistical analyses can more readily evaluate intervention effects than visual inspection. The search for reliable albeit weak intervention effects is especially difficult with visual inspection. These interventions may be important to detect, especially in the early stages of research before the intervention is well understood and developed. Finally, there are several situations in which detecting small changes may be important and statistical analyses may be especially useful here.

Several statistical techniques are available for single-case experimental designs. The appropriateness of any particular test depends on the design, characteristics of the data, and various ways in which the intervention is presented.

Conventional t and F tests, time-series analysis, the R_n ranking test, randomization tests, and the split-middle technique were mentioned. (The tests are illustrated in Appendix B.)

The therapeutic criterion for single-case data is evaluated by determining whether behavior changes are clinically significant. Examining the importance of intervention effects entails *social validation,* i.e., considering social criteria for evaluating treatment outcomes. Two methods of social validation are relevant for evaluating intervention effects, namely, the social comparison and the subject evaluation methods. The *social comparison method* considers whether the intervention has brought the client's behavior to the level of his or her peers who are functioning adequately in the environment. The method is used by assessing the performance of persons not referred for treatment and who are viewed as functioning normally. Presumably, if the intervention is needed and eventually effective, the client's behavior should deviate from the normative group before treatment and fall within the range of this group afterward.

The *subjective evaluation method* consists of having persons who interact with the client or who are in a special position (e.g., through expertise) to judge those behaviors seen in treatment. Global evaluations are made to assess whether the changes in specific overt behaviors are reflected in what others can see in their everyday interactions. Presumably, if a clinically important change has been achieved, persons in contact with the client should be able to detect it.

Social comparison and subjective evaluation represent an important advance in evaluating intervention research. The methods, of course, are not free of problems. Nevertheless, they make an important and crucial attempt to evaluate the magnitude of change in relation to clinical and applied considerations. Both methods consider the impact of treatment in altering dimensions that relate to how well the client functions or is likely to function in the environment.

11

Evaluation of Single-Case Designs: Issues and Limitations

Previous chapters have discussed issues and potential problems peculiar to specific types of single-case designs. For example, in ABAB designs, the irreversibility of behavior in a return-to-baseline (or reversal) phase presents a potential problem for drawing valid inferences. Similarly, in a multiple-baseline design, ambiguities about the demonstration arise if several behaviors change when the intervention has only been introduced to the first behavior. Apart from the problems that are peculiar to specific designs, general issues can be raised that can emerge in all of the designs. In all of the designs, characteristics of the data can raise potential obstacles for interpreting the results.

More general issues can be raised about single-case designs and their limitations. Single-case research generally evaluates interventions designed to alter behavior of applied significance. A variety of research questions can be raised about interventions and the factors that contribute to their effects. Single-case designs may be restricted in the range of questions about intervention effects that can be adequately addressed. Another general issue raised in relation to single-case designs is the generality of the results. Whether the findings can be generalized beyond the subject(s) included in the design and whether the designs can adequately study generality are important issues for single-case research. This chapter discusses problems that may emerge within single-case experiments and more general issues and limitations of this type of research as a whole.

Common Methodological Problems and Obstacles

Traditionally, research designs are preplanned so that most of the details about who receives the intervention and when the intervention is introduced are decided before the subjects participate in the study. In single-case designs, many crucial decisions about the design can be made only as the data are collected. Decisions such as how long baseline data should be collected and when to present or withdraw experimental conditions are made during the investigation itself. The investigator needs to decide when to alter phases in the design in such a way as to maximize the clarity of the demonstration.

Each single-case design usually begins with a baseline phase followed by the intervention phase. The intervention is evaluated by comparing performance across phases. For these comparisons to be made easily, the investigator has to be sure that the changes from one phase to another are likely to be due to the intervention rather than to a continuation of an existing trend or to chance fluctuations (high or low points) in the data. A fundamental design issue is deciding *when to change phases* so as to maximize the clarity of data interpretation.

There are no widely agreed upon rules for altering phases, although alternatives will be discussed below. However, there is general agreement that the point at which the conditions are changed in the design is extremely important because subsequent evaluation of intervention effects depends on how clear the behavior changes are across phases. The usual rule of thumb is to alter conditions (phases) only when the data are stable. As noted earlier, stability refers to the absence of trend and relatively small variability in performance. Trends and excessive variability during any of the phases, particularly during baseline, can interfere with evaluating intervention effects. Although both trend and variability were discussed earlier, it is important to build on that earlier discussion and address problems that may arise and alternative solutions that can facilitate drawing inferences about intervention effects.

Trends in the Data

As noted earlier, drawing inferences about intervention effects is greatly facilitated when baseline levels show no trend or a trend in the direction opposite from that predicted by the intervention. When data show these patterns, it is relatively easy to infer that changes in level and trend are associated with the onset of the intervention. A problem may emerge, at least from the standpoint of the design, when baseline data show a trend in the same direction as expected to result from the intervention. When performance is improving during baseline, it may be difficult to evaluate intervention effects. Changes in level and trend are more difficult to detect during the intervention phase if performance is already improving during baseline.

The difficulty of evaluating intervention effects when baselines show trends in a therapeutic direction has prompted some investigators to recommend waiting for baseline to stabilize so that there will be no trend before intervening (Baer et al., 1968). This cannot be done in many clinical and applied situations in which treatment is needed quickly. Behavior may require intervention even though some improvements are occurring. If prolonged baselines cannot be invoked to wait for stable data, other options are available.

First, the intervention can be implemented even though there is a trend toward improved performance during baseline. After initial baseline (A) and intervention (B) phases, a reversal phase can be used in which behavior is changed in the direction *opposite* from that of the intervention phase. For example, if the intervention consists of providing reinforcement for all rational conversation of a psychotic patient, a reversal phase could be implemented in which all nonrational conversation is reinforced and all rational conversation is ignored (e.g., Ayllon and Haughton, 1964). This reinforcement schedule, referred to earlier as differential reinforcement of other behavior (DRO), has the advantage of quickly reversing the direction (trend) of performance. Hence, across an ABAB design for example, the effects of the intervention on behavior are likely to be readily apparent. In general, use of a DRO schedule in one of the phases, or any other procedure that will alter the direction of performance, can help reduce ambiguities caused by initial baseline performance that shows a trend in a therapeutic direction. Of course, this design option may be methodologically sound but clinically untenable because it includes specific provisions for making the client's behavior worse.

A second alternative for reducing the ambiguity that initial trends in the data may present is to select design options in which such a trend in a therapeutic direction will have little or no impact on drawing conclusions about intervention effects. A number of designs and their variations discussed in previous chapters can be used to draw unambiguous inferences about the intervention even in circumstances where initial trend may be evident. For example, a multiple-baseline design is usually not impeded by initial trends in baseline. It is unlikely that all of the baselines (behaviors, persons, or behaviors in different situations) will show trend in a therapeutic direction. The intervention can be invoked for those behaviors that are relatively stable while baseline conditions are continued for other behaviors in which trends appear. If the need exists to intervene for the behaviors that do show an initial trend, this too is unlikely to interfere with drawing inferences about intervention effects. Conclusions about intervention effects are reached on the basis of the pattern of data across all of the behaviors or baselines in the multiple-baseline design. Ambiguity of the changes across one or two of the baselines may not necessarily impede drawing an overall conclusion, depending on the number of baselines, the magnitude of intervention effects, and similar factors.

Similarly, drawing inferences about intervention effects is usually not threatened by an initial baseline trend in a therapeutic direction in simultaneous-treatment and multiple-schedule designs. In these designs, conclusions are reached on the basis of the effects of different conditions usually implemented in the same phase. The differential effects of alternative interventions can be detected even though there may be an overall trend in the data. The main question is whether differences between or among the alternative interventions occur, and this need not be interfered with by an overall trend in the data. If one of the conditions included in an intervention phase of a simultaneous-treatment design is a continuation of baseline, the investigator can assess directly whether the interventions surpass performance obtained concurrently under the continued baseline conditions.

A trend during baseline may not interfere with drawing conclusions about the intervention evaluated in a changing-criterion design. This design depends on evaluating whether the performance matches a changing criterion. Even if performance improves during baseline, control exerted by the intervention can still be evaluated by comparing the criterion level with performance throughout the design, and if necessary by using bidirectional changes in the criteria, as discussed in an earlier chapter.

Another option for handling initial trend in baseline is to utilize statistical techniques to evaluate the effects of the intervention relative to baseline performance. Specific techniques such as time-series analysis can assess whether the intervention has made reliable changes over and above what would be expected from a continuation of initial trend (see Appendix B). Also, techniques that can describe and plot initial baseline trends such as the split-middle technique (Appendix A) can help examine visually whether an initial trend in baseline is similar to trends during the intervention phase(s).

In general, an initial trend during baseline may not necessarily interfere with drawing inferences about the intervention. Various design options and data evaluation techniques can be used to reduce or eliminate ambiguity about intervention effects. It is crucial for the investigator to have in mind one of the alternatives for reducing ambiguity if an initial trend is evident in baseline. Without taking explicit steps in altering the design or applying special data evaluation techniques, trend in a therapeutic direction during baseline or return-to-baseline phases may compete with obtaining clear effects.

Variability

Evaluation of intervention effects is facilitated by having relatively little variability in the data in a given phase and across all phases. The larger the daily fluctuations, the larger the change needed in behavior to infer a clear effect. Large fluctuations in the data do not always make evaluation of the intervention difficult. For example sometimes baseline performance may show large fluctuations about the mean value. When the intervention is implemented, not only may the mean performance change, but variability may become markedly less as well. Hence, the intervention effect is very clear, because both change in means and a reduction in variability occurred. The difficulties arise primarily when baseline and intervention conditions both evince relatively large fluctuations in performance. As in the case with trend in baseline, the investigator has several options to reduce the ambiguities raised by excessive variability.

One option that is occasionally suggested is to reduce the *appearance* of variability in the data (Sidman, 1960). The appearance of day-to-day variability can be reduced by plotting the data in *blocks of time* rather than on a daily basis. For example, if data are collected every day, they need not be plotted on a daily basis. Data can be averaged over consecutive days and that average can be plotted. By representing two or more days with a single averaged data point, the data appear more stable.

Figure 11-1 presents hypothetical data in one phase that show day-to-day performance that is highly variable (upper panel). The same data appear in the middle panel in which the averages for two-day blocks are plotted. The fluctuation in performance is greatly reduced in the middle panel, giving the appearance of much more stable data. Finally, in the bottom panel the data are averaged into five-day blocks. That is, performance for five consecutive days are averaged into a single data point, which is plotted. The appearance of variability is reduced even further.

In single-case research, consecutive data points can be averaged in the fashion illustrated above. In general, the larger the number of days included in a block, the lower the variability that will appear in the graph. Of course, once the size of the block is decided (e.g., two or three days), all data throughout the investigation need to be plotted in this fashion. It is important to note that the averaging procedure only affects the appearance of variability in the data. When the appearance is altered through the averaging procedure, changes in means, levels, and trends across phases may be easier to detect than when the original data are examined.

A few cautions are worth noting regarding use of the averaging procedure. First, the actual data plotted in blocks distort daily performance. Plotting data on a daily basis rather than in blocks is not inherently superior or more veridical. However, variability in the data evident in daily observations may repre-

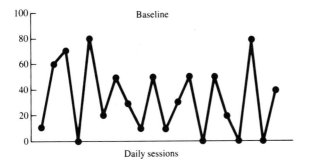

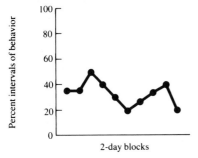

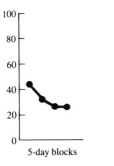

Figure 11–1. Hypothetical data for one phase of a single-case design. *Upper panel* shows data plotted on a daily basis. *Middle panel* shows the same data plotted in two-day blocks. *Lower panel* shows the same data plotted in five-day blocks. Together the figures show that the appearance of variability can be reduced by plotting data into blocks.

sent a meaningful, important, or interesting characteristic of performance. Averaging hides this variability, which, in a particular situation, may obfuscate important information in its own right. For example, a hyperactive child in a classroom situation may show marked differences in how he or she performs from day to day. On some days the child may show very high levels of activity and inappropriate behavior, while on other days his or her behavior may be no different from that of peers. The variability in behavior may be important—or important to alter. The overall activity of the child but also the marked inconsistency (variability) over days represent characteristics that may have implications for designing treatments.

Second, averaging data points into blocks reduces the number of data points in the graph for each of the phases. If ten days of baseline are observed but plotted in blocks of five days, then only two data points (number of days/block size or $10/5 = 2$) will appear in baseline. Unless the data are quite stable, these few data points may not serve as a sufficient basis for predicting performance in subsequent phases. Although blocking the data in the fashion described here reduces the number of data points, the resulting data are usually markedly more stable than the daily data. Thus, what one loses in number of points is compensated for by the stability of the data points based on averages.

Altering how the data appear may serve an important function by clarifying the graphic display. Other options are available for handling excessive variability. Whenever possible, it is better to identify and control sources that may produce variability, rather than merely averaging the data. As Sidman (1960) has noted, excessive variability in the data indicates absence of experimental control over the behavior and lack of understanding of the factors that contribute to performance.

When baseline performance appears highly variable, several factors may be identified that contribute to variability. It is possible that the client is performing relatively consistently, i.e., shows little variability in performance, although this is not accurately reflected in the data. One factor that might hide consistency is the manner in which observations are conducted. Observers may introduce variability in performance to the extent that they score inconsistently or depart (drift) from the original definitions of behavior. Careful checks on interobserver agreement and periodic retraining sessions may help reduce observer deviations from the intended procedures.

Another factor that may contribute to variability in performance is the general conditions under which observations are obtained. Excessive variability may suggest that greater standardization is needed over the conditions in which the observations are obtained. Client performance may vary as a function of the persons present in the situation, the time of day in which observations are obtained, events preceding the observation period or events anticipated after the observation period, and so on. Normally, such factors that naturally vary from day to day can be ignored and baseline observations may still show relatively slight fluctuations. On the other hand, when variability is excessive, the investigator may wish to identify or attempt to identify features of the setting that can be standardized further. Standardization amounts to making the day-to-day situation more homogeneous, which is likely to decrease factors that influence variability. Obviously, some factors that vary on a daily basis (e.g., client's diet, weather) may be less easily controlled than others (e.g., presence of peers in the same room, use of the same or similar activities while the client is being observed).

For whatever reason, behavior may simply be quite variable even after the above procedures have been explored. Indeed, the goal of an intervention program may be to alter the variability of the client's performance (i.e., make performance more consistent), rather than changing the mean rate. Variability may remain relatively large, and the need to intervene cannot be postponed to identify contributory sources. In such cases, the investigator may use aids such as plotting data into blocks, means, and trend to help clarify the pattern of data across phases.

It is important to bear one final point about variability in mind. The extent to which data show excessive variability is difficult to decide early in an investigation. Whether the variability will interfere with evaluation of the intervention effects is determined by the type of changes produced by the intervention. Marked changes in performance may be very clear because of simultaneous changes in the mean, level, and trend across phases. So the extent to which variability interferes with drawing inferences is a function of the magnitude and type of change produced by the intervention. The main point is that with relatively large variability, stronger intervention effects are needed to infer that a systematic change has occurred.

Duration of the Phases

An important issue in single-case research is deciding how long the phases will be over the course of the design. The duration of the phases usually is not specified in advance of the investigation. The reason is that the investigator needs to examine the data and to determine whether the information is sufficiently clear to make predictions about performance. The presence or suggestion of trends or excessive variability during the baseline phase or tentative, weak, or delayed effects during the intervention phase may require more prolonged phases.

A common methodological problem is altering phases before a clear pattern emerges. For example, most of the data may indicate a clear pattern for the baseline phase. Yet, after a few days of relatively stable baseline performance, one or two data points may be higher or lower than all of the previous data. The question that immediately arises is whether a trend is emerging in baseline or whether the data points are merely part of random (unsystematic) variability. To be sure, it is wise to continue the condition without shifting phases. If one or two more days of data reveal that there is no trend, the intervention can be implemented as planned. The few "extra" data points provide increased confidence that there was no emerging trend and can greatly facilitate subsequent evaluation of the intervention.

Occasionally, an investigator may obtain an extreme data point during baseline in the opposite direction of the change anticipated with the intervention. This extreme point may be interpreted as suggesting that if there is any trend, it is in the opposite direction of intervention effects. Investigators may shift phases when an extreme point is noted in the previous phase in the direction opposite from the predicted effects of the phase. Yet extreme scores in one direction are likely to be followed by scores that revert in the direction of the mean, a characteristic known as *statistical regression* (see Chapter 4).

It is important to be alert to the possibility of regression. If an extreme score occurs, it may be unwise to shift phases. Such a shift might capitalize on regression. This immediate "improvement" in performance might be interpreted to be the result of shifting from one condition to another (change in level) when in fact it might be accounted for by regression. As data continue to be collected in the new phase, the investigator could, of course, see if the intervention is having an effect on behavior. Yet, if changes in level or means are examined across phases, shifting phases at points of extreme scores could systematically bias the conclusions that are drawn.

In general, phases in single-case experimental designs need to be continued until data patterns are relatively clear. This does not always mean that phases are long. For example, in some cases, return to baseline or reversal phases in ABAB designs may be very brief such as only one or two days or sessions (e.g., Allison and Ayllon, 1980; Carr, Newsom, and Binkoff, 1980, Exp. 4; Shapiro, 1979). The brevity of each phase is determined in part by the clarity of the data for that phase and for that phase in relation to adjacent phases.

It is difficult to note with great confidence any general rule about how long phases should be in single-case research. Some authors have suggested that three data points within a given phase should serve as an absolute minimum (Barlow and Hersen, 1973). It is easy to identify examples in which remarkably clear intervention effects were demonstrated that included shorter phases (e.g., Harris, Wolf, and Baer, 1964; Rincover, Cook, Peoples, and Packard, 1979), or examples where less clear effects were evident even though phases were longer than the minimum.

Suggesting a requisite number of data points is a useful practical guideline. As a minimum, three to five days is probably useful as a general rule. However, it is much more important to convey the rationale underlying the recommendation, namely, to provide a clear basis for predicting and testing predictions about performance. A simple rule has many problems. For one, it is likely that some phases require longer durations than others. For example, it is usually important to have the initial baseline of a slightly longer duration than return-to-baseline phases in ABAB designs. The initial baseline of any design provides the first information about trends and variability in the data and serves uniquely as an important point of reference for all subsequent phases. On the other hand, in a multiple-baseline design across several behaviors, initial baselines may be very short (e.g., one or a few sessions) because the strength of a demonstration does not depend on any single baseline phase) (e.g., Jones et al., 1981). Hence, rules about the duration of experimental phases in single-case research are difficult to specify and when specified are often difficult to justify without great qualification.

Aside from the duration of individual phases, occasionally it has been recommended to ensure that phases are equal or approximately equal in duration within a given investigation (Barlow and Hersen, 1973; Hersen and Barlow, 1976). The recommendation is based on the view that in a given period of time (e.g., a week or month), maturational or cyclical influences may lead to a certain pattern of performance that is mistaken for intervention effects. If phases are equal in duration, the effects of extraneous events may be roughly constant or equal in each phase and will not be confused with intervention effects.

Although phases of equal or nearly equal duration might be convenient for some purposes (e.g., certain statistical procedures), the logic of single-case designs does not depend on this feature. The manner in which the intervention is replicated in the different designs is quite sufficient to make implausible threats to internal validity such as history and maturation. Phases of equal duration do not necessarily strengthen the design. In fact, if duration is given primacy as a consideration, ambiguity may be introduced by altering or waiting to alter conditions when data patterns are unclear or clear. The majority of single-case reports show dramatic experimental demonstrations when no attempt was made to equalize durations of the phases.

Several comments have noted the methodological issues that arise when considering duration of phases of single-case experimental designs. Typically, the duration of the phases is determined by judgment on the part of the investigator based on his or her view that a clear data pattern is evident. Of course, practical considerations often operate as well (e.g., end of the school year) that place constraints on durations of the phases. From the standpoint of the design, the pattern of the data should dictate decisions to alter the phases. Occasionally, somewhat more objective criteria have been suggested to replace the investigator's judgment in deciding when one phase should be ended and the other phase begun.

Criteria for Shifting Phases

Currently, no agreed-upon objective decision rules exist for altering phases in single-case experimental designs. The duration of phases depends on having stable data. Yet, determination of whether stability has been achieved is usually based on the judgment, intuition, and experience of the investigator (Sidman, 1960). Also, characteristics of performance during baseline and intervention phases determine in any given case the extent to which data in a particular phase are sufficiently stable to progress from one phase to the next. For example, when the intervention produces large effects, the requirements for stable data in baseline and reversal phases are more lenient than when the intervention produces small effects.

In most circumstances, decisions about stability of performance need to be made before the investigator has access to information about the strength and replicability of intervention effects. The results are not known and the investigator needs to decide when to shift from one phase (baseline) to the next (intervention) without a preview of the strength of the intervention. Of course, the investigator, through experience with previous subjects, may have information about the strength of the intervention. This knowledge may be useful in deciding how much instability in the data can be tolerated. However, without prior information, more general guidelines are needed.

Typically, stability of performance in a particular phase can be defined by two characteristics of the data, namely, trend and variability. A criterion or decision rule for shifting phases usually needs to take into account these parameters (Cumming and Schoenfeld, 1960; Sidman, 1960). Different criteria have been proposed, some of which require application of relatively complex statistical formulas to evaluate the extent to which performance approaches asymptotic levels, as, for example, represented by a learning curve (Killeen, 1978).

The usual recommendation has been to define stability of the data in a given phase in terms of a number of consecutive sessions or days that fall within a prespecified range of the mean (Gelfand and Hartmann, 1975; Sidman, 1960). The method can ensure that data do not show a systematic increase or decrease over time (trend) and fall within a particular range (variability). When the specified criteria are met, the phase is terminated and the next condition can be presented.

In both experimental and applied literatures, relatively few investigations have employed prespecified and objective criteria for altering phases. A few illustrations show how the data are evaluated with respect to falling within a prespecified range. In one investigation, the effect of time out from reinforcement on the aggressive behavior of kindergarten children was evaluated in an ABAB design (Wilson, Robertson, Herlong, and Haynes, 1979). A change from one condition to the next was made when the data were stable. Stability was defined as obtaining three consecutive days of data that did not depart more than 10 percent from the mean of all previous days of that phase. The data consisted of the percentage of intervals in which aggressive behavior occurred. To obtain the mean within a given phase, a cumulative average was continually obtained. That is, each successive day was added to all previous days of that phase to obtain a new mean. When three consecutive days fell within 10 percent of that mean, the phase was changed.

Similarly, in another investigation reinforcement and biofeedback were used to decrease the heart rate of a male psychiatric patient who suffered from tachycardia (elevated heart rate) (Scott, Peters, Gillespie, Blanchard, Edmunson, and Young, 1973, Exp. 1). Phases of an ABAB design variation were continued until stability of heart rate was evident. Stability was defined as less than 15 percent departure from the mean for three consecutive trials. Thus, any one trial was required to fall within $\pm$ 7.5 percent of the mean across three trials. A given phase could last a minimum of three trials if all data points fell within this range.

In another study, slightly more complex criteria were invoked to determine when phases could be altered. Wincze, Leitenberg, and Agras (1972) evaluated the effects of token reinforcement and feedback on delusional statements of psychiatric patients in variations of an ABAB design. The investigators specified in advance that each phase would last seven days. However, if either of two conditions were met during an intervention phase, the phase was extended for four more days. The phase was extended (1) if five of the seven data points in one phase were below (i.e., overlapped with) the data points of the previous phase or (2) if there was at least a 20 percent reduction (improvement) in delusional verbalizations on the last day compared with the final day of the preceding phase.

The above examples are exceptions in that criteria were specified in advance that would be used to decide the duration of individual phases. These examples illustrate that when criteria are invoked, they consist of requiring a series of data points that fall within a range of mean performance within a particular phase. The mean of a given phase is constantly changing as a function of each day's data. The range within which data points should fall and the number of consecutive days within this range must be decided in advance.

Specification of criteria for deciding when to alter conditions (phases) is excellent. If criteria are specified in advance, alteration of conditions is less likely to take advantage of chance fluctuations in the data. In general, specifiable criteria will reduce the subjectivity of decision making within the design. Of course, specification of criteria in advance has its risks. A few shifts in performance during a given phase may cause the criteria not to be met. Behavior often oscillates, i.e., goes back and forth between particular values. It may be difficult in advance of the baseline data to determine for a given subject what that range of oscillation or fluctuation will be. Waiting for the subject's performance to fall within a prespecified range may cause the investigator to "spend a lifetime" on the same experiment (Sidman, 1960, p. 260).

Problems may arise when multiple subjects are used. For example, in a multiple-baseline design across subjects (or behaviors, or situations), the observations across different baselines may be quite different and a single criterion may vary in the extent to which it is likely to be met. Some baselines may need to be invoked for extended periods, which raises practical obstacles in most applied settings.

It is important to bear in mind that the purpose of specifying criteria is to have an objective definition of stability. But it is the stability of the data rather than meeting any particular prespecified criterion that is important. Stability is needed to predict performance in subsequent phases. The prediction serves as a basis for detecting departures from this prediction from one phase to the next. It is conceivable that a criterion for shifting phases may not be met even though a reasonably clear pattern is evident that could serve as an adequate basis for predicting future performance. Stated more simply, specification of a criterion is a means toward an end, i.e., defining stability, and not an end in itself. Data points may fall close to but not exactly within the criterion for shifting phases and progress through the investigation may be delayed. In the general case, and perhaps for applied settings in particular, it may be important to specify alternative criteria for shifting phases within a given design so that if the data meet one of the criteria, the phase can be altered (e.g., Doleys et al., 1976). A more flexible criterion or set of criteria may reduce the likelihood that a few data points could continually delay alteration of the phases (Sidman, 1960).

The above comments are not intended to argue against use of stability criteria. Indeed, the use of such criteria is to be encouraged. However, at this point in single-case methodology, very little work has been conducted to examine the stability criteria that investigators implicitly employ in their application of visual inspection or alternative methods for specifying criteria and their impact for shifting phases (see Killeen, 1978). More research is needed to further understand the available options and potential problems that arise in their application.

General Issues and Limitations

The methodological issues discussed above refer to considerations that arise while conducting individual single-case experiments. The methodology of single-case research and its limitations can be examined from a more general perspective. The present discussion addresses major issues and limitations that apply to single-case experimental research.

Range of Outcome Questions

Single-case designs have been used in applied research primarily to evaluate the effectiveness of a variety of interventions. The interventions are typically designed to ameliorate a particular problem or to improve performance in the context of applied, clinical, and naturalistic settings. In the context of treatment, single-case research would fall under the rubric of what has been called *outcome research*. That is, the focus is on the therapeutic effects or results achieved with the intervention. Applied behavior analysis includes but goes beyond *treatment* or *therapy* evaluation because interventions have been evaluated in a variety of settings and for a host of behaviors that traditionally fall outside the realm of psychological or psychiatric treatment. Nevertheless, it is useful to conceive of single-case research in the context of outcome research more generally.

Several different types of outcome questions can be delineated in applied and clinical research. The questions vary in terms of what they ask about a particular intervention and the impact that the intervention has on behavior. The different questions are addressed by various treatment or intervention evaluation strategies. Major treatment strategies are listed briefly in Table 11-1 (see Kazdin, 1980c for elaboration). As is evident in the table, the strategies raise questions about the outcome of a particular intervention and the manner in which the intervention influences behavior change. The questions and treatment evaluation strategies are usually addressed in between-group research. Depending on the particular strategy, alternative groups are included in the design that provide treatment or variations of treatment compared with various control groups. Between-group research can readily address the full gamut of outcome questions, depending on the precise groups that are included in the design (see Kazdin, 1980c).

In single-case research, the range of outcome questions that can be addressed is somewhat more restricted than in between-group research. Most single-case research fits into the *treatment package strategy* in which a particular treatment is compared with no treatment (baseline). The treatment package usually consists of multifaceted packages with several different ingredients (Azrin, 1977). For example, in applied behavior analysis, complex treatments

Table 11-1. Treatment evaluation strategies and the outcome questions they address

Treatment evaluation strategy	Outcome question addressed
1. Treatment package strategy	Does this treatment with all of its components lead to therapeutic change relative to no treatment?
2. Dismantling strategy	What aspects of the treatment package are necessary, sufficient, or facilitative for therapeutic change?
3. Parametric strategy	What variations of the treatment can be made to augment its effectiveness?
4. Constructive strategy	What procedures or techniques can be added to treatment to make it more effective?
5. Comparative strategy	Which treatment is more (or most) effective among a particular set of alternatives?
6. Client-treatment variation strategy	What client characteristics interact with the effects of treatment? Or, for whom is a particular technique effective or more effective?

often include instructions, modeling, feedback, and direct reinforcement to alter behavior. Typical of such interventions are token economies or social skills training programs in which the techniques can be broken down into several parts or components. For purposes of evaluation, the treatment package strategy examines the whole package. The basic question is whether treatment achieves change and does so reliably. Treatments evaluated in variations of ABAB or multiple-baseline designs usually illustrate the treatment package strategy.

The dismantling, parametric, and constructive strategies listed in Table 11-1 are similar to each other in that they attempt to analyze aspects of treatments that contribute to therapeutic change. In its own way, each strategy examines what can be done to make the treatment or intervention more effective. These strategies are often difficult to employ in single-case research because they involve comparisons of the full treatment package with other conditions.

The *dismantling strategy* attempts to compare the full treatment package with another condition, such as the package minus selected ingredients. The *parametric strategy* attempts to compare variations of the same treatment in which one particular dimension is altered to determine if it influences outcome. With the *constructive strategy,* a given intervention is compared with that same intervention plus one or more additional ingredients.

In single-case research, comparisons are difficult to achieve between any two different interventions or variations of a particular intervention, because most of the designs depend on implementing alternative experimental conditions at different points in time. Consider two examples that illustrate the ambiguities associated with alternative treatment evaluation strategies in single-case research. Scott and Bushell (1974) evaluated the effect of duration of teacher contact on off-task behavior (e.g., not working on the assignment, leaving one's seat) in a group of elementary school children. The study illustrates the parametric strategy, because a particular variable was evaluated along some quantitative dimension. The duration of teacher contact was evaluated by having the teacher spend different amounts of time with the children while they worked on math assignments. The teacher went to each child to provide instructions, assistance, or feedback. The investigators compared the effects of having the teacher spend fifty seconds versus twenty seconds in the contacts with each child. During different phases, the teacher either spent approximately fifty or twenty seconds with the child during a particular contact. An observer in the room monitored the time and provided the teacher with cues when to terminate an interaction. The effects of the different durations are illustrated in Figure 11-2. In the first phase, contact was allowed to vary normally (baseline). In the second phase, when teacher contacts each lasted longer, off-task behavior increased. In the final phase, the duration of the contact lasted for approximately twenty seconds, and off-task behavior returned to baseline levels.

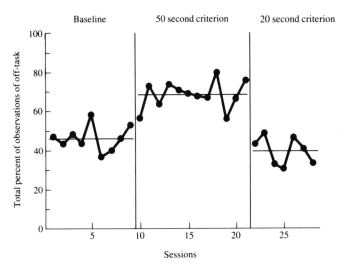

Figure 11–2. Total percent of observations of off-task behavior for the children during the experimental conditions. (*Source:* Scott and Bushell, 1974.)

The results showed that when the duration of teacher-student contact increased over baseline durations, off-task behavior increased, and when the duration decreased, off-task behavior decreased. The investigation shows a strong effect that seemingly has clear implications, namely, that longer teacher-student contacts may produce *more* off-task behavior than shorter contacts. Unfortunately, the effects of the different durations are confounded with sequence effects. It is possible that the effects of the shorter duration would be quite different if that duration had preceded rather than followed the longer one. Indeed, it may have been the *change* in the duration of contacts after baseline that led to an increase in off-task behavior and that this may have had little to do with the longer contact period. Overall, the effects of the two durations of teacher contact are not completely clear. The contribution of sequence effects to the findings remains to be determined.

Another example with a different treatment evaluation strategy also illustrates the potential limits of comparing alternative interventions when sequence effects are not controlled. Bornstein, Hamilton, and Quevillon (1977) evaluated the effects of alternative procedures to reduce the out-of-seat behavior of a nine-year-old third grade boy. This study illustrates the constructive evaluation strategy, because the purpose was to evaluate the effects of a particular intervention with and without added ingredients.

After baseline, positive practice was used to decrease out-of-seat behavior. This consisted of requiring the boy to remain in for recess and to practice stating the rules of the class, raising his hand while seated, and receiving permission to leave his seat. This was conducted for three minutes for each out-of-seat infraction, and minutes were accumulated for the recess period. After a reversal phase, the positive practice procedure was reinstated. Finally, in the next (fifth) phase, additional procedures were added to positive practice. Specifically, the boy was told that positive practice would continue but that now he also was to count instances of his out-of-seat behavior. Also, if his count matched that of the teacher (was within one instance of her count), he would earn extra recess for the entire class. Essentially, this phase included positive practice plus self-observation, group reinforcement, and teacher praise for accurate self-observation.

The effects of the program on out-of-seat behavior are illustrated in Figure 11-3. The first four phases clearly illustrate the functional control that positive practice exerted on performance. The positive practice plus matching phase (which included matching the teacher's tallies of out-of-seat behavior and other contingencies) appears to be more effective than positive practice alone. Apart from the possibility that behavior may have been eliminated completely if the positive practice procedure had been continued by itself (after day twenty), it

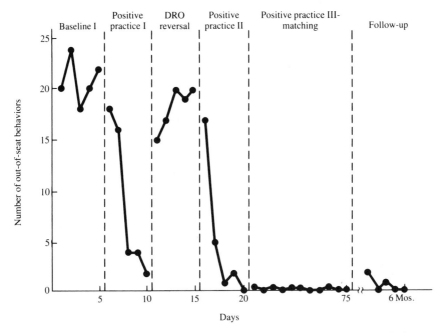

Figure 11-3. Number of out-of-seat behaviors across the six experimental phases. (Although Positive Practice III—Matching actually lasted for 55 days, only 11 data points are presented. These data points represent the mean number of out-of-seat behaviors per day for the 11 weeks of this experimental period.) (*Source:* Bornstein, Hamilton, and Quevillon, 1977.)

is difficult to compare the effects of the different interventions. Positive practice plus matching may have been more effective because it was preceded by several days and two phases of positive practice. The additional contingencies may not have been more effective if they had not been preceded by positive practice alone. Indeed, if positive practice plus the contingencies had preceded positive practice alone or if the two different conditions were given to entirely different subjects (as in between-group research), the pattern of results may have been very different.

In the above examples, alternative interventions or variations of a particular intervention were implemented at different points in time to the same subject(s). The different effects of the alternative conditions might have been due to the specific procedures that were implemented, to the sequence effect, i.e., the particular order in which the interventions appeared, or to the interaction (combined effects) of treatments and the sequence. The first (or second) condition may be more or less effective than the other condition, or equally effective, because of the position in which it appeared within the sequence. With a single case, there is no unambiguous way to evaluate treatments given in consecutive phases because of the treatment $\times$ sequence confound.

An apparent solution to the problem would be to administer two or more treatment conditions in a different order to different subjects. A minimum of two subjects would be needed (if two interventions were compared) so that each subject could receive the alternative interventions but in a different order. Presumably, if both (or all) subjects respond to the interventions consistently, the effects of the sequence in which the treatments appeared can be ruled out as a significant influence. Investigations comparing alternative treatments occasionally have presented the treatments in different orders and have shown consistent effects (e.g., Harris and Wolchick, 1979; Kazdin, 1977d). Yet the order can make a difference when it is examined (e.g., Patterson, Griffin, and Panyan, 1976; White, Nielson, and Johnson, 1972). The difficulty is that the order of the different conditions usually is not balanced (alternated) and conclusions about the differential effects of the conditions cannot be clearly inferred (e.g., Cossairt, Hall, and Hopkins, 1973; Jones and Kazdin, 1975; Kazdin, Silverman and Sittler, 1975; O'Leary, Becker, Evans, and Saudargas, 1969; Walker et al., 1976).

If presentation of the different conditions in different order yields inconsistent effects, then considerable ambiguity is introduced. If two subjects respond differently as a function of the order in which they received treatment, the investigator cannot determine whether it was the sequence that each person received or characteristics of that particular person. The possible interaction (differential effects) of treatment and sequence needs to be evaluated among several subjects to ensure that a particular treatment-sequence combination is not unique to (i.e., does not interact with) characteristics of a particular subject. Simply altering the sequence among a few subjects does not necessarily avoid the sequence problem unless there is a way in the final analyses to separate the effects of treatments, sequences, subjects, and their interactions.

The problem of evaluating variations of treatments as part of the dismantling, parametric, and constructive strategies extends to the *comparative strategy* as well. Even though the comparative strategy does not attempt to analyze alternative variations of a given treatment, it does, of course, examine the relative effectiveness of alternative treatments. In most single-case experimental designs, comparisons of different treatments are obfuscated by the sequence effects noted earlier.

The multiple-schedule and simultaneous-treatment designs attempt to provide an alternative in which two or more treatments or treatment variations can be compared in the same phase but under different or constantly changing stimulus conditions. These designs can resolve the sequence effects associated with presenting different conditions in consecutive phases. However, it is possible that the results are influenced by multiple-treatment interference, i.e., the effects of introducing more than one treatment (Johnson and Bailey, 1977; Shapiro et al., 1982). Interventions, when juxtaposed to other interventions, may have different effects from those obtained if they were administered to entirely different subjects.

Overall, evaluating different interventions introduces ambiguity for single-case research. The possible influence of administering one intervention on all subsequent interventions exists for ABAB, multiple-baseline, and changing-criterion designs. Similarly, the possibility that juxtaposing two or more treatments influences the effects that either treatment exerts is a potential problem for multiple-treatment designs. It should be noted that this ambiguity has not deterred researchers from raising questions that fit into the dismantling, parametric, constructive, or comparative strategies. Yet the conclusions are often ambiguous because of the possible influence of factors discussed above.

The remaining strategy to appear in Table 11-1 is the *client-treatment variation strategy,* which raises questions about the clients for whom the intervention is suited. Specifically, the strategy addresses whether the intervention is more or less effective as a function of particular client characteristics. The usual way that between-group research approaches this question is through factorial designs in which types of subjects and treatment are combined in the design. The analyses examine whether the effectiveness of treatment interacts with the types of clients, where clients are grouped according to such variables as age, diagnosis, socioeconomic status, severity of behavior, or other dimensions that appear to be relevant to treatment. Single-case research usually does not address questions of the characteristics of the client that may interact with treatment effects. If a few subjects are studied and respond differently, the investigator has no systematic way of determining whether treatment was more or less effective as a function of the treatment or the particular characteristics of the subjects.

In general, single-case research designs are highly suited to evaluating particular treatment packages and their effects on performance. Some of the more subtle questions of outcome research may raise difficulties for single-case experimental designs. These designs can address many of the important outcome questions but in so doing raise ambiguities that are not evident in between-group research. In the case of treatment $\times$ subject interactions, i.e., whether treatments are differentially effective as a function of certain subject characteristics, single-case designs are especially weak. Actually, the questions posed by the client-treatment variation strategy address the generality of the results among subjects. Generality of the results in single-case research is an important issue in its own right for evaluating this methodology and hence is discussed separately below.

Generality of the Findings

A major objection levied against single-case research is that the results may not be generalizable to persons other than those included in the design. This objection raises several important issues. To begin with, single-case experimental research grew out of an experimental philosophy that attempts to discover laws of individual performance (Kazdin, 1978c). There is a methodological heritage of examining variables that affect performance of individuals rather than groups of persons. Of course, interest in studying the individual reflects a larger concern with identifying generalizable findings that are not idiosyncratic. Hence, the ultimate goal, even of single-case research, is to discover generalizable relationships.

The generality of findings from single-case research is often discussed in relation to between-group research. Because between-group research uses larger numbers of subjects than does single-case research, the findings are often assumed to be more generalizable. As proponents of the single-case approach have noted, the use of large numbers of subjects in research does not, by itself, ensure generalizable findings (Sidman, 1960). In the vast majority of between-group investigations, results are evaluated on the basis of average *group* performance. The analyses do not shed light on the generality of intervention effects among individuals.

For example, if a group of twenty patients who received treatment show greater change than twenty patients who did not receive treatment, little information is available about the generality of the results. We do not know by this group analysis alone how many persons in the treatment group were affected or affected in an important way. Ambiguity about the generality of findings from between-group research is not inherent in this research approach. However, investigators rarely look at the individual subject data as well as the group data to make inferences about the generality of effects among subjects within a given treatment condition. Certainly, if the individual data were examined in between-group research, a great deal might be said about the generality of the findings.

Often the generality of the findings in between-group research is examined using the client-treatment variation strategy, as outlined above. Individual performance is not examined. Rather, the performance of classes of persons is examined to assess whether treatment(s) are differentially effective as a function of some subject variable. Within single-case demonstrations with one or a few subjects, by definition, there is no immediate possibility to assess generality across subjects. Hence, between-group research certainly can shed more light on the generality of the results than can single-case research. A factorial design examining treatment × subject interactions can provide information about the suitability of treatment for alternative subject populations.

Given the above comments, the generality of results from single-case research would seem to be a severe problem. Actually, inherent features of the single-case approach may increase rather than decrease the generality of the findings. As noted earlier, investigators who use single-case designs have emphasized the need to seek interventions that produce dramatic changes in performance. Thus, visual inspection rather than statistical significance is advocated. Interventions that produce dramatic effects are likely to be more generalizable across individuals than are effects that meet the relatively weaker criterion of statistical significance. Indeed, in any particular between-group investigation, the possibility remains that a statistically significant difference was obtained on the basis of chance. The results may not generalize to other attempts to replicate the study, not to mention to different sorts of subjects. In single-case research, extended assessment across treatment and no-treatment phases, coupled with dramatic effects, makes it implausible that the changes in performance could be attributed to chance.

Proponents of single-case research sometimes have suggested that the results may even be *more* generalizable than those obtained in between-group research because of the methodology and goals of these alternative approaches (e.g., Baer, 1977). The relative generality of findings from one approach over another may not be resolvable on the basis of currently available evidence. Yet it is important to note that generality is not necessarily a problem for single-case research. Findings obtained in single-case demonstrations appear to be highly generalizable because of the types of interventions that are commonly investigated. For example, various techniques based on reinforcement have been effective across an extremely wide range of populations, settings, and target problems (e.g., Kazdin, 1978a).

The problem of single-case research is not that the results lack generality among subjects. Rather, the problem is that there are difficulties largely inherent in the methodology for assessing the dimensions that may dictate generality of the results. Within single-case research designs, there are no provisions for identifying client-treatment interactions within a single case. Focusing on one subject does not allow for the systematic comparison of different treatments among multiple subjects who differ in various characteristics, at least within a single experiment. Examining subject variables is more readily accomplished in between-group research.

Replication

One way to examine the generality of the findings of an investigation is to evaluate a particular treatment as applied to different types of subjects, as noted earlier. When treatment interacts with characteristics of the subject, the investigator has obtained evidence about the external validity or generality of treatment effects. As already discussed, between-group research is uniquely suited to direct evaluation of generality within a single investigation.

For single-case research, the key to evaluate generality is replication (or repetition) of intervention effects across subjects. Indeed, replication is a critical ingredient for all research. Replication can examine the extent to which results obtained in one study extend (can be generalized) across a variety of settings, behaviors, measures, investigators, and other variables that conceivably could influence outcome.

Replication can be accomplished in different ways depending on the precise aspect of generality in which the investigator is interested. To evaluate generality across subjects, the investigator can conduct a direct replication. *Direct replication* consists of applying the same procedures across a number of different subjects. The investigator attempts to evaluate the intervention under exact or almost exact conditions included in the original study. A direct replication determines whether the findings are restricted to the subject(s) that happened to be included in the original demonstration.

To evaluate the generality of findings across a variety of different conditions (e.g., subjects, settings, behaviors), the investigator can conduct a systematic replication. *Systematic replication* consists of repetition of the experiment by purposely allowing features of the original experiment to vary. In a systematic replication, different types of subjects may be studied and the intervention, setting, or target problems may vary from the original experiment. Results from systematic replication research examine the extent to which the findings can be repeated across a variety of different conditions.

Actually, direct and systematic replication are not qualitatively different. An exact replication is not possible in principle since repetition of the experiment involves new subjects tested at different points in time and perhaps by different investigators, all of which conceivably could lead to different results. Thus, all replications necessarily allow some factors to vary; the issue is the extent to which the replication attempt departs from the original experiment.

If the results of direct and systematic replication research show that the intervention affects behaviors in new subjects across different conditions, the generality of the results has been demonstrated. The extent of the generality of the findings, of course, is a function of the range, number, and type of subjects, clinical problems, settings, and other conditions included in the replication studies. In any particular systematic replication study, it is useful to vary only one or a few of the dimensions along which the study could depart from the original experiment. If the results of a replication attempt differ from the original experiment, it is desirable to have a limited number of differences between the experiments so the possible reason(s) for the discrepancy of the results might be more easily identified. If there are multiple differences between the original experiment and replication experiments, discrepancies in results might be due to a host of factors not easily discerned without extensive further experimentation.

A limitation of single-case research occurs in replication attempts in which the results are inconsistent across subjects. For example, the effects of the intervention may be evaluated across several subjects in direct replication attempts. The results may be inconsistent or mixed, i.e., some subjects may have shown clear changes and others may not. In fact, it is likely that direct replication attempts will yield inconsistent results because one would not expect all persons to respond in the same way. Several demonstrations could be cited in single-case research in which all subjects included did not respond (e.g., Herman, Barlow, and Agras, 1974; Kazdin and Erickson, 1975; Wincze, Leitenberg, and Agras, 1972). The problem with inconsistent effects is understanding *why* the results did not generalize across subjects. Here lies the potential limitations of single-case research. When direct replication reveals that some subjects did not respond, the investigator has to speculate on the reasons for lack of generality. There often is no way within a single investigation or even in a series of single-case investigations to identify clearly the basis for the lack of generality.

Consider an example of a direct replication attempt with inconsistent results across subjects. Herman et al. (1974) evaluated a procedure to increase heterosexual arousal among homosexual males who wished to change their sexual orientation. The procedure included showing subjects a film depicting heterosexual scenes (a seductive nude female assuming sexual poses). In single-case designs, subjects were exposed to two erotic films, one of which depicted heterosexual stimuli, noted above, and another that depicted homosexual activities. Sexual arousal was measured directly by changes in penile blood volume (penile plethysmograph).

The intervention was applied to four males ranging in age from eighteen to thirty-eight. The results showed that heterosexual arousal increased during exposure to the heterosexual films, decreased during the homosexual film, and increased again when the heterosexual film was reintroduced. These findings were obtained for three of the four subjects. The fourth subject did not show the same pattern of arousal as the others across the different conditions.

The difficulty arises in identifying what factor(s) accounted for the lack of responsiveness of the fourth subject. The investigators noted that the subject differed from the others in being the only one with a history of active heterosexual experiences (in which he employed homosexual fantasies to produce arousal). Also, this patient was seen for fewer sessions than the others. From the original report, it is evident that this subject was the oldest included in the studies and also had the longest history of homosexuality (twenty-six years). This subject may have differed from the others in a variety of ways, many of which might not even be known to the investigators. How can one identify empirically which factor(s) accounted for the lack of responsiveness? Stated another way, how can one evaluate which factor(s) dictated the generality of the results among subjects?

The above research would need to be followed up with systematic replications across subjects who differed in each of the factors that might contribute to the success or failure of treatment. This is a difficult task, to say the least, and it is perhaps especially so for single-case research. A more manageable alternative would be to identify a limited number of factors according to which subjects could be grouped (e.g., younger versus older, relatively short versus long history of homosexuality, previous heterosexual experience versus no previous heterosexual experience). Whether these factors contribute to change could be systematically evaluated in between-group research. Factorial designs provide a direct way to examine treatment × subject interactions.

If the problem focused on is relatively uncommon, a sufficient number of subjects may not be available for an investigator to conduct factorial designs. The investigator may only see a small number of cases. One alternative is to have several investigators or clinicians collect data on all of the cases seen at different treatment settings and to catalogue subject variables as well as behavior changes. The information, when accumulated across several cases, could be analyzed for treatment × subject interactions (Barlow, 1981).

It is possible that a few systematic replications of a single-case demonstration may show that some subjects (e.g., those with lower IQs, with certain psychiatric diagnoses rather than others) respond less well than others. If the relationship between subject characteristics and response to treatment is obvious, it may be evident with a consistent pattern of data among different types of subjects. It is more likely that direct replication attempts will not show perfectly consistent results depending on the type of subject. Treatment × subject interactions often are difficult to discern from one or a few subjects because these interaction effects themselves may not be consistent. That is, treatment may be more effective with one type of subject rather than another but this will not *always* be true. Group research, with its reliance on statistical analyses, often is useful to evaluate reliable, albeit occasionally subtle, interactions.

General Comments

Generality of the results from single-case research is not an inherent problem with the methodology itself. In fact, it appears that intervention effects demonstrated in single-case research have been highly generalizable across subjects, settings, and other conditions for many interventions. The case is often made that the stringent criteria for evaluating interventions in single-case research identifies interventions with effects that are likely to be more potent and more generalizable than those identified by statistical techniques. The argument is not empirically resolvable at this time but is interesting because it points to the notion that using fewer subjects does not necessarily restrict the generality of the results. In general, investigation of the dimensions or factors that influence the generality of a finding is difficult to accomplish in a single-case study. Systematically evaluating the factors that interact with treatment is more readily accomplished with between-group factorial designs.

Summary and Conclusions

In single-case designs, several problems may emerge as the data are gathered that compete with drawing unambiguous conclusions. Major problems common to each of the designs include ambiguity introduced by trends and variability in the data, particularly during the baseline phases. *Baseline trends* toward improved performance may be handled in various ways, including continuing observations for protracted periods, using procedures to reverse the direction of the trend (e.g., DRO schedule of reinforcement), selecting designs that do not depend on the absence of trends in baseline, or using statistical techniques that take into account initial trends.

Excessive variability in performance also may obscure intervention effects. The appearance of variability can be improved by blocking consecutive data points and plotting blocked averages rather than day-to-day performance. Of course, it is desirable, even if not always feasible, to search for possible contributors to variability, such as characteristics of the assessment procedures (e.g., low interobserver agreement) or the situation (e.g., variation among the environmental stimuli).

A major issue for single-case research is deciding the *duration of phases,* an issue that encompasses problems related to trend and variability. It is difficult to identify rigid rules about the minimum number of data points necessary within a phase because the clarity and utility of a set of observations is a function of the data pattern in adjacent phases. Occasionally, objective criteria have been specified for deciding when to shift phases. Such criteria have the advantage of reducing the subjectivity that can enter into the decisions about shifting phases. Most criteria used in the applied literature are based on obtaining data over consecutive days within a phase that do not deviate beyond a certain level, i.e., fall within a prespecified range, from the mean of that phase. In applied work, it may be useful to include multiple criteria for defining when to shift a phase so that there are options that will help the investigator avoid protracted delays in shifting phases.

Aside from common methodological issues that arise in single-case designs, larger concerns were discussed. A major issue is the range of questions about intervention effects that can be addressed easily by single-case research. Among the many outcome questions that serve as a basis for research, single-case designs are best suited to *treatment package evaluation,* i.e., investigation of the effects of an overall intervention and comparison of that intervention with no treatment (baseline). *Dismantling, parametric, constructive, and comparative treatment evaluation strategies* raise potential problems because they require more than one intervention given to the same subject. The prospect and effects of multiple-treatment interference need to be evaluated as part of the design if unambiguous conclusions are to be reached about the relative merits of alternative procedures.

The *generality of results* from single-case research also is a major issue. Concerns often have been voiced about the fact that only one or two subjects are studied at a time and the extent to which findings extend to other persons is not known. Actually, there is no evidence that findings from single-case research are any less generalizable than findings from between-group research. In fact, because of the type of interventions studied in single-case research, the case is sometimes made that the results may be more generalizable than those obtained in between-group research.

The area in which generality is a problem for single-case research is the investigation of the variables or subject characteristics that contribute to generality. In single-case research, it is difficult to evaluate interactions between treatments and subject characteristics. Between-group factorial designs are more appropriate for such questions and address the generality or external validity of the results directly. For single-case research, generality is usually studied through *replication* of intervention effects across subjects, situations, clinical problems, and other dimensions of interest. Indeed, replication is an important characteristic of all research. The difficulty for single-case research is that replication still does not easily illuminate treatment × subject interactions. Overall, it is not the generality of findings from single-case research that is necessarily a problem. However, the investigation of factors that contribute to generality is more difficult within this methodology than for between-group research.

12

Summing Up:
Single-Case Research in Perspective

The individual subject has been used throughout history as the basis for drawing inferences both in experimental and clinical research, as highlighted in the introductory chapter of the book. Development of single-case designs as a distinct method of experimentation has emerged relatively recently. The designs discussed in previous chapters provide alternative ways of ruling out or making implausible threats to internal validity, a critical feature of experimentation.

Single-case research as an experimental methodology has been associated predominantly with particular areas of investigation. Indeed, it is not difficult to identify a distinct conceptual position, professional journals, and professional organizations with which single-case research is associated.[1] Of course, it is a mistake to imply that single-case research has not proliferated beyond an area with easily identified boundaries. For example, the approach has been extended to diverse disciplines, including clinical psychology, psychiatry, medicine, education, counseling, social work, and law enforcement and corrections (e.g., Kazdin, 1975). (Some of these areas have their own texts on single-case research [e.g., Chassan, 1979; Jayaratne and Levy, 1979; Kratochwill, 1978].)

---

1. The conceptual position is referred to as the experimental and applied analysis of behavior; the professional journals in which single-case designs predominate are the *Journal of the Experimental Analysis of Behavior* and the *Journal of Applied Behavior Analysis;* and the professional organizations in which proponents of single-case research are especially active include Division 25 of the American Psychological Association and the Association for Behavior Analysis.

Despite the extension of the methodology to diverse disciplines and areas of research, the tendency still exists to regard single-case designs as restricted in their focus. It is important to examine single-case designs more generally to convey their essential characteristics apart from any particular conceptual framework. Single-case research occupies an important place in the larger scientific effort of addressing a wide range of questions of basic and applied interest. The relationship of single-case and between-group research, often seen as rival approaches, needs to be considered as well.

Characteristics of Single-Case Research

Previous chapters have detailed the assessment, design, and evaluation techniques of single-case research. After all of the detail, it is useful to look at the designs more generally. Single-case designs are often considered to consist of several distinct characteristics that may limit their relevance for widespread application.

Historically, single-case designs have been closely tied to the experimental and applied analysis of behavior, an approach toward conceptualizing the subject matter of psychology and conducting research. This approach has been elaborated through systematic laboratory research in operant conditioning. The research has become identified with several characteristics, including the investigation of one or a few subjects, examination of the effects of various experimental manipulations on the frequency or rate of responding, evaluation of the data from direct (visual) inspection of changes in performance over time, and others (see Kazdin, 1978c). Because single-case designs frequently have been used to investigate variables important in operant conditioning, the association between the designs and a particular conceptual position has seemed essential. Single-case designs are not necessarily restricted to any particular theoretical approach, however. Many characteristics attributed to single-case designs are more properly tied to the conceptual position of operant conditioning rather than to the designs themselves. Consider the central characteristics of single-case designs.

Of all the characteristics that might be ascribed to single-case research, two seem to be central. First, single-case designs require *continuous assessment* of behavior over time. Measures are administered on multiple occasions within separate phases. Continuous assessment is used as a basis for drawing inferences about intervention effects. Patterns of performance can be detected by obtaining several data points under different conditions. Second, *intervention effects are replicated within the same subject* over time.[2] Subjects serve as their own controls, and comparisons of the subject's performances are made as different conditions are implemented over time. Of course, the designs differ in the precise fashion in which intervention effects are replicated, but each design takes advantage of continuous assessment over time and evaluation of the subject's behavior under different conditions.

Several other characteristics often are associated with single-case designs but do not necessarily constitute defining characteristics. It is important to mention these briefly to dispel misconceptions about the designs and their applicability. Perhaps a characteristic that seems most salient is the *focus on one or a few subjects*. The designs are often referred to as "small-N research," "N-of-one research," or "single-case designs," as in the present text. Certainly it is true that the designs have developed out of concern for investigation of the behavior of individual subjects who are studied intensively over time. However, investigation of one or a few subjects is not a necessary feature of the methodology. The designs refer to particular types of experimental arrangements. The number of subjects included in the design is somewhat arbitrary. So-called single-case research can use a group of subjects in any design (e.g., ABAB) in which the entire group is treated as a subject. Also, one can use several different groups in one of the designs (e.g., multiple-baseline design across classrooms, schools, families, or communities).

The number of subjects included in the design can vary widely. For example, single-case methodology has been used to evaluate procedures in which the actual or potential subjects include thousands or even more than a million subjects (e.g., McSweeney, 1978; Schnelle et al., 1978). Although single-case research has usually been employed with one or a few subjects, this is not a necessary characteristic of the designs.

Another characteristic of single-case research has been the evaluation of interventions on *overt behavior*. The data for single-case research often consist of direct observations of performance. The association of single-case research with assessment of overt behavior is easily understandable from a historical standpoint. The development of single-case research grew out of the research on the *behavior* of organisms (Skinner, 1938). Behavior was defined in experimental research as overt performance measures such as frequency or rate of responding. As single-case designs were extended in applied research, assessment of overt behavior has continued to be associated with the methodology.

---

2. An exception to the replication of intervention effects within the same subject is the multiple-baseline design across subjects. In this instance, subjects serve as their own control in the sense that each subject represents a separate AB design, and the replication of intervention effects is across subjects.

Yet single-case research designs are not necessarily restricted to overt performance. The methodology does require continuous assessment, and measures that can be obtained to meet this requirement can be employed. Other measures than overt performance can be found in single-case investigations. For example, self-report and psychophysiological measures have been included in single-case research (e.g., Alford, Webster, and Sanders, 1980; Hayes et al., 1978). In any case, the assessment of overt behavior is not a necessary characteristic of single-case research.

Another characteristic of research that would seem to be pivotal to single-case designs is the evaluation of data through *visual inspection* rather than statistical analyses. Certainly a strong case might be made for visual inspection as a crucial characteristic of the methodology (Baer, 1977). Indeed, a major purpose of continuous measurement over time is to allow the investigator to *see* changes in the data as a function of stable patterns of performance within different conditions.

Actually, there is no necessary connection between single-case research and visual inspection of the data. Single-case designs refer to the manner in which the experimental situation is arranged to evaluate intervention effects and to rule out threats to internal validity. There is no fixed or necessary relationship between how the situation is arranged (experimental design) and the manner in which the resulting information is evaluated (data analysis). In recent years, statistical analyses have been applied increasingly to single-case investigations. Although visual inspection continues to be the primary method of data evaluation for single-case research, this is not a necessary connection.

A final characteristic is that single-case designs are used to investigate interventions derived from operant conditioning. Historically, operant conditioning and single-case designs developed together, and the substantive content of the former was inextricably bound with the evaluative techniques of the latter (Kazdin, 1978c). Over the years, single-case designs and operant conditioning have proliferated remarkably in both experimental (Honig, 1966; Honig and Staddon, 1977) and applied research (Catania and Brigham, 1978; Leitenberg, 1976). To be sure, most of the interventions evaluated in applied single-case research are derivatives of principles or procedures of operant conditioning, including a variety of reinforcement and punishment techniques. Yet it is not accurate to suggest that the interventions investigated in single-case research must be based on operant conditioning. A number of different types of interventions derived from clinical psychology, medicine, pharmacology, social psychology, and other areas not central to or derived from operant conditioning have been included in single-case research.

Many arguments about the utility and limitations of single-case designs focus on features not central to the designs. For example, objections focus on nonstatistical data evaluation, the use of only one or two subjects, and restricting the evaluation to overt behavior. While these objections can be addressed on their own grounds, there is a larger point that needs to be made. The many characteristics tied to single-case designs have long been associated with a combined methodological and substantive position about research in psychology. Yet the designs can be distinguished from the larger approach. Applied research in clinical, educational, community and other settings can profit greatly from extension of single-case designs. The areas might profit as well from the approach with which such designs have been associated. However, the approach is not essential. It would be unfortunate if investigators eschewed a methodology with potentially broad utility because of antipathy over a particular theoretical position that need not necessarily be embraced.

Single-Case and Between-Group Research

The research questions that prompt clinical or applied experimentation can be addressed in many different ways and at different levels of analysis. First, questions about interventions and their effects can be addressed at the level of the single case. Single-case experimental designs can be used in the multifaceted ways, as discussed throughout previous chapters. Their unique contribution is to provide the means to evaluate interventions experimentally for the individual client.

Second, questions can be addressed at the level of groups. Although groups of subjects can be investigated in single-case designs, the usual methodology is based on between-group designs. In between-group research, one group is compared with one or more other groups. The unique contribution of between-group research is to examine the separate and combined effects of different variables within the same investigation.

Third, questions about intervention effects can be addressed at the level of examining many different between-group studies. Data from several different group studies can serve as the basis for drawing conclusions about different types of interventions, a type of evaluation referred to as *meta-analysis* (Smith and Glass, 1977).[3] Each of the above levels of analysis for evaluating interven-

---

3. For the reader unfamiliar with meta-analysis, other sources can be consulted, including descriptions and illustrations of the technique (Blanchard, Andrasik, Ahles, Teders, and O'Keefe, 1980; Glass, 1976; Smith and Glass, 1977), critiques of the analysis (Gallo, 1978; Eysenck, 1978; Kazdin and Wilson, 1978), and innovative types of meta-analyses to overcome objections to previous versions (Kazrin, Durac, and Agteros, 1979).

tion effects has its assets and liabilities. It is difficult to argue convincingly in favor of one level of analysis to the exclusion of the others.

Psychological research has placed great emphasis on between-group designs and statistical evaluation of the results. Specific limitations have been levied against this methodology by proponents of single-case research (e.g., Hersen and Barlow, 1976; Robinson and Foster, 1979; Sidman, 1960) but by many others as well (e.g., Lykken, 1968; Meehl, 1967). In the larger scheme of research, the particular objections may not be crucial. The general point is that between-group research is one approach; however multifaceted, it is ipso facto limited to some degree in the picture it provides of empirical phenomena. Single-case research represents another level of analysis. This level does not necessarily replace between-group research since it too has its own set of limitations.

In many cases single-case and between-group research have similar goals. For example, both methodologies are suited to evaluating a given intervention package. In single-case research, an intervention can be provided to a particular subject or group and replicated over time or across behaviors, situations, or persons. In between-group research, groups can be divided into treatment and no-treatment conditions. The evidence from both levels can attest to the efficacy or lack of efficacy of the procedures.

In several other instances, single-case and between-group research address different types of questions or can address the different questions with varying degrees of clarity. To object to or refute one type of research is to ignore sets of questions or answers that are encompassed by that approach. One type of methodology cannot address all of the questions that are likely to be of interest. And to apply any single methodology to the full gamut of research questions is to seek answers that are in some cases destined to ambiguity.

If single-case methodology is only one among alternative strategies that should be considered for the questions of applied research, then one might question the advisability of preparing a book devoted narrowly to one type of methodology. Several books have been and continue to be prepared on the fundamentals of between-group design. By their exclusion of single-case designs, such books imply that between-group research is the sole method of scientific research. The view that between-group research is the only research methodology is usually exemplified in undergraduate and graduate curricula in psychology, in which single-case designs are rarely taught. This book was designed to elaborate single-case methodology and to describe design options, their utility, and their limitations. Only when the methodology itself is thoroughly elaborated and taught can its place in the larger schema of scientific research be considered.

Appendix A

Graphic Display of Data
for Visual Inspection

Chapter 10 provided a discussion of visual inspection, its underlying rationale, and how it is invoked in single-case experimental research.[1] As noted earlier, the general criterion for deciding whether the intervention was responsible for change consists of the extent to which the data follow the pattern required by the design. In the concrete case, several characteristics of the data are crucial for reaching this decision, including examining the changes in means, levels, and trends across phases and the rapidity of the changes when experimental conditions (phases) are changed.

Visual inspection requires that the data be graphically displayed so that the various characteristics of the data can be readily examined. This appendix discusses major options for displaying the data to help the investigator apply the criteria of visual inspection to single-case data. Commonly used graphs and descriptive aids that can be added to simple graphs to facilitate interpretation of the results are discussed briefly and illustrated.

Basic Types of Graphs

Data from single-case research can be displayed in several different types of graphs. In each type, the data are plotted in the usual fashion so that the

1. This appendix on visual inspection and the following appendix on statistical analyses are designed to be read after the chapter on data evaluation (Chapter 10). The appendixes are devoted primarily to the mechanics of graphic display, data inspection, and statistical analyses and presuppose mastery of the underlying rationale and points of controversy discussed in the earlier chapter.

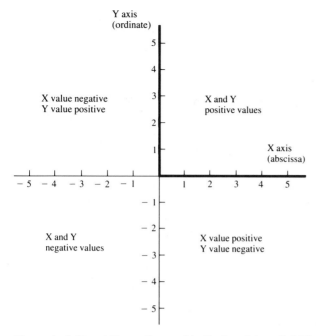

Figure A–1. X and Y axes for graphic display of data. Bold lines indicate the quadrant used in majority of graphs in single-case research.

dependent measure is on the *ordinate* (vertical or y axis) and the data are plotted over time, represented by the *abscissa* (horizontal or x axis). Typical ordinate values include such labels as frequency of responses, percentage of intervals, number of correct responses, and so on. Typical abscissa values or labels include sessions, days, weeks, or months.

As noted in Figure A-1, four quadrants of the graph can be identified in the general case. The quadrants vary as a function of whether the values are negative or positive on each axis. In single-case research, almost all graphs would fit into the top right quadrant (marked by bold lines) where the y axis (ordinate) and x axis (abscissa) values are *positive*. The values for the ordinate range from zero to some higher positive number that reflects interest in responses that occur in varying numbers. Negative response values are usually not possible. Similarly, the focus is usually on performance over time from day one to some point in the future. Hence, the x axis usually is not a negative number, which would go back into history.

A variety of types of graphs can be used to present single-case data (see Parsonson and Baer, 1978). For present purposes, three major types of graphs will be discussed and illustrated. Emphasis will be placed on the use of the graphs in relation to the criteria for invoking visual inspection.

Simple Line Graph

The most commonly used method of plotting data in single-case research consists of noting the level of performance of the subject over time. The data for the subject are plotted each day in a noncumulative fashion. The score for that day can take on any value of the dependent measure and may be higher or lower than values obtained on previous occasions. This method of plotting the data is represented in virtually all of the examples of graphs in previous chapters. However, it is useful to illustrate briefly this type of figure in the general case to examine its characteristics more closely.

Figure A-2 provides a hypothetical example in which data are plotted in a simple line graph. The crucial feature to note is that the data on different days can show an increase or decrease over time. That is, the data points on a given day can be higher or lower than the data points of other days. The actual score that the subject receives for a given day is plotted as such. Hence, performance on a particular occasion is easily discerned from the graph. For example, on day ten of Figure A-2, the reader can easily discern that the target response occurred forty times and on the next day the frequency increased to fifty responses. Hence, the daily level of performance and the pattern of how well or poorly the subject is doing in relation to the dependent values are easily detected.

The obvious advantage of the simple line graph is that one can immediately

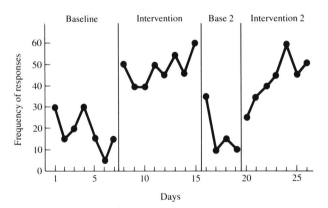

Figure A-2. Hypothetical example of ABAB design as plotted on a simple line graph in which frequency of responses is the ordinate and days is the abscissa.

determine how the subject is performing at a glance. The simple line graph represents a relatively nontechnical format for presenting the session-by-session data. Much of single-case research is conducted in applied settings where the need exists to communicate the results of the intervention to parents, teachers, children, and others who are unfamiliar with alternative data presentation techniques. The simple line graph provides a format that is relatively easy to grasp.

An important feature of the simple line graph, even for the better trained eye, is that it facilitates the evaluation of various characteristics of the data as they relate to visual inspection. Changes in mean, level, slope, and the rapidity of changes in performance are especially easy to examine in simple line graphs. And, as discussed later in this appendix, several descriptive aids can be added to simple line graphs to facilitate decisions about mean, level, and trend changes over time.

Cumulative Graph

The cumulative graph consists of noting the level of performance of the subject over time in an additive fashion. The score the subject receives on one occasion is added to the value of the scores plotted on previous occasions. The score obtained for the subject on a given day may take on any value of the dependent measure. Yet the value of the score that is plotted is *the accumulated total* for all previous days.

Consider as a hypothetical example data plotted in Figure A-3, the same data that were plotted in Figure A-2. On the first day, the subject obtained a score of thirty. On the next day the subject received a score of fifteen. The fifteen is not plotted as such. Rather, it is added to the thirty so that the cumulative graph shows a forty-five for day two. The graph continues in this fashion so that all data are plotted in relation to all previous data.

Data in applied behavior analysis are usually plotted in a noncumulative fashion, although exceptions can be found in the literature.[2] For example, in one investigation, procedures were implemented to reduce shoplifting in a department store (McNees, Egli, Marshall, Schnelle, Schnelle, and Risley, 1976, Exp. 2). The study focused on the shoplifting of women's pants and tops, two types of items shown in preliminary observations to be the most frequently stolen items in the young womens' clothing department where the project was completed. To measure shoplifting, different types of merchandise were

---

2. For additional examples of the use of cumulative graphs in single-case research, several recent sources can be consulted (e.g., Bunck and Iwata, 1978; Burg, Reid, and Lattimore, 1979; Hansen, 1979; Neef, Iwata, and Page, 1980).

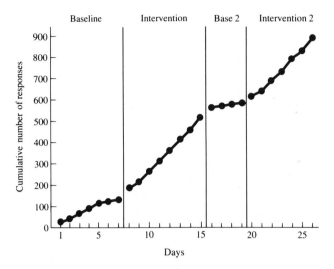

Figure A–3. Hypothetical example of ABAB design as plotted on a cumulative graph. Each data point consists of the data for that day plus the total for all previous days.

counted and tagged each day. The number and type of stolen (missing) items could be derived by counting the number of tags removed when items were sold, the number of tagged items remaining at the end of the day, and the number of total tagged items at the start of the day.

The intervention consisted of placing signs (17.5 by 27.5 cm) on clothing racks and walls of the department that said: "Attention Shoppers and Shop-lifters—The items you see marked with a red star are items that shoplifters frequently take" (p. 403). A special red tag was placed on the two articles of clothing most frequently stolen (pants and tops) in a multiple-baseline design. The effects of identifying the clothing on the amount of theft can be seen in Figure A-4. The cumulative number of thefts of both pants and tops shows a steady increase over the course of baseline (before identification). When the intervention (identification) begins, data show that theft of these items was virtually eliminated (horizontal lines). The effect of the intervention is clear, given the consistent changes when the intervention was introduced. The cumulative graph also is easy to interpret, given the marked changes in rate (and slope) during the AB phases for each type of clothing. (Incidentally, additional data obtained in the study indicated that shoplifting of other items in the store did not increase when the shoplifting of pants and tops was decreased.)

The use of cumulative graphs in single-case research can be traced primarily to infrahuman laboratory research in the experimental analysis of behavior

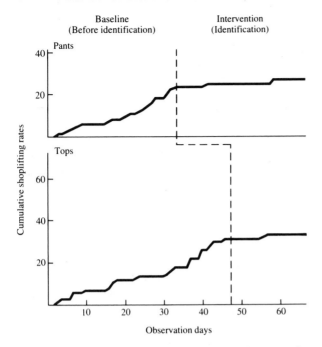

Figure A–4. Cumulative rates of shoplifting for pants (top panel) and tops (lower panel) before and while frequently taken merchandise was publicly identified. (*Source:* McNees, Egli, Marshall, Schnelle, Schnelle, and Risley, 1976.)

(see Kazdin, 1978c). The frequency of responses was often plotted as a function of time (rate) and accumulated over the course of the experiment. Data were recorded automatically on a cumulative record, an apparatus that records accumulated response rates. The cumulative record was a convenient way to plot large numbers of responses over time. The focus of much of the research was on the rate of responding rather than on absolute numbers of responses on discrete occasions such as days or sessions (Skinner, 1938). A simple line graph is not as useful to study rate over time, because the time periods of the investigation are not divided into discrete sessions (e.g., days). The experimenter might study changes in rate over the course of varying time periods rather than discrete sessions.

A cumulative graph was especially useful in detecting patterns of responding and immediate changes over time. For example, in much early work in operant conditioning, schedules of reinforcement were studied in which variations in presenting reinforcing consequences served as the independent variable. Schedule effects can be easily detected in a cumulative graph in which the rate of response changes in response to alterations of reinforcement schedules. The increases in rate are reflected in changes of the slope of the cumulative record; absence of responding is reflected in a horizonal line (see Ferster and Skinner, 1957).

In applied research, cumulative graphs are used only occasionally. Part of the reason is that they are not as easily interpreted as are noncumulative graphs. The cumulative graph does not quickly convey the level of performance on a given day for the subject. For example, a teacher may wish to know how many arithmetic problems a child answered correctly on a particular day. This is not easy to cull from a cumulative graph. The absolute number of responses on a given day may be important to detect and communicate quickly to others. Noncumulative graphs are likely to be more helpful in this regard.

The move away from cumulative graphs also is associated with an expanded range of dependent measures. Cumulative graphs have been used in basic laboratory research to study rate of responding. The parameter of time (frequency/time) was very important to consider in evaluating the effects of the independent variable. In applied research, responses per minute or per session usually are not as crucial as the total number of responses alone. For example, in a clinical setting, the intervention may attempt to reduce the aggressive acts of a violent psychiatric patient. Although the rate of aggressive responses over time and the changes in rate may be of interest, the primary interest usually is simply in the total number of these responses for a given day. The changes in rate during a given session are not as critical as the total number of occurrences. The analysis of moment-to-moment changes, often of great interest in basic laboratory research, usually is of less interest in applied research.

Histogram

A histogram or bar graph provides a simple and relatively clear way of presenting data. The histogram presents vertical or occasionally horizontal columns to represent performance under different conditions. Each bar or column represents the *mean* or average level *of performance* for a separate phase. For example, the mean of all of the data points for baseline would be plotted as a single column; the mean for the intervention and for subsequent phases would be obtained and presented separately in the same fashion. Figure A-5 illustrates a hypothetical ABAB design in which the data are presented in a simple line graph (upper panel); the same data are presented as a histogram (lower panel).

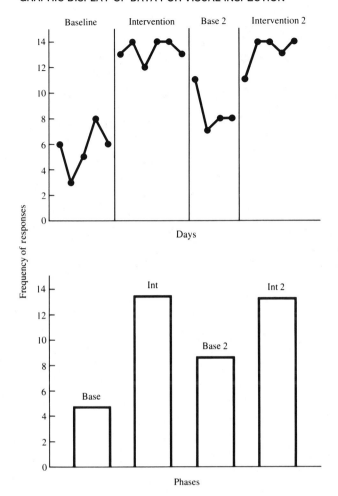

Figure A-5. Hypothetical example of an ABAB design in which the data are represented in a simple line graph *(upper panel)* and a histogram *(lower panel)*.

Histograms are occasionally used to present data in single-case research.[3] An excellent illustration was provided in an investigation that increased the use of language among institutionalized mentally retarded children (Halle, Marshall, and Spradlin, 1979). In many institutions, staff often attend to the needs

3. For additional illustrations of the use of histograms in single-case research, other sources can be consulted (e.g., Barber and Kagey, 1977; Cataldo, Bessman, Parker, Pearson, and Rogers, 1979; Foxx and Hake, 1977).

of the children in such a way that there is no need, opportunity, or demand for the children to express themselves verbally. This investigation attempted to encourage the use of speech at mealtime among several children. During baseline, children picked up their trays in the dining room at mealtime as their names were called. The tray was handed to the child as he or she came up. In the invervention phase, a very brief delay (fifteen seconds) was inserted between the child's appearance and the delivery of the tray. The purpose was to encourage children to make a request for the food before they were given it. As soon as the food was requested, the tray was given. If no response occurred, the food was given anyway as soon as fifteen seconds had elapsed.

The effects of the delay procedure were evaluated on the percentage of meals in which verbal requests for food were made, as the intervention was introduced in a multiple-baseline design across meals (breakfast and lunch). The data for two of the children, plotted in histogram form in Figure A-6, show that requests for food were low for each meal during the baseline phase. When the delay phase was introduced, the percentage of requests increased markedly, showing the pattern expected in a multiple-baseline design.

The advantage of histograms is that they present the results in one of the easiest formats to interpret. Day-to-day performance within a given phase is averaged. The reader is presented with essentially only one characteristic of the data within the phase, namely, the mean. Fluctuations in performance, trends, and information about duration of the phases are usually omitted. The advantage in simplifying the format for presenting the data has a price. The interpretation of data from single-case experiments very much depends on seeing several characteristics (e.g., changes in level, mean, trend). Insofar as histograms exclude portions of the original data, less information is presented to the naive reader from which well-based conclusions can be reached.

The features of the data not revealed by a histogram may contribute to misinterpretations about the pattern of change over time. For example, trends in baseline and/or intervention phases may not be represented in histograms, which could have implications for the conclusions that are reached. Hypothetical data are plotted in Figure A-7 to show the sorts of problems that can arise. In the upper left panel, a continuous improvement is shown over baseline and intervention phases in the simple line graph. The right upper panel plots the same data in a histogram, which suggests that a sharp improvement was associated with the intervention. But the different averages represented by the histogram are a function of the overall trend, which requires the simple line graph to detect. In the lower panel, another set of data is plotted, this time showing that behavior was increasing during baseline (e.g., become worse) and changing in its trend with the intervention. The simple line graph suggests that the

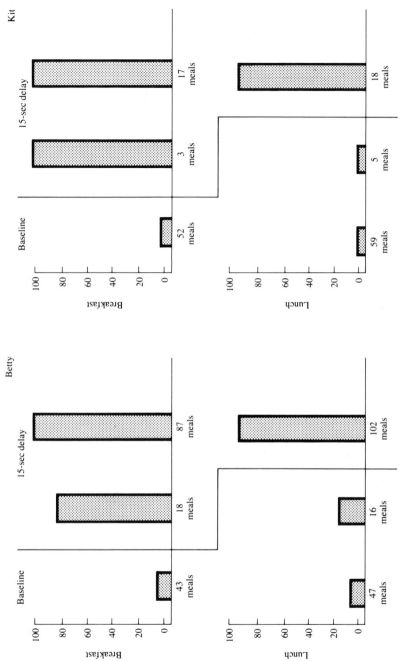

Figure A–6. Percentage of meals requested across conditions for both breakfasts and lunches. (*Source:* Halle, Marshall, and Spradlin, 1979.)

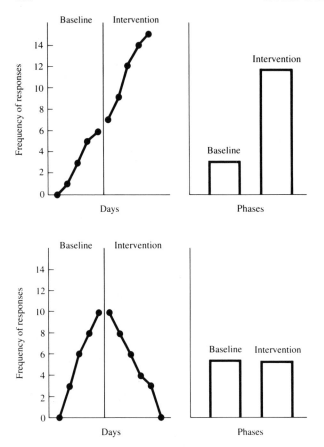

Figure A–7. Hypothetical data from AB phases. The *upper panel* shows the same data plotted in a simple line graph (left) and replotted as a histogram. The histogram suggests large changes in behavior, but the simple line graph suggests the changes were due to a trend beginning in baseline and continuing during the intervention phase. The *lower panel* provides an example in which the intervention was associated with a marked change as shown in the simple line graph (left), but the histogram (right) suggests no change from baseline to intervention phases.

intervention reversed the direction of change. Yet the histogram shows that the averages from the phases are virtually identical. In general, one must be cautious in interpreting histograms without information about trends in the data that may influence the conclusions.

Histograms are especially useful when data are not obtained on a continuous basis within each phase or condition. When performance is assessed on one or a small number of occasions (e.g., before and after intervention), it is useful to represent these in a bar graph. The means are represented graphically and no information is lost about the pattern of data over time within a particular phase. However, the present discussion addresses the use of graphic techniques for continuous data. In these instances, histograms do not convey major characteristics of the data that are usually necessary to apply criteria of visual inspection.

Descriptive Aids for Visual Inspection

As noted earlier, inferences based on visual inspection rely on several characteristics of single-case data. In the usual case, simple line graphs are used to represent the data over time and across phases. The ease of inferring reliable intervention effects depends among other things on evaluating changes in the mean, level, and trend across phases, and the rapidity of changes when conditions are altered. Several aids are available that can permit the investigator to present more information on the simple line graph to address these characteristics.

Changes in Mean

The easiest source of information to add to a simple line graph that can facilitate visual inspection is the plotting of means. The data are presented in the usual way so that day-to-day performance is displayed. The mean for each phase is plotted as a horizontal or solid line within the phase. Plotting these means as horizontal lines or in a similar way readily permits the reader to compare the overall effects of the different conditions, i.e., provides a summary statement.

For example, Barnard, Christophersen, and Wolf (1977) evaluated the effects of a reinforcement and punishment program implemented by parents to control the behavior of their children on shopping trips. The target focus was on staying relatively close to the parent and not disturbing merchandise in the store. Parents provided children with incentive points (exchangeable for privileges and goods), praise, and feedback for behaving appropriately and loss of points (response cost) for misbehavior. The program was evaluated in a multiple-baseline design for three children. The data for one child are presented in Figure A-8, which shows that each behavior improved when the intervention was introduced. Along with the session-by-session data, dotted lines represent the mean levels within each phase and at the follow-up check approximately five months after the program. In this example, the means provide useful information, but the effects are clear without it.

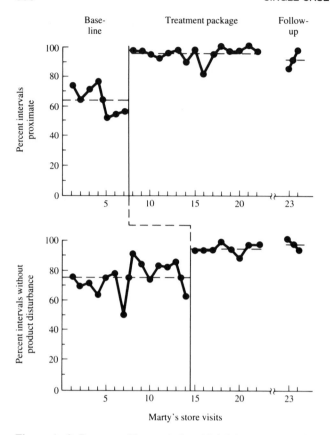

Figure A–8. Percent of intervals in which Marty remained proximate and refrained from disturbing products during store visits. (*Source:* Barnard, Christophersen, and Wolf, 1977.)

Another example provides a demonstration with effects much less clear than the previous example. In this demonstration, feedback was used to improve the performance of boys (nine to ten years old) who participated in a Pop Warner football team (Komaki and Barnett, 1977). The purpose was to improve execution of the plays by selected members of the team (backfield and center). A checklist of players' behaviors was scored after each play to measure if each player did what he was supposed to. During the feedback phase, the coach pointed out what was done correctly and incorrectly after each play. The feedback from the coach was introduced in a multiple-baseline design across various plays.

The results are presented in Figure A-9, which shows that performance

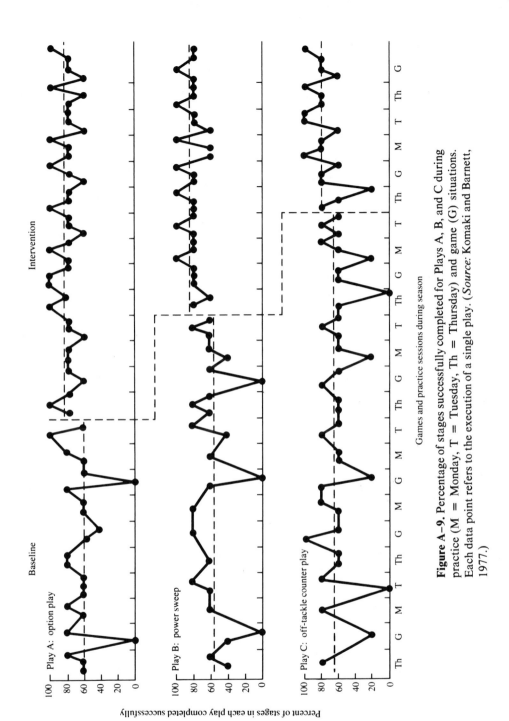

Figure A–9. Percentage of stages successfully completed for Plays A, B, and C during practice (M = Monday, T = Tuesday, Th = Thursday) and game (G) situations. Each data point refers to the execution of a single play. (*Source:* Komaki and Barnett, 1977.)

tended to improve at each point that the intervention was introduced. The means are represented in each phase by the horizontal dotted lines. In this example, the means are especially useful because intervention effects are not very strong. Changes in level or trend are not apparent from baseline to intervention phases. Also, rapid effects associated with implementation of the intervention are not evident either. The plot of means shows a weak but seemingly consistent effect across the baselines. Without the means, it might be much less clear that any change occurred at all.

The plotting of means represents an easy tool for conveying slightly more information in simple line graphs than would otherwise be available. Essentially, plotting of means combines the advantages of simple line graphs and histograms. Although the use of means adds important information to the simple line graph, it is important to note as well that they occasionally may mislead the reader.

The examination of means across phases may suggest that more marked effects were obtained than actually reflected in the day-to-day data, a point already noted in the discussion of histograms. For example, if there is a trend in the data such as a steady improvement over the course of baseline and intervention phases, the means for these phases will suggest a clear and possibly marked improvement in performance. Alternatively, if there is a reverse in trend across baseline and intervention phases, the means may show little or no change. For example, during baseline, a city's crime rate may show a steady increase. An intervention implemented to reduce crime may completely reverse this trend so that a steady decline is evident. The means may be the same across phases but the trends are in opposite directions.

Also, means may misrepresent the data when there are brief phases or when performance is highly variable. With brief phases such as one or two data points or with highly variable performance across phases of longer durations, the means may suggest that a clear change in performance was evident. Too few data points or highly variable performance may suggest that greater experimental control was achieved than is actually evident in the individual data points themselves.

Actually, the means do not *misrepresent* performance in any of the above conditions. The investigator seeing a plot of a mean or the numerical quantity itself may provide an interpretation that is different from the interpretation made if the complete data were examined, i.e., the day-to-day performance. Hence, the cautions do not refer to plotting means but only in making interpretations from them. The advantage of plotting means in a simple line graph rather than a histogram is that the day-to-day performance can be taken into account when interpreting the means.

Changes in Level

Another source of information on which visual inspection often relies is changes in level across phases. Changes in level refer to the discontinuity or shift in the data at each point that the experimental conditions are changed (e.g., change from A to B or from B to A phases). Typically this change refers to the difference in the last day of one phase and the first day of the next. No special technique is needed to describe this change. (One technique to describe the changes in level in ratio form has been devised as part of the split-middle technique of estimating trends, and will be discussed below.)

Of course, the investigator may be interested in going beyond merely *describing* changes in level. The issue is not whether there is simply a shift in performance from the last day of one phase to the first day to the next. Performance normally varies on a daily basis, so it is unlikely that performance will be at the same level two days in a row (unless the behavior never occurs). When conditions are changed, the major interest is whether the change in level is beyond what would be expected from ordinary fluctuations in performance. That is, is the shift in performance large enough to depart from what would be expected given the usual variability in performance?

The *evaluation* of the change in level is different from the description of the change. Whether the change in level represents a veridical change in performance that departs from ordinary variability in the data is a matter of statistical inference and, hence, is beyond the scope of purely visual inspection. (Statistical methods to evaluate changes in level are discussed in Appendix B.)

Changes in Trend

Several procedures have been identified to describe trends in single-case experimental designs (see Parsonson and Baer, 1978). One technique that is worth noting consists of the *split-middle technique* (White, 1972, 1974). This technique permits examination of the trend within each phase and allows comparison of trends across phases. The method has been developed in the context of assessing rate of behavior (frequency/time). The advantage of rate for purposes of plotting trends is that no upper limit exists. That is, theoretically no ceiling effect can limit the responses that occur and hence the slope of the trend. The method can be applied to measures other than rate (e.g., intervals, discrete categorization, duration).

Special charting paper has been advocated for the use of this technique. A chart allows graphing of performance in semilog units, which is a format selected in part because of the ease with which it can be employed by practi-

tioners (White, 1974).[4] However, the split-middle technique can be used with
regular graph paper with arithmetic (equal interval) units rather than log units
on the ordinate. In fact, the use of regular graph paper may facilitate the use
of the procedure because it is readily available. (The present examples given
below rely on semilog units to convey the procedure and to represent the log
units to the reader.)

The data are plotted on the graph on a daily basis by translating frequency
into rate per minute. Once the data are plotted, the split-middle technique
estimates the trend or the "line of progress." The line of progress points in the
direction of behavior change and indicates the rate of change. The line of progress also is referred to as a *celeration line,* a term derived from the notions of
acceleration (if the line of progress is ascending) and deceleration line (if the
line of progress is descending). The celeration line predicts the direction and
rate of behavior change.

Example. To convey computation of the celeration line as an initial step of the
split-middle technique, consider the hypothetical data plotted in Figure A-10.
The data in the upper panel represent a magnified portion of the semilog chart
referred to earlier. The panel represents data from only one phase of an ABAB
or other design. The manner of computing the celeration line can be conveyed
with data from one phase, although in practice this procedure would be done
separately for each phase.

The first step in computing a celeration line is to divide the phase in half by
drawing a vertical line at the *median number of sessions* (or days). The median
is the point that separates the sessions so that half are above and half are below
that point. The second step is to divide each of these halves in half again. The
dividing lines should always be made so that an equal number of data points
exists on each side of the division. The next step is to determine the median
rate of performance for the first and second halves of the phase. This median
refers to the data points that form the dependent measure rather than the sessions or days.

A brief review of the procedure thus far may avoid confusion. The initial
steps of the procedure consist of dividing the number of days or sessions into

---

4. The semilog units refer to the fact that the scale on the ordinate is a logarithmic scale but the
   the scale on the abscissa is not. The effect of the scale is to make it so that there is no zero
   origin on the graph or that low and upper rates of performance can be readily represented.
   The chart can be used for behaviors with extremely high or low rates (see Kazdin, 1976 for
   the chart). The rates of behaviors can vary from .000695 per minute (i.e., one every twenty-
   four hours) to 1000 per minute. (The semilog chart paper has been developed by Behavior
   Research Company, Kansas City, KA.)

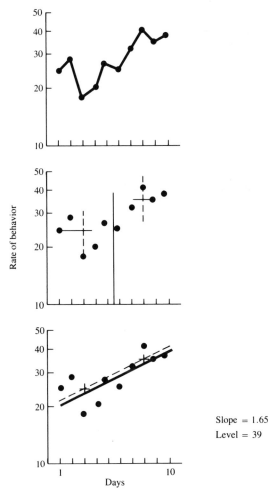

Figure A–10. Hypothetical data during one phase of an ABAB design *(top panel)*, with steps to determine the median data points in each half of the phase *(middle panel)*, and with the original (dashed) and adjusted (solid) celeration line *(bottom panel)*.

quarters for a particular phase. Then the median data value within the first two quarters (or half of the sessions) is identified. This is also done for the second half of the sessions. These medians refer to the dependent variable values (the ordinate) rather than the number of days (the abscissa). To obtain the data point that is the median within each half of the phase, one merely counts from the bottom (ordinate) up toward the top data point for each half-phase.

The data point that constitutes the median value within each half is identified. A horizontal line is drawn through the median at each half of the phase until the line intersects the vertical line that was made from dividing each half.

Figure A-10 shows completion of the above steps, namely, a division of the data (days) into quarters and selection of median values (for the data) within each half. Within each half of the data, vertical and horizontal lines intersect (middle panel, Figure A-10). The next step is finding the slope, which entails drawing a line to connect the points of intersection between the two halves.

The final step is to determine whether the line that results from the above steps "splits" all of the data, i.e., is the split-middle line or slope. The *split-middle slope* is the line that is situated so that 50 percent of the data fall on or above the line and 50 percent fall on or below the line. The line is adjusted (moved up or down) without changing the slope (or angle). The adjustment is intended to divide the data so that the median split is obtained. The adjusted line remains parallel to the original line. Figure A-10 (lower panel) shows the original line (dotted) and the line after it has been adjusted to achieve the split-middle slope (solid line). Note that the original line did not divide the data so that an equal number of points fell above and below the line. The adjustment achieved this middle slope by altering the level of the line but not the slope.

Expressing the Trend and Level. The celeration or split-middle line expresses the rate of behavior change. This rate can be expressed numerically by noting the rate of change for a given time period (e.g., a week). To calculate the rate of change, a point on the celeration line (day x) is identified arbitrarily along with the point on the ordinate through which it passes. The data value on the ordinate for the celeration seven days later (i.e., day $x + 7$) is identified. To compute the rate of change, the numerically larger value is divided by the smaller value.

This procedure can be applied to the data in the lower panel of Figure A-10. At day one the celeration line is at twenty. Seven days later the line is at approximately thirty-three. Applying the above computations, the ratio (33/20) for the rate of change equals 1.65. Because the line is accelerating, this indicates that the average rate of responding for a given week is 1.65 times greater than it was for the prior week. The ratio merely expresses the slope of the line.

The level of the slope can be expressed by noting the level of the celeration line on the last day of the phase. In the above example (lower panel, Figure A-10), the level is approximately thirty-nine. When separate phases are evaluated (e.g., baseline and intervention), the levels of the celeration lines refer to the last day of the first phase and the first day of the second phase (see below). For

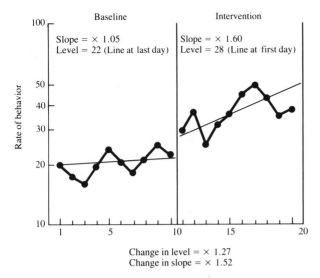

Figure A–11. Hypothetical data across baseline (A) and intervention (B) phases with separate celeration lines for each phase.

each phase in the design, separate celeration lines are drawn. The slope of each line and the initial and final level of each phase can be expressed numerically.

Consider hypothetical data for A and B phases, each with its separate celeration line in Figure A-11. The change in level is estimated by comparing the last data point in baseline (approximately twenty-two) and the first data point in the intervention phase (approximately twenty-eight). The larger value is divided by the smaller, yielding a ratio of 1.27. The ratio expresses how much higher (or lower) the intersection of the different celeration lines is. Similarly, for a change in slope, the larger slope is divided by the smaller slope (1.60 divided by 1.05), yielding 1.52. The changes in level and slope summarize the differences in performance across phases.

Considerations. A few issues are worth noting in passing regarding the split-middle technique. To begin with, the descriptions of the technique have advocated the use of special chart paper to plot trends in the data. Part of the reason is to be able to graph virtually any value (rate) of behavior. When the paper is readily available and understood, plotting of individual data points on a daily basis is relatively simple. However, the special chart paper and the notion of semilog units are currently unfamiliar to most investigators and have impeded extensive use of the procedure. Further, the charting procedure reflects frequency or rate of performance. In applied single-case research, frequency or rate measures are not the most commonly used assessment methods. Interval assessment and discrete categorization constitute a significant segment of the assessment strategies.

The above restrictions need not detract from the use of the split-middle technique. As a descriptive tool, ordinary graph paper can be used to plot trends (celeration lines) across phases. Also, measures other than frequency could be tried as well. These latter uses of the split-middle technique are important to note because they bring the technique more into line with the assessment formats commonly in use in research and clinical situations. If trends are plotted as part of the full range of assessment formats used in applied research, the added information may be very helpful. Trends are often difficult to discern from the data in light of day-to-day variability. The split-middle technique provides one alternative for incorporating this additional descriptive information into simple line graphs.[5]

Rapidity of Change

Another criterion for invoking inspection discussed earlier refers to the latency between the change in experimental conditions and a change in performance. Relatively rapid changes in performance after the intervention is applied or withdrawn contribute to the decision, based on visual inspection, that the intervention may have contributed to change.

One of the difficulties in specifying rapidity of change as a descriptive characteristic of the data pertains to defining a change. Behavior usually changes from one day to the next. But this fluctuation represents ordinary variability. At what point can the change be confidently identified as a departure from this ordinary variability? When experimental conditions are altered, it may be difficult to define objectively the point or points at which changes in performance are evident. Without an agreed upon criterion, the points that define change may be quite subjective. Without knowing when change occurred or agreeing on its point of occurrence, it is difficult to measure how rapidly this change occurred after the intervention was implemented or withdrawn.

Rapidity of change is a difficult notion to specify because it is a joint function of changes in level and slope. A marked change in level and in slope usually reflects a rapid change. For example, baseline may show a stable rate and no trend. The onset of the intervention may show a shift in level of 50 percentage

---

5. Another method of estimating trends that has received recent attention is the method of least squares. For a description of the method and an illustration of its use in single-case research see Parsonson and Baer (1978) and Rogers-Warren and Warren (1980)

points and a steep accelerating trend indicating that the change has occurred quickly and the rate of behavior change from day to day is marked.

Conclusion

This appendix has discussed basic options for graphing data to facilitate application of visual inspection. *Simple line graphs, cumulative graphs,* and *histograms* were discussed briefly. Virtually all of the graphs in single-case research derive from these three types or their combinations. Among the available options and combinations, the simple line graph is the most commonly reported.

As noted in the earlier discussion of data evaluation (Chapter 10), visual inspection is more than simply looking at plotted data and arbitrarily deciding whether the data reflect a reliable effect. Several chracteristics of the data should be examined, including changes in means, levels, and trends, and the rapidity of changes. Selected descriptive aids are available that can be incorporated into simple graphing procedures to facilitate examination of some of these data characteristics. The appendix has discussed *plotting means, computing ratios to express changes in level,* and *plotting trends* as some of the aids to facilitate visual inspection.

Appendix B

Statistical Analyses for Single-Case Designs: Illustrations of Selected Tests

The previous discussion of the use of statistical analyses for single-case experimental designs (see Chapter 10) focused on the controversy surrounding the use of statistical tests and the circumstances in which statistical analyses may be especially useful. Selected statistical tests were mentioned in passing. To the reader interested in using statistical tests, relatively few sources are available that describe alternative tests, their underlying rationale, and how they are computed.

This appendix discusses major statistical options for single-case research and provides examples to convey how the tests are computed and what they can accomplish. The specific tests sampled here have been mentioned earlier in the text and include conventional t and F tests, time-series analyses, randomization tests, a ranking procedure, and the split-middle technique. Of course, each technique cannot be fully elaborated, but examples can convey the steps necessary to use the statistic in commonly used designs.[1]

Conventional t and F Tests
Description

The use of conventional t and F tests for single-case data was discussed in general terms in Chapter 10. As noted there, t and F are not appropriate for

---

1. For additional discussion of statistical tests for single-case research, several sources are available within Kratochwill (1978) and are listed in Hartmann et al. (1980). In addition to these sources, detailed discussions of individual tests presented in this appendix can be found elsewhere (Edgington, 1969; Glass et al., 1975; Kazdin, 1976).

single-case data if serial dependency exists in the data. Such dependency indicates that a major assumption of the tests (independence of error terms) is violated. A number of alternatives have been suggested using conventional t and F to circumvent or minimize this problem (e.g., Gentile, Roden, and Klein, 1972; Shine and Bower, 1971). However, the weight of current opinion is that t and F should be avoided if serial dependency exists.

In fact, t and F tests are appropriate for single-case research in a variety of circumstances, two of which are mentioned in this appendix. One circumstance is the case when there is no serial dependency in the data (for the other circumstance, see the section on randomization below). The basic test for serial dependency is to compute an autocorrelation in which adjacent data points are correlated. Thus, the subject's scores are correlated by pairing days one and two, days two and three, days three and four, and so on. A statistically significant autocorrelation suggests that the dependency is significant and t or F tests should not be used. On the other hand, the absence of significance suggests that the errors are independent and the tests are appropriate.[2]

Example

The use of conventional t and F tests need not be elaborated here to illustrate the procedure. Introductory statistics books convey the tests and how they are computed. However, a brief example is provided to convey a few decision points about applying the test in relation to single-case data. Consider as a hypothetical example that an intervention was applied to improve the social interaction of a withdrawn psychiatric patient. The patient was observed during evenings in the hospital to measure interaction with other patients and with staff. The intervention (e.g., prompts and praise from staff) was evaluated in an ABAB design.

For purposes of the example, we will consider here only the first AB phases, and use a t test. All four phases could be considered with an F test using the same rationale and expansion of the basic computational procedures. Consider the first two phases with several days of the percentage of intervals of appropriate social interaction. Table B-1 presents the means for the baseline and

2. The reliance on a statistically significant correlation to make a decision about serial dependency has its risks. The significance of a correlation is highly dependent on the number of observations (degrees of freedom). If few observations are available to compute autocorrelation, it is quite possible that the resulting correlation would not be statistically significant. Serial dependency might be evident in the series (if that series were continued) but the limited number of observations may make the obtained correlation fail to reach significance.

Table B-1. *t* test comparing hypothetical data for A and B phases for one subject

Baseline (A)		Intervention (B)	
Days	Data	Days	Data
1	12	13	88
2	10	14	28
3	12	15	40
4	22	16	63
5	19	17	86
6	10	18	90
7	14	19	82
8	29	20	95
9	26	21	39
10	5	22	51
11	11	23	56
12	34	24	86
		25	31
		26	77
		27	76

Mean (A) = 17.00   Mean (B) = 65.87

Autocorrelation *r* = .005   Autocorrelation *r* = .010
   (lag 1)   (lag 1)

intervention phases, showing that there was an unequal number of days in each phase.

To determine first whether serial dependency exists, autocorrelations are computed for the separate phases. The autocorrelations are computed separately within each phase rather than for the data as a whole, because the intervention may well affect the relation of the data points to each other (i.e., their dependency). The autocorrelation computed for adjacent points in baseline was $r = .005$ and for adjacent points in the intervention phase was also $r = .01$. These correlations of course are not significant.[3]

A *t* test was computed to find whether different means are significantly dif-

---

3. The autocorrelation here is for adjacent points and is obtained by pairing data from days one and two, two and three, three and four, and so on. Autocorrelations of different intervals (or lags) are sometimes computed, as will be evident below in the discussion of the next statistical test.

ferent.[4] The test is for independent observations (or groups) and for unequal sample sizes. The results indicated that the A and B phases were statistically different (t(25) = 6.86, $p < .01$). Thus, a statistically reliable change has been obtained.

General Comments

As noted earlier, several options for using t and F have been proposed that are more complex than the simple version presented here (Gentile et al., 1972; Shine and Bower, 1971). Several authors have challenged the appropriateness of the different variations because they do not handle the problem of serial dependency in the data (Hartmann, 1974; Kratochwill et al., 1974; Thoresen and Elashoff, 1974). Hence, use of conventional t and F tests for single-case data needs to be preceded by analyses of serial dependency. The absence of dependency would justify use of the tests.

Time-Series Analysis
Description

The general characteristics and purposes of time-series analysis were outlined in Chapter 10. Briefly, time-series analysis provides information about changes in level and trend across phases. Separate t or F tests are computed for changes in level and slope across each set of adjacent phases. t or F tests are computed that take into account the nature of serial dependency in the data. If serial dependency does not exist, ordinary t and F tests can be computed to compare two or more phases for a single subject.

4. The standard t test for independent groups was used where:

$$t = \frac{\overline{X}_1 - \overline{X}_2}{\sqrt{\dfrac{\Sigma X_1^2 - n_1\overline{X}_1^2 + \Sigma X_2^2 - n_2\overline{X}_2^2}{n_1 + n_2 - 2} \left(\dfrac{1}{n_1} + \dfrac{1}{n_2}\right)}}$$

where $\overline{X}_1$ = mean for group 1 (baseline data points)
$\overline{X}_2$ = mean for group 2 (intervention data points)
ΣX_1^2 = sum of squared data points for the baseline phase
ΣX_2^2 = sum of squared data points for the intervention phase
n_1 = sample size (number of data points) for the baseline phase
n_2 = sample size (number of data points) for the intervention phase
(df = for the test = $n_1 + n_2 - 2$)

Time-series t tests cannot be outlined in a way that permits easy computation. The tests depend on more than merely entering raw data into a simple formula. Several models of time-series analysis exist that make different assumptions about the data and require different equations to achieve the statistics. Also, time-series analysis consists of multiple steps that are routinely handled by computer programs. (Information about computer programs available for computing time-series analysis have been enumerated by Hartmann et al. [1980].)

Time-series analysis evaluates changes in the data as a function of the nature of serial dependency. Different patterns of dependency may emerge, depending on the autocorrelations. The autocorrelations are computed with different lags or intervals so that day one is paired with day two, day two with day three, and so on (lag one); day one is paired with day three, day two with day four, and so on (lag two).[5] These correlations for several different lags describe the extent of serial dependency that must be taken into account in the time-series model. The adequacy of a model is based on how well it fits the particular data (see Glass et al., 1975; Gottman and Glass, 1978; Stoline, Huitema, and Mitchell, 1980).

Example

Time-series analysis consists of several steps, including adoption of a model that best fits the data, evaluation of the model, estimation of parameters for the statistic, and generation of t (or F) for level and slope. Several computer programs are available to handle these steps (see Hartmann et al., 1980). It is useful to examine the results of time-series analysis in light of actual data from single-case research.

The application and information provided by time-series analysis can be illustrated by a program in a classroom situation that was designed to reduce inappropriate talking (Hall, Fox, Willard, Goldsmith, Emerson, Owen, Davis, and Porcia, 1971, Exp. 6). Children received praise and other reinforcers for appropriate classroom behavior. Data were collected over the course of a variation of an ABAB experimental design for all children but for the analysis, the group can be treated as a whole.

---

5. In Chapter 10, the discussion noted that a significant autocorrelation by pairing adjacent data points (days one to two, two to three, three to four, ... $n - n+1$) could be used to determine the existence of serial dependency. This is accurate so far as it goes. However, different patterns of dependency can be identified depending on the pattern of correlations with different lags or time intervals over the series. The present discussion elaborates this point more fully. For further discussion, see Gottman and Glass (1978) and Kazdin (1976).

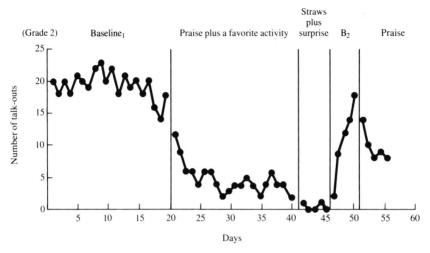

Figure B-1. Daily number of talk-outs in a second grade classroom. Baseline₁—before experimental conditions. Praise plus a favorite activity—systematic praise and permission to engage in a favorite classroom activity contingent on not talking out. Straws plus surprise—systematic praise plus token reinforcement (straws) backed by the promise of a surprise at the end of the week. B₂—withdrawal of reinforcement. Praise—systematic teacher attention and praise for handraising and ignoring talking out. (*Source:* Hall, Fox, Willard, Goldsmith, Emerson, Owen, Davis, and Porcia, 1971.)

The results, plotted in Figure B-1, suggest that inappropriate talking was generally high during the two different baseline phases and was much lower during the different reinforcement (praise, tokens plus a surprise) phases. Consider only the first two phases, which were analyzed by Jones, Vaught, and Reid (1975) using time-series analysis. Using a computer program, the analyses revealed that the data were serially dependent, i.e., adjacent points were correlated. (Autocorrelation for lag 1 was $r = .96$, $p < .01$.) Thus, conventional t and F analyses would be inappropriate. Time-series analysis revealed a significant change in level across the first two AB phases ($t(39) = 3.90$, $p < .01$) but no significant change in slope. The above example illustrates the use of time-series analysis in the first two phases of the design.

The analysis is not restricted to variations of the ABAB design. In any design in which there is a change across phases, time-series analysis provides a potentially useful tool. In multiple-baseline designs, baseline (A) and treatment (B) phases may be implemented across different responses, persons, or situations. Time-series analysis can evaluate each of the baselines to assess whether there is a statistically significant change in level or slope.

General Considerations

In Chapter 10, several of the considerations involved in using time-series analysis were noted. Perhaps the major one is whether a sufficient number of data points is available. The actual number has been debated, but the most agreed-upon range seems to be between fifty and one hundred observation points (e.g., days or sessions). The extended number is needed to provide an estimate of the serial dependency in the data and to identify the appropriate model for the analysis. Data in single-case experiments usually include considerably fewer points than the numbers given above. Time-series analyses have been applied to observations ranging from ten to twenty points and have detected statistically significant changes (Jones et al., 1977).

Time-series analysis has been used increasingly within the last several years, although the tests remain relatively esoteric. Several factors may contribute to the relatively limited use of time-series analysis. The tests are complex; several steps are involved, most of which must be handled by computer. The steps are not easily conveyed in a simple description of the test and how it is computed. Serial dependency and autocorrelation, upon which the analysis depends, are also generally unfamiliar. Finally, the relatively brief phases typically used in single-case experimental designs may make the test difficult to apply. Nevertheless, in cases in which the data requirements can be met, time-series analysis is quite useful in analyzing changes across phases.

Randomization Tests

Description

Randomization tests refer to a series of tests that can be used for single-case experiments (Edgington, 1969, 1980). The tests require that different conditions or interventions be assigned randomly to occasions. At least two conditions are required, one of which may be baseline (A) and the other of which may be an intervention (B). Before the experiment, the total number of treatment occasions (sessions or days) must be specified, along with the number of occasions on which each condition will be administered. Once these decisions are made, A and B (or A, B, C . . . *n*) conditions are assigned randomly to each session or day of the experiment, with the restriction that the number of occasions meets the prespecified total. Each day, one of the conditions is administered according to the randomized schedule planned in advance.

The null hypothesis is that the client's response is due to performance on a particular occasion but is not influenced by particular conditions (e.g., the intervention) that are in effect. If treatment has no systematic effect, performance on any particular day will be a function of factors unrelated to the condition (A or B) that is in effect. The random assignment of conditions to occasions in effect randomly assigns the subject's responses to the different conditions. Any differences in performance on the different occasions summed across A and B conditions is assumed to be a function of chance. The null hypothesis, given random assignment of treatments to occasions, assumes that the measurements of behavior that are obtained are the same as would have been obtained with any random assignment of treatments to occasions. Thus, the null hypothesis attributes differences between conditions to the chance assignment of one condition rather than the other to particular occasions. To test the null hypothesis, a sampling distribution of the differences between the conditions under every equally likely assignment of the same response measures to occasions of A and B is computed. From this distribution, one can determine the probability of obtaining a difference between treatments as large as the one that was actually obtained.[6]

Example

Consider as an example an investigation designed to evaluate the effect of teacher praise on the attentive behavior of a disruptive student. To use the randomization test, the investigator must plan in advance the number of days of the study and the number of days that each of two or more conditions will be administered. Suppose the investigator wishes to compare the effects of the ordinary classroom teaching method (baseline or A condition) and praise (intervention or B condition). To facilitate the computations, suppose that the duration of the study is only eight days and that each condition is in effect an equal number of days. (It is not essential that the conditions be administered an equal number of times.) Each day either condition A or B is in effect and each is administered for four different days. On each day, observations are made of teacher and child performance.

The prediction is that praise (B) will lead to higher levels of attentive behavior than the ordinary classroom procedure (A). Stated as a one-tailed (directional) hypothesis, B is expected to be more effective than A. Under the null hypothesis, any difference between means for the two conditions is due solely to the chance difference in performance on the occasions to which treatments

6. The randomization test discussed here is for a difference between means. Although several other randomization tests are available (Edgington, 1969), the test for differences was selected for illustrative purposes here because it is likely to be the one of greatest interest for comparing performance across phases in single-case experiments.

Table B-2. Percentage of intervals of attentive behavior across days and treatments (hypothetical data)

				Days			
A	B	A	A	B	A	B	B
20	50	15	10	60	25	65	70

Comparing treatment means

A	B
20	50
15	60
10	65
25	70

$\Sigma_A = 70$ $\qquad\qquad\qquad$ $\Sigma_B = 245$
$\overline{X}_A = 17.50$ $\qquad\qquad\quad$ $\overline{X}_B = 61.25$
$$\overline{X}_B > \overline{X}_A = 43.75$$

were randomly assigned. To assess whether the differences are sufficient to reject this hypothesis, the means are computed separately under each treatment and the difference between these means is computed.

Hypothetical raw data for the example appear in Table B-2 (upper portion). The mean difference between A and B is 43.75, as shown in the table (lower portion). Whether this difference is statistically significant is determined by estimating the probability of obtaining scores this discrepant in the predicted direction when treatments have been assigned randomly to occasions. The random assignment of treatments to occasions makes equally probable several combinations of the obtained data. In fact, 70 combinations (8!/4!4!) are possible. The question for computing statistical significance is what proportion of the different combinations would provide as large a difference between means as 43.75.

The critical region used to evaluate the statistical significance is determined by the confidence level. At the .05 level, the critical region of data combinations would be .05 × 70 (or the level of confidence times the number of possible combinations). The result would be 3.5, which needs to be rounded to the next whole number to correspond to a table of values derived for the test (Conover, 1971). With a critical region of four, the four combinations of the obtained data that are the least likely under the null hypothesis must be found. The least likely combination of data, of course, is one in which A and B mean difference in the predicted direction is the greatest possible given the obtained scores or data. The four combinations that maximize the difference between A and B conditions in the predicted direction are computed.

Table B-3. Critical region for the obtained data from the hypothetical example

A				Total for A occasions	$\overline{X}_A$	B				Total for B occasions	$\overline{X}_B$	$\overline{X}_B > \overline{X}_A$
20	10	15	25	(70)	17.50	50	60	65	70	(245)	61.25	43.75
20	10	15	50	(95)	23.75	25	60	65	70	(220)	55.00	31.25
50	10	15	25	(100)	25.00	20	60	65	70	(215)	53.75	28.75
60	10	15	20	(105)	26.25	25	50	65	70	(210)	52.50	26.25

All other combinations of the obtained data (allocated to A and B treatments) are not in the critical region using .05 as the level of significance for a one-tailed test.

Table B-3 presents permutations of the obtained data that reflect the four least likely combinations. The table was derived by first finding the largest combination of data points that would show the greatest difference between A and B, then the combination of data points that would show the next greatest difference, and so on. The total of four combinations was derived because this number of combinations reflected the critical region for the .05 confidence level. The critical region consists of the n set of data combinations in the predicted direction that are the least likely to have occurred by chance (where n = the number of combinations that constitute the critical region).

As noted in Table B-3, the difference of means between treatments for the least likely data combinations is computed. The question for the randomization test is whether the difference between means obtained in the original data is equal to or greater than one of the differences obtained in the critical region. As is obvious, the obtained mean difference equals the most extreme value in the critical region that indicates a statistically significant effect ($p = 1/70$ or .014). In fact, because the data points under A and B conditions did not overlap, there could be no other combination of these scores that yields such an extreme mean difference between groups. When the data represent the least probable combination of data for a one-tailed test, the probability is one over the total number of data combinations possible. (Of course, for a two-tailed test, any probability in the critical region is doubled because the region entails both ends of the distribution.)

Special Considerations

Computational Difficulties and Convenient Approximations. An important issue regarding the use of randomization tests is the computation of the critical region to determine whether the results are statistically significant. For a given confidence level, the investigator must compute the number of different ways in which the obtained scores could result from random assignment of treatment conditions to occasions (e.g., days). In practice, the technique is useful when there is a small number of occasions in which A and B conditions are applied, as in the earlier example. When the number of occasions for assigning treatments exceeds ten or fifteen, even obtaining the possible arrangements of the data on a computer becomes monumental (Conover, 1971; Edgington, 1969). Thus, for most applications, computation of the statistic in the manner described above may be prohibitive.

Fortunately, convenient approximations to the randomization test are available. The approximations depend on the same conditions of the randomization test, namely, the random assignment of treatments to occasions. The approximations include the familiar t and F tests for two or more conditions, respectively. The t and F tests are identical in computation to conventional t and F, discussed earlier. However, there is an important difference. In the conventional t and F, serial dependency in the data make the tests inappropriate. In the present use of t as an approximation to randomization tests, dependency is not a problem. Because the treatments are assigned to occasions in a *random* order across all occasions, t and F provide a close approximation to the randomization distribution (Box and Tiao, 1965; Moses, 1952). Serial dependency does not interfere with this approximation.

Thus, data in the example provided earlier (Table B-3) could be readily tested with a t test for independent groups with degrees of freedom based on the number of A and B occasions ($df = n_1 + n_2 - 2$). The data in the above example yield a ($t(6) = 8.17$, $p < .001$), which is less than the probability obtained with the exact analysis from the randomization test (p = .014). In cases in which the exact critical region is not easily computed, t and F can provide useful approximations. For single-case research, t and F can be readily used with the proviso that randomization of conditions to occasions must be met.

Practical Restrictions. Perhaps the major concerns with randomization tests pertain to the practical constraints that they may impose (Kazdin, 1980b). The test depends on showing that performance can change rapidly (reverse) across conditions. Although reversals are often found when conditions are withdrawn or altered, this is not always the case. Without consistent reversals in performance, differences between A and B conditions may not be detected.

Of even greater concern is the requirement for randomly assigning treatment occasions and alternating these treatments repeatedly. Usually it is not feasible to shift conditions in applied settings in a way to meet the requirements of the statistic. For example, a randomization test might be used to compare baseline (A) and token economy (B) conditions on the performance of hospitalized psychiatric patients. The AB conditions need to be alternated frequently to meet the requirements of the design. To alternate conditions on a daily basis would be extremely difficult in most settings. One cannot easily implement an intervention such as a token economy for one day, remove it on the next, implement it again for two days, and so on, as dictated by randomly assigning conditions to days.

Rather than alternating conditions on a daily basis, a fixed block of time (e.g., three days or one week) could serve as the unit for alternating treatment. Whenever A is implemented it would occur for three consecutive days or a week; when B is assigned, the period would be the same. The mean or total score for each period (rather than each day) serves as the unit for computing the randomization test. The conditions are still assigned in a random order, but treatment continues for a longer period than one day. Thus, the problem of rapidly shifting treatments would be partially ameliorated. Also, occasionally two or more periods of the same condition in a row may be in effect, purely on a random basis. Thus, longer periods of implementing a particular condition will be in effect, which further reduces the rapid shifting of conditions.

R_n Test of Ranks

Description

Revusky (1967) proposed a statistical test referred to as R_n to evaluate data from multiple-baseline designs. The test depends on evaluating the performance of each of the baselines at the point that the intervention is introduced. Consider as an example a multiple-baseline design across persons in which the intervention is introduced to each person at different points in time. The statistical comparison is completed by ranking scores of each subject at the point the intervention is introduced for any one of the subjects. When the intervention is introduced for one subject, the performance of all subjects, including those who have not received the treatment, is ranked. The sum of the ranks across all baselines when treatment is introduced to each baseline forms R_n.

A critical feature of the test is that the intervention is applied to the different baselines in a random order. Because the baseline (e.g., person, behavior) that receives the intervention is randomly determined, the combination of ranks at the point of intervention will be randomly distributed if the intervention has no effect. On the other hand, if the intervention alters performance at the point of intervention, this should be reflected in the ranks. The sum of the ranks (or R_n) conveys the extent to which the ranks are unlikely to be due to random factors.

To use R_n the minimum requirement to detect a difference at the .05 level is four baselines (e.g., four subjects or four behaviors of one subject).

Example

Application of R_n can be seen in a hypothetical example where, say, an intervention is implemented to increase studying among six hyperactive elementary school children. Data are gathered on the number of intervals of studying in a one-hour period for each child. An intervention is introduced to different children at different points in time in the usual fashion of a multiple-baseline design. The child who receives the intervention at a particular point is determined on a random basis, an essential requirement for R_n. Table B-4 provides hypothetical data on the percentage of intervals of study behavior across eleven days. As evident from the table, baseline was in effect for five days for all children. On the sixth day, one subject (child three) was randomly selected to receive the intervention. This child was assigned the intervention while other children continued under baseline conditions. On successive occasions, a different child was exposed to the intervention.

The ranking procedure is applied to each person at the point when the intervention is introduced. Whenever the intervention was introduced, the children were ranked. The lowest rank is given to the child who has the highest score (if a high score is the desired direction).[7] In the example, on days six through eleven, the child with the highest amount of studying at each point would receive the rank of one, the next highest the rank of two, and so on. When the intervention is introduced to the first child, all children are ranked. When the intervention is introduced on subsequent occasions, all children except those who previously received the intervention are ranked. Even though several subjects are ranked when the intervention is introduced, not all ranks are used for R_n. On any given occasion, only the rank for the subject for whom treatment was introduced is used. The ranks for these subjects at the point at which the intervention was introduced are summed across occasions. If treatment is not effective, the ranks should be randomly distributed, i.e., include numbers ranging from one to the *n* number of baselines. If treatment is effective, the point of intervention should result in low ranks for each subject at the point of intervention, if low ranks are assigned to the most extreme score in the predicted direction of change.

7. As a general guideline, ranks are assigned so that the lowest score is given to the behavior that shows the highest level in the desired direction. An easy rule of thumb is to assign first place (rank of one) to the highest or lowest score that represents the "best" performance in terms of the dependent measure; the second, third, and subsequent ranks are assigned accordingly.

Table B-4. Percentage of intervals of study behavior among six children in a multiple-baseline design

	Baseline					Baseline (a) or Intervention (b)					
Days	1	2	3	4	5	6	7	8	9	10	11
1	15	10	5	20	10	30a	*70b*				
2	30	45	50	30	20	70a	50a	65a	70a	*90b*	
3	10	10	15	5	20	*80b*					
4	25	40	25	65	30	40a	75a	*90b*			
5	5	10	10	15	10	30a	30a	40a	35a	35a	*60b*
6	25	15	15	20	25	25a	25a	30a	*80b*		
Ranks =						1	2	1	1	1	1	$\Sigma R = 7$

(Children labels for rows 1–6)

a = control or baseline days, b = point of intervention for a particular child. Days 1 through 5 are baseline days for all children. The italicized data points are the one whose ranks are used for R_n. In each case the highest score in the direction of therapeutic change is given the lowest rank.

Table B-4 shows that with the exception of child one, all children received the lowest rank at the point at which the intervention was introduced. Summing the ranks across children yields $R_n = 7$. The significance of the ranks for designs employing different numbers of subjects (or multiple baselines) can be determined by examining Table B-5. The table provides a one-tailed test for

Table B-5. Values for significance for R_n

Maximum values of R_n significant at the indicated one-tailed probability levels when the experimental scores tend to be smaller than the control scores.

No. of subjects	Significance level				
	0.05	0.025	0.02	0.01	0.005
4	4				
5	6	5	5	5	
6	8	7	7	7	6
7	11	10	10	9	8
8	14	13	13	12	11
9	18	17	16	15	14
10	22	21	20	19	18
11	27	25	24	23	22
12	32	30	29	27	26

Note: Table provides significance for a one-tailed test. The number of subjects in the table also can be used to denote the number of responses or situations across which baseline data are gathered, depending on the variation of the multiple-baseline design. (*Source:* Revusky 1967.)

R_n. (A two-tailed test, of course, can be computed by doubling the probability level of the columns tabled.) To return to the above example, $R_n = 7$ for six subjects (one-tailed test) is equal to the tabled value required for the .01 level. Thus, the data in the hypothetical example, not surprisingly, permit rejection of the null hypothesis of no intervention effect.

Special Considerations

Rapidity of Behavior Change. The above example suggests that the rankings need to be assigned to the different baselines at the point the intervention is introduced (e.g., on the first day). However, it is quite possible and indeed likely that intervention effects would not be evident on the first day the intervention is applied. With some interventions, slow and gradual increments in performance may be expected or performance may even become slightly worse before becoming better. The statistic can be used without necessarily applying the ranks on the first day of the intervention for each baseline.

The intervention may be evaluated on the basis of *mean performance* for a given person (behavior) across several days. For example, the intervention could be introduced for one person and withheld from others for several days (e.g., a week). The rankings might be made on the basis of the mean level of performance across an entire week. The mean performance of the target child would be compared with the mean of the other persons, and ranks would be assigned on the basis of this mean score. Using means across days is likely to provide a more stable estimate of actual performance and to reflect intervention effects more readily than the first day that the intervention is applied. Also, by using averages, the statistic takes into account the usual manner in which multiple-baseline designs are conducted, where the intervention is continued for several days for one person before being introduced to the next. The mean of the several day period, whatever that is, could serve as the basis for assigning ranks.

Response Magnitude. If the scores across the different baselines vary markedly from each other in overall magnitude, it may be difficult to reflect change using R_n. The absolute scores may vary in magnitude to such an extent that when the intervention is introduced to one subject and change occurs, the amount of change does not bring the person's score to the level of another person who has continued in baseline conditions. The intervention may still lead to change, but this is not reflected in rankings because of discrepancies in the magnitude of scores across subjects.

For example in Table B-4, compare the hypothetical data of children one and four. On the seventh day the intervention was introduced to child one, which led to an increase in study behavior relative to his(her) baseline performance. However, the increase did not bring the child to the level of child four, who remained in baseline conditions that day. Hence, child one was not assigned the highest rank, but this was in part an artifact of the different initial magnitudes of responses across subjects. The ranks assigned to the different baselines when the intervention is applied do not take into account the initial differences in baseline magnitudes.

A very simple data transformation can be used to ameliorate the problem of different response magnitudes. The transformation corrects for the different initial baseline responses (Revusky, 1967). The formula for the transformation is:

$$\frac{B_i - A_i}{A_i}$$

Where B_i = performance level for subject i when the experimental intervention is introduced and

A_i = mean performance across all baseline days for the same subject.

The transformation is the same as examining the change in percentage of responding from baseline to treatment. The raw scores for each subject (i.e., for each baseline across which multiple-baseline data are gathered) are transformed when the intervention is introduced to any one subject. The ranks are computed on the basis of the transformed scores. In general, the transformation might be used routinely because of its simplicity and the likelihood that responses will have different magnitudes that could obscure the effects of treatment. Where response levels are vastly different across baselines, the transformation will be especially useful.

Split-Middle Technique
Description

As noted in Appendix A, the split-middle technique provides a systematic way to describe and to summarize the rate of behavior change across phases for a single individual or group (White, 1972, 1974). The technique reveals the nature of the trend in the data and can be used to make and test predictions about changes in performance over time. As noted in the introductory chapter on single-case experimental designs, data from baseline and intervention phases are used to describe the performance and to make predictions about what performance would be like in the future. The intervention is ultimately evaluated by examining the extent to which performance resembles the levels predicted by previous phases. In general, the split-middle technique is well suited to the logic of single-case designs by examining predicted levels of performance.

The split-middle technique has been proposed primarily to describe the process of change across phases rather than to be used as an inferential statistical technique. Nevertheless, statistical significance can be evaluated once the split-middle lines have been determined. White (1972) has proposed a simple technique to consider change across phases. The technique can be illustrated by considering just the changes made from AB phases, although, of course, in practice the changes across all phases would be computed.

The null hypothesis is that there is no change in performance across phases. If this hypothesis is true, then the celeration line of the baseline phase should be an accurate estimate of the celeration line of the intervention phase (see Appendix A). Stated another way, if the intervention has no effect, the split-middle slope of baseline should be the same slope of the intervention phase. Thus, 50 percent of the data in the intervention or B phase should fall on or above and 50 percent of the data should fall on or below the projected baseline slope that has been extrapolated to the intervention phase.

Example

To complete the statistical test, the slope of the baseline phase is extended through the intervention or B phase. Consider the example of hypothetical data in Figure B-2.[8] In the baseline phase, the celeration line was plotted in the manner described in Appendix A. In addition to the celeration line, the figure also shows the extension of this line into the intervention phase. For purposes of the statistical test, it is assumed that the probability of a data point during the intervention phase falling above the projected celeration line of baseline is 50 percent (i.e., $p = .5$) given the null hypothesis. A binomial test can be used to determine whether the number of data points that are above the projected

---

8. The figure is a simplified version of Figure A-11. The figure is simplified here because only the celeration line from baseline is needed for purposes of the statistical analysis described in the present section.

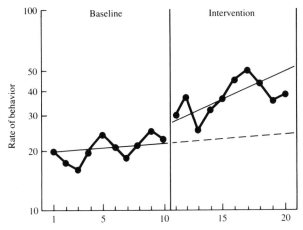

Figure B-2. Hypothetical data across baseline (A) and intervention (B) phases. The dashed line represents an extension of the celeration line for the baseline phase. The binomial test is based on the assumption that if the intervention does not alter behavior, data points in the intervention phase are equally likely to appear above or below the projected celeration line from baseline.

slope in the intervention phase is of a sufficiently low probability to reject the null hypothesis.[9]

Employing the above procedure to the hypothetical data in Figure B-2, there are ten of ten data points during the intervention phase that fall above the projected slope of baseline. Applying the binomial test to determine the probability of obtaining all ten data points above the slope $\left[p = \binom{10}{10} 1/2^{10} \right]$ yields a value of $p < .001$. Thus, the null hypothesis can be rejected and the data in the intervention phase are significantly different from the data of the baseline

---

9. The binomial applied to the split-middle test would be the probability of obtaining x data points above the projected slope:

$$f(x) = \binom{n}{x} p^x q^{n-x} \text{ or simply } \binom{n}{x} p^n$$

Where n = the number of total data points in phase B
x = the number of data points above (or below) the projected slope
$p = q = .5$ by definition of the split-middle slope
p and q = the probability of data points appearing above or below the slope given the null hypothesis.

phase. The results do not convey whether the level and/or slope account for the differences, but only that the data overall depart from one phase to another.

Special Considerations

Utility of the Test. The main purpose of the split-middle technique is to describe the data in a summary fashion and to predict the outcome given the rate of change. The utility of the test is that it provides a computationally simple technique for characterizing the trend in the data and for examining whether trends depart from one another across phases. The rate of change and the level changes are readily described in a summary fashion. In the usual case of data presentation in single-case research, summary statistics are restricted to describing mean changes across phases. The split-middle technique can provide additional descriptive information on the level and slope and on changes in these characteristics over time. These latter features would be of special interest since level and slope changes contribute to inferences drawn using visual inspection.

Statistical Tests. Several different statistical tests have been proposed to assess change (White, 1972), such as changes in slope or change in level. These tests also rely on the binomial discussed here. The use of the binomial in the case of the split-middle technique is a matter of controversy. As Edgington (1974) noted, the binomial may not be valid when applied to data during baseline that show an initial trend. Consider the following circumstances in which the binomial might lead to misinterpretation of intervention effects. A random set of numbers could be assigned randomly as the data points for baseline and intervention phases. On the basis of chance alone, baseline occasionally would show an accelerating or decelerating slope. If the data points in the first phase show a slope, it is unlikely that the data points in the second phase will show the same slope. The randomness of the process of assigning data points to phases in this hypothetical example would make identical trends possible but very unlikely across baseline and intervention phases. Hence, if there is an initial trend in baseline, it is quite possible that data in the intervention phase on chance alone will fall above or below the projected slope of baseline. The binomial test will show a statistically significant effect even though the numbers were assigned randomly and no intervention was implemented. Thus, problems may exist in drawing inferences using the binomial test when initial trend is evident in baseline.

At present, the split-middle technique has not been widely reported in published investigations so the test as either a descriptive or inferential technique remains generally unfamiliar. The paucity of demonstrations raises questions about the statistical techniques and problems they may introduce. The conditions in which the binomial test represents the probability of the distribution of data points across phases, given the null hypothesis, are not well explored. Apart from the binomial test, the split-middle technique can add considerably as a descriptive tool to elaborate characteristics of the data.

Conclusion

This appendix has illustrated a few of the statistical options available for single-case research. The entire area of statistical evaluation for single-case designs has received major attention only recently. The use of these statistical tests, discussion of the problems they raise, and suggestions for the development of alternative statistical techniques are likely to increase greatly in the future.

The issue of major significance is suiting the statistic to the design. Statistical tests for any research may impose special requirements on the design in terms of how, when, to whom, and how long the intervention is to be applied. In basic laboratory research with infrahuman or human subjects, the requirements of the designs can largely dictate how the experiment is arranged and conducted. In applied settings where many single-case designs are used, practical constraints often make it difficult to implement various design requirements such as reversal phases, withholding treatment for an extended period on one of the several baselines, and so on. Some of the statistical tests discussed in this appendix also make special design requirements such as including extended phases (time-series analysis), assigning treatment to persons or baselines randomly (R_n), or repeatedly alternating treatment and no-treatment conditions (randomization tests). A decision must be made well in advance of a single-case investigation as to whether these and other requirements imposed by the design or by a statistical evaluation technique can be implemented.

References

Agras, W. S., Leitenberg, H., Barlow, D. H., & Thomson, L. E. Instructions and reinforcement in the modification of neurotic behavior. *American Journal of Psychiatry,* 1969, *125,* 1435–1439.

Alford, G. W., Webster, J. S., & Sanders, S. H. Covert aversion of two interrelated deviant sexual practices: Obscene phone calling and exhibitionism. A single-case analysis. *Behavior Therapy,* 1980, *11,* 15–25.

Allison, M. G., & Ayllon, T. Behavioral coaching in the development of skills in football, gymnastics and tennis. *Journal of Applied Behavior Analysis,* 1980, *13,* 297–314.

Allport, G. W. *Pattern and growth in personality.* New York: Holt, Rinehart & Winston, 1961.

Ayllon, T. Intensive treatment of psychotic behavior by stimulus satiation and food reinforcement. *Behaviour Research and Therapy,* 1963, *1,* 53–61.

Ayllon, T., & Haughton, E. Modification of symptomatic verbal behavior of mental patients. *Behaviour Research and Therapy,* 1964, *2,* 87–97.

Ayllon, T., & Michael, J. The psychiatric nurse as a behavioral engineer. *Journal of the Experimental Analysis of Behavior,* 1959, *2,* 323–334.

Ayllon, T., & Roberts, M. D. Eliminating discipline problems by strengthening academic performance. *Journal of Applied Behavior Analysis,* 1974, *7,* 71–76.

Azrin, N. H. A strategy for applied research: Learning based but outcome oriented. *American Psychologist,* 1977, *32,* 140–149.

Azrin, N. H., Hontos, P. T., & Besalel-Azrin, V. Elimination of enuresis without a conditioning apparatus: An extension by office instruction of the child and parents. *Behavior Therapy,* 1979, *10,* 14–19.

Baer, D. M. Perhaps it would be better not to know everything. *Journal of Applied Behavior Analysis,* 1977, *10,* 167–172.

Baer, D. M., Rowbury, T. G., & Goetz, E. M. Behavioral traps in the preschool: A proposal for research. *Minnesota Symposia on Child Psychology,* 1976, *10,* 3–27.

Baer, D. M., Wolf, M. M., & Risley, T. R. Some current dimensions of applied behavior analysis. *Journal of Applied Behavior Analysis,* 1968, *1,* 91–97.

Barber, R. M., & Kagey, J. R. Modification of school attendance for an elementary population. *Journal of Applied Behavior Analysis,* 1977, *10,* 41–48.

Barlow, D. H. Behavior therapy: The next decade. *Behavior Therapy,* 1980, *11,* 315–328.

Barlow, D. H. On the relation of clinical research to clinical practice: Current issues, new directions. *Journal of Consulting and Clinical Psychology,* 1981, *49,* 147–155.

Barlow, D. H., & Hayes, S. C. Alternating treatments design: One strategy for comparing the effects of two treatments in a single subject. *Journal of Applied Behavior Analysis,* 1979, *12,* 199–210.

Barlow, D. H., & Hersen, M. Single-case experimental designs. *Archives of General Psychiatry,* 1973, *29,* 319–325.

Barlow, D. H., Leitenberg, H., & Agras, W. S. The experimental control of sexual deviation through manipulation of the noxious scene in covert sensitization. *Journal of Abnormal Psychology,* 1969, *74,* 596–601.

Barlow, D. H., Reynolds, J., & Agras, W. S. Gender identity change in a transsexual. *Archives of General Psychiatry,* 1973, *29,* 569–576.

Barnard, J. D., Christophersen, E. R., & Wolf, M. M. Teaching children appropriate shopping behavior through parent training in the supermarket setting. *Journal of Applied Behavior Analysis,* 1977, *10,* 49–59.

Barrett, B. H., & Lindsley, O. R. Deficits in acquisition of operant discrimination in institutionalized retarded children. *American Journal of Mental Deficiency,* 1962, *67,* 424–436.

Behar, I., & Adams, C. K. Some properties of the reaction time ready signal. *American Journal of Psychology,* 1966, *79,* 419–426.

Beiman, I., Graham, L. E., & Ciminero, A. R. Self-control progressive relaxation training as an alternative nonpharmacological treatment for essential hypertension: Therapeutic effects in the natural environment. *Behaviour Research and Therapy,* 1978, *16,* 371–375.

Bellack, A. S., & Hersen, M. (Eds.). *Research and practice in social skills training.* New York: Plenum, 1979.

Bellack, A. S., Hersen, M., & Lamparski, D. Role-play tests for assessing social skills: Are they valid? Are they useful? *Journal of Consulting and Clinical Psychology,* 1979, *47,* 335–342.

Bellack, A. S., Hersen, M., & Turner, S. M. Role-play tests for assessing social skills: Are they valid? *Behavior Therapy,* 1978, *9,* 448–461.

Bergin, A. E., & Strupp, H. H. New directions in psychotherapy research. *Journal of Abnormal Psychology,* 1970, *76,* 235–246.

Bergin, A. E., & Strupp, H. H. (Eds.). *Changing frontiers in the science of psychotherapy.* Chicago: Aldine-Atherton, 1972.

Bijou, S. W. A systematic approach to an experimental analysis of young children. *Child Development,* 1955, *26,* 161–168.

Bijou, S. W. Patterns of reinforcement and resistance to extinction in young children. *Child Development*, 1957, *28*, 47–54.

Bijou, S. W., Peterson, R. F., & Ault, M. H. A method to integrate descriptive and experimental field studies at the level of data and empirical concepts. *Journal of Applied Behavior Analysis*, 1968, *1*, 175–191.

Bijou, S. W., Peterson, R. F., Harris, F. R., Allen, K. E., & Johnston, M. S. Methodology for experimental studies of young children in natural settings. *Psychological Record*, 1969, *19*, 177–210.

Birkimer, J. C., & Brown, J. H. Back to basics: Percentage agreement measures are adequate, but there are easier ways. *Journal of Applied Behavior Analysis*, 1979, *12*, 535–543. (a)

Birkimer, J. C., & Brown, J. H. A graphical judgmental aid which summarizes obtained and chance reliability data and helps assess the believability of experimental effects. *Journal of Applied Behavior Analysis*, 1979, *12*, 523–533. (b)

Bittle, R., & Hake, D. A multielement design model for component analysis and cross-setting assessment of a treatment package. *Behavior Therapy*, 1977, *8*, 906–914.

Blanchard, E. B., Andrasik, F., Ahles, T. A., Teders, S. J., & O'Keefe, D. Migraine and tension headache: A meta-analytic review. *Behavior Therapy*, 1980, *11*, 613–631.

Blanchard, E. B., & Epstein, L. H. The clinical usefulness of biofeedback. In M. Hersen, R. M. Eisler, & P. M. Miller (Eds.), *Progress in behavior modification, Volume 4*. New York: Academic Press, 1977.

Bolgar, H. The case study method. In B. B. Wolman (Ed.), *Handbook of clinical psychology*. New York: McGraw-Hill, 1965.

Boring, E. G. The nature and history of experimental control. *American Journal of Psychology*, 1964, *67*, 573–589.

Bornstein, M. R., Bellack, A. S., & Hersen, M. Social-skills training for unassertive children: A multiple-baseline analysis. *Journal of Applied Behavior Analysis*, 1977, *10*, 183–195.

Bornstein, P. H., Hamilton, S. B., & Quevillon, R. P. Behavior modification by long-distance: Disruptive behavior in a rural classroom setting. *Behavior Modification*, 1977, *1*, 369–380.

Bornstein, P. H., & Wollersheim, J. P. Scientist-practitioner activities among psychologists of behavioral and nonbehavioral orientations. *Professional Psychology*, 1978, *9*, 659–664.

Box, G. E. P., & Jenkins, G. M. *Time series analysis: Forecasting and control*. San Francisco: Holden-Day, 1970.

Box, G. E. P., & Tiao, G. C. A change in level of non-stationary time series. *Biometrika*, 1965, *52*, 181–192.

Bracht, G. H., & Glass, G. V. The external validity of experiments. *American Educational Research Journal*, 1968, *5*, 437–474.

Breuer, J., & Freud, S. *Studies in hysteria*. New York: Basic Books, 1957.

Brigham, T. A., Graubard, P. S., & Stans, A. Analysis of the effects of sequential reinforcement contingencies on aspects of composition. *Journal of Applied Behavior Analysis*, 1972, *5*, 421–429.

Broden, M., Hall, R. V., Dunlap, A., & Clark, R. Effects of teacher attention and a token reinforcement system in a junior high school special education class. *Exceptional Children,* 1970, *36,* 341–349.

Browning, R. M. A same-subject design for simultaneous comparison of three reinforcement contingencies. *Behaviour Research and Therapy,* 1967, *5,* 237–243.

Browning, R. M., & Stover, D. O. *Behavior modification in child treatment: An experimental and clinical approach.* Chicago: Aldine-Atherton, 1971.

Bunck, T. J., & Iwata, B. A. Increasing senior citizen participation in a community-based nutritious meal program. *Journal of Applied Behavior Analysis,* 1978, *11,* 75–86.

Burg, M. M., Reid, D. H., & Lattimore, J. Use of a self-recording and supervision program to change institutional staff behavior. *Journal of Applied Behavior Analysis,* 1979, *12,* 363–375.

Campbell, D. T., & Stanley, J. C. *Experimental and quasi-experimental designs for research.* Chicago: Rand-McNally, 1963.

Carr, E. G., Newsom, C. D., & Binkoff, J. A. Escape as a factor in the aggressive behavior of two retarded children. *Journal of Applied Behavior Analysis,* 1980, *13,* 101–117.

Cataldo, M. F., Bessman, C. A., Parker, L. H., Pearson, J. E. R., & Rogers, M. C. Behavioral assessment for pediatric intensive care units. *Journal of Applied Behavior Analysis,* 1979, *12,* 83–97.

Catania, A. C., & Brigham, T. A. (Eds.). *Handbook of applied behavior analysis: Social and instructional processes.* New York: Irvington, 1978.

Chaddock, R. E. *Principles and methods of statistics.* Boston: Houghton Mifflin, 1925.

Chapman, C., & Risley, T. R. Anti-litter procedures in an urban high-density area. *Journal of Applied Behavior Analysis,* 1974, *7,* 377–384.

Chassan, J. B. *Research design in clinical psychology and psychiatry.* New York: Appleton-Century-Crofts, 1967.

Chassan, J. B. *Reseach design in clinical psychology and psychiatry* (2nd edition). New York: Irvington, 1979.

Christensen, D. E., & Sprague, R. L. Reduction of hyperactive behavior by conditioning procedures alone and combined with methylphenidate (Ritalin). *Behaviour Research and Therapy,* 1973, *11,* 331–334.

Christophersen, E. R., Arnold, C. M., Hill, D. W., & Quilitch, H. R. The home point system: Token reinforcement procedures for application by parents of children with behavior problems. *Journal of Applied Behavior Analysis,* 1972, *5,* 485–497.

Clark, H. B., Boyd, S. B., & Macrae, J. W. A classroom program teaching disadvantaged youths to write biographic information. *Journal of Applied Behavior Analysis,* 1975, *8,* 67–75.

Clark, H. B., Greene, B. F., Macrae, J. W., McNees, M. P., Davis, J. L., & Risley, T. R. A parent advice package for family shopping trips: Development and evaluation. *Journal of Applied Behavior Analysis,* 1977, *10,* 605–624.

Cohen, J. Some statistical issues in psychological research. In B. B. Wolman (Ed.), *Handbook of clinical psychology.* New York: McGraw-Hill, 1965.

Combs, M. L., & Slaby, D. A. Social-skills training with children. In B. B. Lahey

& A. E. Kazdin (Eds.), *Advances in clinical child psychology, Volume 1.* New York: Plenum, 1977.

Conover, W. J. *Practical nonparametric statistics.* New York: Wiley, 1971.

Cook, T. D., & Campbell, D. T. (Eds.). *Quasi-experimentation: Design and analysis issues for field settings.* Chicago: Rand-McNally, 1979.

Cossairt, A., Hall, R. V., & Hopkins, B. L. The effects of experimenter's instructions, feedback, and praise on teacher praise and student attending behavior. *Journal of Applied Behavior Analysis,* 1973, *6,* 89–100.

Creer, T. L., Chai, H., & Hoffman, A. A single application of an aversive stimulus to eliminate chronic cough. *Journal of Behavior Therapy and Experimental Psychiatry,* 1977, *8,* 107–109.

Cumming, W. W., & Schoenfeld, W. N. Behavior stability under extended exposure to a time-correlated reinforcement contingency. *Journal of the Experimental Analysis of Behavior,* 1960, *3,* 71–82.

Dapcich-Miura, E., & Hovell, M. F. Contingency management of adherence to a complex medical regimen in an elderly heart patient. *Behavior Therapy,* 1979, *10,* 193–201.

Davison, G. C. Homosexuality: The ethical challenge. *Journal of Consulting and Clinical Psychology,* 1976, *44,* 157–162.

Deitz, S. M. An analysis of programming DRL schedules in educational settings. *Behaviour Research and Therapy,* 1977, *15,* 103–111.

Deitz, S. M., & Repp, A. C. Decreasing classroom misbehavior through the use of DRL schedules of reinforcement. *Journal of Applied Behavior Analysis,* 1973, *6,* 457–463.

DeMaster, B., Reid, J., & Twentyman, C. The effects of different amounts of feedback on observer's reliability. *Behavior Therapy,* 1977, *8,* 317–329.

DeProspero, A., & Cohen, S. Inconsistent visual analysis of intrasubject data. *Journal of Applied Behavior Analysis,* 1979, *12,* 573–579.

Dittmer, C. G. *Introduction to social statistics.* Chicago: Shaw, 1926.

Dobes, R. W. Amelioration of psychosomatic dermatosis by reinforced inhibition of scratching. *Journal of Behavior Therapy and Experimental Psychiatry,* 1977, *8,* 185–187.

Doleys, D. M., Wells, K. C., Hobbs, S. A., Roberts, M. W., & Cartelli, L. M. The effects of social punishment on noncompliance: A comparison with timeout and positive practice. *Journal of Applied Behavior Analysis,* 1976, *9,* 471–482.

Dukes, W. F. N = 1. *Psychological Bulletin,* 1965, *64,* 74–79.

Edgington, E. S. *Statistical inference: The distribution-free approach.* New York: McGraw-Hill, 1969.

Edgington, E. S. *Personal communication,* August, 1974.

Edgington, E. S. Validity of randomization tests for one-subject experiments. *Journal of Educational Statistics,* 1980, *5,* 235–251.

Epstein, L. H. Psychophysiological measurement in assessment. In M. Hersen & A. S. Bellack (Eds.), *Behavioral assessment: A practical handbook.* Oxford: Pergamon, 1976.

Epstein, L. H., & Abel, G. G. An analysis of biofeedback training effects for tension headache patients. *Behavior Therapy,* 1977, *8,* 37–47.

Eyberg, S. M., & Johnson, S. M. Multiple assessment of behavior modification with families: Effects of contingency contracting and order of treated problems. *Journal of Consulting and Clinical Psychology,* 1974, *42,* 594–606.

Eysenck, H. J. An exercise in mega-silliness. *American Psychologist,* 1978, *33,* 517.

Favell, J. E., McGimsey, J. F., & Jones, M. L. Rapid eating in the retarded: Reduction by nonaversive procedures. *Behavior Modification,* 1980, *4,* 481–492.

Fawcett, S. B., & Miller, L. K. Training public-speaking behavior: An experimental analysis and social validation. *Journal of Applied Behavior Analysis,* 1975, *8,* 125–135.

Ferritor, D. E., Buckholdt, D., Hamblin, R. L., & Smith, L. The noneffects of contingent reinforcement for attending behavior on work accomplished. *Journal of Applied Behavior Analysis,* 1972, *5,* 7–17.

Ferster, C. B. Positive reinforcement and behavioral deficits of autistic children. *Child Development,* 1961, *32,* 437–456.

Ferster, C. B., & Skinner, B. F. *Schedules of reinforcement.* New York: Appleton-Century-Crofts, 1957.

Fichter, M. M., Wallace, C. J., Liberman, R. P., & Davis, J. R. Improving social interaction in a chronic psychotic using discriminated avoidance ("nagging"): Experimental analysis and generalization. *Journal of Applied Behavior Analysis,* 1976, *9,* 377–386.

Firestone, P. The effects and side effects of timeout on an aggressive nursery school child. *Journal of Behavior Therapy and Experimental Psychiatry,* 1976, *7,* 79–81.

Fisher, R. A. *Statistical methods for research workers.* Edinburgh: Oliver & Boyd, 1925.

Fjellstedt, N., & Sulzer-Azaroff, B. Reducing the latency of a child's responding to instructions by means of a token system. *Journal of Applied Behavior Analysis,* 1973, *6,* 125–130.

Foxx, R. M., & Hake, D. F. Gasoline conservation: A procedure for measuring and reducing the driving of college students. *Journal of Applied Behavior Analysis,* 1977, *10,* 61–74.

Foxx, R. M., & Rubinoff, A. Behavioral treatment of caffeinism: Reducing excessive coffee drinking. *Journal of Applied Behavior Analysis,* 1979, *12,* 335–344.

Foxx, R. M., & Shapiro, S. T. The timeout ribbon: A nonexclusionary timeout procedure. *Journal of Applied Behavior Analysis,* 1978, *11,* 125–136.

Frederiksen, L. W., Jenkins, J. O., Foy, D. W., & Eisler, R. M. Social skills training to modify abusive verbal outbursts in adults. *Journal of Applied Behavior Analysis,* 1976, *9,* 117–125.

Freedman, B. J., Rosenthal, L., Donahoe, C. P., Jr., Schlundt, D. G., & McFall, R. M. A social-behavioral analysis of skill deficits in delinquent and nondelinquent adolescent boys. *Journal of Consulting and Clinical Psychology,* 1978, *46,* 1448–1462.

Friedman, J., & Axelrod, S. The use of a changing-criterion procedure to reduce the frequency of smoking behavior. Unpublished manuscript, Temple University, 1973.

Freud, S. *New introductory lectures in psychoanalysis.* New York: Norton, 1933.

Gallo, P. S., Jr. Meta-analysis—A mixed meta-phor? *American Psychologist,* 1978, *33,* 515–516.

Garfield, S. L., & Kurtz, R. Clinical psychologists in the 1970s. *American Psychologist,* 1976, *31,* 1–9.

Gaul, D. J., Craighead, W. E., & Mahoney, M. J. Relationship between eating rates and obesity. *Journal of Consulting and Clinical Psychology,* 1975, *43,* 123–125.

Gelfand, D. M., & Hartmann, D. P. *Child behavior analysis and therapy.* New York: Pergamon, 1975.

Gentile, J. R., Roden, A. H., & Klein, R. D. An analysis of variance model for the intrasubject replication design. *Journal of Applied Behavior Analysis,* 1972, *5,* 193–198.

Glass, G. V. Primary, secondary and meta-analysis of research. *Educational Researcher,* 1976, *10,* 3–8.

Glass, G. V., Willson, V. L., & Gottman, J. M. *Design and analysis of time-series experiments.* Boulder: Colorado Associated University Press, 1975.

Glenwick, D., & Jason, L. (Eds.). *Behavioral community psychology: Progress and prospects.* New York: Praeger, 1980.

Goetz, E. M., Holmberg, M. C., & LeBlanc, J. M. Differential reinforcement of other behavior and noncontingent reinforcement as control procedures during the modification of a preschooler's compliance. *Journal of Applied Behavior Analysis,* 1975, *8,* 77–82.

Goldiamond, I. The maintenance of ongoing fluent verbal behavior and stuttering. *The Journal of Mathetics,* 1962, *1,* 57–95.

Gottman, J. M., & Glass, G. V. Analysis of interrupted time-series experiments. In T. R. Kratochwill (Ed.), *Single-subject research: Strategies for evaluating change.* New York: Academic Press, 1978.

Greenwood, C. R., Walker, H. M., Todd, N. M., & Hops, H. Validating teacher selection with normative data for preschool social interaction. Paper presented at American Psychological Association, Washington, D.C., September 1976.

Grice, C. R., & Hunter, J. J. Stimulus intensity effects depend upon the type of experimental design. *Psychological Review,* 1964, *71,* 247–256.

Gullick, E. L., & Blanchard, E. B. The use of psychotherapy and behavior therapy in the treatment of an obsessional disorder: An experimental case study. *Journal of Nervous and Mental Disease,* 1973, *156,* 427–433.

Hall, R. V. *Behavior management series: Part II. Basic principles.* Lawrence, Kan.: H & H Enterprises, 1971.

Hall, R. V., & Fox, R. G. Changing-criterion designs: An alternate applied behavior analysis procedure. In B. C. Etzel, J. M. LeBlanc, & D. M. Baer (Eds.), *New developments in behavioral research: Theory, method and application. In honor of Sidney W. Bijou.* Hillsdale, N.J.: Lawrence Erlbaum, 1977.

Hall, R. V., Fox, R., Willard, D., Goldsmith, L., Emerson, M., Owen, M. Davis, F., & Porcia, E. The teacher as observer and experimenter in the modification of disputing and talking-out behaviors. *Journal of Applied Behavior Analysis,* 1971, *4,* 141–149.

Halle, J. W., Marshall, A. M., & Spradlin, J. E. Time delay: A technique to increase language use and facilitate generalization in retarded children. *Journal of Applied Behavior Analysis,* 1979, *12,* 431–439.

Hansen, G. D. Enuresis control through fading, escape and avoidance training. *Journal of Applied Behavior Analysis,* 1979, *12,* 303–307.

Harris, F. C., & Lahey, B. B. A method for combining occurrence and nonoccurrence interobserver agreement scores. *Journal of Applied Behavior Analysis,* 1978, *11,* 523–527.

Harris, F. R., Wolf, M. M., & Baer, D. M. Effects of adult social reinforcement on child behavior. *Young Children,* 1964, *20,* 8–17.

Harris, S. L., & Wolchik, S. Suppression of self-stimulation: Three alternative strategies. *Journal of Applied Behavior Analysis,* 1979, *12,* 185–198.

Harris, V. W., & Sherman, J. A. Homework assignments, consequences, and classroom performance in social studies and mathematics. *Journal of Applied Behavior Analysis,* 1974, *7,* 505–519.

Hartmann, D. P. Forcing square pegs into round holes: Some comments on "An analysis-of-variance model for the intrasubject replication design." *Journal of Applied Behavior Analysis,* 1974, *7,* 635–638.

Hartmann, D. P. Considerations in the choice of interobserver reliability estimates. *Journal of Applied Behavior Analysis,* 1977, *10,* 103–116.

Hartmann, D. P., Gottman, J. M., Jones, R. R., Gardner, W., Kazdin, A. E., & Vaught, R. Interrupted time-series analysis and its application to behavioral data. *Journal of Applied Behavior Analysis,* 1980, *13,* 543–559.

Hartmann, D. P., & Hall, R. V. The changing criterion design. *Journal of Applied Behavior Analysis,* 1976, *9,* 527–532.

Hauserman, N., Walen, S. R., & Behling, M. Reinforced racial integration in the first grade: A study in generalization. *Journal of Applied Behavior Analysis,* 1973, *6,* 193–200.

Hawkins, R. P., & Dobes, R. W. Behavioral definitions in applied behavior analysis: Explicit or implicit. In B. C. Etzel, J. M. LeBlanc, & D. M. Baer (Eds.), *New developments in behavioral research: Theory, methods, and applications. In honor of Sidney W. Bijou.* Hillsdale, N.J.: Lawrence Erlbaum, 1977.

Hawkins, R. P., & Dotson, V. A. Reliability scores that delude: An Alice in Wonderland trip through the misleading characteristics of inter-observer agreement scores in interval recording. In E. Ramp & G. Semb (Eds.), *Behavior analysis: Areas of research and application.* Englewood Cliffs, N.J.: Prentice-Hall, 1975.

Hayes, S. C., Brownell, K. D., & Barlow, D. H. The use of self-administered covert sensitization in the treatment of exhibitionism and sadism. *Behavior Therapy,* 1978, *9,* 283–289.

Herman, S. H., Barlow, D. H., & Agras, W. S. An experimental analysis of exposure to "explicit" heterosexual stimuli as an effective variable in changing arousal patterns of homosexuals. *Behaviour Research and Therapy,* 1974, *12,* 335–346.

Hermann, J. A., de Montes, A. I., Dominguez, B., Montes, F., & Hopkins, B. L. Effects of bonuses for punctuality on the tardiness of industrial workers. *Journal of Applied Behavior Analysis,* 1973, *6,* 563–570.

Hersen, M., & Barlow, D. H. *Single-case experimental designs: Strategies for studying behavior change.* New York: Pergamon, 1976.

Hiss, R. H., & Thomas, D. R. Stimulus generalization as a function of testing procedure and response measure. *Journal of Experimental Psychology,* 1963, *65,* 587–592.

Hollandsworth, J. G., Glazeski, R. C., & Dressel, M. E. Use of social-skills training in the treatment of extreme anxiety and deficient verbal skills in the job-interview setting. *Journal of Applied Behavior Analysis,* 1978, *11,* 259–269.

Honig, W. K. (Ed.). *Operant behavior: Areas of research and application.* New York: Appleton-Century-Crofts, 1966.

Honig, W. K., & Staddon, J. E. R. (Eds.). *Handbook of operant behavior.* Englewood Cliffs, N.J.: Prentice-Hall, 1977.

Hopkins, B. L., & Hermann, J. A. Evaluating interobserver reliability of interval data. *Journal of Applied Behavior Analysis,* 1977, *10,* 121–126.

Horner, R. D., & Baer, D. M. Multiple-probe technique. A variation of the multiple baseline. *Journal of Applied Behavior Analysis,* 1978, *11,* 189–196.

Horner, R. D., & Keilitz, I. Training mentally retarded adolescents to brush their teeth. *Journal of Applied Behavior Analysis,* 1975, *8,* 301–309.

House, B. J., & House, A. E. Frequency, complexity and clarity as covariates of observer reliability. *Journal of Behavioral Assessment,* 1979, *1,* 149–165.

Jackson, J. L., & Calhoun, K. S. Effects of two variable-ratio schedules of timeout: Changes in target and non-target behaviors. *Journal of Behavior Therapy and Experimental Psychiatry,* 1977, *8,* 195–199.

Jayaratne, S., & Levy, R. L. *Empirical clinical practice.* New York: Columbia University Press, 1979.

Johnson, J. L., & Mithaug, D. E. A replication of sheltered workshop entry requirements. *AAESPH Review,* 1978, *3,* 116–122.

Johnson, M. S., & Bailey, J. S. The modification of leisure behavior in a half-way house for retarded women. *Journal of Applied Behavior Analysis,* 1977, *10,* 273–282.

Johnson, S. M., & Bolstad, O. D. Methodological issues in naturalistic observation: Some problems and solutions for field research. In L. A. Hamerlynck, L. C. Handy, & E. J. Mash (Eds.), *Behavior change: Methodology, concepts, and practice.* Champaign, Ill.: Research Press, 1973.

Jones, M. C. A laboratory study of fear: The case of Peter. *Pedagogical Seminary,* 1924, *31,* 308–315.

Jones, R. R., Reid, J. B., & Patterson, G. R. Naturalistic observation in clinical assessment. In P. McReynolds (Ed.), *Advances in psychological assessment, Volume 3.* San Francisco: Jossey-Bass, 1974.

Jones, R. R., Vaught, R. S., & Reid, J. B. Time-series analysis as a substitute for single subject analysis of variance designs. In G. R. Patterson, I. M. Marks, J. D. Matarazzo, R. A. Myers, G. E. Schwartz, & H. H. Strupp, *Behavior change 1974.* Chicago: Aldine, 1975.

Jones, R. R., Vaught, R. S., & Weinrott, M. Time-series analysis in operant research. *Journal of Applied Behavior Analysis,* 1977, *10,* 151–166.

Jones, R. R., Weinrott, M. R., & Vaught, R. S. Effects of serial dependency on the agreement between visual and statistical inference. *Journal of Applied Behavior Analysis,* 1978, *11,* 277–283.

Jones, R. T., & Kazdin, A. E. Programming response maintenance after withdrawing token reinforcement. *Behavior Therapy,* 1975, *6,* 153–164.

Jones, R. T., Kazdin, A. E., & Haney, J. I. Social validation and training of emergency fire safety skills for potential injury prevention and life saving. *Journal of Applied Behavior Analysis,* 1981, *14,* 249–260.

Kallman, W. M., & Feuerstein, M. Psychophysiological procedures. In A. R. Ciminero, K. S. Calhoun, & H. E. Adams (Eds.), *Handbook of behavioral assessment.* New York: Wiley, 1977.

Kandel, H. J., Ayllon, T., & Rosenbaum, M. S. Flooding or systematic exposure in the treatment of extreme social withdrawal in children. *Journal of Behavior Therapy and Experimental Psychiatry,* 1977, *8,* 75–81.

Kazdin, A. E. Role of instructions and reinforcement in behavior change in token reinforcement programs. *Journal of Educational Psychology,* 1973, *64,* 63–71.

Kazdin, A. E. The impact of applied behavior analysis on diverse areas of research. *Journal of Applied Behavior Analysis,* 1975, *8,* 213–229.

Kazdin, A. E. Statistical analyses for single-case experimental designs. In M. Hersen & D. H. Barlow, *Single-case experimental designs: Strategies for studying behavior change.* New York: Pergamon, 1976.

Kazdin, A. E. Artifact, bias, and complexity of assessment. The ABC's of reliability. *Journal of Applied Behavior Analysis,* 1977, *10,* 141–150.(a)

Kazdin, A. E. Assessing the clinical or applied significance of behavior change through social validation. *Behavior Modification,* 1977, *1,* 427–452. (b)

Kazdin, A. E. Extensions of reinforcement techniques to socially and environmentally relevant behaviors. In M. Hersen, R. M. Eisler, & P. M. Miller (Eds.), *Progress in behavior modification, Volume 4.* New York: Academic Press, 1977. (c)

Kazdin, A. E. The influence of behavior preceding a reinforced response on behavior change in the classroom. *Journal of Applied Behavior Analysis,* 1977, *10,* 299–310. (d)

Kazdin, A. E. The application of operant techniques in treatment, rehabilitation, and education. In S. L. Garfield & A. E. Bergin (Eds.), *Handbook of psychotherapy and behavior change* (2nd edition). New York: Wiley, 1978. (a)

Kazdin, A. E. Evaluating the generality of findings in analogue therapy research. *Journal of Consulting and Clinical Psychology,* 1978, *46,* 673–686. (b)

Kazdin, A. E. *History of behavior modification: Experimental foundations of contemporary research.* Baltimore: University Park Press, 1978. (c)

Kazdin, A. E. Direct observations as unobtrusive measures in treatment evaluation. *New Directions for Methodology of Behavioral Science,* 1979, *1,* 19–31. (a)

Kazdin, A. E. Imagery elaboration and self-efficacy in the covert modeling treatment of assertive behavior. *Journal of Consulting and Clinical Psychology,* 1979, *47,* 725–733. (b)

Kazdin, A. E. Unobtrusive measures in behavioral assessment. *Journal of Applied Behavior Analysis,* 1979, *12,* 713–724. (c)

Kazdin, A. E. Vicarious reinforcement and punishment in operant programs for children. *Child Behavior Therapy,* 1979, *1,* 13–36.(d)

Kazdin, A. E. *Behavior modification in applied settings* (2nd edition). Homewood, Ill.: Dorsey, 1980.(a)

Kazdin, A. E. Obstacles in using randomization tests in single-case experimentation. *Journal of Educational Statistics,* 1980, *5,* 253–260. (b)

Kazdin, A. E. *Research design in clinical psychology.* New York: Harper & Row, 1980. (c)

Kazdin, A. E. Drawing valid inferences from case studies. *Journal of Consulting and Clinical Psychology,* 1981, *49,* 183–192.

Kazdin, A. E., & Erickson, L. M. Developing responsiveness to instructions in severely and profoundly retarded residents. *Journal of Behavior Therapy and Experimental Psychiatry,* 1975, *6,* 17–21.

Kazdin, A. E., & Geesey, S. Simultaneous-treatment design comparisons of the effects of earning reinforcers for one's peers versus for oneself. *Behavior Therapy,* 1977, *8,* 682–693.

Kazdin, A. E., & Geesey, S. Enhancing classroom attentiveness by preselection of back-up reinforcers in a token economy. *Behavior Modification,* 1980, *4,* 98–114.

Kazdin, A. E., & Hartmann, D. P. The simultaneous-treatment design. *Behavior Therapy,* 1978, *9,* 912–922.

Kazdin, A. E., & Klock, J. The effects of nonverbal teacher approval on student attentive behavior. *Journal of Applied Behavior Analysis,* 1973, *6,* 643–654.

Kazdin, A. E., & Mascitelli, S. The opportunity to earn oneself off a token system as a reinforcer for attentive behavior. *Behavior Therapy,* 1980, *11,* 68–78.

Kazdin, A. E., & Polster, R. Intermittent token reinforcement and response maintenance in extinction. *Behavior Therapy,* 1973, *4,* 386–391.

Kazdin, A. E., Silverman, N. A., & Sittler, J. L. The use of prompts to enhance vicarious effects of nonverbal approval. *Journal of Applied Behavior Analysis,* 1975, *8,* 279–286.

Kazdin, A. E., & Wilson, G. T. *Evaluation of behavior therapy: Issues, evidence, and research strategies.* Cambridge, Mass.: Ballinger, 1978.

Kazrin, A., Durac, J., & Agteros, T. Meta-meta analysis: A new method for evaluating therapy outcome. *Behaviour Research and Therapy,* 1979, *17,* 397–399.

Kelly, M. B. A review of the observational data-collection and reliability procedures reported in the *Journal of Applied Behavior Analysis. Journal of Applied Behavior Analysis,* 1977, *10,* 97–101.

Kennedy, R. E. The feasibility of time-series analysis of single-case experiments. Unpublished manuscript, The Pennsylvania State University, 1976.

Kent, R. N., & Foster, S. L. Direct observational procedures: Methodological issues in naturalistic settings. In A. R. Ciminero, K. S. Calhoun, & H. E. Adams (Eds.), *Handbook of behavioral assessment.* New York: Wiley, 1977.

Kent, R. N., Kanowitz, J., O'Leary, K. D., & Cheiken, M. Observer reliability as a function of circumstances of assessment. *Journal of Applied Behavior Analysis,* 1977, *10,* 317–324.

Kent, R. N., & O'Leary, K. D. A controlled evaluation of behavior modification with conduct problem children. *Journal of Consulting and Clinical Psychology,* 1976, *44,* 586–596.

Kent, R. N., O'Leary, K. D., Diament, C., & Dietz, A. Expectation biases in observational evaluation of therapeutic change. *Journal of Consulting and Clinical Psychology*, 1974, *42*, 774–780.

Killeen, P. R. Stability criteria. *Journal of the Experimental Analysis of Behavior*, 1978, *29*, 17–25.

King, G. F., Armitage, S. G., & Tilton, J. R. A therapeutic approach to schizophrenics of extreme pathology: An operant-interpersonal method. *Journal of Abnormal and Social Psychology*, 1960, *61*, 276–286.

Knapp, T. J., & Peterson, L. W. Behavior management in medical and nursing practice. In W. E. Craighead, A. E. Kazdin, & M. J. Mahoney (Eds.), *Behavior modification: Principles, issues, and applications*. Boston: Houghton Mifflin, 1976.

Komaki, J., & Barnett, F. T. A behavioral approach to coaching football: Improving the play execution of the offensive backfield on a youth football team. *Journal of Applied Behavior Analysis*, 1977, *10*, 657–664.

Korchin, S. J. *Modern clinical psychology*. New York: Basic Books, 1976.

Kratochwill, T. R. (Ed.). *Single-subject research: Strategies for evaluating change*. New York: Academic Press, 1978.

Kratochwill, T., Alden, K., Demuth, D., Dawson, D., Panicucci, D., Arntson, P., McMurray, N., Hempstead, J., & Levin, J. A further consideration in the application of an analysis-of-variance model for the intrasubject replication design. *Journal of Applied Behavior Analysis*, 1974, *7*, 629–633.

Kratochwill, T. R., & Wetzel, R. J. Observer agreement, credibility, and judgment: Some considerations in presenting observer agreement data. *Journal of Applied Behavior Analysis*, 1977, *10*, 133–139.

Lattal, K. A. Contingency management of tooth-brushing behavior in a summer camp for children. *Journal of Applied Behavior Analysis*, 1969, *2*, 195–198.

Lawson, R. Brightness discrimination performance and secondary reward strength as a function of primary reward amount. *Journal of Comparative and Physiological Psychology*, 1957, *50*, 35–39.

Lazarus, A. A. The results of behaviour therapy in 126 cases of severe neurosis. *Behaviour Research and Therapy*, 1963, *1*, 69–79.

Lazarus, A. A., & Davison, G. C. Clinical innovation in research and practice. In A. E. Bergin & S. L. Garfield (Eds.), *Handbook of psychotherapy and behavior change: An empirical analysis*. New York: Wiley, 1971.

Leitenberg, H. The use of single-case methodology in psychotherapy research. *Journal of Abnormal Psychology*, 1973, *82*, 87–101.

Leitenberg, H. Training clinical researchers in psychology. *Professional Psychology*, 1974, *5*, 59–69.

Leitenberg, H. (Ed.). *Handbook of behavior modification and behavior therapy*. Englewood Cliffs, N.J.: Prentice-Hall, 1976.

Leitenberg, H., Agras, W. S., Thomson, L. E., & Wright, D. E. Feedback in behavior modification: An experimental analysis in two phobic cases. *Journal of Applied Behavior Analysis*, 1968, *1*, 131–137.

Lewin, L. M., & Wakefield, J. A., Jr. Percentage agreement and phi: A conversion table. *Journal of Applied Behavior Analysis*, 1979, *12*, 299–301.

Lindsay, W. R., & Stoffelmayr, B. E. A comparison of the differential effects of three different baseline conditions within an ABA_1B_1 experimental design. *Behaviour Research and Therapy*, 1976, *14*, 169–183.

Lindsley, O. R. Operant conditioning methods applied to research in chronic schizophrenia. *Psychiatric Research Reports*, 1956, *5*, 118–139.

Lindsley, O. R. Characteristics of the behavior of chronic psychotics as revealed by free-operant conditioning methods. *Disease of the Nervous System* (Monograph Supplement), 1960, *21*, 66–78.

Lubar, J. F., & Bahler, W. W. Behavioral management of epileptic seizures following EEG biofeedback training of the sensorimotor rhythm. *Biofeedback and Self-Regulation*, 1976, *1*, 77–104.

Lykken, D. T. Statistical significance in psychological research. *Psychological Bulletin*, 1968, *70*, 151–159.

Maloney, D. M., Harper, T. M., Braukmann, C. J., Fixsen, D. L., Phillips, E. L., & Wolf, M. M. Teaching conversation-related skills to predelinquent girls. *Journal of Applied Behavior Analysis*, 1976, *9*, 371.

Marholin, D., II, Siegel, L. J., & Phillips, D. Treatment and transfer: A search for empirical procedures. In M. Hersen, R. M. Eisler, & P. M. Miller (Eds.), *Progress in behavior modification, Volume 3*. New York: Academic Press, 1976.

Marholin, D., II, Steinman, W. M., McInnis, E. T., & Heads, T. B. The effect of a teacher's presence on the classroom behavior of conduct problem children. *Journal of Abnormal Child Psychology*, 1975, *3*, 11–25.

Martin, G. L., & Osborne, J. G. (Ed.). *Helping in the community: Behavioral applications*. New York: Plenum, 1980.

Martin, J. E., & Sachs, D. A. The effects of a self-control weight loss program on an obese woman. *Journal of Behavior Therapy and Experimental Psychiatry*, 1973, *4*, 155–159.

Mash, E. J., & McElwee, J. Situational effects on observer accuracy: Behavioral predictability, prior experience, and complexity of coding categories. *Child Development*, 1974, *45*, 367–377.

Matson, J. L., Kazdin, A. E., & Esveldt-Dawson, K. Training interpersonal skills among mentally retarded and socially dysfunctional children. *Behaviour Research and Therapy*, 1980, *18*, 419–427.

McAllister, L. W., Stachowiak, J. G., Baer, D. M., & Conderman, L. The application of operant conditioning techniques in a secondary school classroom. *Journal of Applied Behavior Analysis*, 1969, *2*, 277–285.

McCullough, J. P., Cornell, J. E., McDaniel, M. H., & Mueller, R. K. Utilization of the simultaneous treatment design to improve student behavior in a first-grade classroom. *Journal of Consulting and Clinical Psychology*, 1974, *42*, 288–292.

McFall, R. M, & Marston, A. R. An experimental investigation of behavior rehearsal in assertive training. *Journal of Abnormal Psychology*, 1970, *76*, 295–303.

McMahon, R. J., & Forehand, R. Nonprescription behavior therapy: Effectiveness of a brochure in teaching mothers to correct their children's inappropriate mealtime behaviors. *Behavior Therapy*, 1978, *9*, 814–820.

McNees, M. P., Egli, D. S., Marshall, D. S., Schnelle, R. S., Schnelle, J. F., & Risley, T. R. Shoplifting prevention: Providing information through signs. *Journal of Applied Behavior Analysis*, 1976, *9*, 399–405.

McSweeney, A. J. Effects of response cost on the behavior of a million persons: Charging for directory assistance in Cincinnati. *Journal of Applied Behavior Analysis,* 1978, *11,* 47–51.

Meehl, P. E. Theory-testing in psychology and physics: A methodological paradox. *Philosophy of Science,* 1967, *34,* 103–115.

Meyers, A. W., Artz, L. M., & Craighead, W. E. The effects of instructions, incentive, and feedback on a community problem: Dormitory noise. *Journal of Applied Behavior Analysis,* 1976, *9,* 445–457.

Michael, J. Statistical inference for individual organism research: Mixed blessing or curse? *Journal of Applied Behavior Analysis,* 1974, *7,* 647–653.

Minkin, N., Braukmann, C. J., Minkin, B. L., Timbers, G. D., Timbers, B. J., Fixsen, D. L., Phillips, E. L., & Wolf, M. M. The social validation and training of conversational skills. *Journal of Applied Behavior Analysis,* 1976, *9,* 127–139.

Mithaug, D. E., & Hagmeier, L. O. The development of procedures to assess prevocational competencies of severely handicapped young adults. *AAESPH Review,* 1978, *3,* 94–115.

Moses, L. E. Nonparametric statistics for psychological research. *Psychological Bulletin,* 1952, *49,* 112–143.

Neale, J. M., & Liebert, R. M. *Science and behavior: An introduction to methods of research* (2nd edition). Englewood Cliffs, N.J.: Prentice-Hall, 1980.

Neef, N. A., Iwata, B. A., & Page, T. J. Public transportation training: *In vivo* versus classroom instruction. *Journal of Applied Behvior Analysis,* 1978, *11,* 331–344.

Neef, N. A., Iwata, B. A., & Page, T. J. The effects of interpersonal training versus high-density reinforcement on spelling acquisition and retention. *Journal of Applied Behavior Analysis,* 1980, *13,* 153–158.

Nordyke, N. S., Baer, D. M., Etzel, B. C., & LeBlanc, J. M. Implications of the stereotyping and modification of sex role. *Journal of Applied Behavior Analysis,* 1977, *10,* 553–557.

Nutter, D., & Reid, D. H. Teaching retarded women a clothing selection skill using community norms. *Journal of Applied Behavior Analysis,* 1978, *11,* 475–487.

O'Brien, F., & Azrin, N. H. Developing proper mealtime behaviors of the institutionalized retarded. *Journal of Applied Behavior Analysis,* 1972, *5,* 389–399.

O'Leary, K. D., Becker, W. C., Evans, M. B., & Saudargas, R. A. A token reinforcement program in a public school: A replication and systematic analysis. *Journal of Applied Behavior Analysis,* 1969, *2,* 3–13.

O'Leary, K. D., & Kent, R. N. Behavior modification for social action: Research tactics and problems. In L. A. Hamerlynk, P. O. Davidson, & L. E. Acker (Eds.), *Critical issues in research and practice.* Champaign, Ill.: Research Press, 1973.

O'Leary, K. D., Kent, R. N., & Kanowitz, J. Shaping data collection congruent with experimental hypotheses. *Journal of Applied Behavior Analysis,* 1975, *8,* 43–51.

Ollendick, T. H., Shapiro, E. S., & Barrett, R. P. Reducing stereotypic behaviors: An analysis of treatment procedures using an alternating-treatments design. *Behavior Therapy,* 1981, *12,* 570–577.

Page, T. J., Iwata, B. A., & Neef, N. A. Teaching pedestrian skills to retarded persons: Generalization from the classroom to the natural environment. *Journal of Applied Behavior Analysis,* 1976, *9,* 433–444.

Paredes, A., Jones, B. M. & Gregory, D. Blood alcohol discrimination training with alcoholics. In F. A. Seixas (Ed.), *Currents in alcoholism, Volume 2*. New York: Grune & Stratton, 1977.

Parsonson, B. S., & Baer, D. M. The analysis and presentation of graphic data. In T. R. Kratochwill (Ed.), *Single-subject research: Strategies for evaluating change*. New York: Academic Press, 1978.

Patterson, E. T., Griffin, J. C., & Panyan, M. C. Incentive maintenance of self-help skill training programs for non-professional personnel. *Journal of Behavior Therapy and Experimental Psychiatry*, 1976, *7*, 249–253.

Patterson, G. R. Interventions for boys with conduct problems: Multiple settings, treatments, and criteria. *Journal of Consulting and Clinical Psychology*, 1974, *42*, 471–481.

Paul, G. Behavior modification research: Design and tactics. In C. M. Franks (Ed.), *Behavior therapy: Appraisal and status*. New York: McGraw-Hill, 1969.

Paul, G. L., & Lentz, R. J. *Psychosocial treatment of chronic mental patients: Milieu versus social-learning programs*. Cambridge, Mass.: Harvard University Press, 1977.

Peacock, R., Lyman, R. D., & Rickard, H. C. Correspondence between self-report and observer-report as a function of task difficulty. *Behavior Therapy*, 1978, *9*, 578–583.

Perkoff, G. T. The meaning of "experimental." In E. S. Valenstein (Ed.), *The psychosurgery debate: Scientific, legal, and ethical perspectives*. San Francisco: W. H. Freeman, 1980.

Phillips, E. L. Achievement Place: Token reinforcement procedures in a home-style rehabilitation setting for "predelinquent" boys. *Journal of Applied Behavior Analysis*, 1968, *1*, 213–223.

Prince, M. *The dissociation of a personality*. New York: Longmans, Green, 1905.

Raush, H. L. Research, practice and accountability. *American Psychologist*, 1974, *29*, 678–681.

Redd, W. H. Effects of mixed reinforcement contingencies on adults' control of children's behavior. *Journal of Applied Behavior Analysis*, 1969, *2*, 249–254.

Reid, J. B. Reliability assessment of observation data: A possible methodological problem. *Child Development*, 1970, *41*, 1143–1150.

Reid, J. B. (Ed.). *A social learning approach to family intervention. Volume 2: Observation in home settings*. Eugene, Ore.: Castalia, 1978.

Reid, J. B., & DeMaster, B. The efficacy of the spot-check procedure in maintaining the reliability of data collected by observers in quasi-natural settings: Two pilot studies. *Oregon Research Institute Research Bulletin*, 1972, *12*.

Reid, J. B., Skindrud, K. D., Taplin, P. S., & Jones, R. R. The role of complexity in the collection and evaluation of observation data. Paper presented at meeting of the American Psychological Association, Montreal, September 1973.

Rekers, G. A. Atypical gender development and psychosocial adjustment. *Journal of Applied Behavior Analysis*, 1977, *10*, 559–571.

Rekers, G. A., & Lovaas, O. I. Behavioral treatment of deviant sex-role behaviors in a male child. *Journal of Applied Behavior Analysis*, 1974, *7*, 173–190.

Renne, C. M., & Creer, T. L. Training children with asthma to use inhalation therapy equipment. *Journal of Applied Behavior Analysis*, 1976, *9*, 1–11.

Repp, A. C., & Deitz, S. M. Reducing aggressive and self-injurious behavior of institutionalized retarded children through reinforcement of other behaviors. *Journal of Applied Behavior Analysis,* 1974, *7,* 313–325.

Revusky, S. H. Some statistical treatments compatible with individual organism methodology. *Journal of the Experimental Analysis of Behavior,* 1967, *10,* 319–330.

Rincover, A., Cook, R., Peoples, A., & Packard, D. Sensory extinction and sensory reinforcement principles for programming multiple adaptive behavior change. *Journal of Applied Behavior Analysis,* 1979, *12,* 221–233.

Risley, T. R. Behavior modification: An experimental-therapeutic endeavor. In L. A. Hamerlynck, P. O. Davidson, & L. E. Acker (Eds.), *Behavior modification and ideal mental health services.* Calgary, Alberta: University of Calgary Press, 1970.

Robinson, E. A., & Eyberg, S. M. The dyadic parent-child interaction coding system standardization and validation. Unpublished manuscript, University of Washington, 1980.

Robinson, P. W., & Foster, D. F. *Experimental psychology: A small-n approach.* New York: Harper & Row, 1979.

Rogers-Warren, A., & Warren, S. F. Mands for verbalizations: Facilitating the display of newly trained language in children. *Behavior Modification,* 1980, *4,* 361–382.

Romanczyk, R. G., Kent, R. N., Diament, C., & O'Leary, K. D. Measuring the reliability of observational data: A reactive process. *Journal of Applied Behavior Analysis,* 1973, *6,* 175–184.

Ross, J. A. Parents modify thumbsucking: A case study. *Journal of Behavior Therapy and Experimental Psychiatry,* 1975, *6,* 248–249.

Rowbury, T. G., Baer, A. M., & Baer, D. M. Interactions between teacher guidance and contingent access to play in developing preacademic skills of deviant preschool children. *Journal of Applied Behavior Analysis,* 1976, *9,* 85–104.

Rusch, F. R., Connis, R. T., & Sowers, J. The modification and maintenance of time spent attending to task using social reinforcement, token reinforcement and response cost in an applied restaurant setting. *Journal of Special Education Technology,* 1979, *2,* 18–26.

Rusch, F. R., & Kazdin, A. E. Toward a methodology of withdrawal designs for the assessment of response maintenance. *Journal of Applied Behavior Analysis,* 1981, *14,* 131–140.

Russo, D. C., & Koegel, R. L. A method for integrating an autistic child into a normal public school classroom. *Journal of Applied Behavior Analysis,* 1977, *10,* 579–590.

Schmidt, G. W., & Ulrich, R. E. Effects of group contingent events upon classroom noise. *Journal of Applied Behavior Analysis,* 1969, *2,* 171–179.

Schnelle, J. F. A brief report on invalidity of parent evaluations of behavior change. *Journal of Applied Behavior Analysis,* 1974, *7,* 341–343.

Schnelle, J. F., Kirchner, R. E., Macrae, J. W., McNees, M. P., Eck, R. H., Snodgrass, S., Casey, J. D., & Uselton, P. H. Police evaluation research: An experimental and cost-benefit analysis of a helicopter patrol in a high crime area. *Journal of Applied Behavior Analysis,* 1978, *11,* 11–21.

Schnelle, J. F., Kirchner, R. E., McNees, M. P., & Lawler, J. M. Social evaluation research: The evaluation of two police patrolling strategies. *Journal of Applied Behavior Analysis,* 1975, *8,* 353–365.

Schrier, A. M. Comparison of two methods of investigating the effect of amount of reward on performance. *Journal of Comparative and Physiological Psychology,* 1958, *51,* 725–731.

Scott, J. W., & Bushell, D., Jr. The length of teacher contracts and students' off-task behavior. *Journal of Applied Behavior Analysis,* 1974, *7,* 39–44.

Scott, R. W., Peters, R. D., Gillespie, W. J., Blanchard, E. B., Edmunson, E. D., & Young, L. D. The use of shaping and reinforcement in the operant acceleration and deceleration of heart rate. *Behaviour Research and Therapy,* 1973, *11,* 179–185.

Shapiro, E. S. Restitution and positive practice overcorrection in reducing aggressive-disruptive behavior: A long-term follow-up. *Journal of Behavior Therapy and Experimental Psychiatry,* 1979, *10,* 131–134.

Shapiro, E. S., Kazdin, A. E., & McGonigle, J. J. Multiple-treatment interference in the simultaneous- or alternating-treatments design. *Behavioral Assessment,* 1982, in press.

Shapiro, M. B. A method of measuring psychological changes specific to the individual psychiatric patient. *British Journal of Medical Psychology,* 1961, *34,* 151–155. (a)

Shapiro, M. B. The single case in fundamental clinical psychological research. *British Journal of Medical Psychology,* 1961, *34,* 255–262. (b)

Shapiro, M. B., & Ravenette, T. A preliminary experiment of paranoid delusions *Journal of Mental Science,* 1959, *105,* 295–312.

Shine, L. C., & Bower, S. M. A one-way analysis of variance for single-subject designs. *Educational and Psychological Measurement,* 1971, *31,* 105–113.

Sidman, M. *Tactics of scientific research.* New York: Basic Books, 1960.

Singh, N. N., Dawson, M. J., & Gregory, P. R. Suppression of chronic hyperventilation using response-contingent aromatic ammonia. *Behavior Therapy,* 1980, *11,* 561–566.

Skindrud, K. An evaluation of observer bias in experimental-field studies of social interaction. Unpublished doctoral dissertation, University of Oregon, 1972.

Skindrud, K. Field evaluation of observer bias under overt and covert monitoring. In L. A. Hamerlynck, L. C. Handy, & E. J. Mash (Eds.), *Behavior change: Methodology, concepts, and practice.* Champaign, Ill.: Research Press, 1973.

Skinner, B. F. *The behavior of organisms.* New York: Appleton-Century-Crofts, 1938.

Skinner, B. F. *Science and human behavior.* New York: Free Press, 1953. (a)

Skinner, B. F. Some contributions of an experimental analysis of behavior to psychology as a whole. *American Psychologist,* 1953, *8,* 69–78. (b)

Skinner, B. F. A case history in scientific methods. *American Psychologist,* 1956, *11,* 221–233.

Smith, M. L., & Glass, G. V. Meta-analysis of psychotherapy outcome studies. *American Psychologist,* 1977, *32,* 752–760.

Sowers, J., Rusch, F. R., Connis, R. T., & Cummings, L. E. Teaching mentally retarded adults to time-manage in a vocational setting. *Journal of Applied Behavior Analysis,* 1980, *13,* 119–128.

Staats, A. W., Minke, K. A., Finley, J. R., Wolf, M., & Brooks, L. O. A reinforcer system and experimental procedure for the laboratory study of reading acquisition. *Child Development,* 1964, *35,* 209–231.

Staats, A. W., Staats, C. K., Schutz, R. E., & Wolf, M. M. The conditioning of textual responses using "extrinsic" reinforcers. *Journal of the Experimental Analysis of Behavior,* 1962, *5,* 33–40.

Stahl, J. R., Thomson, L. E., Leitenberg, J., & Hasazi, J. E. Establishment of praise as a conditioned reinforcer in socially unresponsive psychiatric patients. *Journal of Abnormal Psychology,* 1974, *83,* 488–496.

Stokes, T. F., & Baer, D. M. An implicit technology of generalization. *Journal of Applied Behavior Analysis,* 1977, *10,* 349–367.

Stokes, T. F., Baer, D. M., & Jackson, R. L. Programming the generalization of a greeting response in four retarded children. *Journal of Applied Behavior Analysis,* 1974, *7,* 599–610.

Stoline, M. R., Huitema, B. E., & Mitchell, B. T. Intervention time-series model with different pre- and postintervention first-order autoregressive parameters. *Psychological Bulletin,* 1980, *88,* 46–53.

Surratt, P. R., Ulrich, R. E., & Hawkins, R. P. An elementary student as a behavioral engineer. *Journal of Applied Behavior Analysis,* 1969, *2,* 85–92.

Switzer, E. B., Deal, T. E., & Bailey, J. S. The reduction of stealing in second graders using a group contingency. *Journal of Applied Behavior Analysis,* 1977, *10,* 267–272.

Taplin, P. S., & Reid, J. B. Effects of instructional set and experimenter influence on observer reliability. *Child Development,* 1973, *44,* 547–554.

Taylor, D. R. An expedient method for calculating the Harris and Lahey weighted agreement formula. *The Behavior Therapist,* 1980, *3* (4), 3.

Thigpen, C. H., & Cleckley, H. M. A case of multiple personality. *Journal of Abnormal and Social Psychology,* 1954, *49,* 135–151.

Thoresen, C. E., & Elashoff, J. D. "An analysis-of-variance model for intrasubject replication designs": Some additional comments. *Journal of Applied Behavior Analysis,* 1974, *7,* 639–641.

Twardosz, S., & Baer, D. M. Training two severely retarded adolescents to ask questions. *Journal of Applied Behavior Analysis,* 1973, *6,* 655–661.

Ullmann, L. P., & Krasner, L. (Eds.). *Case studies in behavior modification.* New York: Holt, Rinehart & Winston, 1965.

Ullmann, L. P., & Krasner, L. *A psychological approach to abnormal behavior* (2nd edition). Englewood Cliffs, N.J.: Prentice-Hall, 1975.

Ulman, J. D., & Sulzer-Azaroff, B. Multielement baseline design in educational research. In E. Ramp & G. Semb (eds.), *Behavior analysis: Areas of research and application.* Englewood Cliffs, N.J.: Prentice-Hall, 1975.

Underwood, B. J., & Shaughnessy, J. J. *Experimentation in psychology.* New York: Wiley, 1975.

Van Houten, R., Morrison, E., Jarvis, R., & McDonald, M. The effects of explicit timing and feedback on compositional response rate in elementary school children. *Journal of Applied Behavior Analysis,* 1974, *7,* 547–555.

Van Houten, R., Nau, P., & Marini, Z. An analysis of public posting in reducing speeding behavior on an urban highway. *Journal of Applied Behavior Analysis,* 1980, *13,* 383–395.

Vogelsberg, T., & Rusch, F. R. Training three severely handicapped young adults to walk, look and cross uncontrolled intersections. *AAESPH Review,* 1979, *4,* 264–273.

Wahler, R. G. Some structural aspects of deviant child behavior. *Journal of Applied Behavior Analysis,* 1975, *8,* 27–42.

Walker, H. M., & Hops, H. Use of normative peer data as a standard for evaluating classroom treatment effects. *Journal of Applied Behavior Analysis,* 1976, *9,* 159–168.

Walker, H. M., Hops, H., & Fiegenbaum, E. Deviant classroom behavior as a function of combinations of social and token reinforcement and cost contingency. *Behavior Therapy,* 1976, *7,* 76–88.

Watson, J. B., & Rayner, R. Conditioned emotional reactions. *Journal of Experimental Psychology,* 1920, *3,* 1–14.

Watson, R. I. *The clinical method in psychology.* New York: Harper, 1951.

Webb, E. J., Campbell, D. T., Schwartz, R. D., Sechrest, L., & Grove, J. B. *Nonreactive measures in the social sciences* (2nd edition). Boston: Houghton Mifflin, 1981.

Wells, K. C., Forehand, R., Hickey, K., & Green, K. D. Effects of a procedure derived from the overcorrection principle on manipulated and nonmanipulated behaviors. *Journal of Applied Behavior Analysis,* 1977, *10,* 679–687.

Werner, J. S., Minkin, N., Minkin, B. L. Fixsen, D. L., Phillips, E. L., & Wolf, M. M. "Intervention package": An analysis to prepare juvenile delinquents for encounters with police officers. *Criminal Justice and Behavior,* 1975, *2,* 55–83.

White, G. D., Nielson, G., & Johnson, S. M. Timeout duration and the suppression of deviant behavior in children. *Journal of Applied Behavior Analysis,* 1972, *5,* 111–120.

White, O. R. A manual for the calculation and use of the median slope—a technique of progress estimation and prediction in the single case. Regional Resource Center for Handicapped Children, University of Oregon, Eugene, Oregon, 1972.

White, O. R. The "split middle" a "quickie" method of trend estimation. University of Washington, Experimental Education Unit, Child Development and Mental Retardation Center, 1974.

Whitman, T. L., Mercurio, J. R., & Caponigri, V. Development of social responses in two severely retarded children. *Journal of Applied Behavior Analysis,* 1970, *3,* 133–138.

Wilson, D. D., Robertson, S. J., Herlong, L. H., & Haynes, S. N. Vicarious effects of time-out in the modification of aggression in the classroom. *Behavior Modification,* 1979, *3,* 97–111.

Wincze, J. P., Leitenberg, H., & Agras, W. S. The effects of token reinforcement and feedback on the delusional verbal behavior of chronic paranoid schizophrenics. *Journal of Applied Behavior Analysis,* 1972, *5,* 247–262.

Winett, R. A. & Winkler, R. C. Current behavior modification in the classroom: Be still, be quiet, be docile. *Journal of Applied Behavior Analysis,* 1972, *5,* 499–504.

Winkler, R. C. What types of sex-role behavior should behavior modifiers promote? *Journal of Applied Behavior Analysis,* 1977, *10,* 549–552.

Wolf, M. M. Social validity: The case for subjective measurement or how applied behavior analysis is finding its heart. *Journal of Applied Behavior Analysis,* 1978, *11*, 203–214.

Wolpe, J. *Psychotherapy by reciprocal inhibition.* Stanford: Stanford University Press, 1958.

Yates, A. J. *Biofeedback and the modification of behavior.* New York: Plenum, 1980,

Yelton, A. R. Reliability in the context of the experiment: A commentary on two articles by Birkimer and Brown. *Journal of Applied Behavior Analysis,* 1979, *12*, 565–569.

Zilboorg, G., & Henry, G. *A history of medical psychology.* New York: Norton, 1941.

Zlutnick, S., Mayville, W. J., & Moffat, S. Modification of seizure disorders: The interruption of behavioral chains. *Journal of Applied Behavior Analysis,* 1975, *8*, 1–12.

Author Index

Abel, G. G., 37
Adams, C. K., 220
Agras, W. S., 32, 37, 44, 174, 175, 177, 228, 273, 285
Agteros, T., 294
Ahles, T. A., 294
Alden, K., 242, 321
Alford, G. W., 293
Allen, K. E., 148
Allison, M. G., 270
Allport, G. W., 7
Andrasik, F., 294
Armitage, S. G., 12
Arnold, C. M., 25
Arntson, P., 242, 321
Artz, L. M., 44, 206
Ault, M. H., 63
Axelrod, S., 164, 166
Ayllon, T., 12, 23, 134, 136, 264, 270
Azrin, N. H., 13, 98, 99, 253, 254, 275

Baer, A. M., 117
Baer, D. M., 12, 18, 24, 116, 117, 122, 146, 148, 208, 226, 227, 232, 233, 237, 240, 241, 242, 264, 270, 283, 293, 297, 311, 316
Bahler, W. W., 35
Bailey, J. S., 29, 137, 138, 193, 195, 207, 281
Barber, R. M., 303
Barlow, D. H., 13, 14, 37, 139, 140, 174, 175, 177, 178, 183, 184, 219, 222, 228, 270, 271, 285, 286, 293, 295

Barnard, J. D., 307, 308
Barnett, F. T., 28, 308, 309
Barrett, B. H., 12
Barrett, R. P., 185, 186, 194
Becker, W. C., 280
Behar, I., 220
Behling, M., 39
Beiman, I., 35
Bellack, A. S., 18, 42, 86, 129, 130
Bergin, A. E., 14
Besalel-Azrin, V., 98, 99
Bessman, C. A., 303
Bijou, S. W., 12, 63
Binkoff, J. A., 270
Birkimer, J. C., 62, 64, 237
Bittle, R., 194, 207
Blanchard, E. B., 35, 36, 273, 294
Bolgar, H., 4, 14
Bolstad, O. D., 53, 56, 60
Boring, E. G., 6
Bornstein, M. R., 129, 130
Bornstein, P. H., 13, 278, 279
Bower, S. M., 319, 321
Box, G. E. P., 250, 328
Boyd, S. B., 136
Bracht, G. H., 81
Braukmann, C. J., 20, 31, 255, 256, 259
Breuer, J., 8
Brigham, T. A., 256, 293
Broden, M., 124
Brooks, L. O., 12
Brown, J. H., 62, 64, 237

Brownell, K. D., 139, 140, 293
Browning, R. M., 177, 178, 183, 194
Buckholdt, D., 23
Bunck, T. J., 29, 299
Burg, M. M., 299
Bushell, D., Jr., 277

Calhoun, K. S., 141
Campbell, D. T., 9, 43, 77, 81, 87, 88, 194, 219
Caponigri, V., 32
Carr, E. G., 270
Cartelli, L. M., 274
Casey, J. D., 34, 244, 292
Cataldo, M. F., 303
Catania, A. C., 293
Chaddock, R. E., 6
Chai, H., 122
Chapman, C., 34
Chassan, J. B., 14, 290
Cheiken, M., 68, 69, 70
Christensen, D. E., 45
Christophersen, E. R., 25, 307, 308
Ciminero, A. R., 35
Clark, H. B., 31, 124, 136
Cleckley, H. M., 8
Cohen, J., 66
Cohen, S., 239
Combs, M. L., 18
Conderman, L., 226, 227
Connis, R. T., 213, 214, 216, 217
Conover, W. J., 326, 328
Cook, R., 270
Cook, T. D., 9, 77, 81
Cornell, J. E., 178
Cossairt, A., 280
Craighead, W. E., 40, 44, 206
Creer, T. L., 122, 129, 131
Cumming, W. W., 272
Cummings, L. E., 216, 217

Dapcich-Miura, E., 202, 203
Davis, F., 322, 323
Davis, J. L., 31
Davis, J. R., 25
Davison, G. C., 14, 18
Dawson, D., 242, 321
Dawson, M. J., 202, 204
Deal, T. E., 137, 138
Deitz, S. M., 25, 113, 114, 162, 163
De Master, B., 69
de Montes, A. I., 225, 226
Demuth, D., 242, 321
De Prospero, A., 239
Diament, C., 68, 259
Dietz, A., 259
Dittmer, C. G., 6

Dobes, R. W., 24, 69, 95, 97
Doleys, D. M., 274
Dominguez, B., 225, 226
Donahoe, C. P., Jr., 21
Dotson, V. A., 60, 61, 62, 64
Dressel, M. E., 41
Dukes, W. F., 4, 6
Dunlap, A., 124
Durac, J., 294

Eck, R. H., 34, 244, 292
Edgington, E. G., 184, 246, 318, 324, 325, 328, 336
Edmunson, E. D., 273
Egli, D. S., 301
Eisler, R. M., 27, 43
Elashoff, J. D., 321
Emerson, M., 322, 323
Epstein, L. H., 35, 36, 37
Erickson, L. M., 144, 145, 285
Esveldt-Dawson, K., 254
Etzel, B. C., 18
Evans, M. B., 280
Eyberg, S. M., 41
Eysenck, H. J., 294

Favell, J. E., 205
Fawcett, S. B., 256
Ferritor, D. E., 23
Ferster, C. B., 12, 302
Feuerstein, M., 35
Fichter, M. M., 25
Fiegenbaum, E., 280
Finley, J. R., 12
Firestone, P., 97, 98
Fisher, R. A., 6
Fixsen, D. L., 20, 22, 31, 255, 256, 259
Fjellstedt, N., 33
Forehand, R., 132, 133, 136
Foster, D. F., 4, 6, 295
Foster, S. L., 60, 68
Fox, R. G., 153, 156, 158, 161, 162, 322, 323
Foxx, R. M., 34, 120, 154, 155, 303
Foy, D. W., 27, 43
Frederiksen, L. W., 27, 43
Freedman, B. J., 21
Freud, S., 8
Friedman, J., 164, 166

Gallo, P. S., Jr., 294
Gardner, W., 246, 248, 250, 318
Garfield, S. L., 13
Gaul, D. J., 40
Geesey, S., 181, 182, 188, 193
Gelfand, D. M., 272
Gentile, J. R., 319, 321
Gillespie, W. J., 273

Glass, G. V., 81, 237, 239, 246, 248, 250, 294, 318, 322
Glazeski, R. C., 41
Glenwick, D., 244
Goetz, E. M., 116, 117, 122
Goldiamond, I., 12
Goldsmith, L., 322, 323
Gottman, J. M., 237, 239, 246, 248, 250, 318, 322
Grahman, L. E., 35
Graubard, P. S., 256
Green, K. D., 136
Greene, B. F., 31
Greenwood, C. R., 258
Gregory, D., 35
Gregory, P. R., 202, 204
Grice, C. R., 220
Griffin, J. C., 280
Grove, J. B., 43
Gullick, E. L., 36

Hagmeier, L. O., 22
Hake, D. F., 34, 194, 207, 303
Hall, R. V., 124, 152, 153, 156, 158, 161, 162, 280, 322, 323
Halle, J. W., 303, 305
Hamblin, R. L., 23
Hamilton, S. B., 278, 279
Haney, J. I., 40, 271
Hansen, G. D., 299
Harper, T. M., 255
Harris, F. C., 148, 270
Harris, F. R., 63
Harris, S. L., 280
Harris, V. W., 23
Hartmann, D. P., 62, 65, 67, 153, 177, 178, 193, 242, 246, 248, 250, 272, 318, 321, 322
Hasazi, J. E., 258
Haughton, E., 264
Hauserman, N., 39
Hawkins, R. P., 24, 32, 60, 61, 64, 69
Hayes, S. C., 139, 140, 178, 183, 184, 293
Haynes, S. N., 273
Heads, T. B., 23
Hempstead, J., 242, 321
Henry, G., 9
Herlong, L. H., 273
Herman, S. H., 285
Hermann, J. A., 60, 61, 62, 65, 225, 226, 285
Hersen, M., 13, 18, 42, 86, 129, 130, 178, 219, 222, 270, 271, 295
Hickey, K., 136
Hill, D. W., 25
Hiss, R. H., 220
Hobbs, S. A., 274
Hoffman, A., 122

Hollandsworth, J. G., 41
Holmberg, M. C., 116, 117
Honig, W. K., 293
Hontos, P. T., 98, 99
Hopkins, B. L., 60, 61, 62, 65, 225, 226, 280
Hops, H., 254, 258, 280
Horner, R. D., 38, 146, 148
House, A. E., 56, 71
House, B. J., 56, 71
Hovel, M. F., 202, 203
Huitema, B. E., 322
Hunter, J. J., 220

Iwata, B. A., 28, 29, 211, 212, 299

Jackson, J. L., 141
Jackson, R. L., 24
Jarvis, R., 256
Jason, L., 244
Jayaratne, S., 290
Jenkins, G. M., 250
Jenkins, J. O., 27, 43
Johnson, J. L., 22
Johnson, M. S., 29, 193, 195, 207, 281
Johnson, S. M., 41, 53, 56, 60, 280
Johnston, M. S., 148
Jones, B. M., 35
Jones, M. C., 8
Jones, M. L., 205
Jones, R. R., 71, 237, 239, 246, 248, 250, 318, 322, 323, 324
Jones, R. T., 40, 271, 280

Kagey, J. R., 303
Kallman, W. M., 35
Kandel, H. J., 134, 136
Kanowitz, J., 68, 70
Kazdin, A. E., 12, 14, 22, 25, 36, 40, 42, 68, 77, 86, 117, 119, 121, 141, 144, 145, 177, 181, 184, 189, 193, 197, 208, 213, 219, 237, 241, 244, 246, 250, 254, 259, 271, 275, 280, 285, 290, 291, 301, 312, 318, 322, 328
Kazrin, A., 294
Keilitz, I., 38, 146
Kelly, M. B., 55
Kennedy, R. E., 248
Kent, R. N., 60, 68, 69, 70, 254, 259
Killeen, P. R., 272, 274
King, G. F., 12
Kirchner, R. E., 34, 244, 249, 292
Klein, R. D., 319, 321
Klock, J., 25
Knapp, T. J., 35
Koegel, R. L., 27
Komaki, J., 28, 308, 309
Korchin, S. J., 7

Krasner, L., 12, 19
Kratochwill, T. R., 64, 177, 178, 242, 246,
     290, 318, 321
Kurtz, R., 13

Lahey, B. B., 63
Lamparski, D., 42, 86
Lattal, K. A., 38
Lattimore, J., 299
Lawler, J. M., 244, 249
Lawson, R., 220
Lazarus, A. A., 14, 88
Le Blanc, J. M., 18, 116, 117
Leitenberg, H., 13, 32, 37, 44, 174, 175, 177,
     213, 258, 273, 285, 293
Lentz, R. J., 31, 223, 224, 225
Levin, J., 242
Levy, R. L., 290, 321
Lewin, L. M., 67
Liberman, R. P., 25
Liebert, R. M., 291
Lindsay, W. R., 116, 117
Lindsley, O. R., 12
Lovaas, O. I., 228
Lubar, J. F., 35
Lykken, D. T., 295
Lyman, R. D., 28

Macrae, J. W., 31, 34, 136, 244, 292
Mahoney, M. J., 40
Maloney, D. M., 255
Marholin, D., II, 23, 208
Marini, Z., 29, 44
Marshall, A. M., 303, 305
Marshall, D. S., 299, 301
Marston, A. R., 43, 255
Martin, G. L., 244
Martin, J. E., 95, 96
Mascitelli, S., 193
Mash, E. J., 71
Matson, J. L., 254
Mayville, W. J., 27, 114, 115
McAllister, L. W., 226, 227
McCullough, J. P., 178
McDaniel, M. H., 178
McDonald, M., 256
McElwee, J., 71
McFall, R. M., 21, 43, 255
McGimsey, J. F., 205
McGonigle, J. J., 195, 197
McInnis, E. T., 23
McMahon, R. J., 132, 133
McMurray, N., 242, 321
McNees, M. P., 31, 34, 244, 249, 292, 299,
     301
McSweeney, A. J., 249, 292
Meehl, P. E., 295

Mercurio, J. R., 32
Meyers, A. W., 44, 206
Michael, J., 12, 232, 241
Miller, L. K., 256
Minke, K. A., 12
Minkin, B. L., 20, 22, 31, 255, 256, 259
Minkin, N., 20, 22, 31, 255, 256, 259
Mitchell, B. T., 322
Mithaug, D. E., 22
Moffat, S., 27, 114, 115
Montes, F., 225, 226
Morrison, E., 256
Moses, L. E., 328
Mueller, R. K., 178

Nau, P., 29, 44
Neale, J. M., 219
Neff, N. A., 28, 211, 212, 299
Newsom, C. D., 270
Nielson, G., 280
Nordyke, N. S., 18
Nutter, D., 20, 209, 210

O'Brien, F., 253, 254
O'Connor, R., 254
O'Keefe, D., 294
O'Leary, K. D., 68, 69, 80, 254, 259, 280
Ollendick, T. H., 185, 186, 194
Osborne, J. G., 244
Owen, M., 322, 323

Packard, D., 270
Page, T. J., 28, 211, 212, 299
Panicucci, D., 242, 321
Panyan, M. D., 280
Paredes, A., 35
Parker, L. H., 303
Parsonson, B. S., 233, 237, 297, 311, 316
Patterson, E. T., 280
Patterson, G. R., 41, 71, 254
Paul, G. L., 31, 88, 223, 224, 225
Peacock, R., 28
Pearson, J. E. R., 303
Peoples, A., 270
Perkoff, G. T., 143
Peters, R. D., 273
Peterson, L. W., 35
Peterson, R. F., 63, 148
Phillips, D., 208
Phillips, E. L., 20, 22, 31, 32, 255, 256,
     259
Polster, R., 118, 119
Porcia, E., 322, 323
Prince, M., 8

Quevillon, R. P., 278, 279
Quilitch, H. R., 25

Raush, H. L., 13
Ravenette, T., 14
Rayner, R., 8
Redd, W. H., 175
Reid, D. H., 20, 209, 210, 299
Reid, J. B., 41, 69, 70, 71, 323
Rekers, G. A., 18, 228
Renne, C. M., 129, 131
Repp, A. C., 25, 162, 163
Revusky, S. H., 247, 329, 331
Reynolds, J., 228
Rickard, H. C., 28
Rincover, A., 270
Risley, T. R., 12, 18, 31, 34, 230, 252, 264, 299, 301
Roberts, M. D., 23
Roberts, M. W., 274
Robertson, S. J., 273
Robinson, E. A., 41
Robinson, P. W., 4, 6, 295
Roden, A. H., 319, 321
Rogers, M. C., 303
Rogers-Warren, A., 316
Romanczyk, R. G., 68
Rosenbaum, M. S., 134, 136
Rosenthal, L., 21
Ross, J. A., 238
Rowbury, T. G., 122
Rubinoff, A., 154, 155
Rusch, F. R., 213, 214, 216, 217, 218
Russo, D. C., 27

Sachs, D. A., 95, 96
Sanders, S. H., 293
Saudargas, R. A., 280
Schlundt, D. G., 21
Schmidt, G. W., 44
Schnelle, J. F., 34, 244, 249, 259, 292, 299, 301
Schnelle, R. S., 299, 301
Schoenfeld, W. N., 272
Schrier, A. M., 220
Schutz, R. E., 12
Schwartz, R. D., 43
Scott, J. W., 277
Scott, R. W., 273
Sechrest, L., 43
Shapiro, E. S., 185, 186, 194, 195, 197, 270
Shapiro, M. B., 14
Shapiro, S. T., 120
Shaughnessy, J. J., 219
Sherman, J. A., 23
Shine, L. C., 319, 321
Sidman, M., 11, 219, 222, 232, 266, 268, 272, 274, 282, 295
Siegel, L. J., 208
Silverman, N. A., 280

Singh, N. N., 202, 204
Sittler, J. L., 280
Skindrud, K. D., 70, 71
Skinner, B. F., 10, 292, 301, 302
Slaby, D. A., 18
Smith, L., 23
Smith, M. L., 294
Snodgrass, S., 34, 244, 292
Sowers, J., 213, 214, 216, 217
Spradlin, J. E., 303, 305
Sprague, R. L., 45
Staats, A. W., 12
Staats, C. K., 12
Stachowiak, J. G., 226, 227
Staddon, J. E. R., 293
Stahl, J. R., 258
Stanley, J. C., 87, 88, 194, 219
Stans, A., 256
Steinman, W. M., 23
Stoffelmayr, B. E., 116, 117
Stokes, T. F., 24, 208
Stoline, M. R., 322
Stover, D. O., 177
Strupp, H. H., 14
Sulzer-Azaroff, B., 33, 178, 197
Surratt, P. R., 32
Switzer, E. B., 137, 138

Taplin, P. S., 69, 71
Taylor, D. R., 63
Teders, S. J., 294
Thigpen, C. H., 8
Thomas, D. R., 220
Thomson, L. E., 32, 44, 174, 175, 177, 258
Thoresen, C. E., 321
Tiao, G. C., 328
Tilton, J. R., 12
Timbers, B. J., 20, 31, 256, 259
Timbers, G. D., 20, 31, 256, 259
Todd, N. M., 258
Turner, S. M., 86
Twardosz, S., 116
Twentyman, C., 70

Ullmann, L. P., 12, 19
Ulman, J. D., 178, 197
Ulrich, R. E., 32, 44
Underwood, B. J., 219
Uselton, P. H., 34, 244, 292

Van Houten, R., 29, 44, 256
Vaught, R. S., 237, 239, 246, 248, 250, 318, 322, 323, 324
Vogelsberg, T., 218

Wahler, R. G., 141
Wakefield, J. A., Jr., 67

Walen, S. R., 39
Walker, H. M., 254, 258, 280
Wallace, C. J., 25
Warren, S. F., 316
Watson, J. B., 8
Watson, R. I., 7
Webb, E. J., 43
Webster, J. S., 293
Weinrott, M. R., 237, 239, 246, 248, 250, 324
Wells, K. C., 274
Werner, J. S., 22, 255
Wetzel, R. J., 64, 246
White, G. D., 280
White, O. R., 247, 311, 312, 333, 334, 336
Whitman, T. L., 32
Willard, D., 322, 323
Willson, V. L., 237, 246, 248, 250, 318, 322

Wilson, D. D., 273
Wilson, G. T., 294
Wincze, J. P., 273, 285
Winett, R. A., 18
Winkler, R. C., 18
Wolchik, S., 280
Wolf, M. M., 12, 18, 20, 22, 31, 252, 255, 256, 259, 264, 270, 307, 308
Wollersheim, J. P., 13
Wolpe, J., 88
Wright, D. E., 32, 44

Yates, A. J., 35
Yelton, A. R., 65
Young, L. D., 273

Zilboorg, G., 9
Zlutnick, S., 27, 114, 115

Subject Index

ABAB designs, 109–10, 126, 128, 153, 163, 169, 188, 194, 220, 239, 245. *See also* Reversal phase
  characteristics of, 110–14
  in combined designs, 202–6
  multiple interventions in, 119–21
  number of phases, 118–19
  order of phases, 117–118
  problems of, 121–24
  underlying rationale, 110–14
  variations of, 115–21
Abscissa, 297
Alternating-treatments design, 178. *See also* Multiple-treatment designs
Analysis of variance, 245. *See also t* and *F* tests
Applied behavior analysis, 11–12, 275, 299
Assessment, 17, 89, 291, 293. *See also* Behavioral assessment; Strategies of assessment
  automated recording, 43–46
  contrived, 39–41
  in natural settings, 41–42
  probes, 148
  reactivity of, 82–84
  strategies of, 26–39
  unobtrusive, 42–43

BABA design, 118
Baseline assessment, 105, 292
  extrapolation of, 105–6, 111
  functions of, 105–6

Baseline phase, 23–24, 105–6, 109, 111, 126–27, 153, 263
  prolonged assessment in, 143–48
  trends in, 263–65
Behavioral assessment, 17–18. *See also* Conditions of assessment
  defining behaviors, 23–25
  focus of, 17–18
  sources of artifact and bias, 67–72
  strategies of, 26–39
Between-group research, 6–7, 219, 228, 231, 275, 294
  combined with single-case designs, 219–27
  contributions of, 220–23, 225–26
  evaluating "interactions," 221–22, 228
  and generality of findings, 282–83
  in relation to single-case research, 103, 228, 294–95

Calculating interobserver agreement, 52–62
  base rates and chance, 59–62
  frequency ratio, 52–53
  point-by-point ratio, 53–56
  product-moment correlation, 56–59
Case studies, 7–9, 14, 87–94, 100
  characteristics of, 88–91
  defined, 87–88
  drawing inferences from, 91–94
  single-case research and, 7–9, 13–15
  types of, 91–94
Categorical assessment, 27–29

Chance agreement, 59–62
  estimates of, 61–62
  methods of handling, 62–67
Changing-criterion design, 152–56, 265
  characteristics of, 153–54
  clinical utility of, 169–70
  correspondence of criteria and behavior,
    160–61
  magnitude of criterion shifts, 165–69
  "mini" reversals in, 157–59
  number of criterion shifts, 164–65
  problems of, 160–69
  rapid changes in performance, 161–64
  underlying rationale, 153–54
  variations of, 157–60
Clinical or applied significance, 14, 251–52
  problems with, 257–59
  social validation, 252–59
Clinical psychology, 7–9, 13–15
Combined designs, 163, 200, 223–28
  between-group research in, 219–27
  description of, 200–201
  problems of, 207–8
  underlying rationale, 200–201
  variations of, 201–7
Concurrent schedule design, 178. *See*
    Multiple-treatment designs
Conditions of assessment, 39–46
  human observers vs. automated recording,
    43–46
  natural vs. laboratory settings, 41–42
  naturalistic vs. contrived, 39–41
  obtrusive vs. unobtrusive, 42–43
Correlational statistics, 56, 65
  kappa, 66–67
  Pearson product-moment correlation, 56–59
  phi, 67n
Criteria for shifting phases, 272–74
  problems in using, 274
Cumulative graph, 299–302

Data evaluation, 230, 296
  changes in level, 234–35, 237–38
  changes in means, 233–34, 237–38
  changes in slope, 235, 237–38
  clinical evaluation, 251–59
  latency of change, 235–38
  statistical evaluation, 241–51, 318–37
  visual inspection, 231–40, 296–316
Display of data, 231, 238. *See also* Graphical
    display of data
  level, 234–35, 237–38
  means, 233–34, 237–38
  trend, 235, 237–38
Duration of phases, 269–72. *See also*
    Stability of performance
  criteria for shifting phases, 272–74
Duration of response, 32–33

Experimental analysis of behavior, 10–13,
    241, 300
Experimental psychology, 4–7
External validity, 81–85
  priority of, 85–87
  threats to, 81–85

Frequency of measures, 26–27, 37

Generality of results, 282–84, 287
  interaction effects and, 281, 283, 286–87
  replication, 284–87
  single-case research and, 282–83
Generalization, 208
  designs to evaluate, 208–19
  and external validity, 81–83
  in multiple-baseline designs, 141–42
Graphical display of data, 296–307
  descriptive aids, 307–17
  types of graphs, 296–302

Histogram, 302–7, 310

Interaction effects, 221–22, 228
  between-group research and, 222, 283
  single-case research and, 222n, 281, 286–
    87
Internal validity, 77, 87, 100–101, 113
  priority of, 85–87
  threats to, 77–81, 91–94
Interobserver agreement, 48–62. *See also*
    Calculating interobserver agreement
  accuracy vs., 49–51
  base rates and chance, 59–62, 64
  acceptable levels of, 72–74
  checking, 51
  methods of estimating, 52–62
  sources of bias in, 67–72
Interval recording, 30–32, 38

Meta-analysis, 294
Multi-element treatment design, 178. *See*
    also Multiple-treatment designs
Multiple-baseline designs, 126, 153, 215–
    16
  across behaviors, 126–31
  across individuals, 132–34
  across situations, 134–35
  characteristics of, 126–29
  clinical utility of, 148–49
  in combined designs, 202–5
  multiple-treatment design and, 187–88
  number of baselines, 135–37
  partial treatment applications, 137–39
  problems of, 141–48
  prolonged baselines, 143–48
  underlying rationale, 126–29
  variations of, 132–39

Multiple-schedule design, 173–77, 189, 193n, 194
  underlying rationale, 173–74
Multiple-treatment designs, 172–73
  advantages of, 196–98
  alternating-treatment design, 178
  characteristics of, 172
  discriminability of treatments, 191–93
  multiple-schedule design, 173–77, 189, 193n
  multiple-treatment interference, 194–96
  number of interventions, 193–94
  problems of, 188–196
  randomization design, 184–85
  simultaneous-treatment design, 177–182, 189, 194, 197
  variations of, 185–88
Multiple-treatment interference, 82, 84, 194–97, 223, 279–81
  ABAB designs and, 194
  simultaneous-treatment designs and, 194–96

Observational data, 26–33
  complexity of, 71–72
  conducting agreement checks, 51
  observer drift, 69–70
Observer drift, 69–70
Operant conditioning, 10–12, 291, 293
Ordinate, 297
Outcome questions, 275–82
  between-group research and, 281
  single-case research and, 276–81
  types of, 275–76, 281

Partial-withdrawal design, 215–16
Pearson product-moment correlation, 56–59
  interpretation of, 58
Pre-experimental designs, 87, 94–100
  case studies and, 87–94
  single-case experiments and, 100–101
  true experiments and, 87
Probe designs, 209–11
Psychophysiological assessment, 34–35, 38
Psychotherapy, 7–9, 275

Randomization design, 184
Randomization tests, 246, 324–29
  approximations of, 327–28
  practical restrictions of, 328–29
Reactivity of assessment, 68–69, 82–84
Regression toward the mean, 78–79, 89, 92, 270
Reliability, 48n. See also Interobserver agreement
  complexity of observations, 71–72
  expectancies and feedback in, 70–71
  observer drift, 69–70
  reactivity in assessing, 68–69

Replication, 231, 284–87
  direct, 284
  inconsistent effects in, 285–86
  systematic, 284
  types of, 284
Response maintenance, 208
  designs to examine, 211–19
Reversal phase, 116–17, 163, 188, 194, 207, 221, 270
  absence of reversal in behavior, 121–23
  in combined designs, 202–5
  duration of, 124, 270
  mini-reversal, 157–59
  procedural options for, 116–17
  undesirability of using, 123–24
R_n test of ranks, 247, 329–33
  considerations in using, 332–33
  data transformation in, 333
  values for significance of, 331

Self-report measures, 35–36, 39
Sequential-withdrawal design, 213–15
Shifting phases, 263–69
  criteria for, 272–74
  duration of the phases, 269–72
Simple line graph, 298–99, 310
Simultaneous-treatment design, 177–182, 189, 194, 197
  multiple-baseline design and, 187–88
  underlying rationale, 177–79
Single-case research, 3–4
  characteristics of, 100, 291–94
  in clinical research, 7–9, 13–15
  contemporary development of, 10–12
  in experimental psychology, 4–7
  limitations of, 219–21, 275–87
  methodological issues, 263–74
  outcome studies and, 275–82
  requirements of, 104–9
Social validation, 19–23, 252
  combined procedures, 256
  to evaluate outcomes, 252–59
  to identify target focus, 19–23, 253n
  problems with, 257–59
  social comparison, 20–21, 252–55, 257–58
  subjective evaluation, 21–23, 255–56, 258–59
Split-middle technique, 247, 250, 311–16
  binomial test, 334–36
  celeration line, 312–15
  to describe data patterns, 311–16, 333–34
  statistical analyses and, 333–37
Stability of performance, 106, 242–43, 263, 272
  criteria to define, 272–74
  trends in the data, 106–9, 263–65
  variability in the data, 109, 167, 266–69

Statistical evaluation, 6–7, 14, 241, 265. *See also* Statistical tests
  problems in using, 250–51
  reasons for using, 242–45
  sources of controversy, 241–42
  tests for the single-case, 245–50
Statistical tests, 231, 240, 245, 318
  randomization tests, 246, 324–29
  R_n test of ranks, 247, 329–33
  split-middle technique, 247, 333–37
  t and *F* tests, 245–48, 250, 318–21, 328
  time-series analysis, 246, 248–50, 321–24
Strategies of assessment, 26–27, 37–39
  discrete categories, 27–29, 38
  duration, 32–33
  frequency, 26–27, 37
  interval, 30–32, 38
  latency, 32–33, 38
  number of clients, 29–30, 38
  psychophysiological measures, 34–35, 38
  response-specific measures, 33–35, 38
  self-report, 36–37, 39

t and *F* tests, 245–48, 250, 318–21, 328
  autocorrelation, 319, 320
  serial dependency and, 245–46, 248, 319–20
  use of, 246
Time-series analysis, 246, 248–50, 251, 265, 321–24
  autocorrelation, 248, 320, 322–23, 324
  level and trend, 246, 248–50, 323
  serial dependency, 248, 324
Transfer of training, 208
  designs to assess, 209–11

Trends in the data, 106–9, 240, 263–65, 271
  split-middle technique and, 311–16
  statistical analysis of, 248–51, 265
Type I and II errors, 241–42n
Types of graphs, 296–98
  cumulative graph, 299–302
  histogram, 302–7, 310
  simple line graph, 298–99, 310

Variability, 109, 167, 240, 263, 266–69, 271
  interobserver agreement and, 48–49, 73, 237
  observer drift, 268
  plotting of data and, 266–68
  statistical analyses and, 243–44
Visual inspection, 231–32, 243–45, 291, 293, 296
  changes in level, 234–35
  changes in means, 233–34
  changes in trend, 235
  consistency of, 239–40
  criteria for, 233–39
  descriptive aids, 307–16
  graphical display and, 296–307
  latency of change, 235–37
  problems with, 239–41, 242–43
  sensitivity of, 232, 240
  underlying rationale, 232–33

Withdrawal designs, 211, 218–19
  combinations of, 216–18
  partial withdrawal, 215–16
  sequential withdrawal, 213–15